CHILDREN WITH AUTISM AND ASPERGER SYNDROME

A Guide for
Practitioners and Carers

CHILDREN WITH AUTISM AND ASPERGER SYNDROME

A Guide for Practitioners and Carers

Patricia Howlin

JOHN WILEY & SONS

Chichester · New York · Weinheim · Brisbane · Singapore · Toronto

Other Wiley Editorial Offices

John Wiley & Sons, Inc., 605 Third Avenue,
New York, NY 10158-0012, USA

WILEY-VCH Verlag GmbH, Pappelallee 3,
D-69469 Weinheim, Germany

Jacaranda Wiley Ltd, 33 Park Road, Milton,
Queensland 4064, Australia

John Wiley & Sons (Asia) Pte Ltd, 2 Clementi Loop #02-01,
Jin Xing Distripark, Singapore 129809

John Wiley & Sons (Canada) Ltd, 22 Worcester Road,
Rexdale, Ontario M9W 1L1, Canada

Library of Congress Cataloging-in-Publication Data

Howlin, Patricia.
    Children with autism and asperger syndrome : a guide for
practitioners and carers / Patricia Howlin.
        p.   cm.
    Includes bibliographical references and index.
    ISBN 0–471–98327–6 (cased). — ISBN 0–471–98328–4 (pbk.)
    1. Autism in children. 2. Asperger's syndrome. 3. Autism.
I. Title.
RJ506.A9H678   1998   98-39196
618.92'8982—dc21   CIP

British Library Cataloguing in Publication Data

A catalogue record for this book is available from the British Library

ISBN 0-471-98328-4

Typeset in 10/12pt Palatino by Dorwyn Ltd, Rowlands Castle, Hants
Printed and bound in Great Britain by Biddles Ltd, Guildford and King's Lynn
This book is printed on acid-free paper responsibly manufactured from sustainable forestry, in which at least two trees are planted for each one used for paper production.

CONTENTS

ABOUT THE AUTHOR

Patricia Howlin is a Consultant Clinical Psychologist and Regional Tutor in the psychology of learning disability, and Professor of Clinical Psychology at St George's Hospital Medical School, London. She has worked in the field of autism for many years, both as a researcher and as a clinician and has collaborated closely with Professor Sir Michael Rutter at the Institute of Psychiatry. She is particularly interested in the problems faced by more able individuals with autism (or those described as having Asperger syndrome). Research has included: long-term follow-ups of individuals with autism and related disorders; the effectiveness of home-based interventions; the outcome of supported employment schemes; specialist programmes designed to improve 'theory of mind' abilities; diagnostic resources; and, most recently, the outcome of early intensive behavioural programmes. Other research interests include disorders that also involve problems of social communication and stereotyped and ritualistic behaviours or interests including Fragile X, Turner's syndrome, Williams' syndrome and Cohen's syndrome.

PREFACE

This book represents many years of working with people with autism, their families and other professionals involved in clinical and research work. It was initially conceived as a re-edition of the book originally written with Michael Rutter and colleagues on the *Treatment of Autistic Children* (1987). However, major advances in knowledge and understanding of autism over the past decade meant that, for the book to have any real practical value, a significant revision was required. Developments in the areas of genetics and neurobiology, refinements in classification systems and progress in diagnostic methodology were all issues that could not be ignored. Over the past 10 years, too, many different treatments claiming to have a major impact on the autistic condition have been reported. An evaluation of such claims was considered to be crucial. Further significant therapeutic innovations have resulted from work on the communicative functions of behaviours initially viewed as maladaptive or inappropriate. Thus, a particular focus of the book is on the underlying *causes* of problems in autism rather than concentrating simply on ways of modifying unwanted behaviours. Much greater emphasis on environmental factors was also considered to be necessary. Autism is a profound and pervasive disability that affects almost all areas of an individual's functioning. Although appropriate management strategies can help to reduce or minimize problems, the fundamental deficits will always remain. It is important to recognize, therefore, that often much can be achieved by changing the behaviour and communication skills of those living with or caring for the child with autism. If they can be helped to provide a more predictable, structured, and understandable world for the child in their care, very many problems can be dealt with more effectively.

Despite the progress made over the last decade, the basic tenets of our earlier book are ones that we believe are still essential for good clinical practice. These include:

—The provision of practical information and advice to parents—about autism in general and their own child in particular, and about relevant social, medical and educational services.

—The direct involvement of parents in therapy and in decision making more generally.

—A focus on changing behaviour by using positive and, as far as possible, naturally occurring reinforcers (such as the child's own special interests or routines).

—The implementation, wherever feasible, of management techniques that are already used within families. This is based on the grounds that the *consistent* application of simple, familiar strategies is more likely to be effective in the long term than the introduction of programmes which, although more sophisticated, may be difficult for families to follow.

—The importance of understanding the role played by the basic 'triad' of impairments (social and communication deficits and the need for ritual and routine).

—A focus on improving communication (in carers as well as the child).

—A graded change approach to the modification of problems so that distress and anxiety are kept to a minimum.

—The need to provide the child with an environment that is appropriately structured and predictable.

—A focus on *prevention* of problems, both by improving facilities for early diagnosis and helping parents to be aware of the types of problems that may emerge over time, and how they might avoid or deal with these.

—Good liaison between families and social, health and education services to ensure that all aspects of the child's needs are satisfactorily met.

—The need to take account of other aspects of home life, so that treatment is family oriented, rather than entirely child focused.

Although much still needs to be known about the causes of autism, and the best ways of helping affected individuals and their families, it is clear that we have come a long way in the half century since autism was first described. However, it is important to be aware that many of these benefits have sprung from close collaboration over the years between researchers, practitioners and families. Thus, it is a cause of considerable concern that, in recent years, some attempts to promote new treatments have resulted in bitterness and recriminations. As this book will, hopefully, make clear, autism is a highly complex condition, affecting individual children in very different ways. Thus, no one treatment approach will be universally effective and liaison, rather than litigation is most likely to improve the lives of children and their families. As long as parents and professionals can continue to work in close collaboration, who knows what improvements the coming century will bring?

ACKNOWLEDGEMENTS

First and foremost, thanks must go to the many families and individuals on whose stories this book relies. All the anecdotal accounts are based on true scenarios, although occasionally circumstances have been altered somewhat to ensure anonymity.

The clinical and research expertise of the other authors involved in the original book (William Yule, Michael Berger and Lionel Hersov) has, of course continued to have a major impact on the present version. In particular, the close collaboration with Michael Rutter on follow-up studies in adulthood, has been an ongoing source of inspiration, as well as providing invaluable information on how much people with autism can achieve if given appropriate help and support. Other colleagues over the years, whose support, advice, and clinical or research experience have proved invaluable, include Simon Baron-Cohen, Sue Goode, Judy Gould, Ann le Couteur, Lynn Mawhood, Lorna Wing and many others, far too numerous to mention.

Special thanks must also go to my secretary Jill Rolfe for her patience and assistance, and to my husband Michael Brammer for 'technical support' (patiently retrieving lost chapters and other computer errors).

Finally, neither this book, nor its predecessor would ever have been written without the invaluable input of Rosemary Hemsley who co-authored the original and was responsible for designing and implementing many of the programmes described. Her loss remains a source of great sadness.

┌─────┐
│ 1 │
└─────┘

THE RANGE OF PROBLEMS IN AUTISM AND ASPERGER SYNDROME

HISTORICAL BACKGROUND

It was in America, in the 1940s that Leo Kanner, a child psychiatrist, first became aware of a group of children 'whose condition differs so markedly and uniquely from anything reported so far, that each case merits . . . a detailed consideration of its fascinating peculiarities'. Three major features distinguished these children from others attending his clinic. The first was the children's inability to relate themselves in the ordinary way to people and to situations from the beginnings of life. Second was their failure to use language for the purpose of communication. Third was their 'anxiously obsessive desire for the maintenance of sameness, resulting in a marked limitation in the variety of spontaneous activity'. Play, too, was characterised by a preoccupation with stereotyped, repetitive activities, lacking any creative or social function. These were the children whom he was later to identify as having 'early infantile autism' (1943).

His was not the first account of this condition. Lorna Wing (1996) and Uta Frith (1991) both provide fascinating case examples, taken from historical accounts, clinical descriptions, novels, and even the Lives of the Saints, all of which indicate that autism has, in fact, been around for a very long time. Nevertheless, it was Kanner who first systematically described the disorder and pointed out the similarities in dysfunction in a *group* of children, rather than simply reporting on individual cases.

It is something of a remarkable coincidence, therefore, that, at much the same time—although separated by an ocean and global war—a very similar group of children was described by another physician, Hans Asperger. Both men had been born around the turn of the century in Austria and had trained in medicine in Vienna. However, unlike Kanner, Asperger remained in Europe where he, too, described in meticulous detail a group of children whose problems had previously been unrecognised by professionals in the fields of paediatrics, child psychiatry or mental retardation. These children were characterised by their social and communication deficits, their obsessional interests and behaviour, their dislike of change and their dependence on rituals and routines. Many were also physically very clumsy, but generally there were no significant delays in early linguistic or cognitive development. Asperger coined the term *autistic psychopathy* to describe their condition.

KANNER'S SYNDROME

'Kanner's syndrome', as it was to become known, was soon acknowledged by many influential clinicians, and was followed by similar accounts by Eisenberg (1956) in the USA and Creak (1963) in the UK. Although the terminology varied (from 'childhood psychosis', to 'infantile autism', to 'early childhood schizophrenia') there was little doubt that the children described exhibited the same characteristic pattern of deficits, related to communication and social difficulties, and obsessional and ritualistic behaviours. Later follow-up studies also confirmed the persisting nature of these problems into older childhood, adolescence and early adulthood (Rutter *et al.*, 1967; Rutter & Lockyer, 1967; Lockyer & Rutter, 1969, 1970; Mittler *et al.*, 1966; DeMyer *et al.*, 1973).

By the end of the 1970s autism was included in the two principal diagnostic systems used to classify illness and disorders in the USA and Europe (American Psychiatric Association: *Diagnostic and Statistical Manual of Mental Disorders*, or DSM-III (APA, 1980); World Health Organisation: *International Classification of Diseases and Related Health Problems*, or ICD-9 (WHO, 1978)). The updated diagnostic criteria for autism, as defined by ICD-10 (WHO, 1992), are presented in Table 1.1. As can be seen, diagnosis remains firmly based in the fundamental areas of deficit identified by Kanner:

- Abnormal communication
- Abnormal social development
- Ritualistic and stereotyped behaviour and resistance to change.

THE RANGE OF PROBLEMS ASSOCIATED WITH AUTISM

Within these three fundamental areas of deficit the range of problems shown can be highly variable. Differences in age and linguistic and cognitive abilities will significantly affect the way in which the condition

Table 1.1: ICD-10 criteria for autism

A. Abnormal or impaired development is evident before the age of 3 years in at least one of the following areas:

   (1) receptive or expressive language as used in social communication;
   (2) the development of selective social attachments or of reciprocal social interaction;
   (3) function or symbolic play.

B. A total of at least six symptoms from (1), (2), and (3) must be present, with at least two from (1) and at least one from each of (2) and (3):

   (1) Qualitative abnormalities in reciprocal social interaction are manifest in at least two of the following areas:

      (a) failure to make adequate use of eye-to-eye gaze, facial expression, body posture, and gesture to regulate social interaction;
      (b) failure to develop (in a manner appropriate to mental age, and despite ample opportunities) peer relationships that involve a mutual sharing of interests, activities and emotions;
      (c) lack of socio-emotional reciprocity as shown by an impaired or deviant response to other people's emotions; or lack of modulation of behaviour according to social context; or a weak integration of social, emotional and communicative behaviours;
      (d) lack of spontaneous seeking to share enjoyment, interests or achievements with other people (e.g. lack of showing, bringing or pointing out to other people objects of interest to the individual).

   (2) Qualitative abnormalities in communication are manifest in at least one of the following areas:

      (a) a delay in, or total lack of, development of spoken language that is *not* accompanied by an attempt to compensate through the use of gesture or mime as an alternative mode of communication (often preceded by a lack of communicative babbling);
      (b) relative failure to initiate or sustain conversational interchange (at whatever level of language skills is present), in which there is reciprocal responsiveness to the communications of the other person;
      (c) stereotyped and repetitive use of language or idiosyncratic use of words or phrases;
      (d) lack of varied spontaneous make-believe or (when young) social imitative play.

   (3) Restricted, repetitive and stereotyped patterns of behaviour, interests and activities are manifest in at least one of the following areas:

      (a) an encompassing preoccupation with one or more stereotyped, restricted patterns of interest that are abnormal in content or focus; or one or more interests that are abnormal in their intensity and circumscribed nature though not in their content or focus;
      (b) apparently compulsive adherence to specific, non-functional routines or rituals;
      (c) stereotyped and repetitive motor mannerisms that involve either hand or finger flapping or twisting, or complex whole body movements;

Table 1.1 (*continued overleaf*)

Table 1.1: (*Continued*)

(d) preoccupations with part-objects or non-functional elements of play materials (such as their odour, the feel of their surface, or the noise or vibration that they generate).

C. The clinical picture is not attributable to the other varieties of pervasive developmental disorders; specific developmental disorder of receptive language with secondary socio-emotional problems; reactive attachment disorder or disinhibited attachment disorder; mental retardation with some associated emotional or behavioural disorder; schizophrenia of unusually early onset; and Rett's syndrome.

---

manifests itself. For many parents, the early childhood years are most difficult, particularly as they may be left to cope with their child with relatively little help or support. If appropriate schooling can be found, which offers the child a suitably stimulating environment in addition to providing parents with practical advice and emotional support, then day-to-day problems of management can be greatly reduced. In adolescence some children may show an increase in problems and more disturbances of mood and behaviour. However, in many other cases, adolescence is a time of greater stability. Improvements in adolescence occur particularly in more able children, who, by this stage are better able to recognise their own difficulties and to devise more effective ways of coping with these. In Kanner's own account of 96 individuals, who were followed up in their twenties and thirties, he described 11 people who had made particularly good progress. Kanner noted that in the majority of these cases 'a remarkable change took place' around their mid-teens. 'Unlike most other autistic children they became uneasily aware of their peculiarities and began to make a conscious effort to do something about them.' In particular they tried to improve their interactions with their peers, often using their obsessional preoccupations or special skills 'to open a door for contact'.

Cognitive ability will also have a major impact on the way in which other deficits are manifest. Thus, the rituals and obsessions of a child who has severe learning disabilities will be far more limited and stereotyped than the obsessional interests shown by a child with an IQ that is well above average. In the following sections, the range of problems associated with impairments in the three main areas of deficit are described.

Communication Skills

Abnormalities of language are often among the first problems to arouse concern in parents of children with autism (Howlin & Moore, 1997;

Gillberg *et al.*, 1990; Frith *et al.*, 1993; Smith *et al.*, 1994). Early babble may be limited in range and complexity, and tends not to be used to initiate or maintain contacts with other people. The pre-linguistic 'conversations' that are well established between normal infants and their caretakers, long before words first appear, do not take place and typically there is a failure to respond either to verbal or non-verbal cues from parents. Babies with autism do not lift up their arms to their parents in anticipation of being picked up, they do not gurgle with delight if other people smile or make noises to them, and they do not attempt to initiate verbal interactions.

Although many children with autism remain mute, a significant minority does begin to speak in the second year of life, perhaps developing a single-word vocabulary of several dozen words. However, at the stage when most normally developing children move on to using simple phrase speech, progress in the child with autism may cease, with a loss of the vocabulary previously acquired (Volkmar & Cohen, 1989; Rogers & DiLalla, 1990; Short & Schopler, 1988). Kurita (1985) in a study of 261 children, found that 37% lost meaningful words before the age of 30 months, and Hoshino *et al.* (1987) reported that over 50% of children who were described as having normal early development showed some form of regression between 15 and 30 months. Rutter and Lord (1987) confirmed that approximately 20% of children begin to lose speech around this time. Some of these children may later regain language but more than half do not, although the reasons for this are poorly understood. Even in those who later regain language, there is some indication that their communication skills remain more impaired than those of children who did not experience a period of regression (Brown & Prelock, 1995).

It is estimated that around half of all children with autism fail to develop functional speech (Lord & Rutter, 1994) and many of these also have little or no understanding of spoken language. Nor, as they grow older, do they attempt to overcome their linguistic deficits by communicating in other ways, such as by gesture, pointing, eye contact or facial expression. If they want something they may simply scream or take the adult's hand and place it on the thing they want. They rarely point their finger to indicate their needs (and almost never point out things of interest to other people) although they may wave their hands vaguely in the direction of the desired object.

Some children are later able to acquire a simple signing vocabulary, and the Makaton system, developed by Margaret Walker (1980), can be particularly helpful for some. However, relatively few children with autism learn to communicate fluently and spontaneously by means of gesture; instead communication tends to be brief, stereotyped and repetitive, and generally restricted to a few essential signs such as those for 'please', 'toilet' or 'food' (Attwood *et al.*, 1988). In contrast, some more able children, as they grow older, do begin to use a greater range of gestures. Unfortunately, these may be too exaggerated, or used out of context, making the child's attempts to communicate appear even more unusual.

In non-speaking children, comprehension usually remains very limited, although most will probably learn to respond to simple commands within a specific and well-rehearsed context, such as 'Get your coat', 'Let's go in the car' or 'Dinner's ready'. Others may learn to follow a few basic signs or gestures. However, most non-verbal children remain unable to follow more complex instructions involving the combination of two or more components. Thus, if asked to 'take your coat upstairs', they may pick up their coat *or* go upstairs but are unlikely to do both.

Even in children who do learn to talk, their understanding of language is often at a much lower level than their spoken vocabulary. Abstract concepts present particular difficulties, and their interpretation of what is said is frequently highly literal. Remarks such as 'It's raining cats and dogs' or 'He laughed his head off' will leave them totally bemused, or desperately searching for the objects in question. An instruction such as 'Ask your dad if he's got a hammer' may result in the child following the explicit command but he or she will be most unlikely to respond to the *implicit* instruction, which is to return with the hammer. In mainstream school this literal interpretation of language can result in numerous problems. Told, in an art lesson, to 'Paint the child sitting next to you' the child with autism is liable to do *exactly* that. He or she will not realise that the instruction really means 'Paint *a picture of* the child sitting next to you'. Asked 'What year is your birthday?', the reply is likely to be 'Every year, of course'.

Among those children who do develop spoken language, the acquisition of first words or phrases is usually delayed, although in some cases, particularly those who are of relatively high cognitive ability, speech may develop around the normal age. However, patterns of language development and language usage tend to be highly unusual.

Firstly, the tone, pitch and modulation of speech can seem very odd. Normal speech cadences are often missing, so that the voice sounds monotonous, staccato or mechanical in quality. Children may speak too loudly or too softly, or develop an accent that is quite different to that of their family or their peers. Janey, for example, who came from a working-class background and attended a primary school in the middle of a south London housing estate, had somehow acquired a very 'posh' accent, which led to her being much teased by other children. In other cases, children with a parent whose first language is not English have acquired the same (often strong) foreign accent, despite the fact they have never lived abroad. Among children who are more able, many also develop a rather formal and pedantic style of speaking, and are often described as 'sounding like little adults' even when they are still very young.

Secondly, a range of different semantic errors, such as neologisms and pronoun reversal, can occur. Children may make up their own words or phrases, such as 'hot raining' for steam, 'lefsocky' for foot, or 'carhome' for garage. They may refer to themselves as you, rather than I: 'You don't want to go swimming' or 'You mustn't say damn to Grandma', or simply use their own name: 'Johnny wants three Mars Bars'. Typically, too, speech tends to be repetitive and echolalic. Children may repeat the same phrases over and over again, or continuously ask the same questions, often for no apparent reason. They may insist that other people say things, or answer their questions, in a particular way. Any deviation from this routine may lead to severe distress and disruption.

Many children echo or repeat back exactly what has been said to them. Asked 'What's your name?', they will repeat the question rather than supplying the answer. Echolalia can be delayed as well as immediate. For example, children may use previously heard questions, such as 'Do you want a biscuit?' or 'Does Johnny want to go out now?' to indicate their own needs. Other children may repeat, verbatim, things that they have heard people say during the day, or even weeks or months ago. Many parents say that the only way they ever know what is happening at school is because their children will repeat back lengthy extracts from classroom conversations. When upset or anxious, children may also repeat things that people have said to them in the past: 'There's no need to upset yourself . . . calm down and count to ten . . .' or 'It wasn't nice to kick daddy in the knee because he stopped you'. If angry they may keep talking, over and over again, about occurrences that had previously annoyed them: '. . . That Lucy took your teddy bear . . . she was a very naughty girl wasn't she?'

In most cases, distinguishing between echolalic and spontaneous utterances is a relatively easy task, either because the remarks are made out of context, because they are so stereotyped, or because the language used is more sophisticated than the child's own speech. However, recognising the extent of echolalic speech in more able children can present a greater challenge. In such cases the remarks echoed may be more or less appropriate to the conversational context; the utterances may not appear noticeably odd or repetitive and, because the child's has an extensive vocabulary, there is little obvious disparity between spontaneous and echoed speech. It is only after the same theme, or even the same sentence structures, appear time after time, with different people and in different contexts, that one becomes aware that the child's 'conversation' actually stems directly from things he or she has heard other adults use, or from TV, radio, video, or books.

The most characteristic feature of the language deficit in autism, what-ever the level of the child's ability, is the failure to use communication for **social** purposes. In infancy, there is rarely any evidence of the 'to and fro' quality of interactions that characterise the speech of normally develop-ing infants. As they grow older, non-verbal children with autism seem to have no motivation to develop alternative means of communication (as, for example, do deaf children, children with expressive language disor-ders, or Down's syndrome children with executive speech problems). More verbal children, in contrast, may become only too willing to talk *at* people, about their obsessions and preoccupations, or to ask repetitive questions, although they continue to show little interest in, or even under-standing of, reciprocal or two-way conversations. Maurice, for example, was an extremely intelligent 14-year-old boy, attending a well-known private school in London. His headmaster suspected that Maurice might have autism and referred him for diagnosis. When his mother was asked, as part of a standard diagnostic interview, whether he ever liked to chat 'just for the sake of it', Maurice looked up in utter disbelief. In a voice of mingled scorn and astonishment he asked 'Why should any one *ever* want to do that? When I talk', he said, 'it's because I want to know something, or because I want someone else to know something. Anything else would just be a complete waste of time!' Not only did he show no desire for communication of this kind, he could not believe that any rational person could want this either.

Play and Imagination

The pervasiveness of the language disorder in autism is also manifest in children's inability to develop normal, imaginative patterns of play. Just as language is stereotyped, repetitive and non-social, so too is their imag-inative play. In children who are least able, 'play' of any kind is usually very limited, often restricted to behaviours such as lining up objects, placing them in set patterns, spinning the wheels of cars and trains, or the objects themselves, or simply dismantling everything. Older and more able children, however, may show apparently quite complex play ac-tivities. Scenes from the classroom, with the child as teacher, may be enacted with teddies or dolls; complex scenarios from Thomas the Tank Engine videos may be played out, with the child copying the voices of the different characters; or 'highlights' from Star Wars or similar programmes may be reproduced. At first sight such activities seem incompatible with the usual accounts of children with autism; they certainly do not fit the classic image of a child 'lost in its own world', sitting silently in a corner while completely absorbed in simple repetitive behaviours. On second or third viewing, however, the repetitive nature of even this type of play activity tends to become apparent. If interrupted for any reason, the child is likely to become extremely distressed, and may well have to return to the very beginning, enacting everything over again. Interruptions from other children are usually particularly unwelcome, and although a few children with autism may actively try to involve their peers or siblings in the action, this is usually done in a very specific way. Any deviation from the 'rules' tends to meet with considerable displeasure. Moreover, the games involved may well be out of keeping with other children's current interests. Jessica, for example, had an obsession with the film 'The Sound of Music'. She had a vast collection of dressing-up clothes and a variety of different scenarios that she liked to act out from the film. She would never go to visit other children 'because they did not have the right clothes', but was constantly inviting them to her house. Immediately they entered they would be made to choose a costume and then follow one of her 'scripts'. Most of them had never even heard of 'The Sound of Music' before, and few willingly returned!

Social Impairments in Autism

Another common and somewhat stereotyped view of a child with autism is of one who refuses to meet eye-gaze, avoids all physical contact and is happiest if left in a corner engaging in repetitive and stereotyped activities. However, although such a picture may occur—particularly in very young children or in those who are also very cognitively impaired—this is by no means invariable. Many years ago Wing and Gould (1979) suggested that children with autism could be subdivided according to three main types of social impairment:

1. *The aloof group.* These, in fact, are the children who do seem happiest if left alone. They will actively avoid eye gaze and may dislike physical contact, although some nevertheless greatly enjoy rough and tumble games. Often they seem to treat people as objects and have no interest in, or understanding of, other people's feelings or emotions. Parents describe them as 'being in a world of their own'. They do not come for comfort if hurt, and indeed may show very little reaction to pain (tales of children who develop dreadful sores or abscesses but never indicate they are in distress are not unusual). When little, they show no distress at being separated from their parents and although, with time, some may begin to develop attachments to familiar adults, they generally continue to show little or no interest in other children. As adults they remain isolated and unresponsive.

2. *The passive group.* Wing and Gould suggest that this is the least common picture. Unlike the aloof group these children do not actively avoid contact but nor do they do anything to initiate this. They will never point out things of interest to others, and if they themselves want something they may simply stand close to someone, or to the desired object, leaving others to find out what they want. One 7-year-old boy, for example, would always cry bitterly if hurt, but when asked what the matter was would only say 'You have to guess'. They may make eye contact as long as reminded to do so, and other children may sometimes make use of them as passive partners in their games.

3. *The active but odd group.* This group tends to consist of children who are more intellectually and cognitively able. They show no sense of social barriers, will talk to (or rather *at*) anyone, and may willingly approach complete strangers. If they have a particular obsession they will involve anyone they can in this. One child, for example, with a fascination for a particular brand of training shoes, would look constantly at people's feet, and even pull up their trousers to see what shoes they were wearing; if he could find someone with the 'right' sort of shoe he would happily follow them along the street. Others will engage anyone they meet in monologues about their particular interests. These may be relatively innocuous topics such as cars, the Eurovision Song contest, or distances, but they can be more embarrassing. One young teenage girl had a fascination with the regularity of other people's menstrual cycles, and was continually questioning any women she met about this. Rather than avoiding eye contact, they may stare long and hard at people, which can be extremely disconcerting. They may be physically very demonstrative, but because they lack any understanding of social 'rules' this is often entirely inappropriate—for example, hugging and kissing virtual strangers, or the school headmaster! Gesture and facial expression, too, may be exaggerated and inappropriate. Instead of avoiding other children they may be desperate to make friends but in trying to do so will barge into other children's groups, disrupt their activities, or try to take their toys. If other children do not respond as they wish they may become even more disruptive and sometimes aggressive. For obvious reasons these children often give rise to far more anxiety for their parents than those who are more withdrawn.

More recently Wing (1996) has added a fourth group to this classification:

4. *The over-formal, stilted group.* This pattern of behaviour tends to be seen in later adolescence or early adulthood, and is more typical in those who are of high IQ and have good expressive language. In contrast to

the active but odd group, who treat everyone they meet as if they were close family members, this group tends to treat family members as if they were distant strangers. One child at boarding school, for example, always began letters home to his mother with 'Dear Mrs Smith', ending them with 'Yours sincerely, Jonathan Smith'. Their behaviour is always excessively polite and formal, which often results in much teasing from their peers. They are extremely punctilious about keeping to rules, and may become very upset and indignant if anyone else infringes these. Again this can lead to considerable problems at school, for example, if the children feel obliged to inform teachers whenever they hear their classmates talking in lessons or see them smoking in the playground.

Although, by definition, all children with autism show social impairments, it is clear that the nature of these impairments can be very variable. Often, too, children change as they grow older, so that an initially aloof child may later become one who is 'active but odd'. Giles, for example, was described by his mother as the perfect baby; he rarely cried and would happily spend hours in his cot alone—indeed the only time he became irritable was when people tried to talk to him or pick him up. Later, at nursery school, he avoided all contact with other children and would shy away if they approached. By adolescence, however, the problems were very different. He would engage anyone he met in 'conversations' about badminton players and whenever he saw a group of children would march up to them, announce his name and ask which of them was going to be his friend. If they did not reply he was quite likely to hit them.

Nevertheless, although the ways in which social problems are manifest may be very different, the core features prevail whatever the child's developmental level. These include lack of reciprocity, impaired empathy, and a lack of joint attention—that is, failure to share their own enjoyment or activities with other people in the normal way. Ever pervasive, too, is what has been described as the child's inability to 'mind-read' (Baron-Cohen, 1995). By this is meant their failure to understand other people's feelings, beliefs or emotions, and their consequent inability to respond to these in an appropriate way. This 'mindblindness' permeates all social interactions, affecting those of very able children as well as those who are most handicapped.

Ritualistic and Stereotyped Interests or Behaviours

Problem behaviours in this area also span a very wide range and tend to vary according to the child's intellectual level.

Stereotyped behaviours

Simple, stereotyped behaviours are most likely to be found in children who are severely cognitively impaired. They may spend hours tearing up pieces of paper, flicking pieces of elastic or string, picking out the threads from clothing or carpets, or even plucking the hairs from the dog. Such items may also be used for visual stimulation, as the child waves them to and fro in front of his or her eyes. Other children may spend hours flicking light switches on and off, opening and shutting doors, or spinning the wheels of toy cars or trains. Some, in fact develop a quite remarkable skill in spinning objects. Gavin, for example, despite having severe learning disabilities, was able, by the age of 3, to spin almost any object set in front of him. These could include bottles, plates, cups, cutlery, even meat pies!

Motor mannerisms, such as rocking or hand flicking or flapping, are also very common in this group and may well interfere with the child's other activities. In children who are more severely retarded there is also a greater risk of self-injurious behaviours. Often these start off as simple stereotyped behaviours, such as rocking or flicking, but they may gradually evolve into much more serious problems, such as head banging, eye poking, skin picking and biting (Hall, 1997).

Other ritualistic behaviours

The complexity of ritualistic and stereotyped behaviours tends to increase as IQ levels rise. Thus, more able children may tend to seek out very specific objects to spin or flick; only using elastic bands of a particular size or thickness, blades of grass or leaves of a certain size or colour, or pieces of cloth or paper of a particular texture. Children may also become very rigid in their acceptance of certain items. Even quite young infants may refuse to take milk, except from bottles of a particular shape or colour. One child would only eat food that was pink or yellow; another would only accept drinks that were clear and uncoloured; another would accept only one brand of orange juice. Others become fixated with particular types of clothing, only wearing navy blue or (more expensively) only clothes with specific logos or designer labels. Although these habits may not sound too difficult to cope with, they can, in fact, lead to great disruption should fashions change or manufacturers alter their packaging. It is not unknown for families to scour the country looking for baby bottles or dummies of a certain shape and/or colour because they dread the crisis that will inevitably occur if these items are no longer available.

Object attachments and collections

Collecting items is typical of many children with autism. These may vary from leaves or pieces of paper of a particular shape, to Star Trek figures,

Thomas the Tank Engine trains, Mr Bean videos, snails and woodlice, coke cans, and many, many more. Although the type of object collected is not necessarily unusual, the number of items collected, or the child's overwhelming interest in these, may well be. Tracey's mother, for example, mentioned that her daughter liked to keep Coca Cola cans. When questioned further, it transpired that, in fact, she had *never* thrown one away, and by the age of 13 had 4,000 cans stacked in her bedroom. Damien, aged 4, not only demanded to wear Thomas the Tank Engine clothes, but he insisted on having a picture of Thomas on everything possible, including books, pencil cases, note-pads, even tea towels. His conversation revolved entirely around Thomas themes, and it was almost impossible to divert him as he was so adept at turning any conversation back to this topic. The obsession was also very expensive for his parents. Another boy, with a penchant for collecting Mr Bean videos, marched into his local police station, demanded to see the Police Inspector and told him he wanted to make an official complaint. When asked the reason for this, he announced it was because no one had informed him that a new Mr Bean video had just been released.

Many young children with autism also insist on carrying around particular items. These are not usually the teddy or piece of blanket beloved of normal toddlers, but are likely to be much more bizarre. One young girl always carried around pieces of her toy animals' tails in glass jars; another always had a woodlouse in a matchbox; another child had a penchant for blue rubber sink plungers; another for left-foot red wellingtons. If the item is lost, broken, or simply unobtainable, the child may become extremely distressed, disrupting all other activities. Alternatively, the number of items can gradually increase over time, so that what began as a fairly innocuous attachment can later become much more difficult to cope with. Jenny had begun carrying around a pair of old spectacles when she was about 2. By 5, she had 10 pairs, tied together on a piece of ribbon, and by 15 she had a carrier bag full.

Routines and resistance to change

The resistance of some children to any change in their routine or environment may become apparent at a very early age. Many infants, still in their pram or baby buggy, became distressed if their parents deviate from their normal route while out shopping. Other children may insist on eating at exactly the same time each day, with the table being laid in a specific way and even other people having to sit in a particular position. Meals in Amanda's house were continually disrupted by the fact that she was constantly peering under the table to ensure that her father's legs were crossed in the 'correct' fashion (right foot over left). Other children become distressed if the house is redecorated, or if furniture or even ornaments are moved. They may insist that curtains are drawn in a particular way, that doors are left open at a specific angle, or that books, records or clothes are always arranged in a set order. Changes that are usually much enjoyed by other children (school holidays, a teacher off sick, parties, even Christmas) may be a nightmare for the child with autism.

At times, the insistence on doing things in a certain way, or having items placed in a set pattern, seems to have an almost compulsive quality so that the child will resist strongly any attempts to prevent him from putting the objects back in their 'right' place. Children may occasionally develop compulsive behaviours involving handwashing or checking lights or door locks and so forth. Obsessional thoughts, concerning death or illness (particularly of their parents) or anxieties that they may inadvertently do something wrong, even commit a crime, can also sometimes occur.

More able children often try to involve other people in their routines. Verbal routines, in which the child repeatedly asks the same questions and then demands that others answer in a specific way, can be particularly exhausting. Indeed many parents find verbal rituals (for example, constantly having to reply to questions about the accuracy of last night's weather forecast, or which famous people have their birthday today) far more disruptive than many other types of obsessional behaviour, simply because they can never escape from them.

Preoccupations and special interests

Although younger, less able children tend to collect or manipulate objects, the preoccupations of those who are older and more able are often much more complex. They may become fascinated with particular topics, such as TV test cards, lighting systems on trains, the underground network, sports players, film stars, pop singers and so forth. They may also collect *facts* rather than objects, and can build up a vast amount of knowledge on particular topics. Unusual preoccupations—with, for instance, street lights, telephone boxes, toilets, men with bald head, people wearing fur coats—are also common. Even when these interests appear to be age appropriate, as for example in sport or computers, they can become so intense and overwhelming that they effectively prevent the child taking part in any other activity.

Although few children show problems in all of the above areas, every child with autism will show some evidence of ritualistic and stereotyped interests or behaviours. In some cases these can be so severe as to disrupt not only the child's own activities, but also many aspects of family life.

The Spectrum of Autistic Disorders

As is apparent from the discussion above, the manifestations of autism are wide and varied. Although the underlying threads of social and communication deficits, and rigid and obsessional behaviours, are forever present, the severity of these problems can vary markedly from one individual to another. As already noted, the age, IQ and language ability of the child will have a major impact on how problems are manifest and the severity of impairment in each of the different domains may also vary within the same individual. Thus, one child may be extremely ritualistic but be relatively responsive in social situations and have quite good speech. Another child may avoid social contact whenever possible and rarely speak, but have only a few rituals or routines. Other children may be severely affected in all areas. The following case studies illustrate just some of the variability that can be found.

Three Case Studies

(1) Jimmy's parents had recognised the fact that his development was unusual by the time he was about 12 weeks of age; he did not smile or look at them, and spent most of the day just staring at his toes. He was late to sit and did not walk until he was almost 2. Now aged 12 he is still not toilet trained, has never learned to speak, and usually just screams if he want something, although occasionally he will take someone's hand (without looking at them) and put it on the object he wants. If distressed he screams or makes a low humming noise. He has little comprehension of speech, although his parents think he can understand one or two simple phrases (such as 'Go get your coat') if these are accompanied by pointing or gesture. Jimmy has never shown any separation anxiety, and he shows no sign of distress when he goes to his 'foster family' once a month for respite care. He shows little curiosity in his environment although he does seem to enjoy being taken out. He has never played with toys and shows no interest in other children. His favourite activity, which he will carry on for hours, is to tear up pieces of paper and cloth and wave these in front of his eyes. His IQ is estimated as being in the severe to profoundly retarded range and he attends the special needs unit at the local school for children with learning disabilities.

(2) Julie is the same age as Jimmy, but her parents noticed nothing unusual in her early development. She smiled and gurgled, made good eye contact and enjoyed rough-and-tumble and chasing games. However, she was never very interested in toys. She was a little slow to use speech, but

by 18 months had a vocabulary of around 20 single words. Between 18 and 24 months she seemed to become less interested in communicating with them and most of the words she had previously used gradually disappeared. Her parents also noted that she became very distressed by change, and whenever they went out they always had to return by the same route. She became distraught when they tried to take her to a pre-school nursery and stripped off all her clothes whenever she was left there. Because of this her mother kept her at home until she was 4. Around this age a few words began to appear again, and now, at 12, she has a vocabulary of around 30 to 40 single words; she also used some Makaton signs. She seems interested in other children and laughs to herself if they are around; however, if they come too close or are very noisy she will scream or bang her head. She enjoys looking at picture books, 'drawing' with coloured pens, and doing jigsaws. She also has an old battered dinosaur puppet that she carries with her everywhere (at school it is kept in a carrier bag). She attends a special school for children with autism and has made good progress there. Her self-help skills are good but, apart from when she is at school, she refuses to be separated from her mother. Her behaviour is said to be good during the school term, but she is upset by change and becomes more disruptive during the vacations. Her non-verbal IQ is around 45–50.

(3) Jason, now aged 11, was thought by his parents to be a very pre-cocious infant. He walked at 9 months, was toilet trained at 2 and showed very advanced constructional skills (30-piece puzzles at the age of 3). Although he was slow to develop speech his parents did not worry be-cause his brother, too, had been very delayed in this area. He began to use words just after his third birthday, although almost everything he said was echoed. At 4, just when his parents began to think he would never learn to talk properly, he began to use spontaneous phrases, although these often sounded very grown up or stilted. He attended nursery school but there were many complaints about his aggressive behaviour towards other children and his inability to play normally. Most of his time was spent jumbling up boxes of jigsaws and then putting them together again. He was moved to a primary unit for children with learning disabilities but an educational assessment revealed that his IQ was just within the normal range. Transfer to a mainstream primary school with individual help was organised, but his progress there has been very variable and much influenced by individual teachers. He has no friends, but does show some imaginative play and is obsessed with enacting scenes from old western films. He will talk about these endlessly, much to the irrita-tion of his family and other children. His reading and maths are good and academically he is able to keep up with his peers. However, both his

parents and teachers are greatly concerned about the forthcoming transfer to secondary school, as they do not feel that he will be able to cope with the social and academic demands there, even with support.

ASPERGER SYNDROME

In contrast to 'Kanner's syndrome', 'Asperger syndrome' remained in relative obscurity for almost 40 years. It was not until 1981, when Lorna Wing published a detailed account of 34 further cases, that interest began to re-emerge. Even then, it was not until the 1990s that the condition was included in DSM or ICD classifications. Table 1.2 gives current ICD-10 criteria for Asperger syndrome; these are very similar to those used in DSM-IV.

Lorna Wing (1981) has summarised the main areas of similarity between the accounts of Kanner and Asperger. These include:

1. A marked preponderance of males.
2. Social isolation, and lack of empathy.
3. Impaired communication skills (e.g. pedantry, abnormal delivery, stereotyped and repetitive utterances) and, above all, the failure to use speech for reciprocal, conversational purposes.

Table 1.2: ICD-10 criteria for Asperger syndrome

A. There is no clinically significant general delay in spoken or receptive language or cognitive development. Diagnosis requires that single words should have developed by 2 years of age or earlier and that communicative phrases be used by 3 years or age or earlier. Self-help skills, adaptive behaviour, and curiosity about the environment during the first 3 years should be at a level consistent with normal intellectual development. However, motor milestones may be somewhat delayed and motor clumsiness is usual (although not a necessary diagnostic feature). Isolated special skills, often related to abnormal preoccupations, are common, but are not required for diagnosis.

B. There are qualitative abnormalities in reciprocal social interaction (criteria as for autism).

C. The individual exhibits an unusually intense, circumscribed interest or restricted, repetitive, and stereotyped patterns of behaviour, interests and activities (criteria as for autism; however it would be less usual for these to include either motor mannerisms or preoccupations with part-objects or non-functional elements of play materials).

D. The disorder is not attributable to the other varieties of pervasive developmental disorder; simple schizophrenia; schizotypal disorder; obsessive–compulsive disorder; anankastic personality disorder; reactive and disinhibited attachment disorders of childhood, respectively.

---

4. Impairments in non-verbal communication, notably eye gaze, gesture and facial expression.
5. A lack of flexible and sociable imaginative play.
6. Repetitive and stereotyped behaviours and resistance to change.
7. Unusual responses to sensory stimuli, including hypersensitivity to noise and fascination with the feel, taste or smell of objects.
8. Gross motor clumsiness and abnormal gait in some cases.
9. Disruptive behaviours, including aggression, destructiveness, and poor co-operation.
10. Uneven patterns of development with many individuals showing particular skills in areas such as memory or mathematics.

However, there are also a number of differences. Firstly, while many of the cases described by Kanner showed clear evidence of mental retardation, Asperger's cases were generally said to be of normal or even superior intelligence (although few were formally assessed). Secondly, whereas many of Kanner's cases had little or no speech, Asperger's individuals tended to have well-developed vocabularies (often unusually so for their age or background). They were, nevertheless, unable to carry out normal social conversations and had profound difficulties in understanding abstract concepts. Jokes, sarcasm, irony or metaphor posed particular problems. Thirdly, although many of Kanner's children tended to avoid social contact, those with Asperger's syndrome were often quite disinhibited, lacking 'completely any respect for the other person'. Finally, outcome in the two groups was very different. Only around 11% of Kanner's cases were reported to have a good outcome in terms of later independence and social functioning (Kanner, 1973). In contrast, Asperger cites examples of many individuals who had done remarkably well in later life, including university professors, mathematicians, chemists, and high-ranking civil servants. Indeed, he suggests that 'able autistic individuals can . . . perform with such outstanding success that one may even conclude that *only* such people are capable of certain achievements (because of) . . . their unswerving determination . . . their narrowness and single mindedness' (see Frith, 1991).

Are Autism and Asperger Syndrome Different Conditions?

Diagnostic criteria

There remains confusion over the diagnostic criteria for Asperger syndrome, particularly as subsequent accounts have not necessarily adhered to the criteria suggested by Asperger himself (Klin & Volkmar, 1997;

Table 1.3: Differing criteria for Asperger syndrome

Reference (N subjects)	Language delay	Cognitive delays	Autistic social impairment	Abnormal communication	All-absorbing interests	Clumsy
Asperger (1944) (>200)	–	Rarely present	+	+	+	+
Wing (1981) (34)	May be present	May be present	+	+	+	+
Gillberg (1989) (23)	May be present	May be present	+	+	+	+
Szatmari et al. (1989) (28)	No mention	No mention	+	+	+	+
Tantam (1991) (85)	May be present	May be present	+	+	+	+
WHO[a] (1992)	–	–	+	Non-verbal impairment implicit	+ (or rigid behaviours patterns)	Usually
APA[b] (1994)	–	–	+	Non-verbal impairment noted	+ (or rigid behaviours patterns)	May be present

+ = Characteristic deemed necessary for diagnosis
– = Characteristic deemed to exclude diagnosis
[a] World Health Organisation; ICD-10
[b] American Psychiatric Association; DSM-IV

Ozonoff & Miller, 1997; Schopler & Mesibov, 1977). America-based DSM criteria exclude the diagnosis of Asperger syndrome if the child also fulfils criteria for autism, whereas ICD 'rules' for this are more equivocal. Some researchers suggest there is little or no justification for using the category of Asperger syndrome at all (Schopler, 1985). Others have used the label to describe a range of different conditions. These have included autistic individuals of higher levels of intelligence and/or language ability; those who have relatively mild obsessional or social difficulties; atypical cases who do not fulfil all the criteria for autism, or even for cases with 'schizoid personality disorders' (Wolff & McGuire, 1995).

Table 1.3 (adapted from Ghaziuddin et al., 1992) summarises the criteria used in the few large-scale studies to date, and those now adopted by ICD-10 (WHO, 1992) and DSM-IV (APA, 1994). As can be seen, the principal areas of inconsistency relate to early cognitive, linguistic and motor development.

Cognitive functioning: Although Asperger's own accounts focus on individuals of relatively high ability, he also refers to cases with 'considerable intellectual retardation' noting 'The fate of (these) cases is often very sad'. Individuals with cognitive delays are also described by other authors (Wing, 1981; Gillberg, 1991; Tantam, 1991). ICD criteria rule out the presence of severe learning disability although they lack any precise definition of what is meant by 'clinically significant cognitive delay'.

Early language delays: Clinical researchers (Wing, 1981; Gillberg, 1991; Tantam, 1991) note the difficulties in establishing whether or not early language development was entirely normal. How, for example, does one classify a child who develops words and phrases at a normal age, but whose *communicative* ability remains very limited? Other children may be slow to use single words, but their phrase speech then develops quite rapidly. Still others, who are described as using words and phrases by the 'normal' time (2 and 3 years respectively) may then be found to have linguistic delays when subsequently assessed on formal language tests.

Motor clumsiness: Neither ICD nor DSM criteria specifically include motor difficulties, and although these are often described, assessment has rarely been based on adequately standardised and validated tests. Well-controlled studies (e.g. Manjiviona & Prior, 1995), have failed to demonstrate that children with Asperger syndrome are consistently impaired in their motor functioning or that clumsiness is a diagnostically differentiating feature. However, there is clearly wide variability and Manjiviona and Prior (1995) found that 50% of children with Asperger syndrome and 67% of children with high-functioning autism had clinically significant levels of motor impairment.

Epidemiology and age of onset

There are a number of other factors that seem to differentiate between autism and Asperger syndrome. Estimates of prevalence rates, for example (based only on small-scale investigations), suggest that the rates for Asperger syndrome may be considerably higher than those for autism, with figures varying between 3 and 7 per 1,000 (Ehlers & Gillberg, 1993). The gender distribution, too, may be rather different. Asperger believed that the typical condition did not occur in girls at all, except following an encephalitic illness. Although later studies have identified females with the disorder it is clear the majority are male. Howlin and Moore (1997) found the ratio of males to females in a sample of 190 individuals diagnosed as having Asperger syndrome was 10.3:1. Other estimates vary from around 4.7:1 (Wing, 1981) to 10:1 (Gillberg, 1991) although, as with the general prevalence data, these figures require confirmation by larger-scale epidemiological studies.

Neither ICD nor DSM systems stipulate the criteria for age of onset but all the children described by Asperger had shown difficulties by the time they were 2. DSM-IV criteria note that recognition of the disorder may be later than for autism, although problems are usually apparent in the pre-school or early school years. In a recent survey of parents of children with autism and related disorders in the UK, Howlin and Moore (1997) examined the average age at which parents first became aware of their children's difficulties. Parents of children with Asperger syndrome were

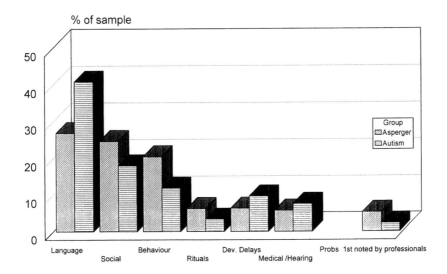

Figure 1.1: First problems to raise parent's concerns

aware of problems at around 2.5 years; in the autism group anxieties first emerged when the children were aged about 18 months. The areas first giving rise to concern were also different. In the autistic group parents were most likely to worry initially about problems related to language development; in the Asperger group problems tended to focus around language *or* social development *or* behavioural difficulties (see Figure 1.1).

There was also a significant difference in the age at which parents received a formal diagnosis for their children. In the autism group the average age of diagnosis was 5.5 years; in the Asperger group it was much later, at 11.3 years. Almost all (88.7%) of the children with autism had been diagnosed before 10 years of age as compared to only 45% of the Asperger group.

Causation

As far as aetiology is concerned, there is widespread agreement (see Chapter 2) that genetic factors predominate. Asperger himself noted that 'in every instance where it was possible to make a close study' similar traits were to be found to some degree in parents and other relatives. Other studies (Wing, 1981; De Long & Dwyer, 1988) also report a high frequency of autistic features in the relatives of individuals with Asperger syndrome. However, whether heritability is greater than in other autistic-spectrum disorders is not clear. Bolton and his colleagues (1994) suggest that genetic susceptibility is actually higher in autistic children of low verbal IQ. In contrast, Gillberg (1991) and Eisenmajer *et al.* (1996) suggest that genetic factors may be particularly strong in individuals who are more able, or those who have Asperger syndrome.

Other research findings

Although Asperger himself believed that autism and Asperger syndrome were very different conditions, the obvious similarities between the two disorders have led many other authors to suggest that they lie on the same continuum, and are only quantitatively different from each other (see Wing, 1981). Recent studies of cognitive profiles in subjects with high-functioning autism and Asperger syndrome illustrate the confusion that exists in distinguishing between them. Some research reports *no differences* in IQ between the two groups (Szatmari *et al.*, 1990); others (Klin *et al.*, 1995; Manjiviona & Prior, 1995) have found significantly higher *non-verbal* IQ scores in the Asperger group; and yet others have found significantly higher *verbal* scores (Ozonoff *et al.*, 1991). Klin *et al.* (1995) suggest that although individuals with autism and Asperger syndrome do have somewhat different profiles, these could be viewed as being similar to 'the phenomenological differences between lower functioning and higher functioning autism'.

Szatmari and his colleagues (1989) conclude: 'Our results indicate that it may be best to think of Asperger's syndrome as a mild form of high functioning autism.' However, Lord and Rutter (1994) note that there have been very few adequately controlled comparative studies and 'research has been plagued from the start by a lack of clear definition of the syndrome'. Klin and Volkmar (1997) also criticise the inherent 'circularity' of many studies, since findings have often simply reflected the criteria adopted in subject selection.

Wing (1981) suggests that the term is helpful 'when explaining the problems of children and adults who have autistic features, but who talk grammatically and who are not socially aloof. Such people are perplexing to parents, teachers and work supervisors who often cannot believe in a diagnosis of autism, which they equate with muteness and total social withdrawal.'

Szatmari and his colleagues (1995) also compared scores on the ADI (Autism Diagnostic Interview) in a group of children with Asperger syndrome, and another of high-functioning children with autism. They found that although many of the Asperger group met full diagnostic criteria for autism (indeed, only one child who met the criteria for social and repetitive impairments did not also meet criteria for communication deficits), there were a number of differences between the groups. Thus, the children with autism were significantly less sociable, more ritualistic and more resistant to change than the children with Asperger syndrome. Although the average IQ in both groups was in the normal range, it was lower in the autism group (86.6 vs 99.3) and language delays and abnormalities were significantly greater.

Eisenmajer and colleagues (1996) attempted to identify the characteristics that were most likely to lead to a diagnosis of Asperger syndrome, rather than autism. Lack of early delays in language was the most significant factor, but the Asperger group also had a higher verbal mental age, tended to be more proactive in their social relationships, were more likely to receive a co-diagnosis of attention deficit disorder and were, generally diagnosed at a later stage (8.88 years compared with 6.02 years). As noted above, there was a raised incidence of autism-spectrum disorders in the families of the Asperger children, but other variables—such as use of medication, perinatal difficulties, early illnesses and most motor milestones—did not differentiate between the groups (although the children with autism were more likely to have been delayed in walking).

Whether or not Asperger syndrome is most appropriately considered as the equivalent of high-functioning autism, or whether it is sufficiently different to warrant a distinct label within the autistic continuum, remains a subject of debate (see Klin & Volkmar (1997) and Schopler & Mesibov (1997) for further discussion of these issues). More research, using much better defined diagnostic criteria, is required before this question can be answered finally. For the time being, however, it is deemed to warrant its own diagnostic classification.

A Typical Case History

As with autism generally—although there is wide variation in the expression of the disorder, depending on age, intellectual ability, language and other skills—there are also many striking similarities between cases. The following case history illustrates a typical pattern of development.

Background

John was not diagnosed as having Asperger syndrome until the age of 16. Prior to this he had been referred to educational psychologists and child psychiatrists on several occasions, primarily because of his poor peer relationships and difficulties in coping with school work. Psychometric assessments consistently showed him to be of above-average intelligence and to have age appropriate skills in reading, spelling and mathematics. The family had been offered family therapy in the past but this had no impact on his behaviour.

Early childhood

John had been a very good baby, and his early milestones had all been normal. He seemed most contented if left alone and did not particularly enjoy being cuddled, but he would respond if picked up and tickled. He would look at his parents and smile at them, but rather less frequently than his siblings. He started to use words at about 9 months, and by the age of 3 years had a very sophisticated vocabulary. He was fascinated by maps and trains and would talk endlessly about these. He was considered to be very intelligent but his mother remembers how hard it was to get him to talk about any other topics and how he was unable to take part in normal conversations.

She also recalls that he tended to interpret every thing that was said very literally. Once, to keep him quiet, she had suggested he paint his Thomas the Tank Engine trains, leaving him with paper and paints. When she returned the paper was blank but all the toy trains were covered in paint.

As he grew older his behaviour became more difficult and he was 'expelled' from two nursery schools before he was 5 because of his disruptive behaviour. His first two years in primary school are described as 'a nightmare' and his mother was continually summoned to the principal's office because of some new misdemeanour. At the age of 7 the educational psychologist recommended transfer to a smaller and more highly structured school. John got on well there and, although he had no friends, his class teacher made use of his skills in spelling and mathematics by encouraging him to help less able children.

He had never shown any imitative or imaginative play until the age of about 6 years, when he began to collect and play with 'Thomas the Tank Engine' railway sets. He would play for hours alone with these, enacting complex scenarios from books or videos. Occasionally he would allow other children to join in but they had to follow his directions exactly, otherwise the game would have to start all over again. It was around this time that the possibility of his having an autistic disorder was first suggested, but his paediatrician dismissed this on the grounds of his complex pretend play, and his good conversational skills. (John had told him about all the Thomas the Tank Engine books he had ever read.)

Gradually the obsession with Thomas the Tank Engine faded, but the interest in trains persisted. John was particularly fascinated by the internal lighting systems of trains and at weekends would insist on travelling on different branch lines to photograph all the lights. He was also extremely knowledgeable about train routes and maps. From the age of 7 he would ask for maps, or books about maps, for every Christmas or birthday.

Socially, he remained a very isolated child and often offended members of his own family by his thoughtless comments or behaviour. In public he would make loud remarks about people's appearance and was particularly fascinated by anyone who was overweight or had a physical handicap. He showed no understanding of why these remarks should be viewed as offensive, insisting 'they were always true!'. He was never demonstrative, never sought or offered comfort and seemed unaware of other people's feelings. On one occasion, his mother fainted while they were eating a sandwich together in the kitchen. Only when he had finished his sandwich did he call his sister to help.

Adolescence

The situation became much more difficult when John moved to secondary school. He had no friends, was badly bullied and was frequently 'set up' by other children. Thus, if they suggested that he trip up the school principal on the way to assembly, or drop his bag on another teacher from the top of the staircase, he would do exactly as he was asked. He was constantly in trouble with his teachers because of his lack of organisation, his lateness, his failure to bring the right books and equipment to school and his erratic approach to homework. His tendency to make loud and personal comments about teachers' appearance, or to correct them in lessons, was also (understandably) resented. Sports activities presented particular problems as he was extremely clumsy and could never grasp the rules of team games. He was, however, remarkably good at maths, French and German.

As time went on he became more anxious and resistant to going to school. He became increasingly withdrawn, spending most of his time alone in his room. His mother became concerned that he might be developing schizophrenia (from which her own brother suffered) and his teachers were worried that he would not be able to cope with the public examinations that were due to take place at the end of the year.

THE OUTCOME FOR ADULTS WITH AUTISM AND ASPERGER SYNDROME

Early follow-up studies of children with autism were largely anecdotal (e.g. Eisenberg, 1956; Creak, 1963) but towards the end of the 1960s Michael Rutter and his colleagues conducted a detailed follow-up of 63 autistic individuals initially diagnosed during the 1950s and early 1960s. Among those who had reached adulthood, over half were in long-stay hospitals, 11 were still living with their parents, and three were placed in special autistic communities; only three were in paid employment (Lockyer & Rutter, 1969, 1970; Rutter & Lockyer, 1967; Rutter et al., 1967).

In a subsequent study, Lotter (1974a, 1974b) followed up 29 young people, aged over 16, with autism. His findings were similar to those of Rutter, although by the 1970s many more had received full-time education. Nevertheless, only one individual had a job and almost half the sample was in long-stay hospital provision; two individuals were living at home and five were attending day training centres.

Throughout the 1980s and 1990s there has continued to be a small number of reports of outcome in adulthood. These include the follow-up study of Chung et al. (1990) in Hong Kong, Gillberg and Steffenburg (1987) in Sweden, Kobayashi et al. (1992) in Japan, and Goode et al. (1994) in England. A follow-up in France has been carried out by Fombonne and his colleagues (1989), although this involves a more heterogeneous group of subjects. There have also been several studies that have focused more specifically on higher functioning individuals with autism or Asperger syndrome: three in the USA or Canada (Rumsey et al., 1985; Szatmari et al., 1989; Venter et al., 1992) and two in the UK (Mawhood et al., 1998; Tantam, 1991).

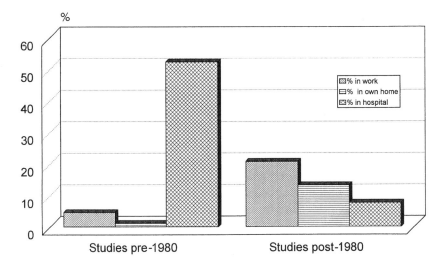

Figure 1.2: Improvements in independent living reported over four decades

Figure 1.2 illustrates some of the changes in outcome that appear to have occurred over the last four decades. The analysis is split into those studies that appeared between 1950 and the end of the 1970s and those completed during the 1980s and 1990s (Howlin & Goode, 1998, provide details of all the studies involved).

Although direct comparisons between studies are complicated because of differences in methodology, in the subjects involved and in data analysis, the overall results indicate that, over the years, there have been improvements in the levels of functioning attained by people with autism. More people are living independently, more are in jobs and far fewer spend their lives in hospitals or similar forms of institutional care. Obviously, these changes cannot be directly attributed to better treatment and education—the decrease in hospital care, for example, is mostly due to the widespread closure of large institutions—but they are encouraging.

Factors Related to Outcome

These studies also suggest that there are a number of factors related to early development that appear to be associated with later outcome. These include the development of at least simple communicative language by the age of 5 or 6 years; the ability to score within the mildly retarded range or above on non-verbal tests of ability; and, in many cases, the presence of *additional* skills or interests (such as specialised knowledge in particular areas or competence in mathematics, music or computing) which make it easier for individuals to find their own 'niche' in life. Kanner (1943, 1973), Rutter *et al.* (1967), Lockyer and Rutter (1970) and Lotter (1974a) also stress the importance of appropriate education. The influence of other factors remains uncertain, such as the severity of autistic symptomatology, the extent of early behavioural difficulties, family factors, or the sex of the child. On the whole, women tend to do less well than men, although this is probably related to IQ differences (Lord & Schopler, 1985). There are no individual symptoms (other than lack of speech) that are related to outcome, although the greater the number of social and behavioural problems, the worse the ultimate outcome. And, although some earlier studies suggested that socio-economic factors and ratings of family adequacy might be *correlated* with outcome (DeMyer *et al.*, 1973; Lotter, 1974a), there is little evidence of any direct causal relationships.

The Impact of Early Intervention on Outcome in Adult Life

In his account of over 90 young adults who had first been diagnosed in childhood, Kanner (1973) noted that 11–12% of the group had done relatively well, despite receiving little in the way of specialist intervention or support. This led him to speculate that prognosis might well improve in future years as recognition of the disorder, and the provision of appropriate educational and therapeutic facilities, increased.

However, despite some improvements in outcome over the past two decades, the majority of adults with autism still remains highly dependent. Despite claims appearing from time to time in the media that particular treatments can have a dramatic impact on outcome, there is little evidence to substantiate such optimism. Moreover, even when there is evidence of short-term gains, information about functioning in adult life is generally non-existent. Later chapters will explore various different approaches to intervention. Some involve therapies that offer parents the hope of 'miracles' or 'cures'; others, although more cautious in their claims, may nevertheless have a significant impact on the lives of children and their families.

2

UNDERSTANDING THE CAUSES OF AUTISM

EARLY THEORIES, PSYCHOGENIC THEORIES AND VIEWS OF 'INADEQUATE PARENTING'

In Kanner's earliest writings on the causation of autism he wrote: 'We must . . . assume that these children have come into the world with an innate ability to form the usual biologically provided affective contact with people, just as other children come into the world with innate physical or mental handicaps.' At that time (1943) he considered autism to be a constitutionally determined developmental disorder, primarily affecting social and emotional understanding.

However, as time went on, his writings begin to reflect the prevalent view that many childhood disorders, and indeed much psychotic illness in adulthood, were a response to dysfunctional patterns of family interaction or inadequate parenting. In 1954 he wrote: 'It should not be forgotten that the emotional refrigeration which children experience from such parents cannot but be a highly pathogenic element in the patient's early personality development.' For two decades or more parents' fate was sealed and it was they who came to be viewed as the primary cause of their children's difficulties. Many other authors began to comment on their apparently cold, detached and obsessive traits (Szurek & Berlin, 1956; Boatman & Szurek, 1960; Goldfarb, 1961; Bettelheim, 1967; O'Gorman, 1970). And treatment, which was largely psychotherapeutic, focused on parents' pathology as much as on disturbance in their child. Indeed, even today in countries with a strong analytic tradition, such as France, parents may still be refused treatment for their child unless they, too, are willing to undergo personal analysis.

Despite the impact of these ideas on both theory and clinical practice, they were, in fact, based on little, if any, experimental evidence, and, when empirical investigations finally began to appear, they provided no support for such views. Cantwell and his colleagues (1979) found that, compared with control families, the families of children with autism did not have higher rates of adverse environmental factors; emotional and personality problems were no more frequent, and there were no differences in patterns of family interaction. Moreover, Rutter (1985) pointed out that psychogenic theories could not possibly explain the very specific nature of children's cognitive, behavioural and communication deficits, especially the marked lack of social responsiveness that is often apparent in the earliest months of life. Rutter and Lord (1987) also noted that the characteristic behaviour patterns of a child with autism were generally very different to those exhibited by children who have been damaged by emotional neglect or abuse of other kinds. Furthermore, Gardner (1976), in a neatly designed study, illustrated that, even if abnormalities in interaction are detected, these may well be attributable to the child, rather than vice-versa. He observed children with and without autism interacting with their mothers. He then asked the mothers of the non-autistic children to interact with a child with autism, while mothers of autistic children were observed with a normal child. When interacting with a child with autism, both groups of mothers showed a number of unusual behaviours; when they were observed interacting with the non-autistic children these abnormal features disappeared. The conclusion was that it was the *child's* behaviour that affected parental responses; not the other way around!

Autism as a Form of Early Schizophrenia

Kanner himself believed that autism was a very early form of schizophrenia, and in 1951 wrote: 'There is no likelihood that early infantile autism will at any future time have to be separated from the schizophrenias.' The use of terms such as 'infantile psychosis' or 'childhood schizophrenia' in many of the early descriptive accounts of children with autism (Creak, 1963; Eisenberg, 1972), or more recent accounts of 'schizoid personality in childhood' (Wolff, 1991) has led to considerable confusion in the minds of professionals and non-professionals alike, regarding the underlying nature of the condition. In fact, there is no evidence that the incidence of schizophrenia in people with autism is any higher than in the general population. As Rutter (1985) makes clear, there are also many features that differentiate between the two disorders. These are summarised in Table 2.1.

Current classificatory systems (DSM-IV; ICD-10) now distinguish clearly between autism as a developmental disorder, with its onset in infancy or early childhood, and schizophrenia, which is a group of diseases of later onset, characterised by particular abnormalities of thinking, perception and emotion. As long as diagnostic procedures are carried out

Table 2.1: A summary of the principal differences between autism and schizophrenia

	Autism	Schizophrenia
Age of onset	Typically before 3 years.	Generally mid-teens or early adulthood.
Course of the disorder	Problems frequently evident in first 9–12 months. Behavioural difficulties often greatest in early years. Tend to stabilise in late adolescence/early adulthood.	Early history appears relatively normal. Although developmental delays, cognitive and attentional difficulties, and poor social relationships are found in pre-morbid stage, *severe* delays in early development rare. In adulthood periodic relapses and remissions are typical.
Symptoms	Severe and pervasive language impairments; lack of social understanding and marked rituals and routines are the main diagnostic features. Delusions and hallucinations rare.	First rank symptoms of delusions and/or hallucinations required for diagnosis.
Cognitive impairments	Around 70% of individuals with autism have an IQ in the retarded range. Significant discrepancies between verbal and non-verbal IQ are typical.	Severe learning disabilities rare, although cognitive impairments may increase with age. Specific deficits in information-processing identified.
Incidence	Figures vary, but rates of approximately 2 to 3 per 1,000 are now widely accepted.	Lifetime prevalence around 1%.
Sex ratio	Typically 4:1 male to female. Fewer females in average IQ range (ratio probably around 9:1); more females in severely retarded range. No overall differences in symptom severity/prognosis.	Overall occurs only slightly more frequently in males than females; males tend to be more severely affected, respond less well to treatment and have worse prognosis.
Family characteristics	Increased genetic risks of cognitive impairments and/or social, linguistic or obsessional difficulties. No increased familial risks for schizophrenia.	Significant genetic heritability; risk of schizophrenia as high as 40% if both parents affected; 55% if identical twin affected.
Organic features	Epilepsy relatively common (around 20–30%). Other neuropathological or biochemical findings inconsistent.	Epilepsy not particularly common; if does occur has different age of onset and is more often of temporal lobe origin. Some evidence of ventricular abnormalities although neuropathological and biochemical findings often inconsistent.
Treatment	No proven successful pharmacological treatments (other than for secondary problems, such as overactivity). Early and appropriate educational and behavioural interventions most important for outcome.	Antipsychotic medication very successful in many cases, although not all. Most effective if used in conjunction with other psychosocial interventions (e.g. family education and cognitive-behavioural approaches).

appropriately, with careful attention being given to early history as well as current state, confusion over differential diagnosis should be avoidable. Problems are most likely to occur not in the diagnosis of children but of adults who come to the attention of services later in life. Many of these cases tend to be of higher intellectual ability or suffer from Asperger syndrome and hence their problems may be misinterpreted. When seen by adult psychiatric services their unusual affect, concrete thought processes, misunderstanding of language, and abnormal preoccupations can still result in a mistaken diagnosis of schizophrenia, even in the absence of any first-rank psychotic symptoms. Such errors can have serious implications for treatment and prognosis (see Howlin, 1997).

RECENT RESEARCH FINDINGS: ORGANIC DYSFUNCTION IN AUTISM

One particular aspect of autism, which psychogenic theories could not attempt to explain, was the strong association with organic factors. A high incidence of pre-natal problems has been recognised for some time (Gillberg & Coleman, 1992). These include pre-maturity, post-maturity, early or mid-trimester bleeding, advanced maternal age and birth order (either first born or fourth born or later). Respiratory and other difficulties at birth also tend to be relatively more frequent. In later childhood, typically around 12 to 14 years of age, around 20% to 30% of children develop epilepsy. Major motor seizures are the most common kind, although complex partial seizures may also occur. The risk of epilepsy is not strongly associated with IQ, except in individuals with profound learning disabilities. Goode and her colleagues (1994) found that 18% of young adults with a non-verbal IQ above 70 had epilepsy compared with 16% of those with an IQ between 50 and 69, and 20% in the 35 to 49 range.

The increased frequency and unusual age of onset of epilepsy in autism (which usually begins in early childhood in non-autistic children) led to research into possible EEG abnormalities. Such abnormalities probably occur in around 50% of people with autism (Bailey *et al.*, 1996) although estimates vary widely, ranging from 10% to 83%. Bilateral, diffuse abnormalities are common (Tsai *et al.*, 1985) but even when unilateral anomalies have been found, no particular part of the brain seems to be involved and no specific EEG patterns have been identified.

In recent years far more complex techniques, such as evoked potential recordings, positron emission tomography (PET), computerised tomography (CT) or structural or functional magnetic resonance imaging (MRI and fMRI) to assess brain dysfunction have become available. Unfortunately, much of the work carried out lacks a clear theoretical basis. Inadequate diagnosis, the failure to include appropriate controls, small sample size, and the heterogeneity of subjects have also given rise to problems. Thus, many potentially interesting results have proved contradictory or inconclusive and few findings have been reliably replicated. The only conclusion that seems to have been fairly consistent is the greater heterogeneity of findings in autistic as compared with control groups (Bailey *et al.*, 1996).

Neurochemical studies of individuals with autism have also failed to produce consistent results. Most of these rely on blood or urine samples, which may not necessarily provide useful information on brain function or structure. Many studies are also flawed because of problems of subject selection, inadequate controls, and the lack of blind evaluations. Again, the only relatively consistent finding relates to raised whole blood serotonin levels (hyperserotonemia). These are elevated in around 25% of individuals with autism and also in some family members. The significance of this is unclear, although Bailey *et al.* (1996) suggest that as serotonin is important for brain development, any causal links (if they exist) may operate through developmental mechanisms.

Various neuropsychological models of dysfunction in autism have been proposed, based on findings from psychological experiments. In a number of studies, subjects (mostly high-functioning adults with autism) have been found to show deficits in tasks related to executive functioning (i.e. planning and organisational abilities; disengaging from external stimuli; inhibiting inappropriate responses; self-monitoring and making use of feedback, and sustaining or switching cognitive set). Executive dysfunction, in turn, has been postulated as being a result of frontal lobe disturbance. Other research has suggested deficits in lateralisation, or in the temporal lobe area. Unfortunately, failure on psychological tests can be due to many different factors and cannot be taken as prima facie evidence of structural brain dysfunction. In most cases, imaging studies have failed to support hypotheses about the involvement of specific brain structures, although very recent work by Simon Baron-Cohen and his colleagues suggests that, unlike normal controls, subjects with autism tend to rely more on pre-frontal areas, rather than the amygdala area, when required to process emotional and social stimuli. However, exciting as these findings may be, it should be remembered that experimental work with very small numbers of young adults does not necessarily provide information on causative factors in infancy.

The other source of information on brain dysfunction derives from more traditional autopsy studies. Work by Bauman (1991) has failed to identify gross lesions or other obvious abnormalities in brain structure; and although reductions in the density of Purkinje cells in the cerebellum have been reported in a number of cases, most of these were in individuals who also had epilepsy. Bauman and Kemper (1994) have also reported the relatively consistent finding of abnormally small and densely packed neurones in the hippocampus, amygdala and elsewhere. This might indicate that the normal 'pruning' of brain cells, which usually occurs in the early months of life and is necessary for more efficient processing, has not occurred. However, as yet, such findings are based on very small numbers of subjects, with no IQ-matched control groups, so that it remains unclear how specific these findings are to autism *per se*.

The only other well-replicated finding is that of increased head circumference (macrocephaly) and brain volume in autism (see Bailey *et al.*, 1996; Piven *et al.*, 1996; Lainhart *et al.*, 1997). Abnormally large head circumference (which has been reported in up to 42% of twins and 37% of singletons with autism below 16 years) contrasts with the more usual finding of smaller or lighter brains in individuals with mental handicap. The larger than usual brain volume tends to be associated with an increase in the cerebral cortex, and analysis of lobe sizes indicates that the temporal, parietal and occipital, but not the frontal lobes, are significantly enlarged. Increased head circumference (but not necessarily brain volume) has been reported slightly more frequently in females than males (Lainhart *et al.*, 1997). Longitudinal studies suggest that in most cases increased head size is not apparent at birth; instead, the rate of head growth increases in early and middle childhood. However, Lainhart and her colleagues did not find any association between head circumference and other clinical features, such as severity of autistic symptoms, or IQ.

Possible Links with Other Medical Conditions and Single Gene or Chromosome Disorders

Autism does not confer immunity from other disorders, and there is probably no single condition that can be considered to be mutually exclusive of autism. For example, although it was once thought that the co-occurrence of autism and Down's syndrome was extremely rare, this is no longer the case. It is true that autism does not seem to occur in children with Down's syndrome as often as in other children with non-specific mental retardation, but there are now a number of reports suggesting that the frequency is probably around 10% (Howlin *et al.*, 1995). Autism has also been reported in association with a range of other syndromes (Gillberg & Coleman, 1992). Table 2.2 gives a brief summary of these (for further details of these conditions see Gillberg & Coleman, 1992, and O'Brien & Yule, 1995).

Table 2.2: Other syndromes in which several cases of autism have been reported (from Gillberg & Coleman, 1992)

Congenital rubella	Results from viral infection during pregnancy; causes sensory impairments, especially deafness, and learning difficulties. When autism occurs this is usually atypical. Now rare in areas where rubella inoculation programmes are routine.
Cornelia de Lange syndrome	Chromosomal disorder (? gene 3q 26.3) with severe growth retardation and specific facial characteristics. Often associated with moderate–severe learning difficulties, behavioural problems and communication problems.
Fetal alcohol syndrome	Damage to foetus caused by excessive alcohol intake during pregnancy. Results in a variety of symptoms including physical, behavioural and learning difficulties. Because relatively common, links with autism may be coincidental.
Fragile X	(FraX-A). Most common inherited cause of mental retardation. FMR-1 gene identified at the Fragile X site (Xq 27.3). Variants include FraX-E and FraX-F. Typical facial and other physical characteristics plus cognitive, language, social and behavioural problems. Once considered to be significant cause of autism; recent reports suggest that association is much less.
Hypomelanosis of Ito	Chromosomal disorder (usually sporadic) with skin and skeletal abnormalities, epilepsy and learning difficulties. Neuro-ectodermal syndrome (as are neuro fibromatosis and tuberous sclerosis).
Joubert syndrome	Autosomal recessive disorder with abnormal motor development and mental retardation.
Lujan-Fryns syndrome	X-linked learning disorder, with physical and voice abnormalities and hyperactivity.
Moebius syndrome	Neurological disorder with congenital bilateral diplegia.
Neuro-fibromatosis	Autosomal dominant disorder or spontaneous genetic mutation (gene on chromosome 17Q 11.2) resulting in proclivity to tumour formation in the skin, CNS and viscera. Associated with behavioural and learning disabilities.
Phenylketonuria	Autosomal recessive disorder (Chromosome 12 q22–q24.1) causes enzyme deficiency resulting in toxic levels of phenylalanine; skin and facial characteristics; physical abnormalities, seizures and learning disabilities. Dietary control in early pregnancy essential to avoid foetal abnormalities.
Sotos syndrome	Cerebral giganticism with hydrocephalus; typical facial features; accelerated growth and developmental delay.

continued overleaf

Table 2.2: (*continued*)

Gilles de la Tourette syndrome	Neurological, genetically linked disorder with involuntary movements.
Tuberous sclerosis	Autosomal dominant disorder with two identified loci; one on chromosome 9q 34.3; the other on 16p 13.3. Characterised by benign tubers in different areas, including skin, kidneys and CNS. Epilepsy and mental retardation occur in over 50% of cases. Degree of impairment associated with number of tubers. High rates of autism, hyperactivity, aggressive and self-injurious behaviours. Risk of autism may be associated with presence of tubers in temporal lobes.
Williams' syndrome	Elastin gene deletion disorder, with distinct facial appearance; and typical pattern of social, communication and behavioural characteristics.

Other conditions in which isolated cases of autism have been reported include Biedl–Bardet syndrome, cerebral palsy, Coffin–Siris syndrome, Cohen syndrome, Duchenne muscular dystrophy, Lawrence–Moon–Biedl syndrome, myotonic dystrophy, oculocutaneous albinoism, Noonan syndrome and Sanfillippo syndrome (Gillberg & Coleman, 1992).

Some authors, such as Gillberg (1992a), have argued that as many as 37% of cases of autism have associated medical conditions of the kind noted above. In view of this, he recommends that detailed and systematic medical investigations, including a lumbar puncture and brain scan, should be carried out as routine clinical practice. In contrast, Rutter and his colleagues (1994) suggest that 'subsequent research has indicated that the actual rates are very much lower than originally claimed' (probably around 10%). They also conclude that the association is higher in cases with profound learning disabilities and in those with atypical forms of autism. For example, they argue that the association with maternal rubella is much lower than claimed in the past; moreover, the picture of autism found in such cases tends to be atypical. An additional problem relates to the fact that the finding of an association between autism and another condition such as Fragile X, neurofibromatosis, phenylketonuria (PKU) or tuberous sclerosis does not necessarily indicate a direct causal link. For instance, many children with autism have some degree of hearing or visual impairment (see Gillberg & Coleman, 1992) but few would suggest that these caused the autism. Instead, a common (though unknown) cause for both sets of problems is most likely to be postulated.

Although associations between autism and some of the syndromes listed above have, in the past, given rise to much excitement in the belief that these might offer some clues to the genetic basis of the disorder, a glance at the variety, complexity and diversity of these conditions suggests that no simple answers are likely to emerge from work of this kind. Lord and Rutter (1994) argue that accounts of associations between autism and other conditions are often based on unsystematic single case studies (or ones involving very small numbers of cases). Such reports are clearly important, but statistical extrapolations based on clinical samples do need to be treated with caution. Rutter and his colleagues (1994) also criticise diagnoses made on the basis of 'clinical impression, rather than systematic standardized assessment', or 'misleadingly . . . loose laboratory criteria' (Lord & Rutter, 1994).

On the other hand, large-scale research studies are unlikely to be sensitive to a wide range of possible additional disorders, nor can they employ all the detailed medical and chromosomal analyses that will be available, perhaps over the course of several years' involvement with a child, to an observant and experienced clinician. Single case studies may have their faults, but they are also a rich source of knowledge and the inspiration for subsequent, more rigorous research. After all, Kanner's early writings on autism consisted primarily of a collection of single case studies. Thus, if resources are available, and as long as the proposed investigations do not cause distress or pose any danger to the child, the routine collection of potentially valuable information can hardly be considered detrimental to progress.

Established Associations between Autism and known Genetic Disorders

Phenylketonuria and neurofibromatosis

Over the years the conditions with which autism has been most frequently associated are phenylketonuria (PKU), neurofibromatosis, tuberous sclerosis, and Fragile X. Lord and Rutter (1994) suggest that the proposed link with PKU is now doubtful, adding that this condition is now so rare because of widespread screening that 'it is of negligible importance . . . as a cause of autism'. Similarly, the association with neurofibromatosis is based, like PKU, on single case reports and since this condition too is very rare, it is unlikely to be a frequent cause.

Tuberous sclerosis

The links with tuberous sclerosis, on the other hand, do appear to be stronger and better documented. Studies in Scotland and Sweden suggest that between 25% and 61% of individuals with tuberous sclerosis meet diagnostic criteria for autism, with an even higher proportion having a broader pervasive developmental disorder (Harrison & Bolton, 1997). The rates of autism are particularly high in children who have tubers present in the temporal lobes of the brain or in those with infantile spasms. The incidence of tuberous sclerosis in samples of children with autism is also relatively high, ranging from 0.4% to 3% (Smalley *et al.*, 1991). There is little doubt that a significant association between the two conditions exists, although there is relatively little information on the pattern of autistic symptomatology found in these cases. There is some suggestion (Smalley *et al.*, 1994) that ritualistic and stereotyped behaviours may be less marked in individuals with tuberous sclerosis and autism, but this finding is based on a very small sample size. Lord and Rutter (1994) proposed that, as most cases with autism and tuberous sclerosis also have learning disabilities, the association could be with the degree of mental handicap not the medical condition *per se*. However, several case reports indicate that co-occurrence is also found in individuals of normal intelligence (Harrison & Bolton, 1997).

Fragile X

Studies of the links between autism and Fragile X have resulted in highly variable estimates of concordance rates, which have progressively reduced over recent years. While early studies (on small samples and using less stringent diagnostic criteria for autism) suggested that the concordance rate might be as high as 60%, this declined to 16% when DSM-III criteria were used (Hagerman, 1990: Bailey *et al.*, 1996). Recent improvements in genetic testing, together with the use of more stringent diagnostic criteria for autism, have resulted in much lower rates than initially suggested—current estimates are around 2.5% (Bailey *et al.*, 1996). Nevertheless, even a 2.5% rate of Fragile X in autism is well above that found in the general population. Thus, the association appears to be significant, although the nature of the relationship remains unclear. Bailey *et al.* (1996) suggest that the link may be indirect, in that, since both autism and Fragile X are associated with mental retardation, the basic association may be between Fragile X and mental retardation. In other words, the link with autism could just be secondary and indirect. Moreover, even if a specific association does exist, this is too weak to indicate any clear genetic mechanism.

Links with other chromosomal abnormalities

A number of other chromosomal abnormalities have also been associated with autism. Probably around 5% of cases have some chromosomal anomaly (in addition to Fragile X) but again the meaning of this association is unclear. Most of the abnormalities reported are of uncertain clinical significance, or are also known to arise in individuals with no apparent handicaps. There *may* be a stronger association with the presence of an extra marker chromosome on chromosome 15 (Hotopf & Bolton, 1995; Gillberg *et al.*, 1991), but since autism has been associated with anomalies involving almost all chromosomes, these reports provide few clues regarding possible genetic mechanisms.

GENETIC INVESTIGATIONS: TWIN AND FAMILY STUDIES OF AUTISM

While the nature of the genetic mechanisms associated with autism remain unclear, there is now little doubt that hereditary factors are of primary importance. The possibility of there being an association with genetic factors first emerged from studies of siblings in the 1960s and 1970s. Although the 2% rate of autism found in siblings seemed very small in absolute terms, this represented a 50- to 100-fold increase over the general population incidence. In order to pursue this line of research further, Folstein and Rutter (1977a, 1977b) conducted the first systematic population-based twin study of autism. They identified 11 monozygotic (identical) and 10 dizygotic (non-identical) same-sex twin pairs, in which one twin had been diagnosed as having autism. Among the monozygotic twins 36% were concordant for autism (i.e. both twins in four of the pairs were autistic); none of the dizygotic twins was concordant. The findings also showed that 9 of the 11 pairs of monozygotic twins, but only 1 of the 10 pairs of dizygotic twins, were concordant for some other cognitive impairment, usually involving language or social deficits. A Scandinavian study (Steffenburg *et al.*, 1989) found even higher concordance rates (91%) for autism in monozygotic twins, but again, zero rates for the dizygotic pairs. Further research on a larger twin sample (28 monozygotic pairs and 20 dizygotic pairs) by Le Couteur and her colleagues (1996) resulted in findings of a pairwise concordance rate for autism or atypical autism of 72% in the monozygotic twins and 0% in dizygotic pairs. When a wider spectrum of problems was studied (i.e. social *or* language *or* obsessional problems) the concordance rates were even higher. In 19 pairs of monozygotic twins, both had autism or atypical autism; in a further 7 pairs the co-twin showed evidence of this broader phenotype. In other words, 26 of the 28 pairs showed concordance for autism or autism-related disorders; but this was the case for only 2 of the 20 dizygotic pairs (see Figure 2.1).

The initial twin studies were closely followed by wider studies of the families of children with autism. Piven and his colleagues in America (1990) reported a 3% rate of autism in siblings and a 4% rate of severe

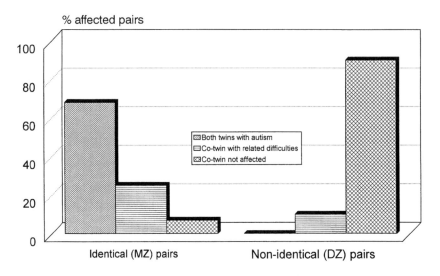

Data from Le Couteur et al., 1996; based on 28 MZ pairs and 20 DZ pairs. Related problems include social difficulties, communication problems and/or repetitive behaviours

Figure 2.1: Autism and related disorders in twins.

social impairment. Szatmari *et al.* (1993) found that 5.3% of siblings had a pervasive developmental disorder, compared with none of the controls. Jorde *et al.* (1991), in a large-scale family study based in Utah, reported a recurrence risk of 3.7% if the first autistic child was male, and 7% if it was female. The most systematic and extensive study was conducted by Patrick Bolton and his co-workers in London (1994). Data were analysed on 195 parents and 137 siblings in the autism sample, and on 72 parents and 64 siblings in the control group (families of a child with Down's syndrome). None of the siblings of the Down's children met diagnostic criteria for autism or other forms of pervasive developmental disorder while four (2.9%) of the siblings of the autistic cases met criteria for autism and four had atypical autism or Asperger syndrome. Thus, while almost 6% of the autism group siblings were diagnosed as having an autistic spectrum disorder, none of the Down's group showed problems of this kind.

Family studies of this kind also began to highlight the fact that, as well as an increased risk of autism occurring in relatives, there was a much higher incidence than expected of problems related to the autistic condition. In their original twin study Folstein and Rutter (1977a, 1977b) became aware that while the characteristic *triad* of impairments found in autism—communication deficits *and* lack of social understanding *and* ritualistic/stereotyped behaviours—did not occur in all monozygotic pairs, problems related to less severe impairments in these domains were

Table 2.3: Criteria for the 'Broader Phenotype' of autism as used in the family study of autism (Bolton *et al.*, 1994)

Inclusion criteria	*Communication deficit*
One item from:	• Language delay (no phrases by 33 months) • Reading delay (needing remedial help) • Articulation disorder (strangers unable to understand by 5 years)
Or two items from:	• Language delay (no words by 24 months) • Reading delay (educational assessment required) • Articulation disorder (speech therapy needed) • Spelling difficulties (frequent errors in common words)
Inclusion criteria	*Social deficit*
One item definitely present *or* two items probably present	*Childhood measures*: • Impaired social play (little/no to and fro social play) • Lack of affection (limited/no affection with caregiver; emotionally aloof/unresponsive) *Adulthood measures*: • Inappropriate or odd behaviour (frequent and pervasive; lacking responsiveness to social cues; intrusive, embarrassing or unacceptable) *Child and adult measures*: • Impaired Conversation (no to & fro chat; does not maintain conversation; monologues; terse replies) • Social dysfunction (awkward, wooden, or limited reciprocal relationships; no contacts outside the family) • Impaired friendships (socially isolated; does not mix; lack of close confiding relationships)
Inclusion criteria	*Repetitive stereotyped behaviour*
One item from:	• Circumscribed interests (odd or socially inappropriate interest; unusual in intensity; excludes other activities) • Rigidity (rigid or perfectionist style of behaviour, associated with social impairment) • Obsessions/compulsions (long standing obsessions or compulsions, associated with impairment or requiring treatment) • Repetitive behaviours (non-functional routines or rituals; preoccupations; motor stereotypes; object attachments; resistance to change)
Or two from:	• Circumscribed interests (as above, but not odd or socially inappropriate) • Rigidity (as above; commented on outside family but not associated with social impairment) • Obsessions/compulsions (as above, but information insufficient/incomplete) • Repetitive behaviours (as above, but information incomplete)

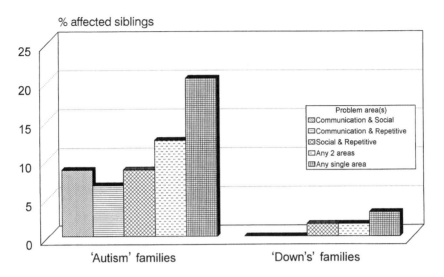

Data from Bolton et al., 1994. Figures based on 137 siblings of autistic children and 64 with a Down's syndrome sibling

Figure 2.2: Autism-related problems in siblings.

very frequent. However, these difficulties did not necessarily become apparent until the supposedly 'unaffected' twin grew older. Thus, in the subsequent family study by Patrick Bolton and his colleagues (1994), research was extended to cover what has become known as the 'broader phenotype' or 'lesser variant' of autism. Using clearly defined criteria (see Table 2.3), and on the basis of a detailed diagnostic interview, the presence of speech, pragmatics and literacy problems, impaired relationships, and restricted patterns of interests or behaviour in family members were assessed. The same data were collected on a control group of families with a Down's syndrome child.

When this wider range of problems related to social, communication or obsessional difficulties was assessed, it was found that 12.4% of siblings of the autistic children had difficulties in any *two* of these areas combined. This was labelled the 'narrow phenotype', meaning that they showed *either* social and communication problems, *or* stereotyped behaviours and social difficulties, *or* communication problems and stereotyped behaviours. Also 20.4% had problems in one of these areas, and this was labelled the 'broad phenotype'. The rates of the 'narrow' and 'broad' phenotypes in the Down's siblings were just 1.6% and 3.1% respectively (see Figure 2.2).

When all first-degree relatives were included (i.e. parents and siblings), 8.7% were found to have communication problems; the same proportion had social difficulties and 5.7% showed obsessional or stereotyped traits.

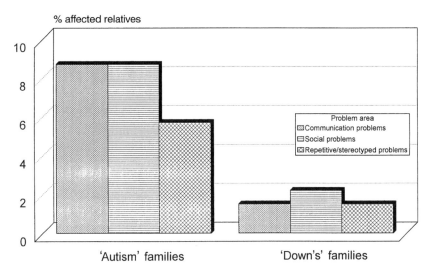

Data from Bolton et al., 1994. Figures based on 332 relatives of children with autism and 136 relatives of children with Down's syndrome

Figure 2.3: Autism-related problems in all first degree relatives.

The comparative figures for the Down's families were 1.5%, 2.2% and 1.5% (see Figure 2.3).

The authors also investigated the association between familial loading and other factors including the sex, IQ, severity of autistic symptoms and history of obstetric complications in the autistic probands. There was no clear association with gender, and although both the broad and narrow phenotypes were significantly more common in male relatives, the male : female ratio tended to decline in those who were very mildly affected. Disorders in siblings were found to be more common and more severe than in parents. Low verbal IQ was associated with a higher family loading but there was only a weak association with performance IQ. Severity of autism (based on the number of ICD-9 symptoms) and history of obstetric problems were only associated with family loading in those autistic probands with speech. There were no clear associations within the non-speaking group.

Taken together, the results from twin and family studies suggest an heritability figure of 91–93% for an underlying liability to autism (Bailey *et al.*, 1996). The association with a much broader phenotype than was once recognised could be due to the fact that relatives with the 'lesser variant' (who unlike those with classical autism tend to be of normal IQ and have no increased risk of epilepsy) have a 'lower dose' of the genetic predisposition. On the other hand, some form of 'two-hit' mechanism might be operating. Thus, one set of causal factors may result in a pre-disposition to the broader phenotype, with a separate set of causal factors being involved in the transition to autism 'proper' (Bailey *et al.*, 1996).

At one time it was suggested that obstetric complications (which tend to be higher in children with autism) may have constituted the 'second hit'. However, the work of Bolton and his colleagues (1997) strongly suggests that these, too, are probably genetically linked. In other words, there seems to be a shared genetic risk for both autism and obstetric problems and, at least in some cases, perinatal difficulties may well stem from abnormalities in the foetus, rather than vice versa.

Another complicating factor has been the finding, now replicated in a number of studies, that rates of major affective disorders (such as depression) are significantly higher (perhaps three times as common) in the families of a child with autism (Bailey *et al.*, 1996). The increase applies to severe unipolar disorders and to milder depressive disorders; it is found in first- and second-degree relatives, and is higher in females than in males. As onset is just as likely to occur prior to the birth of the autistic child as afterwards, it cannot be explained as a response to the strains of having to care for a child with autism. In general, the mechanisms under-lying this association are unclear, and further research is badly needed.

In a recent review article, drawing together the influential work of Michael Rutter and his associates in this area, Bailey *et al.* (1996) state:

> It may be concluded that genetic influences predominate in the aetiology of autism and, moreover, that this is likely to apply to the great majority of cases of autism.

Despite significant advances in molecular research, the actual genetic mechanisms involved remain unclear. Existing data suggest that in most cases autism is *not* due to a single gene operating in a Mendelian fashion (cases in which there is an association with Fragile X or tuberous sclerosis may be the exception). A number of factors, including the reduction in the prevalence of the broader phenotype from first-, through second- to third-degree relatives, suggest that a small number (probably around three or four) of interacting gene loci are probably involved (Pickles *et al.*, 1995; Bailey *et al.*, 1998). There is uncertainty as to whether the very variable clinical picture, and the range of behavioural patterns found within families, indicate genetic heterogeneity (i.e. that different genes or different combinations of genes are responsible for differences in IQ and in behavioural patterns and severity) or whether the findings reflect the variable expression of the same genotype. On the whole, the history of medical genetics would suggest that genetic variability is most likely to be the case. However, the extent of variation in both cognitive and behavioural domains that has been found in twin studies does not seem entirely compatible with this view. It is clear that far more research is needed in order to clarify the way in which autism, and the wider range of problems associated with it, are inherited (Fombonne *et al.*, 1997; Le Couteur *et al.*, 1996).

Practical Implications for Parents

What do these complex data and hypotheses mean, in practice, for parents—especially if they are considering having another child, or if there are grown up siblings or other close relatives who may be planning to start a family? Unfortunately, the genetic information that is available so far is such that it may alarm parents, without being able to provide any clear guidance. There is no diagnostic test for autism (as is now the case for Fragile X); nor is there likely to be one in the near future, if, as seems probable, several different genes are involved. Moreover, the very broad phenotype (the cognitive and behavioural picture that is associated with the condition) means that even if pre-natal testing were ever to become a reality, there would be no way of knowing in advance whether the affected foetus would be born with severe autism, no language and pro-found learning disabilities, or whether he or she would be highly intel-ligent, with a range of highly developed skills.

Some of the main findings of direct, *practical* relevance for families to emerge from research studies so far are presented below.

1. Although a family with one autistic child may have a higher than average risk of having another with this condition (probably around 6%), the most significant risk is of having a child who is not autistic, but who has difficulties related to language, socialisation or rather rigid and stereotyped patterns of behaviour.
2. The risks are probably greater in those families with a stronger genetic history. Thus, if one partner has a family background in which several individuals, particularly first-degree relatives, have a clear history of autistic-spectrum disorders, then the risks to any subsequent offspring are likely to be higher. If both partners have a similar background, the risks would be expected to increase further. In contrast, if within the family there is only one clearly affected individual, and if the autism seems to be attributable to a medical or organic condition with no known genetic cause, the risks to future offspring will probably be much lower.
3. The risks tend to be higher if the sibling is male or if there were several obstetric complications involved in the birth or pregnancy. There is

also an increased risk for families who have a child who is more severely affected. Thus, the lower the proband's verbal IQ, and the higher the number of autistic symptoms he or she shows, the greater may be the genetic risks to subsequent siblings—and it is clear that the development of children who fall within this group should be closely observed.

4. Family studies to date suggest that the risks vary according to the closeness of the relationship with the affected child. Monozygotic twins have the highest risks of all; siblings have a higher risk than parents, and first-degree relatives have a higher risk than second-degree relatives. Hence, if within the family the only clear case of autism had occurred some generations ago, or was the child of a second cousin, rather than a sibling, niece or nephew of one of the putative parents, the risks to a future pregnancy would be expected to be lower.

5. Although the majority of cases of autism may have a genetic component this is not invariably so, and Rutter *et al.* (1994) suggest that around 10% of cases may be associated with a known medical condition (though some of these may have a genetic cause, too). Thus, other factors possibly related to the development of autism in an affected individual, should also be carefully assessed.

Some Examples from Clinical Practice

The following vignettes, taken from actual clinical cases but with individual details changed to ensure anonymity, may help to illustrate the sorts of family picture that may occur.

Family 1

Daniel D first presented for assessment at the age of 9. Although he was of above average IQ and had developed language very early, a formal diagnostic assessment (using the ADI) indicated that he showed very stereotyped and repetitive (albeit apparently sophisticated) speech. His 'conversations' revolved entirely around his obsessional interest (space travel); he had no friends and was badly teased at school. Although he did show some imaginative play this, too, exclusively concerned space travel and totally excluded other children. He had been fascinated by space since he was 2; knew the names of all the major exploration rockets/satellites, etc., spent his free time building huge replicas of these in the (not very large) living room and insisted on keeping all his magazines and space equipment in meticulous order, becoming extremely distressed if they were moved. He was diagnosed as having Asperger syndrome.

When asked about the wider family his mother said that she herself had never been the most sociable of people, although she had always had one or two friends. Her husband, from whom she had been divorced since Daniel was 6, had never had close friends and now lived with his mother. He was an analytic chemist with an 'obsession' for maths. Even when first married he would spend hours on his own, inventing new algebraic systems. On more than one occasion when she had left him to look after the children she returned to find that he had placed the safety-gate across the living room door in order to keep the children out while he solved mathematical equations. He disliked her friends coming to the house and when she finally left home with the children, it was several days before he realised they had all gone. She thinks he was quite relieved when he was left to live by himself and their relationship is now very amicable. The children stay with him twice a month and they all seem fond of him, especially Daniel with whom he shares many common interests. The main problems occur with the paternal grandmother, who has very rigid routines of her own and complains bitterly if the children disrupt them. Mr D's father is described as having been a very rigid disciplinarian and as suffering from prolonged periods of depression. One of Mr D's nephews was diagnosed some years ago as having 'childhood schizophrenia'; another has autism and severe learning disabilities.

Daniel has two siblings. His elder sister had marked articulation problems when little and had needed speech therapy for over a year. However, her mother said that despite this she was always 'a great communicator' and at the age of 16 had no remaining language problems. She was doing well at school and had lots of friends. His brother Winston, who was two years younger than Daniel, had not learned to speak until he was over 3, and had always been a 'difficult' child, but he did have some friends and seemed to be getting on reasonably well at school.

Some years later, when Daniel was 17, the family requested a follow-up appointment. Daniel was doing well at mainstream school and was expected to achieve good marks in his 'A' level exams. He went around with a small group of other boys at school, all of whom were said to be rather odd or eccentric. At weekends, if not studying, he spent most of his time with a local group who organised games on the Internet involving Arthurian legends. His mother felt he had found his 'niche' and was very happy with his progress. In contrast, 15-year-old Winston, who attended the same school, had begun to show increasing problems. His peer relationships had deteriorated and he had few friends. He had great difficulties organising his school work; his output was poor and he was always being given detentions. His teachers viewed him as lazy, and often rude (mainly because of his tone of voice rather than what he said). He had had a prolonged period of depression during which he lost all interest in any activity and refused to get out of bed for days at a time. However, he had responded quite well to a course of medication.

Psychological testing revealed that although Winston's overall IQ was over 125, and his spoken vocabulary was around a 15-year level, his understanding of language was much more limited—only around a 12-year level. Nevertheless, although the school had been remarkably tolerant of Daniel's odd behaviour, Winston had received little help or support. However, when the nature of his difficulties was explained, and when the school became aware of the probable genetic links between the problems of the two boys, they became much more sympathetic towards Winston and began to apply some of the strategies that had previously worked so well with his brother.

Family 2

Margaret M was 18 when first seen and was about to begin a physics degree at university. Her mother was concerned that she might not be able cope because change had always been very difficult for her, and she wanted to organise appropriate support for her at college. Her family doctor had suggested that Margaret might have Asperger syndrome and she and her mother wished to confirm this diagnosis. When seen, Margaret sat with a copy of the journal *Nature* held over her face in order to avoid eye contact. She spoke well and fluently but in a very monotonous voice. The diagnostic interview indicated that, as a young child, she had been very late to develop speech and although she began to use some phrases at 4 years of age these were almost entirely echolalic. The family were posted abroad at this time (father worked for the navy on underwater surveillance systems) and she remained in a small nursery class. Around the age of 5 her speech suddenly improved dramatically, and psychological testing indicated that she was of extremely high intelligence. Thereafter, she attended private schools and, despite her odd behaviour, lack of social awareness and preoccupations (mostly with stick insects and hair ribbons), she was much liked by staff and generally tolerated by the other girls.

Although Margaret's mother had been concerned about her development from an early age, she had not been diagnosed earlier because her father had always insisted 'there was nothing wrong' or 'she'd grow out of it'. He refused to let his wife take her to see a psychiatrist or paediatrician, having an extremely 'dim view' of the usefulness of such professions. The psychological assessment had been conducted without his knowledge. He is described as being a very rigid personality 'who lived for his work'; however, he was largely responsible for fostering Margaret's love of science. The family had split up when his navy contract came up for renewal. His wife, son and three daughters all wanted to return home (he had never allowed members of his wife's family to visit when they lived abroad) but he insisted on renewing the navy contract. He has not seen any of the children for several years. In general, little is known about Mr M's family history, although his mother is described as being a very eccentric person who was continually arguing with the rest of the family and with neighbours. Mr M's brother has an autistic daughter who was diagnosed as having autism many years ago. She has severe learning disabilities and epilepsy, and now lives in a specialist residential home.

The other children are said to be functioning well and to have established good careers in accountancy, astrophysics and theatre, respectively. However, the accountant is described as being something of a 'loner' by her mother.

Family 3

Ms R, a single mother, brought her 4-year-old son Robin for diagnostic assessment. He had been somewhat slow to develop speech, although his development in other areas seemed to be at least age appropriate. She was particularly concerned about his inability to interact with other children at play group, his hyperactivity and destructiveness, severe tantrums if his routine was changed in any way, and his obsessional collecting of elastic bands, which had to be of a particular width and size. Diagnostic assessment confirmed that he had autism.

Ms R said that, as far as she knew there was no one in her family with any obvious learning difficulties, although her younger brother had had reading and spelling problems at school, which persisted into adulthood. Her sister had also suffered severe post-natal depression and had been treated with ECT.

The relationship with Mr T, Robin's father, had been brief and they had never lived together. He had been married at the time they met, but when his wife left him he had never suggested that they move in together. She soon recognised that he had no real commitment to her, although he has maintained very regular contact with his son. He has an older family of his own, none of whom appears to have had any problems. Mr T is described as being an extremely successful software designer, who has written a number of widely used business packages. However, he works independently as his attempts to join forces with larger companies always ended in disaster: 'A company would be very keen for him to come and work for them . . . he was certainly never short of offers . . . Then they would suddenly come and demand his resignation, although he never seemed to have had any idea that things were going wrong, or what had annoyed them.'

He is said to have been a very kind and gentle man in many ways, but very unperceptive of others. For example, he could not seem to understand why she was upset, when on finding that she was pregnant some months after his wife had left him, he made it clear that he had no intention of living with her. Ms R also said that he had a number of obsessions; one was with different filing systems, another was with records (the musical kind) all of which were systematically catalogued and cross-referenced and re-covered in plain black covers with labels of identical shape and size. He also tried to plan his life in 'three-year cycles' and would become upset if these were disrupted. Ms S thinks that one reason he did not want her to live with him was that this was not part of his three-year plan at the time.

Family 4

Joe was a much wanted child, conceived after mother had had several miscarriages. His early development was unremarkable, and videos taken on a family camping holiday when he was about 30 months old show him listening to stories, playing games, and singing and dancing with other children at a fancy dress ball. In the winter of the same year he became feverish, slow and lethargic; he lost weight and spent several days in hospital undergoing tests. Nothing could be identified, and physically he slowly began to improve, However, he lost almost all his speech, began to avoid eye contact, no longer showed any interest in other children, and developed a number of routines, becoming very distressed if these were disrupted in any way. In the following two years he has begun to show more interest in social interactions with adults, but still cannot relate to his peers, and his speech remains limited and largely echolalic. Both parents come from closely knit rural communities and there is no known history of developmental disorders within their extended families.

Vignettes such as these illustrate the variability of the genetic background in many cases of autism or the apparent lack of a family history in others. Many other scenarios also occur. Triplets, as well as twins with autism, are reported in some studies; others describe families in whom several children, or other relatives, with classical autism are found. More commonly however, it is features of the 'broader phenotype' that figure in parental accounts of their family history. Thus, in diagnostic interviews, or when assessing the possible risks for future pregnancies, it is essential to explore the wider phenotype associated with autism, and systematically to question families about problems in any of the three domains, as well as exploring other problems such as cognitive delays and possibly affective disorders too. Genetic counselling, given the present state of knowledge about the inheritance of autism, is far from being an exact science, but even if precise risk figures cannot be given, a thorough exploration of all the factors that might be relevant will give potential parents some basis on which to formulate their decisions.

Such information can be of practical value, too, for siblings. All too often in the past, if a brother or sister of someone with autism had problems at school, had difficulties in reading writing or spelling, or failed to get on well with other children, their difficulties were blamed on the fact that because parents were paying so much attention to the autistic child, the other children were somehow neglected. Family studies now make it clear that laying the blame on the child with autism is neither helpful, nor appropriate. Instead, we know that siblings are at risk of a variety of problems in their own right. It is also evident that in many cases, as long as effective intervention is offered at an early stage, these difficulties can be largely overcome. Even very severe articulation problems, for example, seem to respond well to speech therapy; remedial help for reading and spelling difficulties can help to minimise the impact of these deficits, as well as avoiding the behavioural problems that often follow in their wake. Teachers, and indeed parents themselves, may be more tolerant of social or behavioural problems if these are viewed as a part of the autistic spectrum, rather than as being deliberately provocative.

Bailey *et al.* (1996), conclude that: 'what is universally accepted now is that genetic factors play a very major role in autism. Indeed, it is clear that autism is the most strongly genetic of all multifactorial psychiatric disorders'. Nevertheless, because siblings and other family members will share some genes, this does not mean that they should be left, unsupported to deal with the effects of these. Although there is still much to be learned about the genetics of autism, even with our current state of knowledge it is clear that much practical help and advice can be offered in order to ameliorate the impact of the genetic legacy.

3

IDENTIFYING AND ASSESSING CHILDREN WITH AUTISM OR ASPERGER SYNDROME

HOW COMMON IS AUTISM?

Early epidemiological studies of autism were generally consistent in concluding that the condition was very rare, affecting only 3–4 individuals in every 10,000 (Lotter, 1966; Wing & Gould, 1979). In a much more recent review, involving 19 studies from 10 different countries and covering the period from 1966 to 1996, Fombonne (1998) concluded that the average figure was probably around 5 per 10,000. There was no relationship between the time at which the study was undertaken and the prevalence rates found, and Fombonne suggests that there is no good evidence to support the view that the incidence of autism may have increased in recent years.

Only studies that used strict diagnostic criteria for autism and involved clearly demarcated, non-overlapping samples were included in Fombonne's review. However, other studies suggest that if children within the wider autistic spectrum are included, the rates rise significantly. This term includes individuals who 'share a triad of impaired social interaction, communication, and imagination, associated with a rigid, repetitive pattern of behaviour. . . . The triad can be recognised at all levels of intelligence and can occur alone or together with any other physical or psychological disorder' (Wing, 1996). Wing and Gould (1979) reported that among 3–17-year-old children in one inner London area (an age cohort of 34,700), 17 fulfilled criteria for autism or atypical autism while 57 showed social impairments that were considered to lie within the autistic spectrum. The extrapolated incidence rate was approximately 20 children per 10,000. While their study had focused on children with learning disabilities, a later study by Ehlers and Gillberg (1993) in Sweden concentrated on the higher functioning Asperger group. In a total population study of 1,519 children living in Gothenburg and aged between 7 and 16 they identified five who met criteria for Asperger syndrome and another four who showed many characteristics associated with this condition. This yielded figures of 36 per 10,000 for Asperger syndrome and 35 per 10,000 for other disorders within the spectrum. Combining the figures for both these studies, Wing calculates that the overall estimate for children with autism-spectrum disorders must be over 90 in 10,000; i.e. almost 1% of the population.

There are, of course problems with calculations of this kind. Firstly, the diagnostic assessments used in the two studies were different and hence the figures may not be directly comparable. Secondly, it is possible that there may have been some overlap between the groups (at least one subject in the Swedish sample, for example, appears to have had some degree of learning disability). When working with such a small number of children, misdiagnosis or misclassification of only one or two cases can make a large difference to extrapolated prevalence rates. Thirdly, the number of cases in both the UK and Swedish studies is so small that any extrapolations must be treated with extreme caution. Thus, although recent data from Arvidsson and colleagues (1997) in Sweden appear to support the findings of Wing and Gillberg (suggesting a rate of 31 per 10,000) the 95% confidence limits for a sample of this size indicate that the true figure could actually range from a low of 7 to a high of 55 per 10,000.

Nevertheless, despite the variability in the figures reported it is clear that children with autistic-spectrum disorders are to be found much more frequently than was once thought. It would also seem that the incidence of Asperger syndrome may be considerably higher than that of classic autism (possibly 36 per 10,000 as compared to 5 per 10,000).

DIAGNOSING CHILDREN WITH AUTISM-SPECTRUM DISORDERS

What are the Earliest Signs of Autism or Asperger Syndrome?

It is widely accepted that autism almost always has an onset in infancy (Volkmar *et al.*, 1985) and retrospective studies indicate that many parents have serious concerns about their child's development in the first year of life. These early anxieties tend to focus around abnormalities in communication, play or social responsiveness (Gillberg *et al.*, 1990; Frith *et al.*, 1993; Smith *et al.*, 1994; Howlin & Moore, 1997). In Howlin and Moore's survey of 1,293 families, 41% said that delays or other abnormalities in language development were the first to give rise to concern; in 19% social abnormalities were cited and for 13% it was behavioural problems, such as tantrums. Other difficulties, such as developmental delays, medical problems or ritualistic behaviours were noted far less frequently. However, parents of children who were later diagnosed as having Asperger syndrome tended to worry about their child's social or behavioural development as much as their communication skills (see Figure 1.1).

On the whole, it has not been possible to identify one factor, above all others, that raises parental suspicions. In terms of problem behaviours, babies with autism tend to be at one extreme or the other. Thus, many are described as being extremely good, passive infants who make few if any demands on their carers; others are said always to be fretful, distressed, difficult to comfort, and constantly needing attention.

Most prospective studies have also failed to identify any specific factors that are predictive of later autism (Lister-Brook, 1992; Johnson *et al.*, 1992). The main exception to this is the study of Simon Baron-Cohen and his

Table 3.1: The CHAT (Checklist for Autism in Toddlers) (from Baron-Cohen *et al.*, 1996)

1. Does your child enjoy being swung or bounced on your knee, etc.?
2. Does your child take an interest in other children?
3. Does your child like climbing on things, such as upstairs?
4. Does your child enjoy playing peek-a-boo; hide and seek?
5. *Does your child ever PRETEND, for example, to make a cup of tea using a toy cup, or pretend other things?*
6. Does your child ever use his or her index finger to point, to ASK for something?
7. *Does your child ever use his or her index finger to point, to indicate INTEREST in something?*
8. Can your child play properly with small toys (e.g. cars or bricks) without just mouthing, fiddling or dropping them?
9. Does your child ever bring objects over to you to SHOW you something?

Section B: GP or HV observation
i. During the appointment has the child made eye contact with you?
ii. *Get the child's attention, then point across the room at an interesting object and say 'Oh look! There's a (name toy)'. Watch the child's face. Does the child look across to see what you are pointing at?*
iii. *Get the child's attention, then give the child a miniature toy cup and tea pot and say 'Can you make a cup of tea?'. Does the child pretend to pour it out, drink it, etc.?*
iv. Say to the child 'Where's the light?' or 'Show me the light'. Does the child point with his or her index finger at the light?
v. Can the child build a tower of bricks? (If so how many? Note number of bricks ——)

Note: Items in italics are those that specifically relate to pretence, proto-declarative pointing and joint attention.

colleagues (1996). This work did not directly involve parents but focused instead on the developmental check-up that was routinely used by family doctors and health visitors for 18-month-old infants. The authors added nine questions to those normally asked of parents: four general developmental questions and five additional questions specifically aimed at assessing gaze monitoring, proto-declarative pointing and pretend play. These items are detailed in Table 3.1.

Failure on this group of items was predicted to identify children at risk of having an autistic type disorder. Out of a total of 16,000 children only 12 failed to pass the 5 key items, (presented in italics). The diagnosis of autism was later confirmed in 10 of these children. The screen also proved useful in identifying children with developmental language disorders. At this stage, of course, it is not known whether more children in the sample, who were *not* identified by the screening questionnaire, may eventually be diagnosed as having autism. Nevertheless, since this figure represents a prevalence rate of around 6 per 10,000, such screening may at least result in the identification of those children who are most at risk of developing the more classic forms of autism.

Why is Early Diagnosis Important?

There is little doubt that a diagnosis of autism will have a major impact on any family and there is considerable evidence to show that the *way in which* diagnostic information is conveyed can have a long-term influence on parental attitudes, on families' levels of stress and acceptance, and on coping strategies more generally (Woolley *et al.*, 1989). Satisfaction with the diagnostic process can also affect parents' views of the professionals involved and services provided (Gath, 1985; Cottrell & Summers, 1990; Quine & Pahl, 1987; Stallard & Lenton, 1992; Leff & Walizer, 1992).

Research has consistently shown that delays in obtaining a diagnosis are a particular source of distress for parents. Early diagnosis is also essential if families are to be provided with the help and support they need from the time their child is very young. As will become apparent in later chapters, many day-to-day problems can be minimised or possibly even avoided if appropriate management strategies are developed during the child's earliest years. Problem behaviours that are established at the age of 3 years may well persist until the child is 13, or even 30, and will become increasingly difficult to handle as he or she grows older, bigger and more determined. On the other hand, if effective intervention techniques can be implemented *before* problem behaviours become too difficult to manage, then the outlook, both for the child and his or her family, is likely to be far more positive. Early support can also help to reduce the emotional and personal stress that is associated with bringing up a child with any form of handicap.

Finally, as discussed in Chapter 2, it is now well established that in many cases autism has a strong genetic basis. If one child in the family has autism, this has important implications for parents who may wish to have more children. Failure to diagnose autism early enough in the affected child might well jeopardise parents' chances of obtaining appropriate genetic counselling in the case of future pregnancies. Moreover, given the range of problems that are frequently found in siblings, diagnosis of the autistic child may help parents and others to realise that the somewhat milder difficulties exhibited by brothers or sisters do need to be taken seriously. Early and appropriate intervention or educational programmes for these difficulties are often very effective and can undoubtedly help to avoid the escalation of later difficulties.

WHEN IS AUTISM ACTUALLY DIAGNOSED?

Few would deny the importance of early diagnosis, but although there seem to have been some improvements in this area over the past decade (Pfeiffer & Nelson, 1992) the situation is still far from satisfactory. Parental accounts continue to indicate considerable dissatisfaction and frustration in their attempts to obtain a diagnosis for their child.

Gillberg and his colleagues (1990) in Sweden found that many parents were concerned about their child's development before the child reached his or her first birthday. Other, larger, studies indicate that, on average, parents become anxious when their child is around 18 months (Frith *et al.*, 1993; Smith *et al.*, 1994; Howlin & Moore, 1997). However, diagnosis before 2 years is still uncommon; 70% of the children surveyed by Frith and her colleagues (1993) were over 3 years when diagnosed and the average age of diagnosis reported by Smith *et al.* (1994) was 5 years 3 months.

In our own nationwide survey (Howlin & Moore, 1997) we found that over half of all parents knew that something was wrong well before their

Table 3.2: Age at which parents first became concerned about their child's development

Age of parents' first concerns	Percentage of children diagnosed as autistic	Percentage of children diagnosed as Asperger
Under 1 year	15.1	14.7
1 to 2	36.8	19.5
3 to 5	46.4	54.2
6 to 10	0.5	8.4
11+	1.2	2.2

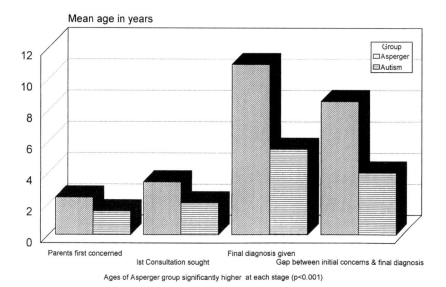

Figure 3.1: Differences in ages between autism and Asperger groups.

child was 2 years old (see Table 3.2). However, although most sought help from their family doctor or some other source fairly soon afterwards (within 6 to 7 months) there were considerable delays, and usually several further consultations with professionals, before their child was finally diagnosed. This delay was even greater in those children who eventually received a diagnosis of Asperger syndrome. Figure 3.1 indicates the average ages at which parents first became anxious about their child's development, when they first sought help and when they eventually obtained a diagnosis. Although some children in both groups were diagnosed quite early, in many cases there were considerable delays, with some individuals not being diagnosed until they were in their forties.

Nevertheless, the good news from this survey was that it confirmed reports from other studies (Pfeiffer & Nelson, 1992; Smith *et al.*, 1994) indicating that the age at which children are diagnosed with an autistic-spectrum disorder has steadily decreased over recent years. Thus, children who were aged under 5 years at the time of the survey had been diagnosed significantly earlier than those who were over 10. However, the survey also indicated that there was considerable regional variation in the age at which diagnosis was made in the UK. Families living in more densely populated areas, which generally had more specialist services, tended to be diagnosed earlier than those in other regions. The diagnosis of Asperger syndrome was given less frequently in areas where fewer professional experts were available; children in these areas were also more likely to receive a non-specific diagnosis, such as 'autistic traits' or 'autistic tendencies' rather than a clear-cut diagnosis of autism or Asperger syndrome.

Not surprisingly, parental satisfaction with the diagnostic process was significantly related to the age at which their child was diagnosed. Those who waited longest, or those who received a vaguer diagnosis (i.e. of autistic features, etc.), were far less satisfied than those who obtained a clear diagnosis relatively quickly.

It is apparent from surveys such as these that parents are, in fact, very astute judges of their children's development. In the majority of cases, they are well aware that all is 'not right' within the first two or three years, and often much earlier. In most cases these anxieties are well founded. Despite this, the time and effort required to obtain a firm diagnosis are often considerable, with some parents struggling on until their son or daughter had reached adulthood before they finally obtained a diagnosis.

HOW IS A DIAGNOSIS MADE?

The principal diagnostic systems used to identify children with autism, and the symptoms on which these are based, are discussed in some detail in Chapter 1. Parents might well be justified in asking, therefore, why they experience such delays in obtaining a diagnosis when so much money has been spent by international organisations on clarifying diagnostic issues. Moreover, it is still not unknown for some parents to be told that autism 'doesn't exist' and that it is simply a middle-class label for children who are mentally retarded, behaviourally disturbed, or even just badly brought up.

The problem is, as Chapter 1 also indicates, that within the three specific areas of deficit associated with autism there can be considerable variation from child to child, and even within the same child over time. Diagnosis, therefore, has to be conducted with care and will need to focus on different areas of the child's functioning. A detailed history from infancy is required in order to trace patterns of early development in communication, social competence, and obsessional or ritualistic behaviours. In that problems in these areas can be found in a range of other disorders (Turk & Graham, 1997) it is also important to be able to define the qualitative aspects that distinguish autistic-type impairments from impairments in other conditions. Hence, the use of a schedule specifically designed to assess the presence of autistic symptomatology is recommended.

Formal cognitive and linguistic assessments are crucial, too, in order to establish whether the difficulties shown might be caused instead by

Table 3.3: Stages required in the diagnostic process for autism (from Lord & Rutter, 1994)

1. Determine intellectual level
2. Determine level of language development
3. Consider whether the child's behaviour is appropriate for his or her:
   (a) chronological age
   (b) mental age
   (c) language age
4. If not, consider special problems in:
   (a) social skills
   (b) play
   (c) communication
   (d) other behaviours
5. Identify any medical conditions
6. Consider other relevant psychosocial factors.

impairments in other areas of functioning. Direct observations of the child are, of course, also essential. However, in a brief, formal interview of the kind that usually takes place in a consultant's office, abnormalities may not necessarily be apparent. It is important, therefore to consolidate this information with data from other sources, such as school records.

Finally, as autistic-spectrum disorders are known to have a strong genetic basis (Bolton *et al.*, 1994) information on relevant aspects of the wider family history is also required.

Lord and Rutter (1994) suggest that the steps indicated in Table 3.3 are needed in order to arrive at a correct diagnosis.

Assessing cognitive ability

In the past it was often claimed that, because of their social and communication difficulties, the use of traditional psychometric tests was inappropriate for children with autism. However, it is now clear that, as long as suitable tests are used, cognitive assessments on autistic children are just as reliable as they are in other groups (Rutter, 1985).

A wide range of different tests is available (see Appendix 1 for some of those in common use) and, if possible, it is preferable to use tests that provide separate assessments for language and non-verbal skills. The Wechsler Scales (Wechsler Intelligence Scale for Children, or WISC; Wechsler Pre-School and Primary Scale of Intelligence or WPPSI) are among the best standardised but they may not be suitable for children who are very young, very handicapped, or have very limited verbal understanding. In such cases, it will be necessary to use tests that require very little verbal understanding and which are more likely to gain the child's co-operation. Of these, the Bayley Scales of Infant Development are useful for children with a mental age below 3 years. For those able to function at a slightly higher level, the Merrill-Palmer Scale has many advantages. Despite the fact that it was last standardised many years ago, most children find the tasks interesting enough to maintain their attention and there is also the advantage, for those who are non-verbal, that verbal tests can be omitted in the calculation of mental age. Early scores on the Merrill-Palmer also tend to correlate well with later scores on other, better standardised tests (Lockyer & Rutter, 1970). More able children may enjoy the Coloured or Board forms of the Ravens Matrices, although these can provide only a very circumscribed assessment of the child's functioning. The Leiter Scales can also be useful for older children who have little spoken language but possess fairly well developed non-verbal and sequencing abilities. For children who are not able to score at all on any tests, even when testing has been attempted over several occasions or in different settings, the Vineland Adaptive Behaviour Scale (Sparrow *et al.*, 1984) can provide a useful alternative form of assessment. This relies on parental accounts of their child's functioning in four separate different domains: Communication, Social, Daily Living Skills and Motor Development. There is also a short section on maladaptive behaviours. However, because it is informant based it lacks the rigour of tests based on the completion of standardised tasks.

Assessing language skills

Unfortunately, the validity and reliability of most language tests is far less well established than that of cognitive assessments. Many have been developed with relatively small numbers of children, the age range that they cover is often limited, and there are very few tests that extend beyond a language age of 7 years (Bishop, 1994). Thus, they cannot be used to provide standard scores for children whose ages fall outside this range; indeed many do not provide standard scores at all, and rely only on age equivalent scores, which are much more difficult to interpret consistently (Howlin & Cross, 1994). Some do not even provide data on age equivalents. Moreover, tests that may be useful for English-speaking children in the UK may well be quite inappropriate for American children, and vice versa.

Appendix 1 lists a number of tests that are commonly used in the UK, and which provide some form of standardised scores. There are many others available, which, although poor in terms of normative data, may be useful in identifying problem areas and in designing intervention programmes (see Chapter 3). Of the better standardised instruments, the Reynell is probably the most informative in the cases of younger children (2–6 years). However, for those with a language age above 7 years, a combination of different tests may have to be used and this can lead to problems when attempting to make comparisons between different areas of skill (for example, expression, comprehension or grammar). Nevertheless, despite such drawbacks, it is always helpful to obtain some objective assessment of the child's linguistic ability, as inferences based only on informal observations of the child may well be misleading. As Bishop (1994) points out, clinicians or practitioners who seldom see normally developing children may have lowered expectations of what should be attained at a particular stage; thus reliance on clinical observation may lead to an overestimation of a child's true language level. Moreover, some children who hardly speak at all may be found to perform quite well on standardised language tests. Others who, because of their tendency to echo, may superficially appear to have well-developed communication skills, may actually be much more impaired in their use of spontaneous language. Many children, too, will be found to show a discrepancy between their receptive and expressive skills, with their understanding of language often being far less well developed than their spoken vocabulary might suggest. (For further details of tests that can be used to assess language, see Bishop, 1994, and Marans, 1997; the latter includes mostly tests with American norms.)

Assessing the presence of autistic symptoms

Although direct observations of the child are an essential part of any clinical assessment, it must be recognised that relatively brief observations in an unfamiliar setting are not necessarily the most reliable means of reaching a firm diagnosis. Those children who are very shy may appear even more withdrawn and aloof than they are in their usual settings. In contrast, others who may have great difficulty dealing with the unpredictable demands of normal social situations may cope surprisingly well when systematically questioned by a sympathetic adult or when presented with formal test materials. Indeed, in such circumstances, particularly when assessing more able children, it may be quite difficult to identify any marked abnormalities. The obvious solution is to carry out observations over several days or even weeks, but for practitioners with a heavy clinical load this can hardly be justified on economic grounds.

Instead, different approaches will be needed to ensure that as much relevant information as possible is collected. Reports from the child's family doctor or other clinicians can be invaluable in providing information about early development. Accounts by nursery or school teachers can also furnish important details about the child's play and social functioning and about communication and cognitive skills. However, whenever possible, reports of this nature should also be supported by objective information, collected in a systematic and rigorous fashion.

Over the years there have been various attempts to develop quick and easy checklists for autism which can be completed in a relatively short time. These include the Autism Behaviour Checklist (Krug *et al.*, 1980), the Childhood Autism Rating Scale (Schopler *et al.*, 1988) and the Behavioral Rating Instrument for Autistic and other Atypical Children (Ruttenberg *et al.*, 1977). However, although these may be useful as screening instruments, in order to indicate whether children *may* fall within the autistic spectrum, they cannot be used for diagnostic purposes. There are no real short cuts, and diagnosis can only be clarified by experienced clinical observation, together with detailed and systematic interview.

There are a number of interview schedules that have been developed to assess the presence or otherwise of autistic behaviours (see Lord, 1997, for review). The Handicaps and Behaviour Schedule (HBS) of Wing and Gould (1978) was one of the earliest of these. It covers the child's development in detail since infancy, and although the focus is on problems related to autism, many other aspects of the child's behaviour are also covered. Many of the items from this schedule are incorporated in the Autism Diagnostic Interview—Revised (ADI-R) of Lord and her colleagues (1994). This focuses predominantly on the child's functioning in three main areas: reciprocal social interactions, communication, and stereotyped patterns of behaviour and interests. Like the HBS, the ADI assesses current functioning and early development in each of these areas. Scores on the ADI can be used to derive an algorithm for ICD-10 criteria for autism, and this can be particularly useful in formulating a diagnosis. Both the HBS and ADI require training before they can be used reliably and both take some time (at least 90–120 minutes to complete). Nevertheless, they provide a valuable framework both for interviewing and for collating the information obtained from the interview. Such instruments may be particularly helpful for clinicians who see only a relatively small number of children with autism, or for those who do not work within a larger, interdisciplinary diagnostic team.

Because informal observations of the child in an unfamiliar setting may provide only limited information, especially if time is short, there have also been attempts to develop more structured observational assessments. The Autism Diagnostic Observation Schedule—which now comes in a number of different versions (Lord *et al.* (1989); PLADOS (Di Lavore *et al.*, 1995); ADOS-G (Lord *et al.*, 1996))—consists of a series of structured tasks that are designed to assess the child's social and communicative functioning. These include constructional and turn-taking activities, imitation, the ability to tell a story, imaginative toy play, gesture and conversational skills. The value of a schedule such as this is that it provides a range of social 'presses', adapted to the developmental level of the individual child, and which encourage interaction with the clinician in a systematic way. The ADOS-G takes around 20–30 minutes to complete, but within this time can provide far more information than might be gleaned from informal observation. However, even if it does not prove practicable to use an instrument of this type because of all the other demands on the clinician's time, then at the very least it is important to spend some time observing the child when he or she is not engaged in formal testing or routine questioning. A child who seems quite 'normal' in one-to-one interactions with an adult may appear very differently in other situations. Robbie, for example, was a boy of 6 who presented for diagnostic assessment. He performed very well on cognitive and language tests, and kept the psychiatrist entertained for over 30 minutes with his tales about space travel and Star Trek. No abnormal behaviours were noted, but later in the crowded waiting room he was observed to sit on the far side of the room from his mother, with a waste paper bin on his head, alternatively repeating items from the psychological tests he had completed earlier and extracts of 'conversation' from a Star Trek video. He seemed totally oblivious to the other occupants of the room, even though he was obviously a source of much amusement to the other children there.

Medical Diagnosis

In Chapter 2 a variety of genetic conditions that are *sometimes* associated with autism were discussed. Although most of these are rare, the possibility of co-existing conditions such as Fragile X and tuberous sclerosis should be considered even if there are no obvious physical characteristics that might give rise to suspicion. For example, if there is a history of learning disabilities in the family, then Fragile X could be implicated; a history of epilepsy might also indicate tuberous sclerosis. Because testing for Fragile X is now so much more reliable, and not particularly expensive, then routine testing for this, as well as for other relatively common or potentially relevant chromosomal abnormalities, would always seem to be advisable.

Christopher Gillberg and Mary Coleman (1992) describe a number of other conditions that may be causally associated with autism. Metabolic disorders include phenylketonuria, errors of purine metabolism and diseases related to carbohydrate and lipid metabolism. Among possible prenatal causes are rubella, rubeola virus, syphilis, cytomagalovirus and herpes simplex virus. Post-natally, encephalitic illnesses resulting from the herpes simplex virus have also been suggested as giving rise to all the classic symptoms of autism in a number of children, some as old as 14. As noted in Chapter 2, Rutter and his colleagues (Lord & Rutter, 1994; Bailey *et al.*, 1996) have expressed considerable scepticism about the high rates (almost 40%) of associated medical disorders reported by Gillberg and his associates. However, even if the rates are much lower than this—at around 10% as Rutter and his colleagues suggest—this still warrants a careful medical examination for all children. This should include a detailed birth history and details of any subsequent medical disorders, such as fits, developmental delays, loss of skills or periods of regression, head injuries or severe infectious illnesses. Details of any similar problems within the wider family should also be explored for genetic reasons, as should the mother's history of miscarriages, still births or neonatal deaths.

As far as assessment of the child is concerned, a thorough medical examination may prove difficult for the doctor, and possibly very distressing for a child who dislikes physical contact. However, measures of height, weight and head circumference are all important. As noted in the previous chapter, there is increasing evidence that children with autism may have a larger than normal head size, while growth retardation, excessive growth or obesity are all associated with a variety of genetic disorders. Any abnormalities in facial appearance or in skin pigmentation should also be carefully noted, as these, too, are often linked with genetic abnormalities.

On the whole, because of problems of technology and interpretation, there would seem to be little rationale for insisting on more complex testing on a *routine* basis. Magnetic Resonance Imaging (MRI), whether structural or functional, remains expensive and may distress some children because of the noise. Moreover, as brain mapping in normal children is still at a somewhat preliminary stage, judgements about abnormality need to be viewed with caution and these techniques should not be used unless there are specific hypotheses to be tested. CT (Computerised Tomography) and PET (Positron Emission Tomography) scans may require relatively long periods of immobility and higher levels of co-operation from the child than are feasible; the latter also involves the need to take blood samples. EEG measures are simpler, but again require good co-operation and some children cannot bear having the electrodes attached to their hair. However, if there is a history of brain damage or seizures, or of a period of regression following normal development, or evidence of any sudden and marked changes in behaviour, then such assessments should be given serious consideration.

Psychosocial Factors

Finally, attention needs to be paid to other factors that may have an impact on the child's development and progress. Although there is no evidence that family discord or disadvantage can cause autism, the presence of additional stressors can certainly exacerbate an already difficult situation. Systematic information should therefore be gathered on family relationships, other support networks, difficulties at work, financial worries and the need for benefits, etc. Problems with neighbours are not uncommon in families with an autistic child (prolonged night-time screaming can easily lead to friction, or even to complaints of child abuse) and again can result in additional, and sometimes avoidable, stress. The ability of parents to have some time to themselves, and the need for respite care, should also be carefully and sensitively explored.

Who can Diagnose?

As is apparent from the preceding sections, diagnosing a child with autism is by no means a simple task. Ideally a multidisciplinary professional team should be involved—a psychiatrist or paediatrician to complete the developmental history; a psychologist to carry out psychometric testing; a language therapist to assess communication skills; and a social worker to examine other aspects of family functioning. A neurologist or geneticist may also be involved in more complex or technological investigations. In practice, however, it may prove impossible, or too expensive to assemble a team of this size and this degree of expertise. When professional input is limited it becomes even more important to back up clinical judgement with the use of assessment measures of established reliability and validity and to base diagnosis on agreed criteria. It is also essential to supplement current information with objective and contemporary accounts of the child's functioning in other areas.

In a recent survey of 70 centres with a specialist interest in autism in the UK it was found that almost all of those seeing 20 or more such children a

Table 3.4: Professional groups in UK clinics involved in diagnostic assessments

Profession	% of services employing
Psychologist	90.6
Speech therapist	75.0
Psychiatrist	75.0
Paediatrician	62.5
Social worker	43.8
Education (teacher, etc.)	21.9
Occupational therapist	12.5
Nurse/health visitor	9.1
Other (physiotherapist, art/play therapist, audiologist, psychotherapist, etc.	18.7

Table 3.5: Diagnostic instruments used in assessment

Diagnostic instruments	% of services using
Standard diagnostic interview	68.8
Psychometric assessment	81.5
Language assessment	90.6
Developmental history	96.9
Family/genetic history	90.6
Neurological assessment	65.7
Other assessments (Medical; EEG, chromosomes, etc.)	12.5
Play, Portage, theory of mind, etc.	18.6

Diagnostic interviews used	% of services using
ADI	28.0
ADOS	3.1
HBS/DISCO	15.6
Other questionnaire (CARS, etc.)	3.1
Other interview (no details)	26.0

year offered a multidisciplinary diagnostic service—only 12.5% were single discipline; 25% involved two to three different professional groups; 40.6% involved four to five different groups of professionals; and 21.9% employed six or more professional groups, at least on a part-time basis. The main professional groups involved (in some or all diagnostic assessments) are detailed in Table 3.4. Almost all centres (90.6%) involved *either* a paediatrician *or* a psychiatrist in their diagnostic assessments (Howlin, 1998). The majority of these centres also employed some form of formal assessment as part of their diagnostic procedure. The different types of diagnostic procedures in use are detailed in Table 3.5.

THE PROBLEMS OF DIFFERENTIAL DIAGNOSIS

Although the diagnostic criteria for autism are now well established, it is also important to recognise that there are many other conditions that may be associated with delays or impairments in social and communication skills, or with obsessional and ritualistic behaviours. The problems that arise in differentiating autism from Asperger syndrome have been discussed in Chapter 1, and the early confusion between autism and schizophrenia is also noted in Chapter 2. However, deficits in the areas listed above may also be due to other types of developmental disorders, generalised cognitive delays, developmental language disorders, neurological dysfunction, genetic abnormalities, visual or hearing impairments, specific learning disorders, motor and attention deficit disorders and psychosocial deprivation.

Atypical Autism

ICD and DSM criteria suggest that this term should be used in cases where some, but not all, of the criteria for autism are met. Thus, a child who meets criteria for abnormalities in each of the three principal domains (communication, social and obsessional) but who did not exhibit difficulties in these areas before the age of three might be diagnosed as having 'atypical autism'. The same label may also be used for a child who meets, say, criteria for communication and social impairments, but who does not show clear evidence of obsessional or ritualistic behaviours. The term may be used, too, for children who show the primary symptoms of autism but who also have severe to profound mental retardation (and do not, therefore, show marked discrepancies between their cognitive and social communication skills).

For many reasons, it is important to ensure that children whose needs are *generally* similar to those who meet full criteria for autism do receive an appropriate diagnosis. Thus, the use of this term can have important practical and educational implications for children and their families (Rutter & Schopler, 1992). However, indiscriminate use can also give rise to problems. It is difficult to accept, for example, that a child whose social relationships appear entirely normal, but who shows problems with language and stereotyped behaviour patterns, should be classified as having the same type of impairment as a child with severe social and communicative deficits who *just* fails to meet criteria for stereotyped and ritualistic behaviours. In such cases, the causes and outcome of the disorder could be quite different, and the educational and management strategies required might also vary considerably. Furthermore, because current ICD and DSM criteria suggest that children who exhibit only *one* out of the three principal areas of deficit may be included within this category, the term could clearly encompass children with widely differing types of problem and levels of severity.

Pervasive Developmental Disorder—Not Otherwise Specified (PDD-NOS)

This is a label that is often used (particularly in the USA) to categorise children who show some but not all of the characteristics of autism. The term is sometimes used as an alternative to 'atypical autism', or even

Asperger syndrome. Indeed, Szatmari and his colleagues (1989) suggest that 'whether Asperger syndrome or PDD-NOS is used to denote children at the mildest end of the (autistic) spectrum is of little consequence'. However, few parents would probably agree with this statement. Such a classification does little to clarify the nature of the disorder; practically, it means little or nothing to teachers or others who may be called upon to help, and parents are unlikely to gain much sympathy or understanding by explaining 'I have a child with a Pervasive Developmental Disorder— Not Otherwise Specified'. On the whole, as noted earlier in this chapter, parents do not tend to find diagnoses of this vague and non-specific type very satisfactory. Of course, there may be occasions when, because of the nature of the child's problems, it is *not* possible to provide a clear-cut diagnosis of autism or Asperger syndrome. However, whenever possible, it seems best for the sake of families and teachers to provide them with a diagnostic label that gives at least some guidelines as to the true nature of the condition. A diagnosis, after all, is only useful (a) if it leads families forwards, (b) if it provides teachers and others with a 'shorthand label' indicating what the condition is and possible associated problems, and (c) if it helps to point the way to more effective teaching and management strategies. A label that gives rise only to confusion and dissatisfaction is likely to result in few benefits.

Mental Retardation or Learning Disability

Although autism has a strong association with learning disability the two do not necessarily go together. Thus, although around 70% of children with autism have additional cognitive impairments, most children who are within the mild to moderate range of mental retardation (IQ 35–69) do not have autism. These children, while relatively impaired in all areas of their functioning, do not tend to show the same discrepancy between verbal and non-verbal skills as is found in autism. And, although the gap between language and other skills tends to widen as IQ levels fall, non-verbal communication skills, imaginative play, and interest in social interactions are usually commensurate with the child's development in other areas.

However, the incidence of autism increases substantially in individuals who are severely or profoundly retarded (IQ below 35). Wing and Gould (1979) found that 50–60% of children within this IQ range showed the typical triad of autistic impairments; in the profoundly retarded group separately (IQ below 20) the figure rose to 82%. Differential diagnosis in this group, therefore, can pose considerable difficulties for the clinician. However, because prognosis will be affected mainly by the child's very severe cognitive impairments, and because such children will inevitably require specialist education, the distinction here may have only limited practical impact. The important issue in such cases is to identify the extent of the child's deficits in crucial areas of functioning—self-help, occupation, communication, etc.—and to ensure that the educational and social provisions available are appropriate to meet the needs of the child and his or her parents.

Developmental Language Disorders

Another condition that shares several common features with autism is that of developmental language disorders (Bishop, 1994). Children with *expressive* language delays tend to compensate for their lack of speech by means of gesture and other forms of non-verbal communication; they also show relatively normal patterns of imaginative play, and there is clear reciprocity in their social interactions with adults, although peer relationships are inevitably affected to some degree. Children with more severe receptive language disorders, however, quite frequently show impairments in reciprocal social relations; imaginative play may be limited, with some evidence of ritualistic behaviours, and they may show unusual language features, such as echolalic and stereotyped speech. Generally, as their understanding of language improves, so does their functioning in other areas and ritualistic and obsessional behaviours are rarely as marked as in autism. Nevertheless, in early childhood in particular, it can sometimes be very difficult to differentiate between a child with a severe receptive language disorder and one with a milder form of autism. Some individuals, too, have long-term social difficulties and in adulthood they may experience problems in finding work or in living independently (Mawhood *et al.*, in preparation; Haynes & Naidoo, 1991).

Another condition, which continues to provoke disagreement among professionals, is that of Semantic Pragmatic Syndrome. This term was first used by Rapin and Allen in 1983 to describe a group of children who showed deficits in comprehension, and in the semantic and pragmatic aspects of language and communication, but in whom the structural aspects of language, such as syntax and prosody were well preserved. However, in a recent review of studies in this area, Gagnon and her colleagues (1997) conclude that there is no evidence to differentiate Semantic Pragmatic Syndrome from high-functioning autism. They suggest that this diagnosis does nothing more than arbitrarily group together, under a separate category, the verbal communication deficits present in autism. More importantly, they warn that the use of this label can prevent children who are autistic from receiving the intervention and educational provision that they need.

Selective (Elective) Mutism

This is a condition in which the child, although he or she has developed language, talks only under certain conditions. Thus, children may speak to family or very close friends, but refuse to talk to strangers or when at school. Because the child communicates, at least in certain circumstances, it is usually fairly easy to differentiate this from autism (in which communication is impaired in all settings, Bishop, 1994). Nevertheless, these children often show some delays in their language development and social isolation and poor peer relationships are also found.

Neurological Disorders

There are a number of conditions, linked to organic brain dysfunction, that can also produce impairments similar to those found in autism.

Rett's syndrome
This condition (Olsson & Rett, 1990) is almost exclusively found in girls. Development in the first year of life appears normal, but then head growth tends to decline and there is loss of motor control, with both walking and grasp being affected. Repetitive and stereotyped hand movements are typical, and communication, imaginative play and social interactions are all severely impaired. There are many additional physical problems such as hyperventilation, ataxia, scoliosis and a high rate of epilepsy. Motor and cognitive impairments tend to increase as childhood progresses, although the girls' interest in social interactions may improve.

Landau–Kleffner syndrome
This is another disorder in which early development appears normal. Onset usually occurs between 3 and 6 years, with a progressive loss of expressive and receptive language, typically in association with EEG abnormalities or epilepsy. Non-verbal cognitive functioning tends to remain relatively intact, and social relationships, at least with familiar adults, are maintained. Prognosis is poorest for cases with an early onset (before 5) and although a few children do recover speech, most remain linguistically very handicapped (Bishop, 1994).

Other disintegrative disorders
Heller's disease is a rare form of disintegrative disorder, which is sometimes linked to measles encephalitis, cerebral lipoidoses or leukodystrophies, although in most cases no specific cause can be found. After apparently normal development in the first 18 months to 2 years, children

show marked developmental regression, often involving a loss of continence and motor control. Self-help, communication and social skills are lost, and stereotypies and motor mannerisms appear. In many cases the regression continues over a period of several months and then reaches a plateau, although the child does not regain lost skills. The picture at this stage is often very similar to that found in autism. In other cases the child may continue to deteriorate, with motor function becoming increasingly impaired and other signs of neurological dysfunction, such as seizures, increasing (Lord & Rutter, 1994).

Genetic Abnormalities

Although there are many different genetic conditions that may occasionally be linked with autism (such as phenylketonuria, tuberous sclerosis, neurofibromatosis and a number of chromosomal abnormalities—see Gillberg and Coleman, 1992) in most of these the co-occurrence is very rare and the nature of the association uncertain. However, as noted in Chapter 2, there are two conditions that do seem to be linked more frequently than might be expected by chance; these are tuberous sclerosis and Fragile X. The association with tuberous sclerosis (which may be caused either by a spontaneous mutation or inherited in an autosomal dominant fashion) is by far the stronger of the two and, as already discussed, a significant number of individuals with this condition also meet diagnostic criteria for autism. Many other individuals also have symptoms, which although not meeting strict criteria for autism, fall within the wider autistic spectrum.

In the case of Fragile X, although this was once considered to be a significant cause of autism, the association now appears much more tenuous than previously thought. Improvements in the technology used to identify the Fragile X site, and in the clarification of diagnostic features, have resulted in better understanding of the link between the two conditions. It is now recognised that the Fragile X anomaly probably accounts for only a small proportion of cases with autism (around 2 to 3%). In a recent study, designed to examine in detail the differences between children with Fragile X and those with autism, Turk and Graham (1997) found that although the Fragile X group showed some autistic-like features, notably gaze avoidance, delayed echolalia, repetitive speech and hand flapping, only a minority actually met diagnostic criteria for autism. Moreover, although children with Fragile X undoubtedly show problems of social communication, these are different in kind to those shown by children with autism. Thus, social anxiety seems to lie at the basis of many of the problems shown by a child with Fragile X whereas it is lack of social understanding that is the core deficit in autism.

Severe Visual and Hearing Impairments

Visual and auditory impairments are frequently reported in studies of children with autism. In a French study (Garreau *et al.*, 1984), 7% of the children were found to be blind and 5% severely deaf. In a Swedish study by Steffenburg (1990), 24% of children identified as being autistic had a hearing loss of more than 25 decibels, and 50% had some form of visual impairment (such as myopia or astigmatism). Conversely, high rates of autism have been found in children who are born totally blind. Those with Leber's amaurosis, in particular, are very likely to meet full criteria for autism. Children with conditions such as retrolental fibroplasia, congenital glaucoma or corneal lens opacity, very often show stereotypical behaviours, but do not usually show marked social communication disorders (see Gillberg & Coleman, 1992).

Specific Learning Disorders; Motor and Attention Disorders

Recently, Klin and his colleagues (1995) have pointed to the similarities between some of the difficulties shown by children with Asperger syndrome and those with 'Non-Verbal Learning Disabilities Syndrome'. This is a disorder described by Rourke (1989), which is characterised by deficits in tactile perception, psychomotor co-ordination, visuo-spatial organisation, non-verbal problem solving, and appreciation of incongruities and humour. These children may also have problems in adapting to change; they have difficulties in social interaction and understanding, and often serious mood disorders. However, on the whole they do not show the preoccupations and stereotyped interests that are characteristic of Asperger children.

Christopher Gillberg (1992a) has documented similarities with another group of children who have deficits in attention, motor control and perception (the so-called DAMP syndrome); many of these are also hyperactive. Gillberg suggests that a small proportion of these children meet criteria for autism and substantially more for Asperger syndrome.

Psychosocial Deprivation

There is no evidence that a less than optimum environment (such as having a mother who is suffering from depression, or living in a rather unstimulating home) can cause autism. However, children who have been exposed to severe neglect do show delays in language development, they may be withdrawn and unresponsive and often have ritualistic or stereotyped behaviours. Recent studies of the children rescued from Romanian orphanages, for example, suggest that many exhibited a number of clearly autistic features (Rutter, personal communication).

On the whole, however, children whose development has been affected by cruelty or neglect do not have marked difficulties of comprehension, nor do they exhibit the broader communication problems associated with autism. After some time spent in a supportive environment they generally show improvements in areas such as play and social interaction, and in their development generally. Ritualistic and obsessional behaviours also tend to decline. Of course, in some instances, children may have been neglected or abused *because* of their abnormal behaviours—for example, the Wild Boy of Aveyron, described by Itard. In such cases, cognitive and behavioural improvements would be unlikely to be marked, even following a dramatic change in living conditions.

Other Conditions that have been Linked with Autism

In the previous chapter, a variety of other conditions that have, from time to time, been associated with autism were discussed. However, few conclusions can be drawn from findings of this kind and although the co-occurrence of one fairly rare condition with an even rarer one may be very unusual it is not necessarily significant. Of far greater *practical* importance is the need for clinicians and educators to be aware of the fact that autism can occur with all sorts of other conditions, and that it is crucial to separate the specific problems associated with autism from those associated with the additional disorder. Often, when a more easily identifiable condition is present, almost all the child's problems may be attributed to this, so that the existence or impact of autism will be missed. Children with autism who also have Down's syndrome or severe visual or hearing problems, for example, may be far more handicapped by their autism than by their other impairments. But, if educational and health services concentrate on the non-autistic condition and fail to address the problems related specifically to the autism, this can lead to many subsequent difficulties. Parents begin to feel guilty because their child is so much more difficult than (say) the other Down's or hearing impaired children in the classroom. Alternatively, because they are constantly being told 'He's like that/not making progress because he's deaf/can't see/has Down's syndrome' and so on, they may fail to respond in the most effective way to the problems that arise because of the autism. Howlin *et al.* (1995) describe four cases of children with Down's syndrome, in which their autism had failed to be identified. All had severe

Table 3.6: Characteristics of autism and other conditions affecting social-communication development

Impaired in:	Clinical diagnosis									
	1 Aut	2 Asp	3 LD IQ <35	4 DLD	5 SPS	6 Fra X	7 Blind	8 Deaf	9 Non-verbal LD	10 Psycho-social
Language comprehension	***	**	**	***	*	**	*	***	*	(***)
Language Grammar/vocab	***	*	***	***	*	**	*	***		(***)
Reciprocal conversation	***	***	**	***	***	*	*	**	*	(**)
Gesture	***	**	**	*		*	*	*	*	(**)
Imagination	***	**	**	**	*	*	*	*	*	(*)
Shared attention	***	***	**	**	**	**	*	*		(**)
Social reciprocity	***	***	**	**	**	**	*	*	*	(**)
Understanding emotions	***	**	**	**	**	*	*		**	
Peer relationships	***	**	**	**	**	**	**	*	**	**
Obsessions & Rituals	***	***	*	*	*	*	*	*	*	(**)
Stereotypies	**	*	***			***	**			(***)
Motor skills	*	**	**			*			**	(**)
Behaviour problems	***	**	**	*	*	*	*	*	*	**

Key: * At least some children reported as showing problems in this area.
** Many children show problems in this area.
*** Almost all children show problems in this area.

1&2 Autism and Asperger syndrome.
3 Mental retardation (severe–profound).
4 Severe developmental receptive language disorder.
5 Semantic pragmatic syndrome.
6 Fragile X.
7&8 Severe visual and hearing impairments. Children with rubella or Leber's amaurosis are excluded as many will show at least atypical autism.
9 'Non-verbal learning disabilities syndrome.'
10 Severe psychosocial deprivation. (*NB*: Many of these symptoms disappear or are significantly reduced once care improves.)

problems over schooling, and in each case the behavioural problems were extremely difficult to manage. Early identification, and hence educational services better geared to meet the special needs of a child with autism, might have helped to reduce or even avoid these problems.

The overlap between autism and other disorders

In Table 3.6 an attempt is made to summarise the overlap between autism and several of the conditions listed above, which are also associated with communication and social impairments or stereotyped and ritualistic behaviours. The ratings are based on both clinical and research studies. As can be seen, it is the severity, pervasiveness or persistence of many of these features that tends to distinguish the autism group from the others. This illustrates the problems that are likely to be inherent in using symptom checklists, since many non-autistic children would also be likely to score positively on these tests. It is evident that there can be no substitute for careful, detailed and individually based diagnostic assessments that can take account of the qualitative nature of the child's difficulties rather than focusing simply on the presence or absence of particular symptoms.

<table><tr><td>

4

</td></tr></table>

TREATMENTS FOR AUTISM[1]

'THE SOUNDS OF MIRACLES'

Few readers can be unaware of the dramatic claims that appear from time to time in the popular press or on television, concerning treatments that are said to have a significant impact on the outcome for children with autism. Parents are promised 'miracles' if they, too, undertake a particular form of therapy, while sceptical professionals may be castigated for their intolerance and short-sightedness. Although there is often little evidence to substantiate such optimism (and on the whole, the more extravagant the promises made, the more limited are the data on which they are based) parents understandably find such claims highly seductive. After all, who could easily turn their back on a treatment that could change the course of their child's life for ever? As one parent with a 22-year-old son writes:

> Nobody wants to give up without a good fight . . . We weren't so much searching for a miracle. Really, we were just looking for something—anything—because to do nothing had become intolerable. Perhaps that is the case for all parents. If you had a child like this you would try everything. For one mother 'everything' means to go into debt, fly to a foreign country, put her child into a tank with dolphins. . . .
>
> For our family it meant different things at different times: pounds of bitter tasting vitamins, rigid behaviour modification, spinning in a suspended net, doing what the doctor didn't say, travelling 2,500 miles across the country to a new home, keeping him at home, giving him over into the care of others.
>
> I try not to think too much about what would or would not have happened had we tried or not tried a particular treatment. But each time I hear of something new—often a therapy we could not even have imagined—a little spark inside my brain briefly ignites and I wonder once again, what if . . . ? (Muller, 1993)

---

[1] This chapter is based on an earlier paper, published in *European Child and Adolescent Psychiatry*; 1997.

This chapter explores a number of treatments that have risen to prominence over recent years. It is by no means all inclusive but attempts to cover those interventions that have received most publicity; no doubt, by the time it appears in print, new therapies will already have hit the headlines. The treatments are arranged alphabetically and contain as much reliable information about their benefits, or otherwise, as it has been possible to find. Further details of a range of other, less widely publicised, interventions can be obtained from the National Autistic Society (1997).

AUDITORY INTEGRATION TRAINING

In her book *The Sound of a Miracle: A Child's Triumph over Autism* (1992), Annabel Stehli describes her daughter Georgie's response to auditory integration training, based on the theories of Dr Berard, a French ear, nose and throat specialist. He postulated that sound sensitivity, and hence behavioural disturbance in autism, could result from distortions in hearing. Such distortions can be identified by peaks in the child's audiogram. Treatment involves the use of filters to eliminate these peaks. If the child cannot tolerate audiometric testing, a standardised programme of Auditory Integration Training is given. This involves listening to electronically processed music through headphones for a total of 10 hours (usually in 2 × 30 minute sessions over a 10-day period). Similar procedures, but using rather different equipment, have been developed by Tomatis in Paris. The latter places more emphasis on supposed psychological and emotional factors in autism, and until recently training necessitated 6–12 months of intervention although this has now apparently been reduced to 12 days.

Most of the evidence in support of this approach is based on subjective and unsystematic parental reports, although not all of these are positive. Arrow (1993), for example, describes the effect on her own daughter:

> The treatment went on for ten gruelling days . . . The effects were immediate. From Day Two (she) became hyperactive, where she had been passive and placid. She didn't go to bed until 11.00 . . . She was more frustrated and threw temper tantrums. She looked 'high' all the time. It took twelve weeks for these effects to disappear, and there was no evidence of any improvements in communication.

Rimland and Edelson (1995) compared 8 children receiving 20 sessions of AIT with 8 who did not. Following treatment there was no evidence of any decrease in sound sensitivity, which is supposedly one of the main functions of AIT. And, although the experimental group showed significant improvements on the Aberrant Behaviour Checklist (ABC) the change was, in real terms, small (a difference between initial and final scores of less than half a point). In a further study (1994) the authors report on outcome in 445 children and adults with autism, with an age range of 4 to 41 years. Again the average ABC score improved by around 0.4 points and there was a small but significant reduction in parental reports of sound sensitivity. In addition, slight improvements in hearing acuity and a reduction in variability on audiogram measures were recorded.

Although positive, the results of these studies need to be treated with caution for a number of reasons. Firstly, it is important to be aware that results that are *statistically significant* are not necessarily of major practical value. Secondly, there was no difference in outcome according to the different types of AIT device used. Thirdly, the investigators found that most change occurred in the first five sessions of treatment, which raises questions about the need for more prolonged therapy. Fourthly, reliance on measures that are based on the accounts of parents who have already invested considerable money, time and emotional energy in the treatment, casts doubts on the validity of the findings more generally. The most puzzling finding, however, was that outcome did not depend on whether or not filtering was used, although the whole rationale of AIT is supposedly based on the removal of frequencies to which the individual is sensitive.

Two other recent studies have failed to confirm the effectiveness of AIT. Bettison (1996) found that structured listening had as much impact on children's behaviour as auditory integration training. Gillberg and his colleagues (1997) also failed to find any significant change in autistic symptomatology after therapy. Furthermore, at least within the UK, auditory integration tends to be combined with other therapies, including vitamin treatment, light therapy and facilitated communication (Howlin, 1997b), so that it is impossible to determine which components of treatment, if any, are effective.

In summary, there is little evidence of any long-term benefits of this approach, and even the short-term findings are, at least at the time of writing, equivocal. It is possible that the main value of this technique lies in encouraging children to sit quietly and listen through headphones. Learning to attend and to co-operate to this extent is a major achievement, and once established such behaviours may open the door to new learning and greater behavioural change.

BEHAVIOURAL APPROACHES: EARLY INTENSIVE INTERVENTIONS

There can be little doubt that the use of behavioural procedures has resulted in major improvements in the education, management and treatment of children with autism over the last three decades (Howlin & Rutter, 1987a; Short, 1984). Such techniques are now widely accepted as playing a crucial role in intervention and it is clear that behaviourally based strategies can be used to reduce many behavioural difficulties or to improve certain aspects of social, communicative and cognitive impairments. However, until recently they have been viewed as a means of ameliorating some of the deficits and difficulties associated with autism, not as a cure for the fundamental disorder. In 1987, however, Ivar Lovaas, long an ardent proponent of behavioural methods, published a paper reporting far more dramatic outcomes. A group of 19 pre-school children who had been involved in intensive home-based behavioural programmes (40 plus hours a week, for two years or more) was followed up at the age of 7, and progress compared with that of a less intensively treated control group (receiving 10 hours or less intervention a week). Children were aged around 2½ to 3 years when the therapy began. The mean IQ of the experimental group was 53 (range 30–82); that of the control group 46 (range 30–80). At follow-up the experimental children were found to have gained and maintained 20 IQ points; 9 children were placed in mainstream schools and several were described as being 'indistinguishable from their normal peers'. In contrast, the IQ of the control children had actually fallen slightly and all but one child remained in a special school placement.

McEachin *et al.* (1993) followed-up the same children some years later, when the experimental group had mean age of 13 years (range 9–19) and the controls a mean age of 10 (range 6–13). The mean IQ of the intensively treated children was 84.5; that of the controls 54.9. Vineland Adaptive Behaviour composite scores were superior in the experimental group as compared to the controls (71.6 : 45.7) and Maladaptive Behaviour scores were significantly lower (10.6 : 17.1). A wide range of other measures also indicated that the experimental group was functioning at a much higher level. Approximately half (9 children) had done particularly well and 8 were described as having 'normal functioning' and as being 'indistinguishable from average children on tests of intelligence and adaptive behaviour'. A later paper by Perry *et al.* (1995) also claims 'recovery from autism' in two siblings with autism exposed to the Lovaas programme. (For further information on treatment techniques and outcomes, see Maurice *et al.*, 1996.)

Perhaps not surprisingly, these reports have given rise to considerable controversy. Previous studies of behavioural interventions had generally indicated that although behavioural improvements were relatively easy to achieve using these techniques, there was little change in cognitive levels (Howlin & Rutter, 1987a; Short, 1984). Moreover, as noted above, the emphasis had always been on the *reduction* of problems, rather than *cures.* Particular concerns have been raised about the lack of random assignment to treatment and control groups and the comparability of the groups of children involved (Mesibov, 1993). Although the authors claim to have matched cases and controls as well as possible, there are some indications that the control group contained fewer high-functioning children than would be expected. Other questions relate to the use of different cut-off ages for the selection of echolalic and non-speaking children and the use of a variety of test protocols as initial and outcome measures. The failure to use independent assessors in the evaluation of the programme is another problem, and one that is fully acknowledged by the authors themselves.

By far the greatest controversy, however, has arisen over the use of terms such as 'recovery' or 'normal functioning'. It is highly likely that children exposed to such intensive treatment would, at least in the short term, show improvements in adaptive behaviour and possibly, too, in their scores on IQ tests. Certainly, other studies have reported marked improvements in IQ scores *in some children* following pre-school intervention programmes (Harris *et al.*, 1990). However, important as such gains are, they do not indicate normal or even near normal functioning. As Mesibov (1993) points out,

> There are many high functioning people with autism with near-normal IQ's and adaptive behaviour participating in regular public school programs who remain severely handicapped. To think otherwise is to minimize the severity of the social, cognitive, and communicative aspects of autism.

Mesibov, together with Mundy (1993), also notes that many of the skills required for normal functioning are not assessed. Thus, there are no measures of social interaction, friendships, conceptual abilities, social communication, obsessional and ritualistic behaviours, or disturbances of mood, all of which are important aspects of autism.

Lovaas (1993) points to other caveats concerning the outcome of treatment. Firstly, the very intensity of the therapy makes it very difficult at times to recruit adequate numbers of therapists and even more difficult for others to attempt to replicate this work. Secondly, although almost half of the children involved in the intervention programme made good progress, this leaves almost half who did not. Lovaas notes: 'What is left to do is to be of more help to the other half . . . and this may be a much more time consuming and challenging job.' He suggests that the subjects who did best were those who acquired verbal imitation within the first three months of intensive treatment; those who did not appeared to be more dependent on visual learning and for them, perhaps, 'basic research in areas other than reinforcement theory may play an important role in the future'.

Other comparative studies of this approach have been relatively short term or have involved only small numbers of children. Birnbrauer and Leach (1993), working in Australia, compared progress in nine pre-school children receiving 1 : 1 behavioural interventions at home (on average for 18.7 hours per week) with that of five children not involved in therapy. After two years, progress in the treated group was greater in terms of IQ, communication, play, social skills, self-help and tantrums. Stereotyped behaviours did not change and even those children who showed most improvement did not achieve normal functioning. However, direct comparisons with the Lovaas programme are difficult, in that intervention was somewhat less intensive, therapists were less experienced and there was no use of aversive procedures.

Sheinkopf and Siegel (1998; also reported in Green, 1996), in a retrospective study, assessed progress in 11 matched pairs of 2- to 3-year-old children. One member of each pair had received 1:1 behavioural intervention for an average of just under 20 hours per week (range 9.4–38.8 hours) for periods ranging from seven months to two years. After therapy the IQ and mental ages of the treated children were significantly higher than controls. In seven pairs the treated child made greater progress than his or her untreated partner; in two pairs progress was much the same, and in one case progress was greater in the control child (no follow-up data were available for one pair). However, no information is provided on adaptive behaviour, language or social skills, or on educational performance, and although the *severity* of autistic symptoms was lower in the experimental group, there was no difference in the *frequency* of these symptoms. Details of the behavioural programmes carried out at home are also sparse although children receiving around 30 hours of therapy each week tended to improve more than those receiving around 20 hours.

Green (1996) suggests that although many questions remain to be answered about this approach to intervention, the best outcomes seem to be achieved (a) if therapists (both parents and others) are appropriately trained and professionally supervised throughout; (b) if therapy begins before the age of 5 and lasts for two years or more; and (c) if intervention takes place for at least 30 hours a week, initially. She concludes that 'for children with autism and their families the benefits could be priceless . . . the payoffs potentially monumental'. However, while such studies clearly illustrate the power of behavioural interventions, the extent of the potential benefits still requires more systematic and scientifically sound exploration. Longer term evaluations, covering many different aspects of functioning, are also needed if the true cost-effectiveness of the time, effort and energy expended by families involved in such treatment is to be adequately assessed.

CRANIAL OSTEOPATHY

This involves very gentle manipulation being given to various parts of the body, particularly the head. It is claimed that a disturbed pattern of motion in the frontal lobes of the brain can sometimes be identified, or that the whole head is tight and unyielding. Treatment may last for several months, and the effects are said to range from minor reductions in hyperactivity to major improvements in communication (National Autistic Society, 1997). However, there are no adequate evaluative studies of this approach, and claims for success remain subjective and anecdotal.

DAILY LIFE THERAPY AND THE HIGASHI SCHOOLS

'Daily Life Therapy', as practised in the Japanese-run Higashi schools, has been claimed to produce unprecedented progress in children with autism (Kitahara, 1983, 1984a, 1984b). It is postulated that the high anxiety levels of many children with autism can be reduced by physical exercise, which in turn is said to release endorphins controlling anxiety and frustration. Daily Life Therapy consists of three complementary elements—building physical strength, stabilising the emotions and normalising intellectual interests. The focus of the curriculum is on group work, with a vigourous physical education programme, much music, art and drama, and a rigorous control of challenging and inappropriate behaviours. There is much less emphasis on the development of spontaneous communication skills or on the encouragement of individuality.

Early promotional publicity suggested that Daily Life Therapy could 'cure' autism, although claims are now more modest and focus on the reduction of behavioural problems. Unlike the schools in Japan, which emphasise the importance of integration, the Boston-based Higashi school offers only segregated provision for students with autism. The Boston school, which also accepts pupils from Europe, has around 100 students aged between 3 and 21 years, and with a wide range of ability and disability. The fees are expensive, and because most of the children are boarders, this means they are separated from their families. Parental accounts generally suggest that, in the short term at least, behavioural difficulties decrease, often very markedly, and compliance improves, although there are fewer reports of dramatic improvements in social communication skills. As one mother said, 'When I sent my child over there he was a little monster, when he came back he was a little robot. On the whole I preferred the robot but I had hoped for something in between.'

There have been no long-term or controlled evaluations of the success of the programme, and although there are positive reports of the extent of control over behavioural problems, concerns have been expressed about the rigidity of the approach, the lack of emphasis on individual development, and the rather sparse living conditions (Gould *et al.*, 1991; Quill *et al.*, 1989). There have even been reports of physical abuse (Cook *et al.*, 1993). Nevertheless, a number of observers have suggested that there may well be components of the regime (such as the high level of routine, and the emphasis on physical exercise) that could be of benefit if introduced into existing education programmes (Quill *et al.*, 1989; Bignell, 1991). At the same time it has been suggested that the Higashi philosophy could profit from incorporating strategies derived from more general educational practice.

Despite the fact that 'Daily Life Therapy has opened many doors of enquiry, and offers . . . professionals the challenge of exploration' (Quill *et al.*, 1989), few as yet appear to have taken up this challenge, and there is little hard evidence of the longer term benefits of this approach, or of the advantages or possible limitations for individual students.

DIETARY AND VITAMIN TREATMENTS

Dietary Restrictions

Several researchers have suggested that food intolerance or allergic responses may be responsible for at least some of the behavioural disturbances observed in autism. Bidet *et al.* (1993), for example, tested 10 individuals with autism and found that seven exhibited at least one positive test towards an allergen and five towards at least one food allergen. On the basis of such findings they recommend that the effectiveness of allergen-free diets should be further explored. Rimland (1994a) also notes that around 40–50% of parents who had removed milk, wheat or sugar from their children's diet felt that this had been beneficial. However, Renzoni *et al.* (1995) failed to find evidence of food hypersensitivity in children with autism when compared to age- and sex-matched controls.

As in any group of children, a small minority of individuals may show abnormal reactions to specific substances, but in many cases children are incorrectly identified as being 'allergic'. Moreover, Taylor (1998) concludes that special diets are of limited value for children who are severely hyperactive. Unsupported generalisations about food intolerance in autism are unlikely to prove helpful but if sensitivity is suspected in an individual child this will need to be systematically tested. This is usually done by means of exclusion diets, which require the support of a qualified dietician and which may well prove difficult for many children to accept. It is important to remember that for some autistic children food, often of a rather limited variety, may be a very important source of motivation and reward. To remove favoured items unnecessarily from the child's menu could result in an increase rather than a reduction in disturbance and distress.

Vitamins

Despite concerns that the limited and restricted diets of some children with autism might result in problems related to nutritional deficiencies, in fact there is little, if any, evidence that their food intake is inadequate. Indeed, when Raiten and Massaro (1986) compared the diets of 40 autistic and 34 control children over one week, they found that the autistic group had significantly greater intake of all nutrients, with the exception of vitamins A and C, and fat. Overall, adequacy of diets was similar for both groups. Nevertheless, vitamin treatments, especially those involving vitamin B6 (pyridoxine) have been recommended in a number of reports (Rimland, 1995). Experiments conducted in France (Lelord et al., 1982) indicated that treatment with B6 resulted in behavioural improvements in 15 out of 44 autistic children. In later studies, Martineau et al. (1985, 1988) demonstrated that the combination of B6 with magnesium resulted in greater change than if used individually. Of 318 parents who responded to a questionnaire on the use of vitamin and other treatments (Rimland, 1988a), 43% reported improvements in their child's behaviour, and in subsequent surveys the rates of positive responding are said to have risen to 46% (Rimland & Baker, 1996).

However, not all children respond positively to therapy; 5% of children in the Rimland survey, and around 9% of the Lelord cases, showed a worsening in their behaviour. Side-effects such as sensory neuropathy, headache, depression, vomiting and photosensitivity have also been reported in other studies. Pfeiffer and colleagues (1995), reviewing recent evidence for the efficacy of B6 and magnesium, note the methodological problems of many investigations (small sample size, lack of clear information on dosage, dubious reliability and validity of outcome measures, and insufficient long-term follow-up data). Because of experimental flaws of this kind, none of the 12 studies reviewed was able to demonstrate that treatment produced statistically significant, or clinically valuable changes.

As with any other treatment, high doses of vitamins should not be given casually or indiscriminately, and the possibility of unwanted side-effects should not be discounted. What is helpful for one child may not be so for another, and individual monitoring and close attention to possible negative responses should always be an integral part of the treatment regime.

EARLY INTERVENTION PROGRAMMES

The highly intensive, behaviourally based programmes of Lovaas and his colleagues have not been the only ones to indicate the importance of early intervention. Rogers (1996) reviewed the outcome of six early intervention projects for children with autism, conducted between 1985 and 1993, including those of Lovaas and McEachin, described above. Fenske and colleagues (1985) compared the outcome of home- and school-based behavioural programmes, involving 27 hours intervention per week for two years or more, in two groups of children aged above or below 5 years. Outcome was far better in the younger group, with 44% in mainstream classes at follow-up, as compared with only 11% of the older children. Rogers and her team (see Rogers & DiLalla, 1991) compared progress in 49 4-year-old children exposed to 6–12 months of developmentally based group teaching, for 22 hours a week, with that of a control group of 27 children. Developmental rates doubled in the experimental group and there were significant increases in symbolic play, language and social interaction.

Some other studies, while not incorporating control groups, have assessed the progress of their experimental children before and after intervention. Hoyson et al. (1984) studied the progress of 3–4-year-old children enrolled in a 15-hour school-based programme over 6–16 months. Intervention was conducted in a group setting, and utilised both behavioural and developmental strategies. Again, the authors report a doubling in developmental rates during the treatment period. Anderson et al. (1987) conducted a similar type of programme, but in the home and on an individual basis, with 14 children also aged around 3–4. Their programme lasted 12–24 months and involved 15–25 hours of therapy each week. Here, too, there was an escalation in developmental growth, with normal rates of development being recorded during intervention. Harris et al. (1990) assessed linguistic progress in 10 4–5-year-old children attending specialist pre-school classes. Half were in an integrated class, the rest in an autistic setting. There were no differences between integrated and segregated children, and the progress of the autistic subjects remained well below that of a normal peer group. However, the rate of language development in the children with autism increased considerably and there were significant gains in language age over the treatment period.

As Rogers points out in her review, all the studies suffer from important methodological flaws, including the failure to assign children randomly to treatment or control groups, and a lack of blind evaluations. Many are based on very small samples and the numerous different components involved in therapy also complicate the analysis. The length and intensity of therapist involvement is also variable, ranging from 15 to 40 hours a week, and from six months to over two years. Nevertheless, it would seem that children who begin receiving intervention between the ages of 2 and 4 make better progress than those who receive similar help at a later age. Successful interventions also involve intensive support (of 15 or more hours per week), tend to last at least six months and require a high adult : child ratio. However, as Rogers notes, many more questions remain to be answered before the specific effects of early intervention can be determined (or more generous funding obtained). These include the effects of different types of treatment and the responses of different sub-groups of children within the autistic spectrum. More information is needed, too, on the specific treatment variables responsible for change, the comparative roles of home-based and school-based intervention, the value of one-to-one versus group teaching, and the optimum timing, intensity and length of intervention programmes. There is also an urgent need for better experimental and evaluative research with random as-signment of children to different conditions, blind evaluations, and much more tightly controlled (and more precisely described) models of treat-ment. Finally, outcome studies need to span a much longer time period and some form of standardised evaluation database is necessary if com-parisons across programmes can be reliably and validly made.

FACILITATED COMMUNICATION

Facilitated Communication (FC) first rose to fame in the early 1990s fol-lowing highly publicised claims for its effectiveness in the USA (Biklen, 1990) and Australia (Crossley & Remington-Gurley, 1992). The technique involves a facilitator who supports the client's hand, wrist or arm while that individual uses a keyboard, or letter board, to spell out words, phrases or sentences. Its use with people with autism is based on the theory that many of their difficulties result from a movement disorder, rather than social or communication deficits. The facilitator should pre-sume that the client possesses unrecognised literacy skills; the provision of physical support can then lead to 'Communication Unbound' (Biklen, 1990).

What is perhaps unique about this form of therapy is the extraordinary degree of success claimed. Thus, while using FC, people with autism were said to demonstrate levels of knowledge, understanding, or literary skills, that were not only much greater than they had ever previously exhibited, but which would be remarkable even for individuals of superior intellec-tual ability and education: 'Many are now communicating . . . and produc-ing written language of such complexity as to challenge commonly held beliefs about the language of people diagnosed as autistic or significantly intellectually impaired' (Crossley & Remington-Gurley, 1992).

However, for many reasons, there arose increasing concerns about this form of intervention. Firstly, there were serious doubts that FC could lead to independent communication. Despite the claims for success, there was considerable reluctance on the part of many advocates to submit the procedures to external validation, on the grounds that this would adversely affect the essential relationship of trust between facilitator and client. When independent evaluations have taken place, these have generally assessed the accuracy of clients' responses under separate conditions:

(a) when both the facilitator and client hear/see the same questions
(b) when the facilitator and client hear/see different questions
(c) when the facilitator is prevented from hearing or seeing the question in some way (e.g. by the use of white noise or visual screening).

Although much criticised by proponents of FC, on the grounds that such techniques are artificial and may lead to stress or non-compliance on the part of the subject with autism, many different evaluation paradigms have been employed over recent years, with experimenters doing their utmost to ensure that conditions were comfortable and acceptable to facilitators and clients alike. The cumulative results of all the evaluative studies to date are striking. When both client and facilitator are provided with the same information, success is relatively good; if they are provided with different information, the rate of correct responding is often lower than might have been expected on a chance basis alone.

In a review of the literature up to 1996 (Howlin, 1997b), 45 control trials of FC were identified, involving over 350 subjects. These studies assessed the numbers of correct responses made by subjects when facilitators and clients were presented with *different* stimuli. Independent communication was confirmed in only around 6% of subjects and in well over 90% of cases the responses were found to be influenced (albeit unwittingly) by the facilitators rather than by the clients. When independent client responses could be demonstrated these were often only partially correct or consisted of minimal, one-word answers.

Recent evaluation studies have become more sophisticated, in an attempt to overcome the criticisms raised by those working as facilitators. Bebko and his colleagues (1996) employed multiple assessment methods with 20 students on two separate occasions. Findings differed across methods and between occasions, but unlike many previous studies the authors did find some evidence of independent communication in nine subjects. However, the most significant finding was that among students who were clearly capable of responding independently, their responses under facilitated conditions were actually inferior to their unsupported responses! The authors suggest that such students may become more passive in their responding when under the control of a facilitator, and they concluded that in a quarter of their sample there was evidence that facilitation hindered rather than enhanced communication.

Furthermore, in line with the findings of Bebko *et al.* (1996), there are suggestions that indiscriminate or widespread use of FC can actually have a negative impact on children's progress. Thus, there are indications that in schools where there has been a major transfer of resources and enthusiasm into FC this has been to the detriment of the wider curriculum. There is also anecdotal evidence to suggest that the remarkable typescripts sometimes produced have led to children being inappropriately transferred to mainstream, and often unduly academic courses with which they are unable to cope (Howlin & Jones, 1996).

Finally, and most disturbingly, there are the concerns about unfounded accusations of sexual abuse, against parents or other carers, made by children in the course of facilitation sessions (Rimland, 1992; Howlin & Jones, 1996).

There is, of course, no doubt that augmentative communication techniques, using signs, symbols, pictures, writing or computers can be crucial in helping many autistic children to improve their communicative competence. By making use of appropriate technology, coupled with shaping and prompting procedures, even the most profoundly disabled of individuals can often be helped to develop some form of independent communication over time (Shane, 1994). However, continuing dependence on the support of a facilitator is likely to be counter-productive, and it is now clear that the success of this method is far more limited than its proponents claim. Moreover, unquestioning acceptance of children's facilitated communications can lead to inappropriate educational placements, misplaced beliefs in their potential ability, and even, as in the cases of accusations of abuse, to the disruption of families and the break up of homes.

So extensive have been the concerns over its use that, in 1994, the American Psychological Association adopted the resolution that: 'Facilitated Communication is a controversial and unproved procedure with no scientifically demonstrated support for its efficacy.' Rather than insisting, in the face of now overwhelming evidence to the contrary, that most children can profit from such methods, proponents need to demonstrate objectively the circumstances in which FC *may* work; which subgroups of children it may work for; what can be done to improve generalisation; and how reliance on facilitators' support can be effectively modified. Until such questions can be satisfactorily answered there would seem to be no case for the further introduction of these methods into children's schools or homes.

GENTLE TEACHING

The term 'Gentle Teaching' was first used by McGee (1985) and, as a therapy, was claimed to be successful for all individuals with learning difficulties and challenging behaviours. It is defined by Jones and McCaughey (1992) as 'a non-aversive method of reducing challenging behaviour that aims to teach bonding and interdependence through gentleness, respect and solidarity. Emphasis is placed on the importance of unconditional valuing in the caregiving and therapeutic process.' The technique rose to popularity in the wake of growing concerns about the use of aversive procedures in the treatment of individuals with autism or other learning disabilities, but has generated anything but gentle arguments. Its proponents have variously denounced behavioural interventions as 'sinful', as a 'culture of death' and even 'deliberate torture' (McGee et al., 1987). In turn, gentle teaching has been dismissed as 'biased, unscientific and naive (or) . . . as a mere recombinant of positive reinforcement, manual guidance, prompting and extinction' (Barrera & Teodoro, 1990).

At the heart of the approach is the belief (similar to that of the Option Method, described below) that bonding between client and therapist is essential for progress. The therapist must learn to value and respond with affection to the client and to recognise 'the inherent dignity of each (mentally handicapped) person' (McGee et al., 1987). Another fundamental assumption is that challenging behaviours are communicative messages, which may indicate distress, discomfort, anxiety or anger.

The therapeutic techniques involved include reinforcement, extinction, interruption and redirection of responses, environmental and stimulus control, errorless learning, shaping and fading, teaching quietly, and feedback and assistance. McGee (1985) states that although the techniques themselves are obviously not new, 'what is new is that mixtures of these techniques enable us to avoid using punishment and, more importantly, teach interactional control which leads to bonding'. The strength of gentle teaching lies in its aim to improve the quality of life for people with learning difficulties, by concentrating on environmental and interpersonal factors rather than focusing specifically on maladaptive behaviours. The emphasis on the *mutual* relationship between client and caregiver, and the need to improve the quality of life for both partners, is also important. However, as Jones and McCaughey (1992) point out, there are weaknesses, too. Firstly, clear and explicit definitions of what the technique actually entails are difficult to find, and this problem is exacerbated by the use of excessive and unnecessary jargon. Secondly, the emphasis on different components of the treatment seems to have shifted over time (the term 'bonding', for example, has been dropped in recent reports) resulting in a number of apparent inconsistencies. Thirdly, attacks on individuals, using a more traditional behavioural approach, have been unwarranted in their viciousness. Accusing those who are trying to reduce challenging behaviours of being 'torturers' is not particularly helpful, and there are also many examples of inaccurate and unfair reporting. Fourthly, despite its professed horror of all things aversive, uncritical acceptance of terms such as reward or punishment can clearly lead to problems. Thus, for an individual whose self-injury is used specifically to escape from social situations, the gentle teaching process, with its emphasis on interaction, may in fact be highly punitive and aversive (Emerson, 1990). Moreover, untested assumptions about the underlying causes of challenging behaviour can also be dangerous. Aggression or self-injury, for example, may often be indicators of pain or illness; they are not always an attempt to communicate unhappiness or frustration.

The effectiveness of this approach has still to be demonstrated. McGee and Gonzalez (1990) claim that aggressive, self-injurious or withdrawn behaviours can be reduced, on average, by 74%, but a number of small-scale controlled studies have indicated that gentle teaching is actually less effective than other techniques, including visual screening, differential reinforcement, graduated guidance, edible reinforcers and restraint (Barrera & Teodoro, 1990; Jordan et al., 1989; Paisey et al., 1989; Jones et al., 1990, 1991). Jones and McCaughey (1992), in a well-balanced review of this topic, conclude that there are, in fact, far fewer differences between gentle teaching and traditional behavioural strategies than is often claimed. Recognition of the positive aspects of both these approaches, and an end to rhetoric, misinformation and personal abuse, might lead to far more benefits for people with autism and other learning difficulties.

HOLDING THERAPY

In their book *Autistic Children: New Hope for a Cure* (1983) Niko and Elizabeth Tinbergen suggested that the autistic condition is caused, not by genetic or neurological factors, but by 'an anxiety dominated emotional imbalance, which leads to social withdrawal and . . . a failure to learn from social interaction'. This imbalance was said to result through a lack of bonding between mother and infant, but 'once the mother–child bond has been established or restored, from that point normal development proceeds'. The Tinbergens suggested that one of the most successful treatments for restoring this bond was 'Holding Therapy'.

'Holding' was initially promoted in the USA by Martha Welch (1988), who claimed it could be effective for an astonishing range of problems, from autism to marital difficulties. It was also publicised widely in

Germany (Prekop, 1984), Italy (Zappella, 1988) and the UK (Richer & Zappella, 1989). As the name indicates, therapy involves holding the child tightly until he or she accepts comfort. Central to this is the need to provoke a state of distress in order that the child will need to be comforted. Often the adult would lie on top of the child, holding the head in order to ensure eye-to-eye contact, although sessions might also be conducted with the child held on the adult's knee. Sessions would typically last for around 45 minutes and in many cases children would clearly be extremely distressed for much of this time.

Richer and Zappella (1989), reviewing research into holding therapy, claimed that it had 'a major contribution to make to the treatment of autistic children' and that it could result in children becoming 'entirely normal'. Wimpory and Cochrane (1991) severely criticised this review, noting that the authors do not properly report on the nature of the studies involved (many were not research articles, as claimed; others involved a combination of different strategies); on the subjects used (many were not actually autistic); or on the results (the percentages of children who were said to have improved were lower than the figures given in the source articles, and reports of adverse effects were considerably higher than cited).

Holding therapy generated a great deal of controversy in the late 1980s, and was taken up by large numbers of parents. Promised evaluative studies never emerged, and, as with so many other much publicised treatments, it has now disappeared virtually without trace. There are no data to show that children who experienced holding are any more or less disturbed in later life than those who did not.

MUSIC THERAPY

Music therapy makes no claims to be able to 'cure' autism, but it is said to have a significant impact on many problem behaviours. Alvin (1968) was one of the first to report the use of music therapy with severely handicapped autistic children, and subsequent studies (see Trevarthen *et al.*, 1996, for review) also claim to demonstrate the effectiveness of this approach. However, in most cases, the accounts have been entirely anecdotal and subjective, and/or based on single-case reports. For example, in one study of a 10-year-old girl it is inferred that 'Through music she has laid the foundation for communicating her needs and incorporating her energies creatively' (Agrotou, 1988). Similarly, Trevarthen *et al.* (1996) claim 'music therapy played a significant role in developing . . . emotional, integrative and self organisational experiences'.

Even in more objective investigations, the evaluative techniques employed have been seriously flawed. Comparisons between studies are made difficult because of the variety of different techniques used; thus, while some have incorporated a psychoanalytic approach, others have involved additional interventions such as play therapy. Muller (1993), using rather more rigorous evaluation procedures, found an increase in turn-taking behaviour and some decrease in socially avoidant behaviour following music therapy, However, there was considerable individual variation: while some children appeared to improve, others showed little change and in some there was a definite deterioration in behaviour. To some extent, children who had higher verbal ability and were less obsessional and ritualistic in their behaviours, tended to respond better than others but these findings were not clear cut and the results were complicated by the fact that several children were also involved in holding therapy during the same period of time.

Overall, it seems that musically based interventions, *as one component of a wider educational curriculum,* may be helpful for some children, presumably because of the emphasis on listening skills, turn taking and social reciprocity within situations that avoid the need for complex language or verbal understanding. The fact that certain children with autism also demonstrate particular skills or interests in music may be another reason why, for some, therapies using this medium may be particularly effective. However, once again, there is no evidence of any long-term benefits and it seems that for some children interventions of this kind may have no, or even a negative, impact.

THE OPTION METHOD

The Option Institute in Sheffield, Massachusetts, was founded by Suzi and Barry Kaufman, parents of an autistic son. The Option process is said to be more a philosophy of life than a specific treatment. Its main aim is to promote happiness among clients by helping them discover the underlying belief systems that may be fostering unhappiness and enabling them to discard these.

Within the field of autism, the Option method is based on the premise that the child finds the world confusing and distressing and hence attempts to shut it out. This then starves the brain of the stimuli needed to develop social interaction skills, thereby further increasing confusion and reinforcing the desire for isolation. Attempts at intervention frequently strengthen the child's experience that interaction is unpleasant and result in further withdrawal. The essential principle underlying treatment is to make social interactions pleasurable, and to ensure that involvement with *people* becomes more attractive than involvement in obsessional or ritualistic behaviours. The approach also emphasises the importance of *acceptance*; that the child's behaviours must not be judged as deviant or inappropriate, and that such behaviours should be viewed as an understandable reaction to their difficulties in making sense of or controlling their world (Kaufman, 1977, 1981). In order to 'reach' the child with autism, adults must be prepared to join in with and enjoy the activities that the child finds pleasurable (very often his or her obsessional activities). Once the child's confidence has been developed in this way, other activities may very gradually be encouraged. Parents are taught to become more aware of and to respond more effectively to the cues given by their own children.

Training at the Option Institute is expensive, especially if families have to travel from abroad. It involves a week's course during which parents sleep, eat, work and exercise in the same room as the child (Hamilton-Ely, 1990). Subsequently, families are encouraged to continue the process at home, and this can mean adapting the house to ensure that they have a distraction free area in which to work—if possible, with a one-way screen through which therapy can be observed. Intensive, one-to-one interaction lies at the heart of the Option method, although the amount of time required for this seems to be variable, with some families managing to fit therapy around other activities, others spending many hours a day with their child and requiring additional assistance from volunteers (Jordan, 1990; Macdonald & Macdonald, 1991). After 9,000 hours of such treatment the Kaufmans' own son is said to have progressed from being 'a severely autistic child . . . with an IQ of about 30' to a completely normal young man with 'a near genius IQ' (Hamilton-Ely, 1990). Parents' own accounts suggest that their children became more co-operative, calmer and happier as a result of therapy. 'He now asks us to join in his obsessions, where previously they were exclusive' (Macdonald & Macdonald, 1991).

Although the Kaufmans are said to make no untoward promises about the effectiveness of their approach, the titles of some of their books (e.g. *A Miracle to Believe In*, 1981), the fact that children in treatment wear T-shirts proclaiming 'Miracle in Progress', and the statement in the brochures that this is 'A place for miracles' rather belie this claim. Moreover, while some observers have concluded that this is 'an unproven but hopeful method that is unlikely to do harm' (Jordan, 1990), anecdotal reports from teachers indicate that some children returning from the Institute have had considerable difficulties in returning to their regular school routines and that their ritualistic behaviours have, if anything, become more difficult to deal with. Apart from occasional reports of successful outcome appearing in the press from time to time, there are no controlled investigations of this form of treatment and, apart from the Kaufmans' own books, no reports of the long-term effects of intervention.

PET THERAPIES

Although claims of apparently dramatic improvements in behaviour after exposure to pet therapy of various kinds also occasionally appear in press reports, there are no satisfactory experimental evaluations of this approach to intervention. Swimming with dolphins, or communicating via the family dog, *may* be helpful for some children, but on the whole there are no properly conducted trials of such approaches to intervention.

Redefer and Goodman (1989) report on improvements in social interactions and reductions in stereotyped behaviours after children with autism were exposed to a dog (breed unspecified) for 18 sessions each of 20 minutes duration. However, the role of the human therapist in this experiment could not be disentangled, and although the authors suggest that a combination of animal therapy and peer-mediated intervention might be 'maximally productive' there seems to be little practical or theoretical evidence to support such a view.

PHYSICAL EXERCISE

'Patterning' or the hands-on systematic exercising of autistic children by their parents, and usually teams of volunteers as advocated by Glenn Doman and Carl Delacato, was once viewed as another possible cure for autism (Delacato, 1974; Cummins, 1988; Yule, 1993). By stimulating muscle activity in a controlled way, often throughout many hours of the day, it was claimed that this could repair damaged or non-functional neural networks. Although any intervention involving such intensive one-to-one therapy is almost bound to have some positive effects, evidence for permanent change or any concomitant neurological improvements has never been forthcoming. Moreover, the enormous demands (both financial and physical) made on families undertaking this form of therapy have tended to result in a steady decline in its popularity.

Nevertheless, vigorous exercise has been reported in a number of studies to have a positive effect on behavioural problems. It is, of course, a crucial component in Daily Life Therapy, as practised in the Higashi schools, and Martha Welch also suggested that it might play some role in the effectiveness of holding therapy. Rimland (1988b) found that 48% of a total of 1,286 parents reported improvements following physical exercise, and reductions in stereotyped, disruptive and hyperactive behaviours, sleep disturbance, aggression, anxiety, self-injury and depression have been noted in other studies. Exercise has also been claimed to improve attention span, social skills, work performance and cognitive functioning, and to reduce self-stimulatory behaviours in subjects with autism, as well as other forms of learning disability (see Elliott *et al.*, 1994; Rosenthal-Malek & Mitchell, 1997). Elliott *et al.* (1994) used a variety of techniques to elevate heart rates in six adults with autism and then compared general motor training (elevating heart beats to 90–120 beats per minute) with more vigourous exercise (elevating heart beats to above 130). Only the latter resulted in any significant reductions in stereotyped behaviours or improvements in other areas. On the basis of these results the authors suggest that *vigorous* aerobic exercise may be a useful component of integration programmes.

Rosenthal-Malek and Mitchell (1997) also report a significant decrease in self-stimulatory behaviour and a concomitant rise in work-related performance following aerobic exercise (20-minute jogging sessions). They suggest that the inclusion of systematic physical exercise sessions into students' curricula could be an easy, cost-effective way to improve positive functioning. However, they also note that more information is needed on the optimal intensity and duration of such programmes.

PSYCHOTHERAPY

Although, in his original writings on autism, it is clear that Kanner believed the disorder to be biologically determined, his comments on the lack of warmth shown by parents, and their tendency towards a 'mechanization of human contacts' (Kanner, 1943) led many to view the condition as being predominantly psychogenic in origin. It was variously suggested that autism was due to a lack of stimulation, parental rejection, lack of warmth, or deviant family interactions (Bettleheim, 1967; Boatman & Szurek, 1960; O'Gorman, 1970). Such theories had a profound and widespread influence on therapeutic practice, and throughout the 1950s and 1960s individual psychotherapy (mainly in the form of psychoanalytically oriented non-directive play therapy) was considered the treatment of choice (Szurek & Berlin, 1956; Goldfarb, 1961). Almost all reports of this form of intervention have been single-case studies and there have been virtually no systematic attempts at evaluation. In 1987, Howlin and Rutter noted 'one cannot conclude with certainty that it does not work, nevertheless, there is little evidence . . . to suggest that it does'. Almost 10 years later, Campbell *et al.* (1996) concluded that 'psychoanalysis as a treatment for autism has a limited value', although they also observed that Hobson (1990) had discussed some possible strengths of this approach, including the emphasis on object relations and affective contact.

For older, more able people with autism, individual psychotherapy or counselling may be useful in helping them to deal more effectively with anxiety or depression, and the pain that comes from realising how different they are from their peers. However, anecdotal evidence suggests that unless therapy is combined with direct practical advice on how to deal with problems, the outcome may be disastrous. Simply taking an individual back to his or her early childhood, or focusing (for example) on disturbed mother–child interactions, is more likely to result in obsessional ruminations and laying the blame for all current problems on other people, rather than encouraging effective coping strategies.

SCOTOPIC SENSITIVITY TRAINING

Scotopic sensitivity, or sensitivity to certain wavelengths of light, is said to result in a variety of symptoms, including reading and communication difficulties, spatial and perceptual deficits, and attentional problems. Special spectacles, incorporating lenses of a variety of different colours, can be designed to provide the 'optimum' tint for each individual in order to improve visual skills; they are also reported to bring about improvements in body and spatial awareness, eye contact, communication and self-control (Irlen, 1995). The spectacles have been used for some time with people with learning disabilities and have recently been claimed to offer help to people with autism: 'We are still at the beginning stages (but) . . . we are amazed by the results. All the senses are connected so that visual perception can affect thought processes which influence auditory perception and, in turn, language' (Irlen, 1995). The most important role of the spectacles is said to be the calming effect that they produce.

Donna Williams, a successful author who also has autism, is said to have found the results 'close to miraculous . . . she was able to listen and concentrate better; her speech became more fluent and spontaneous'. However, other than reports from a small number of individuals who have worn the spectacles, and the writings of Irlen herself, little is known about the relative merits of this form of treatment, and nothing about its long-term effectiveness.

SENSORY INTEGRATION THERAPY

Sensory integration is the ability to process, immediately and simultaneously, the many different sensory messages—smell, hearing, vision, touch, or taste—that may result from even the simplest action. It is well established that many children with autism have problems in dealing with complex sensory stimuli (Minshew et al., 1997) or they may be particularly sensitive to specific types of stimuli (such as sound or texture).

Sensory integration therapy has been recommended as a possible treatment for sensory disturbances of this kind. It aims to improve sensory processing by using a variety of stimuli, such as swings, balls, trampolines, soft brushes and cloths for rubbing the skin, perfume, massage, coloured lights or objects with unusual textures, in order to increase sensory awareness and responsivity (Ayres, 1979). 'Deep pressure therapy' (rolling children up tightly in mats or mattresses) may also be involved.

There are a few small-scale reports of the effectiveness of these techniques. Brocklehurst-Woods (1990) and Dura *et al.* (1988) found that tactile and vestibular stimulation reduced stereotyped or self-injurious behaviours in three subjects with learning disabilities. Temple Grandin, an accomplished animal psychologist, who herself has autism, also claims that deep-pressure therapy has been effective in reducing stress and anxiety (Grandin, 1992a, 1992b, 1995). However, a number of reviews (Arendt *et al.*, 1991; Mason & Iwata, 1990) have pointed to the totally inadequate experimental design of most studies. Despite such criticism there has been an extraordinary growth in the use of these techniques in recent years and Rimland (1995a) suggests that around a quarter of programmes for autistic children in the USA were utilising this approach, albeit with few attempts being made to investigate its effectiveness.

WHAT ARE THE COMMON FACTORS IN THESE TREATMENTS?

Although the treatments described above might seem, at first glance, to be highly variable, closer study reveals a number of common characteristics.

Firstly, many of these programmes claim to be successful for *all* (or almost all) children with autism, but there are few data on which children respond well and which do not, as treatment is often assumed to be equally effective for everyone. There are few detailed, individual assessments of the children involved and, typically, there is little effort to relate individual characteristics to outcome. Indeed some of these treatments for autism—such as holding therapy, cranial osteopathy or auditory integration training—claim to be equally effective for a whole range of other problems from depression to dysfunctional family life.

Secondly, many of these programmes involve highly intensive, one-to-one interaction with parents or other professionals. The interaction may last for relatively brief periods of time (as in auditory integration training or holding therapy) or may be much more prolonged (as in the Lovaas or Options programmes). It would be *most unlikely* that a highly intensive programme would fail to have some positive effects in the short term. The crucial, but unanswered, question is whether or not these effects endure.

Thirdly, and perhaps most importantly, many of these programmes offer parents clear and explicit guidelines on what they can do to help their child. Parents are encouraged to value their child as a person in his or her own right and to expect significant improvements (even though these expectations may sometimes be unrealistic). Moreover, parents themselves are often given much more time, care, attention and encouragement than is usually offered by hard-pressed professionals working in state-run health, social services or educational settings. The importance of giving parents faith in themselves and in their own ability to help their child should never be underestimated.

It is also important to recognise that (almost) all these approaches utilise therapeutic strategies that will be of practical help for at least some of the children who undergo them. The emphasis on physical contact or exercise involved in holding therapy, the Doman–Delacato techniques or Daily Life Therapy may benefit many children. The focus on communication skills and the emphasis on augmentative forms of communication is one positive feature of Facilitated Communication. The use of stereotyped behaviours as rewards, or as a means of establishing the child's co-operation, is an undoubted strength of the Options method. Music therapy may be an excellent way of encouraging reciprocity in some children, and programmes that emphasise more effective ways of integrating sensory input may be of value for others. Similarly, the avoidance of aversive procedures whenever possible, and the emphasis on personal worth as embodied in Gentle Teaching, are clearly important elements in any intervention programme.

COULD SUCH TREATMENTS HELP MY CHILD?

No matter how seductive the claims, no matter how glowing the unsolicited testimonials from satisfied parents, it is essential to remember that there is no such thing as a universal panacea. Even within physical medicine, drugs that have brought widespread advantages to many, such as aspirin or penicillin, may have no effects in certain conditions, and for some individuals or some illnesses they may actually prove dangerous and harmful.

Before being tempted by promises of miracles and before parting from large amounts of money or in some cases (as in specialist boarding school provision), from their own child, parents must be encouraged to seek information on basic issues related to therapy. Brua and Link (1997) have designed a checklist that parents might use when considering an alternative therapy (see Table 4.1).

At the very least parents must attempt to obtain the answers to the following questions:

Table 4.1: A checklist for parents considering an alternative therapy (Brua & Link, 1997)

About the therapy
1. How long has this therapy been used?
2. How does the therapy work?
3. What types of difficulties do the people who have received this therapy have?
4. How many people with my child's disability have received this therapy and what were the results?
5. What research is available that I can see which shows how effective this therapy is for people with my child's disability?
6. How will you decide whether this therapy is appropriate for my child?
7. Will you consult his or her general practitioner or other professionals for his or her medical/personal history?
8. Is the therapy unsuitable for certain people? Who? Why?
9. Are there many side-effects? If yes, what are they?
10. How will you tell whether the therapy has been successful with my child? What sign will you look for?
11. Will you compare his or her behaviour/condition before and after the therapy? How?
12. Will you be following up my child to see if any change has been long-lasting?

About the therapist
1. How long have you been using this therapy? How many people have you treated using this therapy?
2. How were you trained in using this therapy? Who trained you? How long did the training last? What qualifications are needed to undergo training?
3. Can I see your certificate?
4. Does anyone still monitor you to see if you are still doing the therapy correctly?
5. My child is . . . years old and has problems in these areas:
   * language
   * behaviour
   * learning
   * etc. (describe)
   How many people have you treated who had the same problems as my child and what were the results?
6. Can you give me the names and telephone numbers of any other parents/carers who have a child who is similar to my child and has received this therapy?

About the arrangements for therapy
1. How much will the therapy cost in total?
2. Where will the therapy take place?
3. Will I have to arrange transport and/or accommodation for myself and my child? How much will this cost?
4. When will the therapy take place? Dates, times, time span, time off school/work?
5. Do I have to pay for the therapy in advance?
6. What happens if I wish to abandon the therapy before the course of treatment is completed? How much would I have to pay?
7. Will we have a written agreement about the terms and conditions of the therapy?
8. If my child gets worse, can I have my money back? Will I be entitled to compensation?
9. If my child's condition does not change after therapy, can I have my money back?

- *For whom does this programme work best?* Is it more effective for children of high or low ability? Is it more effective for those with good or poor communication skills? Does it work better with younger or older children? Are there any family factors that seem to be related to outcome?
- *With which children does it work less well?* Are there any medical or physical risks, or any particular subgroups of children who should be excluded?
- *What assessments are carried out on individual children prior to treatment?* What are the criteria for acceptance into treatment? What are the exclusion criteria?
- *What evaluation methods have been used to assess the outcome of treatment?* What *objective and scientific* evidence is there that children undergoing this therapy do better over time than those who have no special treatment, or who are involved in treatments of other kinds?
- *What is known about the likely prognosis for my child* (in the absence of any special treatments) as he or she grows older, given my child's age, and his or her intellectual and linguistic functioning? Bearing this in mind, what is known about the long-term effects of this particular treatment? What difference is it likely to make to my child as he or she reaches adolescence or adulthood?
- *How much does it cost?* How much time will be involved? What will be the pressures or restrictions on other aspects of family life?
- *What alternative interventions might be tried?* What information is there concerning the relative effectiveness of those alternatives?

If these questions cannot be answered satisfactorily, if there are no individual assessments before treatment begins and no formal outcome measures when it is ended, if the results are claimed to be universally successful for any child or any level of disability, then it is important to be aware that money may be wasted, valuable time lost and much disappointment and heartbreak may be the eventual result.

Individualised Approaches to Treatment

Of course, the vast majority of those who are involved in the teaching and therapy of children with autism make no extravagant claims for success. Professionals with skill and knowledge in this area recognise the enormous individual differences between children and the need for any programme to be specifically tailored to meet the needs of each child and his or her family. Those programmes that have proved most successful acknowledge the variety and pervasiveness of the deficits in autism and accept the need to employ a range of different techniques. There are no magic answers, no 'quick fixes', no infallible recipes. Instead, the choice of treatment will depend on individual patterns of skills and abilities, as well as family circumstances, all of which will influence the ways in which various techniques or strategies can be employed. Any successful intervention must take account, too, of the role that the fundamental deficits associated with autism—the communication and social impairments and the need for ritual and routine—will play in causing and maintaining behavioural problems. In the following chapters alternative approaches to treatment that offer not cures, but more general ways of improving the quality of life for all concerned, are explored. However, it is important to bear in mind that although there are many anecdotal reports of the success of these strategies—and often several single case or small group studies, using multiple baseline or ABA-type designs, that testify to their effectiveness—few, if any, have been exposed to randomised, control treatment trials. Thus, information on overall success rates, or on the types of children or problems for which the treatments are most/least successful, remains very limited. Carers and clinicians still lack the scientific information that they really need in order to help them decide that a given strategy will be most likely to work with a particular child and a specific problem. A certain degree of trial-and-error is, therefore, still inevitable, but with sensitivity to the needs of the child *and his or her family* progress can be made and unnecessary problems avoided.

UNDERSTANDING THE PROBLEMS OF CHILDREN WITH AUTISM

Articles on the association between autism and 'challenging' behaviour appear throughout the child psychiatric literature. Similarly, behavioural journals abound with detailed accounts of the techniques that have been successful in modifying aggressive, destructive and (although to a lesser extent) self-injurious behaviours. However, while the seriousness of such problems cannot be underrated, it is also important to recognise that, given the severity of their social and communication deficits and their need for ritual and routine, many children with autism show *fewer* challenges than might be expected. Imagine for a moment how 'normal' people might react to a world in which: (1) they are able to understand almost nothing of what is happening around them; (2) they are thrown daily into an ever-changing and unpredictable environment; (3) they lack even the rudimentary verbal skills necessary to make their needs known; and (4) they have no access to the internalised, imaginative facilities that are so crucial for dealing effectively with anxiety, uncertainty and distress. Most 'normal' individuals in such circumstances would rapidly

Table 4.2: The principal diagnostic features of autism and their association with behaviour problems

Area of deficit	Associated problems	
	Less able children	More able children
Impairments in communication and understanding		
● Inadequate language	Frustration, aggression; unacceptable attempts to control environment.	Inappropriate use of speech (echolalia, verbal routines, obsessional questions, etc.)
● Poor comprehension	Anxiety, distress and disruptive behaviours.	Apparent lack of co-operation.
● Lack of internal language	No ability to play or occupy self.	Poor imaginative skills; limited self-control.
Impairments in social understanding		
Lack of social awareness	Withdrawal and isolation. Disturbed/ disruptive and inappropriate behaviours in public.	Attempts to socialise are often inappropriate; may offend or antagonise others. Inability to 'read' others' feelings makes them appear insensitive, callous, even cruel.
Obsessional and ritualistic behaviours		
● Obsessional behaviour patterns	Can severely limit the acquisition of other more productive behaviours/ skills.	May involve other people in routines/ rituals; can impose major limitations on other people's activities too.
● Disruption of routines	Can result in serious distress, disruption and aggression.	
● Dislike of change	Leads to very rigid and inflexible patterns of behaviour and great distress and anxiety if change is necessary.	
● Obsessional Interests		May be pursued regardless of the consequences. Constant talk about these can antagonise others.

resort to a whole range of retaliatory behaviours which, if simply responded to by 'time out' or 'extinction' or even rewards for 'incompatible behaviour', would probably escalate dramatically. Of course, problem behaviours in autism, as in any other condition, will be maintained or increased by the attention or reinforcement they receive, and techniques such as time out, extinction or differential reinforcement can serve an important role (see Emerson, 1995). However, they are not specific to the treatment of autism. The focus of the following chapters, therefore, will be on the underlying causes of behavioural disturbances and on the roles played by social, communication and obsessional difficulties (see Table 4.2). Intervention strategies, too, will concentrate on the need to improve functioning in these areas, rather than on the direct elimination of problems.

Assessment for Intervention

Pre-treatment assessments

Before embarking on any treatment programme it is essential to obtain adequate information, not only on the behaviours to be modified, but also on the child. This is because problems that are apparently similar can have very different causes in different children, and within the same child at different times. For example, 'aggressive behaviour' may result from a child's inability to communicate; because he or she lacks more effective strategies to control the environment; because of the attention such behaviours receive; because of frustration, distress, anxiety or physical illness; or because of disruption to rituals and routines. Moreover, in many instances, a combination of such factors may be operating.

Individual assessment
Autism is frequently referred to as a 'spectrum' disorder (Wing, 1996), in that it can range from relatively mild to profoundly handicapping; similarly, it can affect children across the entire cognitive continuum and is found in those who are non-verbal as well as those whose spoken language is apparently very advanced.

Dealing with the temper tantrums of a non-speaking 4-year-old child with an IQ of 30 will require very different strategies to those appropriate for a highly verbal 14-year-old with an IQ of 130. Programmes that are pitched inappropriately high or low will be unlikely to succeed, and just as formal cognitive and linguistic assessments are essential components of the diagnostic process (see Chapter 3) they are also crucial for planning appropriate interventions. Informal observations, alone, can give a misleading impression of intellectual ability. Thus, children who appear alert and interested in their environment, or who have one or two isolated skills, may be mistakenly viewed as very intelligent; those who are able to follow simple instructions (often only with accompanying gesture or other cues) may be described, quite erroneously, as 'understanding every word you say'; children who have a very good expressive vocabulary may actually have far more limited comprehension skills. Conversely, children whose speech is slow and halting, and who appear to show little interest in the activities around them, may be classified as having severe learning difficulties when, in fact, many aspects of their cognitive development lie within the normal range.

Unfortunately, because of the social and communication difficulties associated with autism, it is often believed that traditional psychometric testing has little or no role to play in assessment. Many psychologists, especially within the educational system, still tend to rely on unstructured observations. While these are undoubtedly important, a relatively brief testing session may reveal unsuspected areas of skill or deficit, which may be very relevant for intervention. (For suggestions on useful tests see Appendix 1.)

Behavioural assessment
Traditional behavioural therapy has long espoused the ABC approach to the analysis of behavioural problems. Thus, following precise delineation of the Behaviour to be modified, attempts are made to identify the Antecedents and the Consequences of that behaviour. However, in the case of many children with autism, a focus on the observed behaviour does not necessarily lead to the most appropriate form of treatment (Emerson & Bromley, 1995); it may also be extremely difficult to establish, with any degree of certainty, either the antecedents or the consequences of the behaviour *as perceived by the child*. For example, a child might begin to self-injure in a particular setting, because he or she has been reminded of an earlier (but no longer existing) distressing occurrence which had previously ceased when self-injury commenced. In such a case, direct observations will be of little use in identifying the relevant variables.

Because the observed *form* of a challenging behaviour may give few clues as to its real role, recent intervention studies have focused instead on the *function* or 'message' of that behaviour. The aim is to establish what it achieves for all the individuals concerned (carers as well as children) and to develop alternative behaviours that might replace it (Sturmey, 1996). The following chapters explore ways in which this approach can be utilised in the treatment of children throughout the autistic spectrum—including those with classic Kanner's syndrome, those with Asperger syndrome, and those with more pervasive learning disabilities.

IMPROVING COMMUNICATION SKILLS

EARLY BEHAVIOURAL STUDIES

'To work most efficiently with a deviant child . . . the speech training should be carried out in a room containing as few distractions as possible' (Risley & Wolf, 1967).

Comprehension training
First, remove the child with autism to a quiet room free from all other distractions. The therapist should sit opposite the child at a desk or table. On the desk place an array of pictures or objects chosen by the therapist. The therapist names one or other object, and by using physical, gestural or verbal prompts as necessary, encourages the child to identify the named item. Errors should be avoided by the use of physical and verbal guidance (e.g. a sharp 'no') from the therapist. Correct responses should be rewarded immediately, usually by small pieces of sweets or other food. Gradually the size of the display should be increased, as should the complexity of the commands given. Thus, with time, the child should progress from being able to select (say) a ball or car from the table or tray, to being able to identify a **red** ball, or a **big** car from a larger display. To ensure generalisation, the programme should be extended to other teaching staff, and eventually, to the child's home environment.

Expressive language training
Again, ensure that the child is in a distraction-free environment, in one-to-one contact with the therapist. The therapist may demonstrate a particular sound, such as 'aah' and prompt the child to repeat this. Physical prompts may be used to ensure that the child's mouth is in the correct shape. Praise, together with small items of food should be used to reward acceptable attempts. Once a single sound has been established other sounds can be trained in the same way. Sounds can then be paired together, and used to identify items selected by the therapist. For example, if the child can make the sounds 'K' and 'aah', he or she can be prompted to combine these in an approximation to 'Car'. Once an extensive naming vocabulary has been established, the therapist can progress to using published language programmes or packages, in order to enhance grammatical complexity.

For readers unfamiliar with the use of early behavioural techniques to improve language skills in autism, the fact that such approaches were widely advocated and practised throughout the 1960s and much of the 1970s may come as something of a surprise. Even more surprising is the fact that these techniques were said to have a significant impact on language acquisition. Single-case studies reported highly successful outcomes in a wide range of children, of varying ages and cognitive abilities (see Howlin, 1989, for review). Some studies even claimed to have established 'near normal speech' in less than a year (Marshall & Hegrenes, 1970; Daley et al., 1972). As time went on, however, it became increasingly apparent that outcome was far from being universally successful. Hingtgen and Churchill (1968), for example, found no improvement in one child following 600 hours of therapy. Lovaas (1977) reported that over 90,000 trials were needed to teach one child just two simple word approximations. Other, even less successful, studies were presumably never published at all.

Problems of maintenance and generalisation also became increasingly apparent. The majority of these early intervention studies were conducted in specialist settings, with little or no parental involvement. Thus, even if improvements were reported these often disappeared once the child was returned home (Lovaas, 1978; Lovaas et al., 1973). Subsequently, emphasis shifted to the use of school and home-based programmes, with close liaison between parents and teachers becoming a central part of most successful interventions. Even so, there were very few controlled trials of language intervention programmes and those that were conducted suggested that the results were not entirely consistent. Hemsley and her colleagues (1978) found that there were clearly short-term gains, both in the frequency and complexity of children's speech, following the implementation of a behaviourally based programme at home. After six months, children in treatment used significantly more spontaneous speech and less echolalia than controls, phrase speech improved, their language was more complex and informative, and they responded more to their mothers' speech. However, over the following year progress tended to plateau and by the end of the intervention period there were few significant differences between cases and individually matched controls in level or frequency of speech, although treated children did use more socialised and communicative utterances.

This study also found considerable variability between children in their response to intervention. Those who were initially using phrase speech, even if much of this were echolalic, tended to make good progress, whether or not they were involved in treatment. In contrast, those who were initially mute at the time the project began, remained severely impaired. The effects of intervention seemed to be greatest in those children who had some single words or word approximations at the outset. While, in the non-treatment group, few children at this level showed any significant improvements over time, children in the therapy group showed much greater change.

Individual variation in responsiveness to treatment was also noted by Lovaas in his follow-up of children exposed to early and very intensive behavioural programmes (Lovaas, 1993, 1996). Although around half of the children involved in this programme made remarkably good progress, around half did not. Those who did best were those who acquired verbal imitation within the first three months of treatment.

INDIVIDUALISED APPROACHES TO LANGUAGE INTERVENTION

Recognition of individual variability in response to treatment has led in recent years to a shift towards much more individually based language programmes. Gone are the artificial, often arbitrarily designed language packages of the past, which sometimes attempted to teach language structures that were quite inappropriate to the child's developmental level or home environment. They have been replaced by more flexible intervention strategies which are not recipes as such, and hence may lack the intrinsic simplicity and appeal of the earlier programmes. Instead, they offer a potential *framework* for therapy, in which success depends heavily on the initiative and imagination of therapists, and their ability to adapt treatment approaches to the needs and skills of the individual child.

Enhancing Communication in Non-verbal Children

Analysing communicative intent

Although many children with autism are non-verbal, this does not mean that they are non-communicating. Most communicate a great deal, although *how* they attempt to communicate may not always be socially desirable, and *what* they are attempting to communicate may prove difficult to establish. If a child in the classroom pulls his neighbour's hair, he is almost certainly communicating something: it may be that he is bored, agitated or distressed; that he is ill or in pain; that he dislikes the child involved; that the work he has been given is too difficult; that he has just been bullied in the playground; that his morning routine had been upset before he left for school; that his parents are always fighting, or that his father has left home.

Table 5.1: Assessing communicative intentions (from Schuler et al., 1989)

CUE QUESTIONS	Crying	Aggression	Tantrums/self-injury	Passive gaze	Proximity	Pulling other's hands	Touching/moving other's face	Grabs/reaches	Enactment	Removes self/walks away	Vocalization/noise	Active gaze	Gives object	Gestures/pointing	Facial expression	Shakes 'no'/nods 'yes'	Intonation	Inappropriate echolalia	Appropriate echolalia	One-word speech	One-word signs	Complex speech	Complex signs
1. Requests for affection/interaction: WHAT IF S WANTS																							
adult to sit near?																							
peer to sit near																							
non-hand, peer to sit near?																							
adult to look at him?																							
adult to tickle him?																							
to cuddle/embrace?																							
to sit on adult's lap?																							
other:																							
2. Requests for adult action: WHAT IF S WANTS																							
help with dressing?																							
to be read a book?																							
to play ball/a game?																							
to go outside to store?																							
other:																							

3. Requests for object, food or things: WHAT IF S WANTS

an object out of reach?				
a door/container opened?				
a favourite food?				
music/radio/TV?				
keys/toys/book?				
other:				

4. Protest: WHAT IF

common routine is dropped?				
favourite toy/food taken away?				
taken for ride without desire?				
adult terminates interaction?				
required to do something doesn't want to?				
other:				

5. Declaration/Comment: WHAT IF S WANTS

to show you something?				
you to look at something?				
other:				

Establishing the true reason for isolated incidents of behaviour such as this can prove very difficult. However, semi-standardised questionnaires can be used in order to obtain a more generalised profile of the child's communicative attempts. One example of this is the schedule developed by Schuler and her colleagues (1989). This can be used with parents or teachers and by systematically exploring how the child expresses his or her need to do something (sit by someone; get attention; obtain food or other object; protest if something is taken away, etc.) the process can help to identify the types of communicative behaviour that are typically used by an individual child. It can also illustrate how behaviours that are often viewed as 'inappropriate' (screaming, self-injury, tantrums, aggression, etc.) may have important communicative functions (see Table 5.1).

Developed along similar lines, but in a slightly different format, is the interview protocol devised by Finnerty and Quill (1991). This uses many of the items in the Schuler schedule, but questions are grouped into 23 communicative functions, with sample scenarios provided to guide the interview. The interview describes a situation that is likely to encourage some form of communication. For example, to assess how the child obtains attention, the interviewee is asked 'You are giving your attention to another child . . . what does X do (or say, in the case of a verbal child)? Descriptions of the child's verbal or non-verbal responses are collated and, if used as described, the authors suggest that this tool can be used to summarise the child's skills in several different areas including the range of communicative means and of communicative functions, the ability to use more than one means to convey each function, the ability to repair strategies and to identify different communicative styles with different people or in different situations (Quill, 1995)—see Table 5.2.

Watson (1987) also describes the approach used within the TEACCH programme to analyse spontaneous language usage. This identifies the *form* of communication used (motor acts, speech vocalisations and gestures) the *target* of the interaction (peer, teacher, other adult, etc.) and the *function* of the interaction. Functions include: getting attention, part of a social routine, requesting, commenting, refusing/rejecting, giving information, seeking information, expressing feelings, and social interaction. Using this system with autistic children, Stone & Caro-Martinez (1990) found that the first three functions—(getting attention, social routine and requesting) together accounted for approximately two-thirds of their communicative acts. The final four (seeking information, expressing feelings and social interaction) accounted for only around 10%.

Once the child's current communicative modes and functions are identified, information gathered in this way can be used to plan ways in which alternative and perhaps more acceptable responses might be established. Moreover, by helping parents or teachers to appreciate that

Table 5.2: Communicative means–functions questionnaire (from Finnerty & Quill, 1991)

Function	Sample communicative context	What does the child do/say?
Request attention	You are giving your attention to another child.	
Request affection	You approach child after he/she has been hurt.	
Request assistance	Child needs help putting on shoes.	
Request information	Child sees a picture of something or someone new.	
Request permission	Child wants to go outside.	
Request peer interaction	Child sees another child playing with one of his/her favourite toys.	
Request adult interaction	You tickle child a few times and then pause.	
Request food or object	Child wants a toy that is out of reach.	
Refusal	You offer child a food that he/she doesn't like.	
Protest	You want child to go to sleep and he/she doesn't want to.	
Cessation	Child wants to be finished with a meal or task.	
Greetings	A family member or friend comes to visit.	
Affirmation	You ask child if he/she wants a favourite toy.	
Comment : object	Child sees an interesting person or object in a book.	
Comment : action	You sit with child while he/she is playing with a favourite toy.	
Comment : mistake	Child accidentally spills his/her drink.	
Express humour	You laugh unexpectedly when child does something.	
Express confusion	Child is given a task that he/she does not understand.	
Express fear	Child sees or hears something that frightens him/her.	
Express frustration	Child is having difficulty completing a task.	
Express anger	You make child stop doing a favourite activity.	
Express happiness	Child is doing a favourite activity.	
Express sadness	Child experiences something sad.	

certain behaviours may be a function of poor *communication* skills rather than being 'deliberate' acts of aggression or provocation, this approach can also have a very positive effect on other people's attitudes and their responses towards the child. Katy, for example, would tend to bite (herself, teachers or other pupils) whenever she was upset. By working through an adaptation of the 'Means and Functions' interview, staff identified that such behaviours tended to occur either when she was sitting near a particularly noisy child, or when she was given a new or difficult task to complete. Attention to her physical placement in the classroom helped to reduce the impact of the first problem; more gradual introduction of new materials reduced the second problem and, at the same time, if agitated, Katy was prompted to bang her hand on the table. Her teachers were warned to respond *instantly* to this, and the frequency of her biting was greatly reduced.

IMPROVING NON-VERBAL COMMUNICATION: SIGNS, SYMBOLS, PICTURES AND OBJECTS

Another major shift in communication training that occurred in the mid 1970s was the move towards alternative or augmentative systems of communication. Before this, alternative approaches tended to be introduced on a somewhat ad-hoc basis—often only after prolonged attempts at spoken language training had failed. However, follow-up studies of children with autism consistently indicated that if a child had not acquired useful speech by the age of 6 or 7 the chances of subsequently developing effective spoken language were very low (Rutter *et al.*, 1967). Children with severely impaired cognitive abilities and those with little or no comprehension of language were least likely to develop speech. For such children, the early introduction of an alternative communication system was needed, both to encourage social interactions and to reduce the behavioural problems resulting from the inability to communicate.

Signing Systems

Initially, the most widely used alternative systems were based on sign languages used within deaf communities (American Sign Language in the USA and British Sign Language, or Paget Gorman, in the UK). Nevertheless, although in some ways simpler than speech, such systems can make considerable demands on users. Signs are often abstract, may require the use of both hands in order for their meaning to be clear, and relatively discrete changes in hand movement can significantly alter the meaning. Studies of children with autism or other learning disabilities indicated that simple, iconic signs (i.e. ones in which the meaning is apparent from the action, such as raising a hand towards the mouth for 'cup') were generally much easier to acquire than more abstract ones (Konstantareas *et al.*, 1978; Kiernan, 1983). The Makaton system, devised by Margaret Walker (1980), was developed specifically for children with additional learning disabilities who were unable to cope with traditional signing systems. This system is now widely used in schools in the UK and has several different levels of complexity. In the early stages, however, it is characterised by signs that are very simple, concrete and require the use of only one hand.

The main advantages of signs are that they can be more easily shaped and prompted than speech and, at least at the single sign stage, the hands can remain in a set position, thereby making fewer demands on memory. There is little doubt that the use of signs has enabled large numbers of children who were previously without language to communicate some-what more effectively. Unfortunately, in the case of children with autism, the evidence to show that communication can be significantly enhanced in this way is somewhat limited. Kiernan (1983), reviewing the outcome of signing programmes, found that these were very variable. After two to three years, some children had acquired an extensive signing vocabulary (400 sign combinations) or had begun to use speech; in contrast, some had managed to learn only one or two signs. Other studies indicate that problems of generalisation and maintenance are similar to those experienced in verbal training programmes and that there is often a close relationship between the ability to use signs and the acquisition of language. The *communicative* use of signs may also remain very limited. Thus, Attwood and his colleagues (1988) found that the signing of children with autism was very similar to their use of language—i.e. it was stereotyped, repetitive and used mainly to achieve the child's immediate goals. Signing was rarely used to share experiences, to express feelings or emotions, or to communicate in a reciprocal and spontaneous fashion. Clinical experience also suggests that many children prefer to use the most 'telegraphic' style of signing that they can get away with, and although this may be understood by familiar adults, it is hardly likely to enhance general communication. Multipurpose signs such as 'Please' are probably best avoided, since children rapidly learn that only the one gesture is needed to obtain anything from toys, food, physical interaction or a visit to the lavatory.

Many parents worry that by introducing signing the child's chances of ever developing spoken language will be further reduced. In fact, the opposite appears to be the case, with many children who become competent signers then beginning to communicate verbally. Work by Layton and others (Layton, 1988; Yoder & Layton, 1989) suggests that once children have acquired around 200 signs, and can use some sign combinations, they are very likely to begin to speak. The problem is that many children fail to reach this stage, and even after intensive training may acquire only one or two signs. Moreover, because of lack of information on the characteristics of children who do, or do not, become proficient signers, or subsequently develop speech, it is not possible to identify, in advance, the children who are most likely to profit from this approach.

A further problem related to signing is the fact that the majority of people in the child's environment will not know how to sign, and will therefore be unable to respond to the child's attempts to communicate. Although exposure to signing is highly related to outcome, often the only people who can sign with or to the child are parents or teachers. Konstantareas (1987) found that the amount of parental involvement was crucial for establishing competent signing but most parents tended to use signs far less frequently than speech. Udwin (1986) found that the average length of direct exposure to alternative communication systems in schools was approximately *12 minutes* a day. Under such conditions it is hardly surprising that children fail to become effective communicators. Quill (1995) suggests that the more people who are willing to learn to sign, the more proficient the child will become, and this in turn will increase the chances of developing spoken language. One particular way of encouraging the wider use of signs is through songs and videos, and the Makaton system now incorporates a number of videos, using nursery rhymes and action songs to encourage joint signing between the child with autism and peers, siblings and parents.

Symbols

Because of the demands that even simple signing makes on memory and motor skills, more permanent systems involving symbols of various kinds also began to appear in the 1970s. Premack and Premack (1974) used plastic symbols in studies of children with autism (as well as with chimpanzees) and these were employed in a number of subsequent studies (see Howlin, 1989, for review). However, although they were found to be successful in experimental conditions, and there was some indication that they could facilitate the transfer to written words (Kuntz *et al.*, 1978), they had little general appeal because of their artificiality and their limited application in naturalistic settings. In contrast, systems such as Rebus and Bliss symbols and Makaton, which combine pictographic symbols with the spoken and/or signed word, have become much more widely used.

These types of symbol system offer a number of advantages over signs alone, especially when working with less able children with autism. Firstly, because they depend on recognition rather than recall, they make few demands on memory or cognitive skills. Secondly, they can be made permanently available to the child in some form or other (on paper or card, on communication boards or on computer). Thirdly, the vocabulary can be easily adapted and modified to ensure that the symbols used are directly relevant to the child's individual environment, needs and interests. 'Word combinations' are also easy to form. Recent developments in computer software (e.g. Boardmaker or Picture Communication Systems; Mayer-Johnson, 1997) mean that it is now possible to create large numbers of different symbols quickly and early. These can be automatically scaled to different sizes to suit different purposes (from classroom displays to individual 'diaries') and can also be used as overlays for computer keyboards. Finally, symbols require only minimal motor skill on the part of the user and (because they are usually accompanied by written labels) are easily understood by untrained observers.

On the other hand, there are also a number of disadvantages. They are a relatively slow and inflexible means of communication, and it is difficult to convey syntactic or semantic relations with ease. Moreover, if children do become proficient in using them difficulties arise because of the size of lexicon that needs to be transported. Computerised systems can now help to overcome many of these difficulties, but they are expensive, and unless they are continuously available to the child, can limit the range of situations in which he or she is able to communicate. Moreover, unless carefully designed software is used, the child's need for direct personal interactions may be reduced, and fascination with the technology can easily take over.

Pictures and Objects

For many children even the simplest of sign or symbol systems will be far too complex and demanding. Alternative systems that use pictures or photographs to assist the child's communicative efforts may be more appropriate, particularly in the early stages of teaching. These make very few demands on the child's cognitive, linguistic or memory skills and can be used or understood equally well by strangers as by familiar adults. Again, it is essential that the materials used reflect the child's particular interests and needs. Once a basic 'vocabulary' has been chosen, children can be provided with their own personal set of photographs or pictures to enable them to indicate basic needs or wishes (for example, to leave the building, have a drink, go to the toilet, etc.). Parents and teachers can also use photographs or pictures to indicate to the child what they are going to do, who they will see, or where they will be going next. Once the child's favourite objects or activities have been identified and portrayed in this way, he or she can be physically prompted to point to the appropriate picture before the relevant object or activity is made available. Gradually verbal prompts, e.g. 'Point to what you want to play with', may be substituted until eventually the child begins to point spontaneously.

Whatever pictures are used, the format should be simple, clear and uncluttered. It may be very difficult for a child to understand why a fuzzy photo of a small plate of chips, against a complex background of tables, chairs and other furniture, should be used to indicate food. The square format and restricted focal length of 'Polaroid' photographs produces very clear pictures that are often very suitable for a child with autism. They also have the advantage that they can be produced almost instantaneously, thereby making it much easier for the child to associate the picture with an actual object or scene. A 'Triple Print' film-processing system (which provides one large photo and two smaller copies for every negative) is also useful, as this provides several identical pictures that can be used in different settings. Once the child is able to use or respond to photographs of real objects then hand-drawn pictures can be introduced. Over time these may become progressively less life-like and more representational, until they are, in fact, more like symbols. Computers can also be used to develop a range of different displays. 'Boardmaker' for example (which currently costs around £240) is a graphics database that contains 3,000 picture communication symbols, as well as drawing and scanning software. It can be used to make pictures of any size as well as to build communication boards, posters or simple books.

Once the association between the activity/object and picture/symbol/ chart is established, individualised sets of photographs or pictures can be used very effectively to increase both communication and understanding (Quill, 1995). For example, in the kitchen, there might be a wall chart (at child height) displaying different foods, so that the child can indicate what he or she would like to eat. In the bedroom, there might be pictures of different items of clothing indicating what the child should put on in the morning. The front door might display a set of pictures illustrating the main activities to be done at school that day. Picture systems can also be used to indicate *sequences* of activities. Thus, a chart in the kitchen might illustrate, in three or four stages, the items that need to be selected in order to set the table for breakfast. In the bathroom, there might be a chart showing a sequence of activities, such as hand and face washing, teeth brushing and hair combing.

Whatever system is used must be readily available to the child and his carers. Possible ways of ensuring easy access are to have the cards in a simple 'Filofax'-type system; attached to a key-ring on the child's belt; in a hip bag; or worn, like an identity badge, on a chain. Picture or symbol cards should be added to, updated and replaced as necessary. Materials need to be properly mounted, using strong card and plasticised coverings and they should be quickly replaceable. Equipment that is forever getting lost, or dog-eared cards that no one can read, are of little use.

The Picture Exchange Communication System (or PECS) of Bondy and Frost (1996) is based on the use of cards to encourage communication in the classroom. The teacher first identifies the items that are needed for communication in the child's environment, and the child is taught to associate a picture with the appropriate item. The child is required to pick up the picture and hand it to the teacher who then exchanges it for the item in question. This approach also stresses the need for the child actively to handle the pictures and remove them from a Velcro communication board before giving them to the teacher. Bondy and Frost consider that the exchange, or handing the picture to the teacher, results in more effective communication than simply having the child point to the picture, and it is said that within the first day of training 'many children are able to calmly and clearly make a request'.

Some children, of course, never reach this stage of spontaneous communication. However, even so, adult-to-child communication may be enhanced by teachers or carers using pictures to indicate what will be happening next, thereby helping to establish the link between the picture and the resulting activity. And, for children who remain unable to make the connection between pictures and events or objects, an *object*-exchange system might be tried instead (Quill, 1995). Thus, the child can be provided with a set of objects that are directly related to items in which he or she is interested; the child then needs to give the object to someone in order to obtain what he or she wants. Handing the adult a cup, for example, can serve as a request for fruit juice; a key might indicate the wish to open the toy cupboard; or a coat the desire to go outside. Quill points out that many children with autism spontaneously use objects to indicate their needs, although they tend to place the object near the required item (putting a cup on a table, or by the tap) rather than handing it directly to someone. This approach capitalises on children's tendency to use objects in this way, and shaping and prompting procedures can then be utilised to encourage the child to give these objects to someone else. Objects can also be used as visual prompts for the child—to indicate where he should be going or what she should be doing. For example, a small ball might be handed to the child to indicate that it is time for games. As with any non-speech system, however, it is crucial that all the adults involved in the child's environment are aware of the meaning of different items. Blank looks or a negative response will rapidly discourage the child's efforts.

COMPUTERISED SYSTEMS

The ever-increasing range of computerised devices—many developed initially for use by individuals with severe physical impairments—can also help to enhance the communicative competence of children with autism (Shane, 1994). Some systems are now specially designed for use with this group of children, in that they have a specific focus on turn taking and reciprocal interaction. Interchangeable keyboards, and overlays that can be readily used to upgrade and modify keyboard displays, make it possible for children to progress steadily from using single symbol boards (with, for example, a large red square or circle that will emit a sound to attract attention) to complex, multi-symbol displays using pictures, symbols or written words. The output produced may be in visual form on the screen, or as written printout, or in synthesised voice format. Computers may be particularly valuable teaching aids for more able children who sometimes respond better to information on the screen than to information given verbally. It is now relatively easy to obtain software that can be adapted to the child's linguistic, cognitive or academic level. Interactive programs are also available to ensure that the child cannot become totally immersed in the computer, to the exclusion of interpersonal contacts.

Despite recent technological progress in this field, there are still relatively few studies of the use of computers with children with autism. Most are single case or small group reports and have tended to involve more able children, especially those with precocious reading skills (Jordan & Powell, 1990a, 1990b; Bernard-Opitz *et al.*, 1990; Quill, 1995). Coldwell (1991a, 1991b), working in Australia, has demonstrated their use with non-speaking children, and in recent Swedish studies (Heimann *et al.*, 1995; Tjus *et al.*, 1998) it was found that interactive, multi-media computer programs were effective in improving both communication and reading skills. However, Chen and Bernard-Opitz (1993) report that, although computers seem to have advantages in terms of motivation and behaviour, learning outcomes are unlikely to be significantly affected.

The use of specialist equipment of this kind, with the aim of encouraging *independent* communication, should not be confused with the use of 'Facilitated Communication', discussed in the previous chapter. Although this, too, makes use of computerised systems, clients remain heavily dependent on the physical support of facilitators and there is little evidence to suggest that this technique enhances spontaneous communication.

MAKING USE OF SPECIAL SKILLS

Despite their many communication difficulties, a number of children with autism show evidence of advanced reading abilities, or hyperlexia.

Many in this group seem to learn to read by means of TV adverts, or familiar product labels or logos. For example, Jonathon's parents suddenly realised, when he was aged 4, that he could read any words associated with the names of cars. Teachers may be sceptical about the value of encouraging such isolated skills, especially if they are aware that the child understands little or nothing of what is read. However, if the child possesses such ability, and is motivated to use it, then, with assistance, it can be usefully shaped into more communicative activities. In Jonathon's case, his parents used car names and model cars to motivate him to follow written instructions: 'Find the Volvo'; 'Give Daddy the BMW'; 'Put the Ford in the cupboard'. Eventually, written instructions that did not involve cars were introduced and Jonathon himself began to use a few written signs to communicate. He was then given a computer with a voice simulator, and this amused him so much that he began to copy the computer's voice. By the age of 6 he was speaking in simple sentences, albeit with a very mechanical tone of voice.

Howlin and Rutter (1987a) describe the stages used to teach Thomas, a 4-year-old boy with a high non-verbal IQ, to progress from picture-matching tasks, which he loved, to using an electronic 'Communicator' to communicate. From picture-matching games he moved on to 'games' that involved the matching of pictures to toy objects. Then, using shaping and fading procedures, he was taught to match written labels to pictures and objects, and eventually progressed to matching two or three word labels to the appropriate object (e.g. big red car). This was then extended to household activities, and his parents began to use written cards to encourage him to carry out a number of tasks around the house (e.g. 'Get your coat'). Although he would not use the cards to communicate himself, he remained fascinated by the written word, and did eventually progress to using an electronic 'Communicator' which produced a written type-script. Other examples of the use of written and computerised systems are described by Quill (1995).

CHOOSING THE MOST EFFECTIVE SYSTEM

Formerly, when the goal of almost any intervention programme was to improve spoken language, the initial emphasis was invariably on teaching *verbal* communication. Only if this failed (sometimes after many months or even years of therapy) would an alternative system be considered. However, in recent years there has been increasing awareness that for older non-speaking children (those aged beyond 7 years or so), for those of very low cognitive ability, for those who produce almost no spontaneous sounds, and for those who have little or no understanding of

Table 5.3: Assessment for choosing alternative communication strategies (from Layton & Watson, 1995)

Characteristics	Signing	Pictures/ pictographs	Writing
Easily shaped	Yes	Yes	Fairly
Portability	High	Moderate	High
Permanence	No	Yes	Yes
Speed	Moderate/Low	Low	High/Moderate
Phrases possible	Moderate	Limited	Yes
Iconicity	Some	Yes	No
Reciprocity	Limited	Limited	High
Skills required			
Motor skills	Yes	No	Yes
High co-operation	Not initially	Not initially	Moderate
Demands on others' understanding	Yes	No	No

speech and show minimal interest in communication of any kind, verbally based programmes are unlikely to produce rapid or significant effects. Rather than turning to non-verbal systems only after prolonged failure with a verbal system, it now seems to be more effective to *begin* by utilising simpler systems, better suited to the individual child's developmental level. This approach is more likely to enhance communication and increase the child's motivation for interaction and, if successful, as noted above, the teaching of alternative methods does not seem to inhibit the later use of spoken language; if anything it may well encourage it.

Nevertheless, the choice of an appropriate system can present difficulties, and will involve a thorough assessment of the child's cognitive abilities, visual, memory and motor skills and general motivation to communicate (see Prizant *et al.*, 1997, and Schuler *et al.*, 1997, for further details). Layton and Watson (1995) provide a useful breakdown of the different skills required for using signs, pictures or written words in children who are non-verbal (Table 5.3). On the whole, a picture-based system makes least demands on cognitive, linguistic or memory skills although it is essential that the pictures or photographs used reflect the individual's particular interests or needs.

Increasing the Motivation to Communicate

Let the child choose
No matter how effective, in principle, a particular method of communication may be, unless the individual child has a powerful incentive to make use of it the results are likely to be very limited. Early intervention

programmes made considerable use of extrinsic reinforcers (especially of the edible kind) to reward the child's attempts at communication. Apart from the fact that these did little to improve dental health, they could actually interrupt the child's verbalisation. It became apparent, too, that the unnecessary use of extrinsic reinforcers can impede progress and limit generalisation (Lepper, 1981). Such programmes also tended to recommend that particular linguistic structures should be taught before others. Some suggested that the programme should follow a strict developmental sequence; others that only the names of concrete, tangible objects should be taught; others recommended teaching only functional nouns, as these are the earliest words to be acquired by normally developing children (Nelson, 1973); other clinicians even suggested that teaching should focus initially on names of food (Quill, 1995). As time has gone on it has become apparent that the choice of structure should be determined not by the clinician but by the children. If the child loves, above all else, to be tickled, then the first sign, symbol, word or picture might best be one that indicates 'Tickle me'. If he or she prefers to be left alone for much of the time, then the most effective 'phrase' to teach initially might be 'Go away'. In the case of one non-verbal 5-year-old who had an overwhelming fascination with all things mathematical, his communication cards predominantly portrayed decimal numbers or fractions. If he handed these to his parents they would then provide him with a sheet of calculations to complete! Another carried around a book of log tables, and would use this to indicate that he wanted his father to do mathematical problems on the computer with him.

The success of this approach to intervention is obviously dependent on careful observations and on teachers' and parents' intimate knowledge and understanding of the child's likes and dislikes. However, it is clear from evaluative studies (e.g. Stone & Caro-Martinez, 1990) that most spontaneous attempts to communicate are likely to involve the child's need for attention or for objects, or to be used as part of a social routine. Once the role of a particular behaviour is identified then alternative forms of communication can be taught in order to replace this. Thus, pointing, and subsequently verbal requests, might be taught to replace non-verbal attempts to communicate such as leading an adult by the hand. Koegel *et al.* (1988) note that reinforcement of these spontaneous attempts at communication (by sounds and/or orientation towards the adult or materials needed) was more likely to lead to the production of speech than the reinforcement of prompted speech sounds. As the child learns that the use of a particular sign, word, symbol or picture produces the desired effect in one situation, then he or she will be more likely to use this form of communication more widely (see also Schuler *et al.*, 1997).

Errors can be helpful
Early intervention programmes tended to stress the importance of error-less learning in order to avoid incorrect attempts to communicate. However, in fact, if the child is really motivated to obtain what he or she wants, then the experience of choosing the wrong symbol, or of using the wrong sign (so that an unwanted item is received instead), can be an extremely effective way of ensuring that greater attention is paid to using the correct form in future.

Make communication fun
'Enjoyment' is not a word that appears often in early language teaching manuals. Nevertheless, although many children with autism may not be particularly interested in speech sounds, they may enjoy songs, animal sounds or other noises. At the age of 3, Oliver had no speech but was fascinated with all forms of transport. His parents found an audio tape containing different vehicle sounds (police and ambulance sirens, tractors, racing cars, etc.) and Oliver soon learned to copy these. Indeed his imitation of emergency sirens was so good that neighbours in his home village would run into the street to look for an ambulance. As time went on he began to copy other sounds and eventually words. Susie was fascinated by animal noises, and her imitative skills began to develop after her parents bought her a computerised game that would make the appropriate animal noise when a particular key (e.g. with a picture of a cat, pig, etc.) was pressed. Other children have learned to hum tunes long before they could speak, and again, encouraging vocal imitation of this kind has sometimes proved the first stage in encouraging more extensive imitation.

Make communication necessary
Children with autism, especially those who are older or more cognitively able, often learn to manage quite well without speech. Food is provided at regular times; routines can be adhered to without hindrance; the daily timetable and environment are subject to few changes; and items such as toys, food, or favourite objects are generally kept within easy reach. There may be little pressure to communicate, as the child is easily able to manipulate his or her environment in other ways. And, if things do go wrong, a loud scream or major tantrum will usually do the trick!

In a number of recent studies it has been shown that routines, or rather the disruption of routines, can be a very effective means of increasing communication. McClenny *et al.* (1992) investigated children's responses to 'infringements' of previously well-established joint action routines. These included making a desired object inaccessible (placing it in a locked box, or on a high shelf), violating object function (using a spoon too large to fit in a jar of yoghurt or one with holes to serve liquid, or attempting to scoop out peanut butter with a broken plastic knife), or mislabelling objects or actions (e.g. calling a cup an elephant). They found that children communicated more frequently during sessions when these unexpected events occurred. Withholding objects resulted in the highest frequency of communicative attempts, and violations of object function were more effective than mislabelling objects. Quill (1995) describes another situation in which a young boy's regular routine of eating crackers and peanut butter was disrupted in a number of different ways. Firstly, although his knife, plate and peanut butter were provided as usual, the crackers were missing and he had to indicate his need for these. The crackers would then be hidden in different places so that he had to indicate that they were missing. His comment 'No crackers' was the first time he had ever used a negative conjunction. On another occasion the knife was missing; on another it was broken; on another the peanut butter jar actually contained something else. In surprise the child commented 'No peanut butter'. Other 'unexpected' events that may elicit communication include switching the contents or labels of well-known containers, demonstrating a wind-up toy but then handing the child a broken one, handing out a container of juice but not providing any cups.

Hawkins (1995) also suggests other changes to routines that naturally occur within the child's environment. These can include removing an item (such as soap) that is required to complete a daily routine such as hand washing, or delaying access to a particular item (e.g. offering one glove but not the other). Autistic rituals might also be disrupted in a similar way. For example, 10-year-old James had a set routine of closing every door in the school corridor before eating his school lunch. His teacher placed a catch on the top of the final door, which meant that he could not close it without assistance. Disconcerted, James immediately insisted 'shut door'. On subsequent days, different doors were held open, and in order to complete his routine he needed to ask for these to be shut on each occasion. Other rituals were gradually disrupted in a similar fashion, and could not be completed unless James asked for changes to be made. Removal of attachment objects to positions where they are beyond the child's reach may also help to elicit communicative responses. Lenny was a 12-year-old boy who was non-verbal and had severe learning disabilities. He had a strong attachment for tape measures, which he would constantly carry around and twiddle; he also had a special tape that he kept in the car. Although his parents were not willing to restrict access to his tapes in the house, they did agree to conceal the one in the car in the glove compartment. Dismayed by this, Lenny actually took his father's hand and placed it on the glove compartment—the first time that he had ever attempted to communicate in such a way. Thereafter, the tape was only made available in the car when he took his father's hand.

'Naturalistic' approaches to communication training clearly have many advantages over techniques that rely on artificial settings, methods and materials. Moreover, as well as increasing the child's attempts to communicate, they are also likely to be more effective in reducing disruptive behaviours. Koegel and colleagues (1992b) suggest that this is because the reinforcement procedures used are so effective, motivation to co-operate with communication programmes is high, and so children will be less likely to use disruptive behaviours in order to escape. Certainly, as long as there is close co-operation and agreement among the adults in the child's environment, this approach seems more likely to ensure generalisation and maintenance of communication skills. Although parents might hesitate before embarking on such strategies for fear of the tantrums that might ensue when daily routines are disrupted, it is possible sometimes to introduce them as a sort of 'game', especially when using unexpected containers and contents. And, initially, any changes or intrusion should be kept very small, so that only a minimal communicative attempt by the child is required to restore them. The modifications to routine should also be presented gradually, in a way least likely to cause distress. Otherwise anger rather than reciprocal interaction is liable to be the result. Ideally, too, interventions of this kind should be introduced when the child is relatively young. A teenager who has always been provided with exactly what he or she wants, or has always been able to obtain food or toys at will, is liable to react in a very negative fashion to sudden restrictions of this kind.

IMPROVING COMPREHENSION

Some children, especially those who are more severely intellectually handicapped, may never learn to communicate effectively or may only acquire one or two signs, pictures or symbols despite many years of teaching. In such cases the daily frustrations that must inevitably be experienced by a child who can neither communicate effectively himself nor understand what others are trying to communicate, may be reduced if attention is focused instead on improving understanding.

Reliance on non-verbal cues may help the child to understand what he or she is expected to do, where it should be done, or what will happen afterwards. Instead of verbal instructions to the child to put away toys or clothing, or lay the table, these can be translated into non-verbal matching tasks that make few, if any, demands on verbal ability. Tasks such as 'tidying up' can be made a great deal easier if the child learns that socks always go in the drawer that has a sock (or picture of a sock) pinned to the outside, or pants go in a drawer that is similarly identified, or jigsaws always go in a box that displays their picture, and trains go in the container showing a train. Setting the table can also become a relatively easy task if the outline of all the necessary plates and cutlery is drawn clearly on plastic mats, placed in the appropriate positions. If dressing or washing are activities that present problems, the order in which clothes should be put on, or the sequence of activities that need to be followed while brushing teeth or washing one's face, can also be indicated in a series of photographs or cartoon-type pictures. As each stage is completed, the relevant picture can then be removed. Problems in putting clothes on the right way round can be avoided by having a badge or coloured label attached to the inside front (so that the child can see it clearly as he or she dresses). Shoes are more likely to go on the correct foot if they are colour coded in some way, or if a large outline of a big toe is drawn in the appropriate place on each insole. A clockwork timer or other device (such as containers filled with different coloured sands or liquids that gradually move from top to bottom) may help the child to tolerate delays. For example, having to wait until the timer rings, or the liquids have reached the bottom, may be a much more comprehensible (and less boring) task than being told to 'Wait 5 minutes'. Howlin and Rutter (1987) illustrate how a simple mechanical timer was used to encourage a teenage boy to sit still for increasing periods of time. Initially he was highly resistant to being made to sit still at all, a situation that was made worse by the fact that he had virtually no understanding of the concept of time. To begin with the timer was set for the minimum time (30 seconds) and as he was

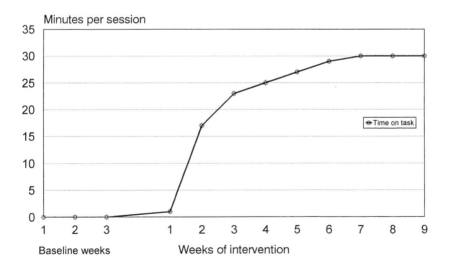

Figure 5.1: Increasing time on task using mechanical timer

quite interested in waiting for the 'ping' he was willing to sit and watch it go round. The time interval was gradually increased and by the end of two months he would sit and co-operate for two 30-minute periods a day (see Figure 5.1).

Picture charts can also help to illustrate longer term sequences of activities. The school timetable may be illustrated on a daily or weekly basis; and may contain individual activities or activities that will be common to the whole class. The various school events leading up to the weekend, or to the vacation, can also be indicated in this way, and photographs can be used to indicate which members of staff will be involved. If holidays are planned, pictures of the places to be visited, or of the people who will be met there, can be helpful.

Obviously, initially, when such charts are used they are unlikely to mean very much to the child. However, after the event, the pictures or photographs can be referred to again, to remind the child what has happened. With time and repetition it should then become easier for the child to make the association between the chart and the events that are about to happen.

Reliance on visual cues of this kind is one of the principal mainstays of the TEACCH educational programme initially developed in North Carolina (Schopler *et al.*, 1995). It is also fundamental to the 'visually mediated instruction' methods used by Peeters (see Powell & Jordan, 1997). The TEACCH method relies heavily on visual cues or 'jigs', so that, throughout the child's school day, different coloured work areas or different coloured containers are used to indicate where the child should be; what he or she should be doing; where work should begin or be placed when finished; even where to play. This combination of a highly structured and visually based programme can be very successful in improving work related skills and reducing inappropriate behaviours (Jordan & Powell, 1995). However, as with any treatment package, it is important that the basic components are adapted to suit the needs of the individual and his or her environment. It is also important to plan for the gradual reduction of such cues if the child is eventually to function effectively in less structured surroundings.

With imagination, initiative and a close understanding of the child's difficulties and needs, visually based methods of communication have many advantages (see Schopler, 1995). The disadvantage is that they do not come in a neat, ready packaged form—if they do they will have only limited impact.

INCREASING COMMUNICATIVE SKILLS IN VERBAL CHILDREN

Lord and Rutter (1994) suggest that around 50% of children with autism remain without useful speech. However, even among those with a good expressive vocabulary there are persisting and pervasive impairments in the communicative use of language, and in understanding complex or abstract concepts.

For younger children who are able to use some words or sounds spontaneously, individualised language programmes may well be helpful, both for improving comprehension, increasing the complexity of speech, enhancing social communication skills or correcting problems of intonation or articulation. It is crucial that such programmes are aimed at a level that is appropriate to the child's cognitive and linguistic development and that the words or concepts involved are of direct and immediate relevance to the child. As in working with non-verbal children, the importance of capitalising on the child's own interests, needs and desires cannot be over-emphasised. As long as the words or sounds taught are of practical value to the child, in that they allow him or her more rapid access to desired objects or activities, then artificial rewards should not prove necessary.

Programmes for improving language competence in verbal children will obviously vary according to the intellectual and linguistic levels of the individual child. There are many assessment tools now available that can be used to guide teaching (see Bishop, 1994, and Marans, 1997, for more details). In the UK, for example, descriptive assessments of the way in which children use and understand language—such as the Derbyshire Language Scheme or the Pragmatics Profile of Early Communication Skills (Dewart & Summers, 1988)—can be used to provide guidelines for improving receptive and conversational abilities. Schemes such as the Social Use of Language Programme (Rinaldi, 1992) have also been successfully used to assess and develop interactive language skills, and this latter programme is one of the few tools developed specifically for children with learning disabilities.

In other cases intervention may begin by teaching the child simple phrases to ask for things he or she wants. If the child is able to combine set phrases such as 'I want' with words such as 'Sweet' or 'Teddy' or 'Out', these can be used to obtain immediate access to the desired object or activity (Charlop et al., 1985). Koegel and Koegel (1995) describe the teaching of question phrases such as 'What's that?', 'Where is . . . ?', 'Whose is it?', 'What happened?'. Using toys, games and books, children are prompted and rewarded for using questions of this kind. Then, as the frequency of questioning increases, prompts are faded until the child is using the questions spontaneously. The authors suggest that this approach works best with children who can already use simple phrases or sentences, and that in this group such teaching can result in very rapid learning and enhanced grammatical skills.

As in work with non-verbal children, it is also important not to neglect the use of visual or other cues. Although a child with autism may possess the vocabulary needed to express his or her needs, using spoken language, especially if under stress or in novel situations, may just prove too difficult. Twachtman (1995) describes how a written cue—a sign indicating 'My turn'—was used to improve a child's ability to take part in reciprocal games. In another example, a red or green circle was used to indicate whether or not it was appropriate for the child to speak in class. In neither of these cases had previous attempts to improve verbal communication or understanding in these situations proved effective.

It is particularly important to be aware that children with no *apparent* spoken language difficulties may also require some augmentative communication systems from time to time. Almost all children with autism, no matter how able, have difficulties with abstract language or in dealing with complex sequences of instructions. Thus, although they may understand the *individual words* spoken, they may well misinterpret or fail to understand the underlying meaning of what is said. Their failure to respond appropriately is, in turn, likely to be misconstrued as negativity or lack of co-operation. Thus, if asked 'Go and ask your mum if she wants a cup of tea' the child may well do so, but is unlikely to bring back any reply! If told 'Take this towel upstairs' the towel may be left on the top stair but is unlikely to be taken into the bathroom. In such circumstances the focus of intervention may need to be on the speaker, not on the child. The speaker needs to examine carefully the way in which the message has been given and make sure that the words used adequately convey what is wanted. Relatively minor modifications to the above instructions, such as 'Go and ask your mum if she wants a cup of tea. Then come back and tell if she said Yes or No' or 'Take this towel upstairs and put it in the bathroom cupboard' may have a major impact on the child's responses. In addition, especially when the task requirements are more complex, checklists of instructions, picture or cartoon sequences of the activities to be completed, or symbols designating the tasks to be done, can all help greatly to improve co-operation.

A variety of different approaches has been reported as successful in increasing communication skills in more linguistically able children. Loveland and Tunali (1991) used social 'scripts' and role-play situations, involving potentially distressing situations (e.g. losing one's purse) to prompt children to use more sympathetic or helpful remarks. Krantz and McClannahan (1993) also used written scripts, which were gradually faded from end to beginning, to encourage conversational initiations (about recently completed activities) with peers. Twachtman (1995), too, recommends the use of scripts (which may be a combination of written and pictorial instructions) to indicate what children should say and do in particular circumstances.

'Joint action routines' such as those involved at mealtimes, preparing food or visiting the shops are another means of increasing verbal skills.

Once the task is clearly delineated, each of the partners in the routine has set questions to ask or comments to make (e.g. 'Come and get it!'). Over time these interactive routines can be expanded, so that the social use of language becomes more complex and flexible (Twachtman, 1995).

Video modelling of conversational exchanges has also been found to be effective in some studies (Charlop & Milstein, 1989). This may involve children watching tapes of their own activities or those of their peers. Twachtman (1995) suggests the use of other techniques such as acting out well-known children's stories, using visual props (3 chairs, 3 bowls, 3 toy bears, etc.), adult modelling, and simple scripts if necessary. Reciprocal reading activities—using stories that are highly repetitive and predictable—are another means of encouraging interactive discourse (Kirchner, 1991; McCracken & McKracken, 1986; Tomkins & Webeler, 1983). The 'Thomas the Tank Engine' series, for example, seems to have a particular attraction for children with autism in the UK. The simplicity of the dialogue and characterisation (engines are identified principally by their colours) means that even very young children can understand the limited number of scenarios with little difficulty. They may spontaneously act out specific scenes (especially if they also have access to videos) and parents can use the books to encourage the child to take part in simple dialogues, or even to talk about emotional responses and feelings. Books may also be used to encourage children to act out themes, such as going to the doctor, while doll house miniatures or other toys can be used to act out specific activities, accompanied by a set dialogue (Twachtman, 1995).

The interruption of daily routines, or the use of time-delay procedures, have been found to be effective in increasing children's spontaneous use of language (Matson *et al.*, 1990; Ingenmey & van Houten, 1991; Charlop & Trasowech, 1991; Taylor & Harris, 1995). Essentially, time-delay procedures involve the establishment or teaching of a specific routine which results in the child obtaining a particular reward or activity at the end. For example, the child may be presented with a favourite object, asked 'What do you want?' and then prompted with the appropriate response. The delay between the presentation of the object and the prompt is then gradually increased until the child spontaneously requests the object. This approach has also been used to increase spontaneous speech, such as saying 'Good morning' to parents, or to increase question-asking and requests for information.

As with less verbally competent children, disruption of routine or ritualised activities may also be effective in increasing the frequency of language used by children who have speech, but are generally reluctant to use this. For, example, Jo had a daily ritual involving his large collection of spectacles. Every day, when he returned from school, he would count these and then transfer them from one plastic bag to another. His mother usually ensured that 'new' plastic bags were in easy reach. However, following discussion with the speech therapist she removed the supply of bags to a high cupboard which Jo was unable to reach; in order to complete his ritual, he had to ask her to pass him a bag. Subsequently, she began to remove several pairs of spectacles into another container, so he then had to ask for these as well. Eventually, when Jo returned from school he was required to ask for both the spectacles *and* the plastic bags in order to pursue his routines.

REDUCING ECHOLALIC SPEECH

Echolalia, both immediate and delayed, is a common feature of autism. Although often considered as inappropriate and non-communicative, as well as frequently being extremely irritating, closer analysis indicates that much echoing serves identifiable and important communicative functions. These include turn taking, declaratives, rehearsal, self-regulatory utterances, requests or answers (Rydell & Prizant, 1995). The amount of echolalia is related to the child's comprehension and overall developmental level, so that as cognitive and linguistic skills increase, the proportion of echolalia used generally declines. The occurrence of echolalia is also associated with adult speech styles. Rydell and Mirenda (1994) found that the majority of children's echolalic utterances followed high constraint utterances by parents (i.e. instructions, direct questions, verbal prompts and attention devices). Echolalia was least likely to occur following low constraint utterances (general comments, positive remarks or reflective questions). Echoing is also usually more frequent in unfamiliar settings and with unfamiliar adults (Charlop, 1986).

As with any other 'autistic' behaviour, it is crucial to assess the role that echolalia serves, and the situations in which it occurs, before attempts are made to modify it (Prizant *et al.*, 1997). Echoing may be an indication of children's lack of understanding; it may be important in helping them to consolidate what they hear, as well as providing them with the opportunity to practise new words or expressions. Moreover, as echolalia is likely to increase when children are distressed or anxious, it may signify that they are experiencing undue pressure (Rydell & Mirenda, 1994).

Repetition can also play a role in rehearsing potentially worrying situations, in dealing with feelings of anger, or in helping to allay anxiety. Greater understanding of *why* such behaviours may occur, and recognition of the potential importance of these, should lead to more appropriate intervention strategies, with a focus on altering the factors causing the echolalia, rather than on the symptom itself.

Ensuring that instructions or questions are fully understood, by simplifying the language used, or supplementing this with pictures, written instructions or other cues, may significantly reduce stereotyped and echolalic speech. Repetitive questioning (which often tends to escalate the more adults respond to it) may also be reduced by directing the child to charts, pictures, calendars or lists, which provide him or her with the information required in a more permanent form. Sonia was a 13-year-old girl with an obsession with petrol stations. She was allowed to go with the school bus every Friday to have it filled with diesel, but every day, particularly as the week progressed, she would anxiously interrogate staff about what day it was, and when she would be allowed to go to the garage. A weekly chart, illustrating clearly the activities for each day and culminating with a photo of the garage, was drawn up and whenever the obsessional questioning began Sonia was sent off to look at her chart. Fascination with the photograph of the petrol station, as well as the clear visual information that the chart displayed, helped greatly to diminish both her anxiety and her repetitive and intrusive questioning.

Dealing with unnecessary stress, by supplying the child with the appropriate help in cognitively or socially demanding situations, may also have considerable impact. Minimising disruption to daily routine, carefully structuring the environment, ensuring that daily life is as predictable and as consistent as possible, and that necessary changes are predicted well in advance are all factors that can help to decrease the frequency of repetitive speech.

Modifying Echolalia

In less verbally able children, echolalia may occur as a way of consolidating what has been said, or it may be an effective way of avoiding having to answer the adult's question. In such circumstances, a further prompt supplied by the adult can help to avoid inappropriate echoing. Thus, instead of asking simply 'What do you want?' (which the child may just echo verbatim) the adult might immediately and firmly prompt 'I want a . . .', so that the child echoes the answer rather than the question. Prompts can then be gradually faded until the child is able to answer the question appropriately without repetition.

In other cases, delayed echolalia may be the only means by which parents are able to know what has happened or what their children have done at school that day. Children who may never respond to a direct question such as 'What did you do in school' may indicate what has been going on by repeating, sometimes word for word and in the exact accent or tone of the original speakers, exactly what has happened. It may also be possible for parents to intrude into these monologues, in order to encourage more reciprocal speech. Thus, by responding with prompts such as 'Oh, why was Mrs Smith cross with Monica?' or 'Why did she say you were a naughty boy?', the child may be diverted from his or her echoing into answering questions that are directly relevant to the situation about which he or she is talking.

Utilising Echolalia

It may also be possible to use delayed echoing as a means of helping the child control and monitor his or her own behaviour. When language development is impaired, internal language controls are also affected, and hence behaviour is likely to be more impulsive and less well controlled (Howlin & Rutter, 1987a). Some children with autism can be encouraged to develop greater self-control if they are taught to 'talk through' activities, and to tell themselves what to do or how to correct mistakes. Jonathon, for example, learned to complete complex jigsaw puzzles in this way. Although he had well-developed visuo-spatial skills, he tended to panic if given tasks that were too complex. Shaping procedures were used to help him progress from simple form-boards to 10–20 piece puzzles, but the move to larger ones proved much more difficult. His teachers used direct verbal prompts: find the four 'corner' bits; look for the straight edges; find the blue pieces, etc., to help him develop effective strategies and eventually he began to give himself the same instructions. Rehearsing, out loud, well-established instructions may also be helpful in other, more complex social situations. Quirk-Hodgson (1995) describes a number of methods by which children can be taught to react more appropriately when distressed. These might involve a series of instructions, usually accompanied by simple pictures, to indicate what to do if upset: 'Don't cry; Don't hit; Relax; Put your head down; Speak quietly.' Or, if the child is angry, to 'Move away; Count to 10; Tell the teacher or Go to your desk.' If it is too noisy: 'Sit at the table in the corner; Put on the earphones; Go for a walk.'

A similar approach was used to reduce violent outbursts in Thomas, an 8-year-old boy in mainstream school. In a one-to-one situation the teachers worked on self-control strategies, initially using pictures, to rehearse what he should or should not do when angry (Don't throw bricks at Damien; Don't scream; Don't kick the desk; Don't bang your head; Go to Mrs Jones and tell her what happened; Leave the room till you feel better). Because visual cues could not be made continuously available (this was felt to be difficult in an open-plan classroom) he was encouraged at the same time to whisper the instructions to himself. Gradually his attacks on other pupils reduced, although not necessarily because he had developed greater self-control (he would be repeating 'Don't throw bricks at Damien' while doing just that). Instead, his teachers learned to intervene immediately whenever they heard him talking to himself in this way!

Identifying Echolalic Speech

In children whose language is poorly developed there are usually no problems in recognising when their speech is echolalic and when it is spontaneous. However, in children of higher levels of ability it may prove much more difficult to distinguish between echoed and non-echoed utterances. It is often difficult for unfamiliar (or even familiar) adults to appreciate that a child who speaks knowledgeably about sport, music or astronomy, perhaps using complex vocabulary and syntax, may actually be copying things that he has heard other people say, either in real life or on the TV, or that he may be repeating verbatim from books, magazines or newspapers. As well as hampering reciprocal conversation, the nature of the language used can give a very misleading impression of the child's true level of linguistic competence. Thus, even if the child's expressive language skills appear to be very complex, because of the echoed components, the appropriate level of language input required may need to be far simpler. Formal linguistic assessments of the child's expressive and receptive language skills (see Chapter 3) can be helpful in identifying possible discrepancies in linguistic function, but even if specific deficits in understanding are identified it can still be very difficult for adults consistently to respond at an appropriate level. In most social interactions, the level of language used by the adult is automatically adapted to the level of language used by the child. Appreciating that a child with an exceptionally good vocabulary needs to be spoken to in very simple language can be a surprisingly difficult goal to achieve.

Improving Other Communicative Skills

Stereotyped speech (bombarding visitors with questions about the make of their car, or lengthy monologues about the lighting systems on particular railway networks) may also be an indication that, although the child wishes to make social contact, he or she lacks the necessary conversational skills. Again, help to initiate and cope with basic conversational exchanges—perhaps by utilising role-play or drama techniques—is often a very effective way of addressing problems of this kind. This may involve teaching children how to answer particular questions (Secan *et al.*, 1989) or might require the teaching of 'set' phrases, such as 'Hello, my name is John. I'm 7 and I go to Doubleday school. What is your name?' In the classroom visual cues, such as pictures of red or green traffic lights or a large Stop/Go sign, might also be used to indicate when individual children should pause and when they should speak, thereby improving turn taking. Although the use of set phrases in this way may result in utterances that are somewhat stilted and inflexible, such procedures can be important in reducing inappropriate social initiations (see also Schopler, 1995).

Correcting Echolalic and Inappropriate Speech

In some cases repetitive, inappropriate utterances continue because the child is simply not provided with the feedback necessary to make improvements. Howlin and Rutter (1987a) cite the example of a 12-year-old boy, Simon, who still used the words 'Morris Mummy' to indicate that he wanted to go out—much to the puzzlement of strangers. The phrase originated many years earlier when the family owned a Morris Traveller van and hence they readily understood a request of this kind. His junior school teachers, too, soon learned what he meant. However, once the original car was replaced the meaning of the phrase became far more obscure, and when Simon was transferred to senior school no one knew what he was talking about. Simon himself was not able to recognise why a previously useful phrase was no longer understood and became very distressed. Only when staff at the new school were informed of the background to the phrase and began to prompt him to say, instead, 'Can I go out now', did the problem diminish.

When children are just beginning to learn to talk, parents are usually so delighted by what is said that they rarely correct grammatical or semantic structures (although they may well correct the truth of what is said). Normally developing children, however, soon learn to alter their speech according to the social context, and rapidly abandon babyish styles of language—at least when they are away from home. Such awareness does not develop in children with autism. Having once been reinforced for using particular utterances, immature speech patterns are likely to continue, even though they become progressively more inappropriate as the child grows older. Parents, too, may become so used to the way in which the child speaks that they are hardly aware that it is not age appropriate, and make no attempt to alter this. However, if the child is consistently prompted with the correct form of utterance, and of course is immediately reinforced for using this form, immature speech can be markedly

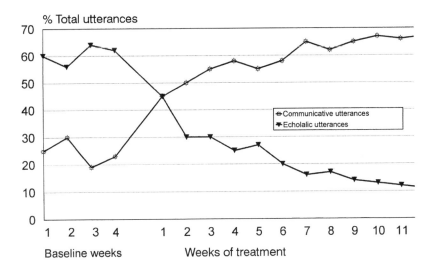

Data based on 30-minute recordings

Figure 5.2: Changes in echolalic and communicative utterances during intervention.

reduced. Figure 5.2, taken from Howlin and Rutter (1987a), illustrates how echolalic utterances ('Do you want to go out?', 'Would you like to go to the swings now?'), when corrected, were steadily replaced by more appropriate sentences such as 'Can I go out?' or 'I want to go on the swing'.

Echoing to Gain Attention

Of course, sometimes, stereotyped speech may be used deliberately because of the attention it generates. Repetitive phrases, swearing or other provocative utterances often provoke a rapid response from adults and other children, and are all too easy to reinforce. In such cases, as well as increasing the child's repertoire of appropriate speech, strategies involving extinction (ignoring) or 'time out' (removal of ongoing rewards) may be necessary. Howlin and Rutter (1987a) describe the strategies used to reduce deliberately provocative remarks by a 7-year-old boy. Living in very cramped, inadequate conditions his mother struggled against the odds to keep the house and children as clean and as orderly as possible. His most effective way of getting her attention was to describe everything as 'dirty'. Physical punishment had no effect and, recognising this, his mother eventually learned to ignore these remarks. From time to time he would try out new and equally annoying phrases, but after an initial reaction his mother

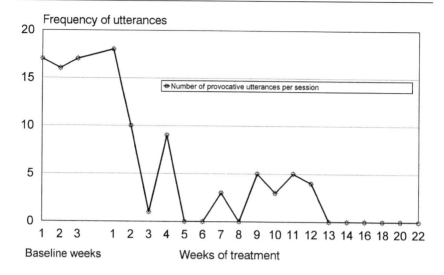

Figure 5.3: Decrease in provocative and stereotyped utterances during 'extinction' programme

managed to ignore these too. The frequency of such remarks declined rapidly and they were eventually overcome entirely when his mother encouraged him to *write them* rather than say them (see Figure 5.3).

There is little doubt that by *consistently* ignoring inappropriate speech, such behaviour can be very effectively modified—the problem lies in being consistent. Swearing or other abusive language may be relatively easy to ignore by parents who are relaxed and in control. After a sleepless night, when under stress, or in conditions where they have little control (e.g. in church, on the top of a bus, or in a supermarket queue) it can be almost impossible not to respond. Moreover, even if parents and siblings manage not to react to swear words or the like, the same will not be true of other children, elderly relatives, fellow-travellers on buses, or worshippers in church. Intermittent reinforcement of this kind will actually result in an increase in unwanted behaviour; hence, extinction programmes, although highly effective in principle, can prove much more difficult to carry out in practice. Daisy, for example, following some 'sex education' classes in school, began to comment loudly on the physical characteristics of men and women whom she saw in the street. Although, to begin with, these remarks were quite innocent, the prompt reaction that they drew from adults led to a rapid escalation, as Daisy realised that they were an extremely effective way of obtaining attention. Even when her family began to try to ignore these utterances, attention from strangers was inevitable and made outings a source of great embarrassment to her parents and siblings. Once behaviours of this kind are established parents will need a great deal of support to cope with them effectively, particularly in the early stages when the so-called 'extinction burst' (an initial increase in the behaviour when reinforcement is first withdrawn) may occur. In Daisy's case, the comments only diminished significantly following the restriction of outings and the introduction of an additional reward system. Socially embarrassing remarks would result in Daisy's outing being terminated (but this involved careful planning between her parents to ensure that the other members of the family were not penalised); if no remarks were made the outing would continue and she was also allowed to watch a favourite video when they returned home. (For many other examples of ways to deal with repetitive and stereotyped speech, see Prizant *et al.*, 1997.)

A Note of Caution

Although many different methods have been tried and found to be effective in improving the language used by children with autism, it is still important to be aware that most studies of this kind involve only individual cases, or very small groups of subjects. The differential benefits of these approaches for different groups of children remain largely unexplored and generalisation to other settings is often limited. There is no real way of knowing how many unsuccessful programmes have been conducted and in the absence of randomised control trials—that is the random allocation of children to different treatment procedures—it is not possible to compare the effectiveness of the various programmes. It remains very much up to individual parents and practitioners to decide which methods to try, and success can still be a matter of trial and error.

What has become clearer, in the course of recent research, is that the focus of attention needs to shift, at least to some extent, away from the child and that greater emphasis needs to be placed on improving the language of other people in his or her environment.

IMPROVING THE COMMUNICATION SKILLS OF OTHERS

Although specialist language programmes can help to improve receptive and expressive skills in children with autism, the communication deficit remains central to the disorder and no amount of therapy will overcome this entirely. Nevertheless, much can be achieved by making the adults in the child's environment more attentive to the language that they themselves use. They also need constantly to bear in mind the potential problems related to the child's literal interpretation of language and difficulties with abstract or metaphorical concepts.

Instructions should be simple and concise, with every attempt being made to ensure that the words used actually mean what they say. Metaphor, slang and colloquialisms are all best avoided. Unwitting remarks such as 'He lost his head', 'Pick your feet up', 'It's raining buckets' can lead to hours of searching (for spare hands and heads) or demands for explanation. Irony, sarcasm or threats such as 'I'll kill you if you do that again' can cause untold distress. Janice, a 14-year-old, was once told by her teacher to make sure that she dried herself thoroughly after swimming 'otherwise your clothes will stick to your skin'. She was so terrified by this possibility that she refused to enter the swimming pool again. Even vague concepts such as 'Perhaps', 'I'll think about it', 'We'll see' are liable to produce confusion and anxiety. If the child is required to do something, an unambiguous request such as 'Please give me the bread' will be more productive than a phrase such as 'Can you pass the bread?' (which might well be answered in the affirmative but without resulting in any action). Questions, too, need to be carefully worded. One little boy, whose visit to the lavatory seemed rather prolonged, was asked by his concerned teacher 'Do you need a hand?'. 'No thank you,' came the polite reply from behind the door, 'there's plenty of paper in here.' Other apparently minor changes in wording can have major effects: one girl's severe distress at being told, prior to a trip to France, that she would be 'going to sleep on the train' changed to pleasure and relief when this was altered to 'going to bed in the train'. A teenage boy who became rude and abusive if ever he was asked by teachers or doctors 'What year is your birthday?' (the obvious answer, to him, was 'Every year') answered politely if they asked instead, 'What year were you born?' In another case, 9-year-old Ashton was told to write an essay 'on the unknown'. He refused steadfastly to do this, on the grounds that he couldn't possibly produce an essay on something he didn't know about. When sent to the headmaster for his refusal to do as he was told, he launched into a verbal attack on his teacher for giving him such a stupid and unreasonable thing to do. Fortunately, the Head was aware of his problems in abstract understanding, and after a rebuke for being so rude about his teacher, he suggested to Ashton that he should go away and write an essay on 'mysteries' instead.

Unfortunately, predicting in advance, what particular turn of phrase is likely to give rise to problems is very much a matter of trial and error. However, whenever a request is not complied with, or if a statement meets with an upsurge in echolalia, irritation or anxiety, the speaker should first assume that what he or she has said has been misunderstood or misinterpreted. Simplifying or changing the words that are used may have a much greater impact than attempts to modify the child's response.

And again, the value of written or pictorial cues to augment the words used, cannot be overemphasised.

It can be surprisingly difficult even for parents or skilled professionals to ensure that they do keep language as concrete and as simple as possible and that they do really say what they mean. Indeed, in mainstream school, children may often get into trouble for doing exactly what they are told. The instruction to 'Paint the child sitting next to you', for example, can result in a major incident in the classroom. In another case, a teenage boy became extremely distressed, hitting both his teachers and fellow pupils when asked to 'Measure the area of tarmac in the playground'. When he eventually calmed down several days later, he explained that he had hit out because he had been asked to do something that was impossible—the tarmac was three dimensional and therefore the *volume* not the *area* needed to be measured.

It is also crucial to ensure that the child's own attempts to communicate are responded to consistently and appropriately. Observations of teachers in special classrooms or day care centres (Sigafoos *et al.*, 1994a, 1994b) have indicated that only a small proportion of the school day (as little as 14%) may provide the child with opportunities for communication. Moreover, when communication is encouraged, teachers tended to focus on the naming of objects or events, rather than on structures that are more useful for the child. Sigafoos and his colleagues found that approximately 55% of communicative opportunities involved labelling, 25% requests, 15% answers to teachers questions and 5% imitations. As noted earlier, this is *not* the pattern of communication that tends to occur spontaneously in the speech of children with autism. Labelling is not a high-frequency activity and may mean very little to the child. On the other hand, offering greater opportunity for requesting would seem to be important, as this is more likely to provide the child with direct reinforcement and to increase his or her control over the environment. The Sigafoos study also showed that although teachers usually responded appropriately to the children's utterances, in 9% of interactions the response was inappropriate, and in 29% there was no response at all.

WHAT PARENTS CAN DO

Much of the work on language development in children with autism has focused on school- or clinic-based programmes, but it is clear that unless families are also actively involved, progress is always likely to be limited and generalisation restricted (Lovaas, 1973). Moreover, although, even relatively recently, it has been suggested that the verbal interaction between young children with autism and their mothers may be less than

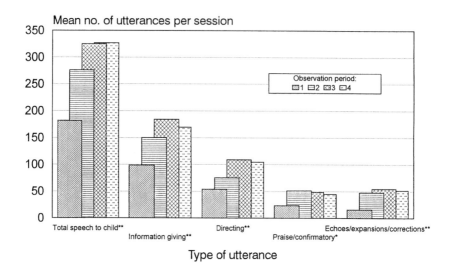

Figure 5.4: Changes in mothers' speech to their children over 18 months. Data based on 90-minute observation sessions. ** Change over occasions significant at $p<0.01$; * significant at $p<0.05$

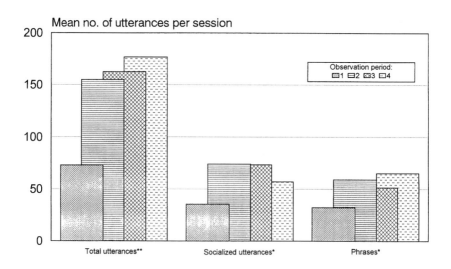

Figure 5.5: Changes in children's speech over 18 months. Data based on 30-minute recordings. ** Change over occasions significant at $p<0.01$; * significant at $p<0.05$

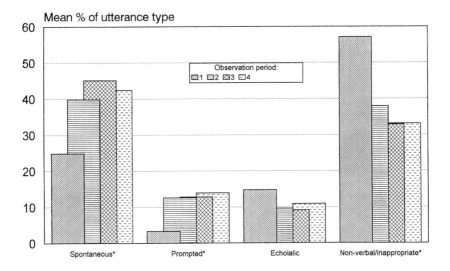

Data based on 30-minute recordings. * Change over 18 months significant at
$p < 0.05$

Figure 5.6: Changes in children's speech style over 18 months.

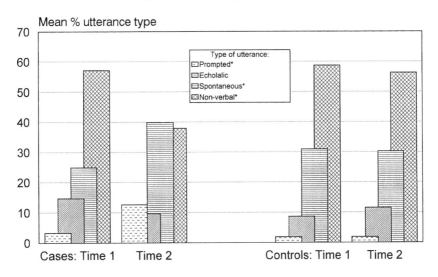

Data based on 30-minute recordings. * Change scores between groups significant at $p < 0.05$

Figure 5.7: Changes in the speech of treatment and control children over 6
months.

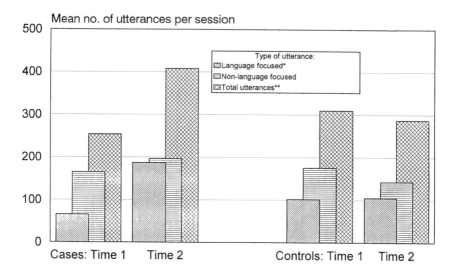

Data based on 30-minute recordings. Change scores between groups significant
at *$p<0.05$ or **$p<0.01$

Figure 5.8: Changes in the speech of treatment and control mothers over
6 months.

optimal (Trevarthen *et al.*, 1996) there is, in fact, little to support such
hypotheses. Most experimental work in this area suggests that mothers
are generally sensitive to their children's communication; they respond
appropriately to the child's level of linguistic ability and provide good
language models themselves.

Nevertheless, there is no doubt that with additional help and guidance,
parents can become even more effective in developing linguistic competence in their children. As an integral part of a home-based intervention
programme Howlin and Rutter (1987a) set out to increase the use of utterances specifically designed to encourage speech or to correct inappropriate language usage in children with autism. In the experimental group, not
only did the amount of speech used by mothers to their children increase
over the 18 months of the project, but the proportion of 'language directed
remarks' also rose significantly. These included questions and corrections,
repetitions, expansions, reductions or reinforcements of the child's utterances. As mothers' speech style changed, concomitant improvements
were also found in their children. The total amount of children's speech
increased substantially, as did their use of socialised utterances (spontaneous speech and prompted repetitions). Over the same period the
relative frequency of phrase speech improved, while echolalic and inappropriate utterances declined (see Figures 5.4 to 5.6).

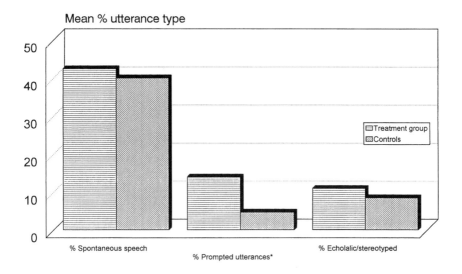

Data based on 30-minute recordings. Difference between groups significant at
*$p<0.05$

Figure 5.9: Language in treatment group and long-term controls at end
of intervention period.

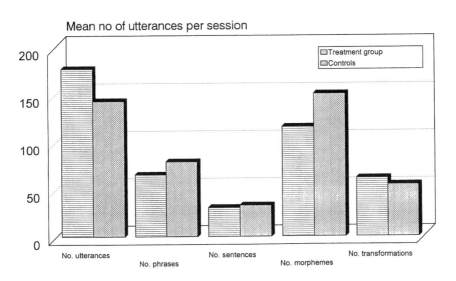

Data based on 30-minute recordings. No significant differences between groups

Figure 5.10: Complexity of language in treatment group and long-term
controls at end of intervention period.

A short-term (6 month) comparison of change in experimental and control families showed that there were few changes in language usage or language complexity in the control children, and no significant changes in the amount or type of speech used by their mothers (see Figures 5.7 and 5.8)

Comparisons with a longer term, individually matched control group indicated that while some of the short-term gains diminished as time went on, the experimental group continued to use significantly more prompted speech. Compared with their matched controls experimental children also tended to be superior in the amount of speech they used, although there were few differences in their use of more complex grammatical structures (see Figures 5.9 and 5.10). Although there were considerable individual differences in the children's response to the intervention programme, a close relationship was found between children's language level and maternal speech styles, in both cases and controls (see also Howlin & Rutter, 1987a, for further details).

These data illustrate how relatively minor changes to parental speech (making this clearer, simpler, and placing the emphasis on encouraging the child to communicate more effectively and appropriately) can have a significant and long-lasting impact on children's social language. No complex intervention programmes are required although professional support is needed to advise parents on the most effective ways of interacting with their child and in helping them to maintain consistency in this.

6

PROBLEMS OF SOCIAL UNDERSTANDING

INTERVENTIONS FOR SOCIAL DIFFICULTIES

The social impairment in autism affects almost every aspect of the child's functioning, whatever his or her intellectual ability. In children who are more severely handicapped, unacceptable or inappropriate behaviours, such as screaming, undressing or masturbating in public, may be a major cause of difficulty for parents. In the case of those who are more able, the problems tend to be much more subtle, and relate to impairments in empathy, social understanding, or reciprocity and synchronisation (i.e. saying or doing things that in themselves are not unacceptable, but at the wrong time, in the wrong place or with the wrong person).

As with any form of intervention, the approaches used to help cope with social difficulties will vary according to age, ability and the nature of the social impairment. An intervention programme for a young child who is very withdrawn and actively resists social contact will need to be very different from one designed for an older child who shows little social shyness or discrimination.

DEALING WITH SOCIAL ISOLATION

For many parents, it is the remoteness and lack of responsiveness in their infant that first alerts them to the fact that all is not well. In retrospect, parents frequently note that their infant was 'happiest if left alone', 'lived in a world of his own', . . ., 'only cried when I talked to him or picked him up'. Understandably, because of this, many mothers try to avoid causing distress, leaving the child undisturbed for much of the time and minimising demands for close physical or social contact. Later, of course, they then experience feelings of profound guilt, often attributing their child's subsequent difficulties to this early lack of pressure or stimulation. However, Cantwell and his colleagues (1979) found no evidence of pathological patterns of family life or interactions among parents with an autistic child, and there are certainly no data to support early theories suggesting that inadequate parenting could cause autism or that autistic withdrawal may become worse if deliberate attempts are made to foster interaction (cf. Tinbergen & Tinbergen, 1983). In fact, isolated and stereotyped behaviours are likely to increase if no attempts are made to intervene. Both clinical and experimental research indicates that deliberate intrusion into the child's solitary world can be an important means of helping this 'socially aloof' group of children. Rutter and Sussenwein (1971) were among the first to describe the use of this approach, and Howlin and Rutter (1987a) also illustrate the effectiveness of these methods. Thus, parents can be given guidance on how to 'interfere' in solitary and repetitive play activities so that the child needs to interact in some way in order to complete these. For example, they might withhold the last piece of a familiar jigsaw puzzle, store a particular attachment object just out of the child's reach, deliberately place an obstacle in the way of the child's ritualistic line up of cars, or remove part of a construction kit so that the item cannot be completed. In order to finish the routine or activity the child is obliged to make some form of contact—perhaps looking towards the adults, reaching out to them, or verbalising his needs in some way. With more handicapped children, just accepting contact may be sufficient. Lewis, for example, simply had to tolerate his mother putting her arm round him for a few seconds on his return from school before he was allowed to return to his perennial paper shredding.

Over time, the degree of interference imposed by parents can be gradually increased. Sarah, a young girl with an intense attraction to pieces of paper and card, was not allowed access to these on her return from school until she had answered a question (subsequently increased to several questions) from her mother about the activities of the day. Robin was not able to play with his collection of toy London buses until he had rolled them back and forth to his parents several times; later he also had to place passengers appropriately in the buses. Martin was prevented from watching his Thomas the Tank Engine videos until he had read his mother a page (later increased to several pages) from his large selection of Thomas the Tank Engine books.

Joint play with peers or siblings can be encouraged by similar means. Howlin and Rutter (1987a) describe the case of an intelligent but very solitary child named Thomas, who resented any approaches from his younger sister. His mother manipulated some of his puzzles and constructional games, so that his sister had access to a number of the pieces. In order to complete the game Thomas had to wait for his sister to place her piece (prompting from her mother ensured that this was done without delay or disruption). Gradually the sister was given more pieces to place, and prompting was reduced until the two were able to co-operate well together. From constructional games they then moved on to less structured activities, including musical and ball games, bubble blowing, and simple card games. Eventually his other sister also became involved, and the time spent in solitary activities steadily reduced.

Intrusive techniques may also be successful in encouraging imaginative play. Martin, who continually lined up Thomas the Tank Engine trains, was encouraged to provide them with passengers, or to have pretend crashes, before continuing with his usual routine. As time went on his parents prompted him to re-enact scenes he had watched on the video; he would always be 'Thomas', while they took the role of one of the other trains, or the Fat Controller. Jake, a child with a fascination for carrying around bags of toy dinosaurs, was encouraged by his parents to take part in a variety of games involving these. Jake insisted that the game always had to end with an extra large dinosaur who gobbled up everyone for his dinner, but within this confine they were able to prompt him to join in an increasing range of imaginative activities.

Although 'forced' social interactions of this kind may seem very artificial initially, as time goes on, involvement becomes more natural, and often more enjoyable on both sides. As children learn to tolerate the intrusion they may become more responsive to parents, who in turn will be encouraged to initiate more activities of this kind. Recent work, by Willemsen-Swinkels *et al.* (1997) also indicates that as parents introduce greater structure into social situations the frequency of eye-gaze and social bids made by their child increases. Thus, what begins as a very simple and artificial interaction may ultimately become the basis of much more sociable, pleasurable and spontaneous activities for children and parents. Even Lewis, the very handicapped child described above, eventually learned 'spontaneously' to give his mother a brief hug when he returned from school, before he moved on to his solitary and ritualistic activities, and this was a source of immense pleasure for her.

PROBLEMS OF SOCIAL DISINHIBITION

As many children with autism grow older, parents' worries begin to focus not on their social isolation but on their lack of social discrimination. A number of examples, taken from clinical practice, illustrate the potential dangers of this:

> Sally, a well-built 14-year-old, will pull up her clothing any time she meets anyone new in order to show them her appendix scar.

Daniel, an 8-year-old with an obsession for excavating machines, spends all his free time on building sites and takes any opportunity he can to gain access to the cab of 'diggers'.

William, a 13-year-old with a fascination for rugby; at matches wanders in and out of players' changing rooms.

Gillian, a 15-year-old with an obsession for certain makes of wrist watch, will approach strangers, roll up their sleeves and then follow them if they are wearing her favourite make.

Lorraine, a pubescent 13-year-old, who, because of her reluctance to wear new clothes, dresses in extremely short and skimpy skirts and dresses. Calls any male she meets her 'boyfriend' and will sit on their knees and cuddle them, whether they be 6 or 60.

In such cases, it is the need to discourage, rather than encourage social initiations that presents problems. Moreover, because the behaviour has often been present for some time before parents realise its potential danger, change can be much more difficult to implement. Nevertheless, there are a number of guidelines that can help to minimise difficulties.

SOME GUIDELINES FOR INTERVENTION

Try to Predict Problems in Advance

Parents need to be aware of behaviours, which, although not necessarily inappropriate in a young child, may become progressively more unacceptable as he or she grows older. A young girl who warmly hugs and kisses everyone she meets, or a little boy who loves the feel of women's tights, may be treated with fond indulgence. The same behaviours in an older teenager will provoke a very different response! Difficulties in social understanding and awareness mean that the child with autism will be either impervious to other people's changed reactions, or totally confused by the fact that behaviours that were once tolerated, even encouraged, are suddenly deemed to be 'wrong'.

Keep to Firm, Simple and Initially Invariable Rules

In many ways, the more obvious social problems are often easier to deal with. With small children it is important to begin with clear and invariable rules—such as never undress or masturbate in public; never speak to, or touch, strangers (or their belongings). The child also needs to learn that if these rules are infringed, this may result in the cessation of ongoing activities. Children with autism, by definition, have a tendency towards rigid behaviour patterns, so that, as long as acceptable behaviours are established in early childhood, they will be less likely to give rise to problems later. The converse, of course, is also true, so that once unacceptable behaviours take hold, they will be very difficult to shift in later years, especially as the child becomes bigger.

On the whole, it is preferable to begin with rather rigid and inflexible rules (You only kiss people in the family; you can only touch mummy's tights, and only in the house; you never talk about your periods to men, except daddy) which may be relaxed in later years if necessary. This approach is less likely to result in difficulties than having initially very lax guidelines, which suddenly have to be made more restrictive. A toddler who has been allowed to take off all his clothes whenever he wanted will find it very difficult to change this behaviour when he begins attending school; on the other hand, a child who has only ever been allowed to take her clothes off in the house, when no visitors are around, can be taught, as she grows older, that it may be acceptable to remove her clothes in certain *specified* situations, such as the family doctor's surgery.

Not all rules, of course, are easy to teach, and because normal social interactions are not based on overt rules, it can be difficult even to decide what or how to teach. Some rules are probably best never taught at all. Insisting that a child should 'look at people when they talk to you', for example, is likely to lead to them staring fixedly at every one they meet, which is far more disconcerting than someone who makes only fleeting eye contact. Other 'rules' that are applicable in one situation may not be so in another. 'Why?' asked one puzzled 7-year-old, who had just started junior school, having lived next door to the head teacher all his life, 'Why can I give her a kiss and call her Sarah on Saturday and Sunday but on Monday I have to call her Mrs Pye and I mustn't even shake her hand?' Ben, who suffered from diabetes, having been lectured at school about the dangers of injecting drugs, immediately came home and refused to continue with his daily insulin injections.

Another boy, Darren, aged 9, asked his therapist to teach him when to laugh. He had realised at school that the teacher appreciated the children laughing at her jokes, and he, too, soon learned to respond in this way. Unfortunately, he had little idea what a joke really was, and so also tended to laugh uproariously if asked to get out his pencil box or tie his shoe lace. This was clearly not so popular with his teacher—hence his request for help! As the therapist was quite unable to formulate the rules governing laughter he suggested, instead, that Darren should never laugh unless other children did so first. Although his laughter remained somewhat exaggerated, this advice did help to reduce the disruption he caused in class.

Understanding about Friends or Strangers

Even if explicit rules can be formulated, those that work well with normally developing children may backfire if applied to children with autism, largely because they are unable to understand the basic concepts underlying these rules. A warning 'never to talk to strangers' may lead to the child refusing to go out at all, because he or she is unable to distinguish between who is a stranger and who is not. In such cases parents may have to try to define exactly what they mean by 'stranger', which is by no means an easy task. Thus, they may need to specify that relatives, family friends, bus or taxi drivers, shop workers, school teachers, doctors, etc., are NOT strangers, and may therefore be talked to. On the other hand, unknown people who approach you in the street or on your way home from school should not be spoken to—instead it is important to run straight home and tell parents. Even this sort of rule can go wrong, of course. Bob, for example, would rush home yelling loudly to his parents if anyone ever spoke to him in the street, even if this was just an elderly woman who was clearly lost.

Understanding about friendships may pose even greater problems, and indeed the factors governing successful social engagement are so complex that even normal children are unlikely fully to understand them (although they will recognise immediately any infringements of such unspoken 'rules'). For the autistic child, however, the most 'ordinary' of social behaviours can cause immense problems. Some children appear to think that all they have to do to get a friend is to march up to a group of children in the playground and demand 'Will you be my friend?'. Others, desperate for friendship, will do anything other children ask. This can range from laying concrete blocks across the railway line, putting a brick through the video shop window, marching up to the head teacher in assembly and asking a highly personal question, urinating openly in the playground as the teacher walks by, or handing over lunch or pocket money to 'friends'. One 8-year-old boy was urged by other children in the neighbourhood to say 'hello' to a large alsatian dog by barking at it. They knew that this would incense the animal, but even when the dog began to growl threateningly the child made no attempt to get away. He was badly mauled and in hospital for several days, having required several stitches to his face and arms.

From the earliest years children will need help to appreciate that friendship cannot be earned by doing what other children say. Even if they are aware that what is suggested is silly, rude or dangerous, they may well need help to say 'no', especially if under pressure, and are unlikely to be able to manage without adult support. It is crucial that parents and teachers are aware of this potential vulnerability to teasing, bullying or being 'set up' and that they are able to intervene immediately they become aware that this might be happening. Some children have great difficulties in working out whether a request from other children is reasonable or not, and if possible there should be someone at home or school to whom they can turn for advice on such issues. Telling a child with autism to 'Stand up for yourself' is of no use at all. If the child does try to fight back, his or her attempts will almost invariably be feeble, mistimed or misplaced. Josh, for example was seriously bullied at school, often returning home with bruises and ripped clothes. His father showed little sympathy over this, and insisted he should 'act like a man'. Finally, one day Josh did give vent to his feelings, but instead of hitting the child responsible he attacked one of the least aggressive children in the school, just as the head teacher was walking by. Another child, also driven to distraction by bullying, turned round one day and, without warning, bit his teacher. In general, in situations where bullying is a real or potential problem, the social competence and understanding required to deal with this is almost certain to be beyond the child's capability. The onus for protection, therefore, must lie with adult carers.

Dealing with Other Social Problems

As children grow older many social difficulties can arise from their stereotyped and ritualistic behaviours. It may become almost impossible to take children out because of demands that they always take a particular direction or follow a set routine. If certain items have been purchased in the supermarket on one occasion they may have to be bought there on every subsequent visit; some children may also become distressed if the same staff are not there on each occasion. Other children may draw attention to themselves by making strange noises, by carrying unusual objects, or by their odd appearance. Jeffrey, for example, always insisted on wearing sun glasses in winter and gloves and overcoat in summer. Susanne carried on a low 'mooing' noise all the time she was out. This did not particularly bother passers-by but was said to 'drive her mother mad'. In other cases, behaviours that are quite acceptable for a young child, such as going unannounced into neighbours' houses to look at their washing machines, can become very unacceptable as they grow older. Parents may need a great deal of help and support during these early years if they are to develop effective management strategies, especially as different problems may require very different intervention techniques. Moreover, because young children with autism are frequently deeply disturbed and confused anyway, most parents, unwilling to increase this distress, tend to give into many of their demands. Helping parents to know what they should do, and how they can decide when it is accept-able or necessary to say 'No', is crucial if social difficulties are not to escalate. Removing a screaming 3-year-old from a shop because he cannot have what he wants may be embarrassing enough; attempts to remove a screaming 13-year-old will prove far more difficult.

Joanna's parents began to realise her resistance to changing the dir-ection in which they walked when she was barely 18 months old. They began to make slight detours, such as crossing over the road and then crossing back again, whenever they went out. Although Joanna would scream loudly at these detours, she would quickly calm down again when they returned back to the usual route. Gradually they increased the length and frequency of detours, at the same time attempting to combine these with something else that Joanna enjoyed—watching the ducks in a nearby pond, having an ice-cream or going on the swings. Although she would often grizzle miserably to herself during these deviations, the piercing screams ceased and eventually she was able to tolerate, if not enjoy, variations in her daily outings.

Bobby was another child who made trips to buy clothes a 'nightmare' for his mother because of his tantrums if she did not buy clothes with a specific sports logo on. To begin with his parents and grandparents had indulged this taste, but over time the clothes became increasingly difficult to find, and also extremely expensive. His mother cut off the logos from worn out garments, and attached them to pieces of Velcro; when out shopping she would then surreptitiously stick these onto appropriate garments and he soon learned to accept clothes with these stick-on logos.

In Jeffrey's case, the attachment to his winter coat was solved when his mother simply refused to buy him a new one. That summer was particularly hot, and at the same time Jeffrey grew considerably larger. Eventually he gave up the struggle to get into the coat and in subsequent years his mother always supplied him with a range of different (usually second-hand) jackets, so that he was never able to get strongly attached to any one in particular. However, he still wears his sun glasses throughout the winter.

As for Susanne, her 'mooing' was dealt with in a very different way. Her mother learned that staff at the nursery she attended were very amused by this noise and would often encourage her to do it. Discussion with the head of the nursery quickly solved this part of the problem. It then became apparent that the noise was much louder in certain super-markets, and avoiding these helped to reduce it further. However, it was still impossible for her mother entirely to ignore the noise so she bought a personal stereo for herself, and a small but very strong cassette player with some of Susanne's favourite nursery rhyme tapes that she attached to her pram. The 'mooing' soon decreased significantly, and most shop-ping trips could take place without disruption.

There are no right and wrong answers to dealing with the social difficulties shown by children with autism. The problems themselves may have very different underlying causes, and hence require very different approaches. However, the one crucial component of any intervention programme is consistency. If parents decide that they will *always* resist the child's demands to turn right out of the house rather than left; if they determine that sweets will *never* be bought at the check-out counter, or that clothes can never be removed in public they must do their utmost to keep to these resolutions. Giving in just once will almost certainly strengthen the child's protests on the next occasion. Parents may also need to persuade aunts, uncles, grandparents or family friends to do the same, and this can prove very difficult. The attempts by Jeffrey's mother to wean him off his overcoat were almost thwarted by her own mother who was so horrified that her grandson should be dressed so badly, that she had to be restrained from buying him a new one.

Understanding when Rules may be Broken

Having stressed the need for consistency in the initial stages of reducing unacceptable social behaviours, it is also necessary to turn, paradoxically, to the need to infringe rules from time to time. This is because, as noted above, the 'rules' of social behaviour are very difficult, if not impossible, to define comprehensively. A rule that works well in one setting may not work in another situation or with another person. Responses that are acceptable in one context may be inappropriate if the social context, or even the topic of conversation, changes. Simon, for example, had constantly been coached by his mother to put his arm around her or his sister if he knew they were upset, and indeed he became rather better than his older brother at offering comfort in this way. When he responded in the same way to his class teacher, who was clearly upset by the behaviour of his fellow pupils, he got into considerable trouble for this 'inappropriate' response.

Because of Michael's propensity to remove his clothes in primary school his parents and teachers had enforced the rule that no clothes could be removed unless his parents or a teacher from his school gave permission. This worked well, even in senior school, until he broke his leg while racing at another school. The sports master there immediately took him to hospital, but because neither he nor the doctor in the emergency clinic quite fitted the rule's specifications, Michael refused to undress until someone from his own school, several miles away, was sent for.

Similarly, staff at Billy's school had become concerned after a number of students had been approached by a man offering them trips in his car.

Billy's vulnerability, together with his love of cars, clearly placed him at risk and so the head teacher gave him a long talk on how he must not talk to strangers, and how he must never go in a car unless it was driven by a relative, a close family friend, or someone connected with the school. A few weeks later, when the school bus failed to arrive, his mother called a taxi to take him instead. Billy, sticking steadfastly to his teacher's warning, became very agitated and refused to enter it. Subsequently, his parents had to work extremely hard to convince him that taxis were acceptable, even though the Head had not originally mentioned these in his list of 'specifications'.

On the whole, rules *without* explanations tend to work best in the early years, when the child's linguistic capacities are fairly limited. Attempts to explain *why* something should not be done or said may be totally beyond the child's ability to understand, and may simply deteriorate into lengthy and fruitless arguments. In particular, the children's lack of social understanding means that explanations concerning people's feelings or sensitivities have little impact. Moreover, the strict 'moral' code which some children develop can lead to them become very upset if they think they are being asked to be less than truthful. Gabriel, a 13-year-old at mainstream school, was in frequent trouble with his teachers and classmates because of his insistence on always telling the truth. If teachers made a mistake in a lesson, or if their appearance was in any way less than perfect, Gabriel would immediately draw attention to this. If other children were surreptitiously talking or eating in class, if they had copied someone else's homework, or if they were seen smoking outside, Gabriel was the first to tell. When, after a number of physical attacks by his peers, his mother and headmaster tried to explain that it would be better to keep quiet about these things, he became quite distraught, insisting it was his duty to tell people the truth. Explanations about hurting people's feelings had no impact on him whatsoever. Instead the headteacher drew up a list of behaviours that he should NOT comment on out loud (spelling or handwriting errors by teachers, people's dress or appearance, other children talking, eating or smoking) and a list of those that he could mention (factual errors by teachers in lessons, physical bullying by other children). For the other 'misdemeanours' Gabriel was allowed to keep a written record, which he could then take to discuss with the Head at the end of each week. His silence in class was also rewarded by a bonus point for his own tutor group, which helped marginally to increase his popularity.

Other 'rules' may be made more complex over time. Definitions of 'strangers' may be expanded, or what topics of conversation are acceptable in what circumstances may be clarified. One child, for example, came home utterly distraught after his first human biology lesson at school because his parents had once told him that if anyone ever spoke to him about intimate body parts he was immediately to run away. He then needed to learn that it was permissible for certain teachers to talk about such topics. A child who has learned never to remove his or her clothes in public may eventually be taught that it is permissible to take them off in the doctor's surgery or in hospital, in the school changing room, at a swimming pool or on the beach. Or there may be explicit rules that although it is *not* permissible to make comments about people's weight, size, the colour of their skin, or any obvious disability, or if they have spots, a bald head, or are wearing clothing of which the child does not approve, it is acceptable to make positive remarks to familiar adults, such as 'that's a nice dress'.

Other children may need to accept that although they should not talk about their obsessional interests to their peer group as this will only lead to teasing or bullying, they can talk about the topic to particular adults, but only for a specified period of time.

There is little doubt that rules of this kind, despite their inadequacy, are a great deal better than no rules at all. Nevertheless, parents and others always need to be aware that they are never likely to be able to predict all the situations in which problems can arise. John, for example, having learned that he could take off his clothes on the beach, invariably did so, regardless of whether it was summer or winter. Rosie, a young teenager, knew that she could strip off at the seaside or swimming pool, but she did this without any shyness whatsoever, removing all her clothes with a flourish before putting on her swimming costume. Another, older teenager, who had been taught to try to compliment people when he met them, horrified his parents at a social gathering by announcing loudly that one of the guests (an elderly woman with white hair, large ears and protruding teeth) 'looked just like a rabbit'. When hauled from the room he protested that he had not said anything wrong as rabbits were his favourite animal.

Developing Socially Acceptable Routines

As they grow older many children with autism run into difficulties because of very basic problems, such as dressing inappropriately, failing to pay attention to personal hygiene, or being unable to greet people in an acceptable way. Ways of establishing simple verbal routines that can be used on a daily basis, or when meeting strangers, have been described in the previous chapter. However, it is also important to work on non-verbal aspects of social behaviour. All but the most handicapped children with autism can be taught basic self-help skills and routines, which most of them can eventually learn to carry out independently. Schopler (1995) provides many innovative ideas on how these skills can be encouraged. Daily washing, grooming, bathing and tooth-cleaning habits should be established as early as possible; children also need to learn to change their clothes on a regular basis. Although this will require considerable parental input initially it is important that, over time, direct prompts and guidance are gradually faded so that the behaviours are under the child's own control. Continued reliance on parents can otherwise lead to a variety of problems. Either children remain unable to carry out these tasks for themselves or, in some cases, they may suddenly decide, as teenagers, that they should no longer have to carry out such 'childish' activities at all. Eighteen-year-old Aaron, for example, was able to travel independently to his community college without difficulty, but was still washed, dressed and shaved every day by his mother before he left. In contrast, Sarah decided that at the age of 15 her parents should treat her more like an adult, and that they had no right to tell her how to dress or when to wash. Her personal hygiene rapidly declined to such an extent that the school began to complain, and eventually insisted on her having a shower there before she was allowed into lessons.

Many children have no interest in clothes, or in their appearance generally, or they may insist on wearing particular types of clothing, which may be very unfashionable or inappropriate for their age. Terry, an 8-year-old attending a school for children with mild learning difficulties, insisted on wearing grey shorts, a white shirt and tie, and lace up shoes with grey socks; all the other children wore jeans and trainers. Sophie, a 13-year-old who had just begun secondary school, sported a bizarre assortment of multi-coloured hair ribbons. Jake, whose parents were trying to settle him in yet another secondary school, appeared on his first day there with a smart brief case, impeccable, if rather old-fashioned clothes and large, horn-rimmed spectacles. These may sound trivial enough, but were viewed with contempt by other pupils. As a result, all three children were unmercifully teased and bullied. On one occasion, on a school trip, several girls got together and tore out all Sophie's ribbons. In Jake's case, his rejection was made worse by the fact that he also spoke in a very 'posh' accent, and a pedantic manner. His teachers became so concerned for his safety that they would not allow him out into the playground at break or lunchtimes, and insisted on his parents coming to meet him at the school door at the end of the day.

Another mother inadvertently found out that her 6-year-old son was a source of great amusement to all the other children in the school. When he used the urinal it was noticed that he always pulled down his pants and trousers to his ankles and soon there were queues of giggling children around to watch him each time he visited the lavatory. He became the butt of all the children's jokes and was constantly teased and bullied because of this.

In order to minimise problems of this kind it is important that parents are aware of how children in the wider peer group dress, or what sorts of equipment they use. Information about the latest 'fads' or favourite pop, film or sports stars can also be valuable in helping the child to 'fit in', or at least to be less instantly identifiable as an outsider.

INCREASING INDEPENDENCE

Although severe bullying and rejection may be minimised by such means, most children with autism will remain relatively isolated, and few develop close friendships. Because of this it is important, particularly with more able children, to try to increase their independence and the range of activities in which they can become involved. These will, of course, depend on individual skills and interests, but some children may be able to join chess, computer or musical clubs; some have done surprisingly well in activities such as judo or badminton or table tennis. Sympathetic scout, Woodcraft or cub-group leaders may also be able to encourage a range of different activities, and the badges awarded for these can be an important means of building self-esteem. Less able children may be able to take part in local groups for children with other forms of disability. Cycling proficiency courses can help to increase independence, while holiday schemes, such as those organised by MENCAP or AFASIC, can offer valuable opportunities for trips away from home for older children.

Obviously, it is important that the organisers of these groups or courses have some information about the nature of the children's difficulties in order to help them understand their sometimes unusual behaviour, and to assist them to structure activities appropriately. It is also important, when developing independence skills, to ensure that the process is gradual and that the child has adequate support at every stage.

Shopping skills, for example, can be developed by speaking to the local shopkeeper before taking the child to buy specific items. Initially he or she might be provided with the exact money, but later they can be prompted to wait for change. The parent might accompany the child initially, prompting him through each stage of choosing and paying for the required items. Prompts can then be faded, perhaps with the parent waiting outside the shop, then on the corner, then at the end of the street, until eventually the child is able to visit the shop alone (although perhaps with a written note, just in case).

Travel skills can also be taught in a similar way. Johann learned to take the bus home alone during one school holiday. He was first accompanied all the way by his father, although Johann himself had to identify and stop the correct bus (a few long waits soon established this behaviour). His father then got off one stop before home, leaving Johann to get to the next stop alone; the driver was also asked to remind him to get off. Later, Johann made the whole journey alone, having been put on the bus outside school. Initially his father followed at a discrete distance in his car to ensure that no problems arose, but by the time term started again Johann was able to travel by himself. Travel cards avoided the need to find the correct money, and a phone card—which was only valid for phoning home—could alert his parents if problems occurred.

Some parents provide children with an identity chain, with their telephone number, in case they get lost or are unable to say where they live. In the final resort, too, children should be taught how to contact the police. However, as always, such instructions can sometimes go awry. Dora, having been told by her parents what to do if ever she saw a fire, immediately rang the emergency services whenever the neighbours had a small bonfire, or if she saw smoke coming out of a chimney. Stevie, who had gradually learned to travel farther afield on his bike, had been taught that he should go into a police station if ever he got really lost. On one occasion this did happen, but Stevie did not panic, did exactly as he had been told, and was brought home in a police car. Unfortunately, he was so thrilled by the experience that each weekend he began to go further and further away from home, seeking out new police stations to whom he could turn for help.

There are, of course, many other ways of helping to improve self-help and independence skills. Shaping and prompting procedures can be used with less able children to teach basic feeding, washing, toileting and dressing skills. Carr (1995) provides detailed advice on procedures that are very effective with this group. Schoen and Sivil (1989) also illustrate how a combination of procedures, involving increased assistance, time delay and observational learning can help even pre-school children to develop self-help skills. Other examples can be found in Schopler (1995).

OTHER WAYS OF IMPROVING SOCIAL INTERACTIONS AND SOCIAL UNDERSTANDING

Quirk-Hodgson (1995) and Groden and Le Vasseur (1995) provide helpful suggestions on how picture scripts—illustrating situations that present problems for the child, together with guidance on how they should or should not behave in these circumstances—can be used to rehearse difficult situations and to develop more effective strategies for self-control. Greater participation in family activities, including leisure pursuits, social interactions, self-care and housekeeping tasks, may also be encouraged by using photographic activity schedules, illustrating the procedures to be followed. Krantz and her co-workers (1993) found that, by following schedules of this kind, children could learn to take part in a range of different work and play activities. These were well maintained over the course of the following year, and also resulted in a diminution in behavioural problems.

Gray (1995) describes the use of 'Social stories' that can help children understand social situations on an individual basis. The construction and use of the stories involves four basic processes. Firstly, a situation that is difficult for the child is targeted. Next, detailed information is obtained concerning the situation, the child's abilities and interests, and possible reasons for his or her current responses. These are then gathered together in the form of a story. In the next stage the child is provided with information regarding the target situation and expected responses, and finally new responses are identified and clearly defined, and potential strategies supported by individualised teaching materials. Pictures or photographs can be used to illustrate the stories; audio cassettes may be used for children who cannot read independently, or video-taped stories may be used instead. The story also needs to be shared with relevant individuals in the child's environment. Stories can be used to establish social routines (using 'fill in the blank' procedures) and to improve the ability to make social judgements. They may also be useful in helping others better to understand the child's perceptions and responses.

Quill (1995) suggests a number of other ways of promoting social interactions, both with adults and other children. These include activity routines, involving activities that are highly motivating for the child, have clear goals, shared roles and a set script to follow, and which, while being repetitive and predictable, also allow scope for expansion and flexibility. The need to establish joint attention is stressed, as is the importance of clear communication and modelling. Environmental supports such as cue cards, message boards, writing pads and so forth are also advised as a way of generalising and maintaining skills.

The importance of environmental supports to improve flexibility and independence in social functioning is also stressed by Dalrymple (1995). These can include timers (digital, sand, oil or clockwork) to indicate when an activity should be begun or completed; jigs, markers or positional cues to indicate where or what should be done; cues (such as particular songs or an action by the teacher) that indicate that an activity has come to an end; pictures or charts to indicate the daily routine, or changes to this routine; labels to identify personal property; and a whole range of other cues that avoid the need for complex verbal explanations or instructions.

Video feedback can prove useful for older children, who may be much more able to identify, and hence modify, unusual social behaviours if they see themselves on the screen. Fifteen-year-old Gordon, who greatly enjoyed role-play activities, always denied that he had any social problems—difficulties were due to the fact that 'other people were stupid' or 'didn't understand' him. However, if shown a video of himself, he was quite willing to identify behaviours that were 'not quite perfect' and would then try to remedy them. Kern and colleagues (1995) have also reported on the value of video feedback for improving peer interactions between students with other social and behavioural difficulties.

Awareness of problems may be enhanced, too, by feedback from other people. Simon was a young teenager who shared a number of common interests with his two brothers, including cycling and going to the cinema. However, they became increasingly embarrassed by his tendency to grimace and mutter to himself if he were bored or angry. They helped to overcome this problem by handing him a newspaper or magazine to cover his face every time he began to grimace. As reading also distracted him the behaviour would usually cease quite quickly. Simply nagging him, on the other hand, tended to raise his anxiety and resulted in an increase in mannerisms.

Although the methods described above are all suggested as useful ways of improving social competence in children with autism, none has been systematically evaluated on a large sample, many are based on anecdotal reports and there is little information about which techniques are likely to be most effective for particular children. The overall message, however, is that social development will not be enhanced simply by telling the child what to do. Prompting and fading techniques, modelling and direct teaching will be required and, as far as possible, non-verbal cues will be needed either to supplement or to replace verbal instruction.

INCREASING SOCIAL ACCEPTANCE

Many children with autism, unless they also have severe learning disabilities, tend to have isolated areas of skill, such as memory or number. In that normal children will be more willing to tolerate a peer who is 'different' if he or she has some special abilities it is important to try to develop such skills as far as possible. With guidance from teachers, children can be helped to use these skills in order to foster social interactions or to increase their acceptance within the classroom. For example, allowing a student who is good at spelling or arithmetic to help other less able pupils can greatly enhance self-esteem; while someone with a particular skill in drawing, or extensive knowledge of specific topics may be a useful contributor to class projects. (Chapter 7 describes how even stereotyped activities might be used in this way.)

SOCIAL SKILLS GROUPS

As already stressed, the rules of social behaviour are not easy to define. If such rules do exist they are highly complex, and constantly changing according to the social context. This is particularly so when dealing with more complex and subtle social skills. Knowing how to make friends, recognising how other people are feeling or thinking, and being able to react appropriately, are fundamental human aptitudes; they are not rule-based skills that are acquired through teaching. Thus, interventions designed to overcome such basic deficits are almost certain to be limited in their effectiveness. Nevertheless, there is some evidence that social skills groups, specifically designed for individuals with autism can improve certain aspects of social functioning (Williams, 1989; Howlin, 1997a; Mesibov, 1983). Tim Williams used procedures adapted from Spence (1980) for teaching social skills to autistic children and adolescents, over a four-year period. The children, aged between 9 and 15 years when the study began, showed improvements in verbal interactions with both adults and peers; their non-verbal communication skills also improved. Most children seemed to enjoy the sessions (although one child referred to them as 'Social Kills') but in this, as in other studies, generalisation to untrained settings was limited. This is probably because no two social situations are absolutely identical, and unless the child is able to *modify* learned skills in order to meet the demands of the new situation, training of this sort will have only a limited impact. In reality, to have optimum effect, social skills training is best conducted in each and every situation to which the child is exposed, so that he or she learns how to respond appropriately at home, with relatives, in shops, at school, or with the peer group. Each of these situations will require different social strategies. Teaching new skills, or correcting errors in situ, is far more likely to be effective than teaching in the relative isolation of a 'social skills group'.

INVOLVEMENT OF PEERS

One of the most difficult and demanding tasks for children with autism is learning how to interact appropriately with children of their own age. It may be relatively easy to learn and employ social skills strategies with adults, who are generally more understanding and tolerant of the child's problems. Harris and her colleagues (1990) found that adolescents with autism could be taught to recognise the need for help and to offer assistance to adults who made it clear that they were unable to complete a task. Simpler co-operative tasks with adults can also be systematically shaped—although sometimes even this can take many hours of teaching.

Coe and his colleagues (1990) for example, found that up to 50 sessions were required to teach children to take part in a ball-throwing task.

Peers, however, are notoriously intolerant of behaviours that are different or unusual in any way. The 'rules' of engagement: of knowing how to enter a group of children, how to join in with their activities, how to talk to them, are all highly complex, unwritten and generally poorly understood (Dodge *et al.*, 1983) and hence far more difficult to teach. Because of this, some researchers have shifted the focus of attention onto non-autistic peers—helping them to play and interact more effectively with the child with autism (Lord, 1996; Wolfberg & Schuler, 1993).

Roeyers (1996) has shown that providing non-handicapped peers with information about children with autism, and general instructions about ways to encourage them to play, could improve the frequency and style of joint interactions. Incidental teaching by peers can also be helpful. In order to achieve longer term success in such programmes, however, the setting needs to be carefully structured and highly skilled input from teachers is required if the interactions are to be effective. Hauck and her co-workers (1995) found that autistic children would only attend to social situations when these were well structured and when adults actively directed them into closer proximity with peers. Zanolli *et al.* (1996) also found that in order to increase social initiations by young autistic children it was necessary to use high levels of prompts, modelling and reinforcement, as well as training peers how to respond. Krantz and McClannahan (1993) recommend the use of written scripts to encourage social interactions. They found that when scripts were introduced (e.g. suggestions to ask for items or comment on other children's activities, such as 'Can I have . . .?' or 'I like your picture'), peer initiations increased and, as the use of scripts was faded, unscripted initiations increased.

Careful attention needs to be given, too, to the play environment and to the types of play material available (Schleien *et al.*, 1995; Wolfberg, 1995). If these are novel and interesting for autistic and non-autistic children alike, and necessitate some degree of co-operation, interaction is more likely to be enhanced. Wolfberg and Schuler (1993) have conducted extensive research on promoting play activities in integrated play groups. They suggest that in order to enhance play activities the following stages are required: careful analysis of the child's spontaneous play levels; adult support to model, direct and guide play activities; enlisting peers to initiate play activities; teaching the autistic child to respond to initiations or cues from peers; and teaching them how to maintain or expand interactions with peers. Specific strategies needed to improve the ability to play include teaching the autistic children to tolerate proximity to peers; mirroring the child's own actions; encouraging parallel play; teaching children to attend to different aspects of the same play activity (joint focus);

teaching them to co-ordinate play activities and to take turns (joint action); portraying real life activities, such as cooking, shopping or feeding dolls (role enactment); and finally role playing involving more complex and interactive scenarios (Wolfberg, 1995).

Schreibman and her colleagues (Oke & Schreibman, 1990; Pierce & Schreibman, 1995) also report increases in complex social behaviours— including joint attention and play initiations—after peers were taught to initiate and encourage play by using role-play, modelling and instructional techniques. It is evident that a variety of different strategies can be implemented in order to improve social interactions between children with autism and their peers. These can result in important short-term gains and are clearly important for improving opportunities for integration. Nevertheless, even with intensive support, it can prove difficult to maintain peers' enthusiasm over the longer term (Lord, 1984).

Another approach aimed at enhancing interactions between more able children with autism and their peers involves the setting up of a 'circle of friends' (Newton *et al.*, 1996). 'Circles' originated in the USA as a means of promoting the inclusion into mainstream schools of children with disabilities and behavioural difficulties. A circle usually consists of six or eight volunteers, usually from the same class or tutor group, who meet regularly with the focus child and an adult facilitator. The circle has three main tasks: (1) to identify difficulties; (2) to set targets and devise strategies for achieving these, and help put these ideas into practice; (3) to offer encouragement and recognition for success and progress. Among the reported benefits for the focus child are improved social integration, higher levels of peer contact and reduced anxiety. The interpersonal skills of non-autistic circle members also seem to improve.

INCREASING SPONTANEOUS PLAY

The lack of imaginative play shown by most children with autism is one of the characteristics that most marks them out from other children and one that further impairs their ability to interact with peers. However, pretend activities can be increased using a variety of different strategies, including modelling, shaping and instructional procedures. The activities can range from simple actions such as 'Show me how you laugh . . . Show me how you cry . . . Show me how to be a horse . . . Show me how to be a car' to more complex activities, such as 'Put dolly to bed . . . Make mummy a cup of tea . . . Give teddy his medicine'. Van Berkalaer-Onnes (1994) describes the stages that might be followed in moving from simple toy manipulations to pretend play. Board games involving some element of imagination, such as Monopoly or Cluedo, can be helpful with older children as can modified versions of games such as charades (Howlin & Rutter, 1987a).

Role-play activities have been reported as helpful in other cases (Howlin & Rutter, 1987a; McGhee, 1983). Thorp *et al.* (1995) found that training in socio-dramatic play techniques was helpful while Stahmer (1995) used 'Pivotal Response Training' (which involves turn taking, reinforcement, frequent task variation, encouraging individual choice and using natural consequences) to increase both elicited and spontaneous symbolic play. The children involved generalised their skills to new situations and also developed new, and untrained play themes. However, interactions with peers showed only minimal change.

Libby and colleagues (1996) have used photographs of children engaged in different activities to promote pretend play, although the play themes subsequently enacted tended to be exact replications of those shown on the photographs, rather than demonstrating spontaneous or novel themes. Modifications of popular card games, such as Happy Families, have been reported by Jordan and Libby (1997) to improve interactive abilities (as well as communication, classification and memory skills).

CAN CHILDREN BE TAUGHT TO UNDERSTAND MINDS?

Despite the success of such approaches in helping to improve play and social skills, the results reported have generally been specific to the activities taught, and there are few indications of widespread generalisation to other aspects of social or imaginative functioning. Some recent studies, therefore, have tried to address the more fundamental deficits which are postulated to underlie children's problems in social understanding and imagination.

The inability of children with autism to 'mind-read', i.e. to understand other people's beliefs, ideas, thoughts or feelings, has received much attention over recent years (see Baron-Cohen, 1995, for an excellent summary) and several researchers have attempted to develop intervention procedures based on this work. These have confirmed that even after relatively brief treatment programmes, involving computers, pictures, photographs, toys or actors, children with autism can show improvements in their ability to understand beliefs and emotions. Swettenham (1995), using a specially designed computer, found that young, normally developing children, and those with autism or Down's syndrome, could be trained to pass a false belief task (understanding that a character *thinks* that an object is in a particular place, even though in reality the child knows it is somewhere else). However, unlike the other two groups, the

Table 6.1: Different levels of ability in three domains—understanding emotions, beliefs and pretence (data from Hadwin *et al.* 1996)

Level	Emotion	Belief	Pretence
1	Face recognition	Simple perspective taking	Sensorimotor play
2	Schematic facial recognition	Complex perspective taking	Functional play (≤ 2 examples)
3	Situation based	Seeing leads to knowing	Functional play (> 2 examples)
4	Desire based	True belief/action prediction	Pretend play (< 2 examples)
5	Belief based	False belief	Pretend play (> 2 examples)

children with autism were unable to generalise this ability to new tasks. Ozonoff and Miller (1995), in a small-scale study of five boys, used a variety of training techniques to improve children's ability to understand mental states, as well as teaching specific interactional and conversational skills. In comparison with the control group, the treated children showed significant improvements in their understanding of other people's (false) beliefs. However, there were no changes in parental or teacher ratings of overall social competence.

Using a much larger sample and a greater range of teaching techniques, together with a developmental approach to teaching, Hadwin *et al.* (1996) set out to try to improve children's functioning in areas associated with the ability to understand minds. In one group teaching focused on developing the ability to understand informational states, such as beliefs; in another, to understand emotions; and, in a third, to improve pretend play. The different stages of teaching are summarised in Table 6.1 and the characteristics of the children involved described in Table 6.2.

These stages were based on what is known about the development of mental state understanding in normal children (Wellman, 1990) and this also ensured that teaching followed a developmental sequence. In order to make learning as 'naturalistic' as possible the teaching environment was enhanced by using a broad range of methods, including play, pictures, computers and games. The tasks themselves were designed to be as rewarding as possible for the children, and the materials used offered rapid and clear feedback on the children's performance. Praise and encouragement were given at every stage. If errors were made the child was immediately prompted with the correct response in order to avoid any perseveration of mistakes, or misunderstanding.

Table 6.2: Characteristics of children involved in 'Theory of mind' training

N = 30*	Mean	Range
Age	9.02 years	4.04–13.07 years
Receptive grammar	5.03 years	2.00–11.0 years
Expressive language	5.21 years	2.75–12.0 years

* Three training groups: Emotion, Belief and Pretence; 10 subjects in each training group.

In addition, the teaching procedures attempted to overcome at least some of the problems of generalisation that have occurred in other studies of this kind. Evidence suggests that teaching children about the *principles* that underlie concepts is more effective than simple instruction, as it helps them to generalise what they learn more effectively (Perry, 1991). For many children, of course, such principles do not need to be made explicit, but when there is a failure to learn by normal means, as is the case for children with autism, these principles may need to be taught 'inductively' through intensive training with many examples, and by means of a variety of different techniques (e.g. dolls and puppet stories, role play, picture stories, etc.). In this study children were provided with *general principles* in order to help them learn specific mental state concepts (Baron-Cohen & Howlin, 1993). In doing so an attempt was made to formalise and make explicit principles which, in normal development, are presumably implicit (Perner, 1991; Wellman, 1990).

As indicated above, teaching was aimed at a range of different mental state concepts: emotion, informational states and pretence. The extent to which teaching in one area resulted in the generalisation of learning to other aspects of the children's development was evaluated in a number of different ways. The first, termed 'near generalisation', assessed performance on tasks involving the specific concept taught (pretence, belief or emotion) using novel materials after teaching. The second, called 'distant generalisation', checked if teaching in one area of mental state understanding (e.g. emotion) would have beneficial effects for understanding areas where no teaching had been given (e.g. pretence). In addition, given the recognised social and communicative deficits in autism, assessments also addressed the issues of whether learning about mental state terms would result in improvements in communication skills generally and whether, more specifically, children would increase their spontaneous use of mental state terms.

Understanding Emotions

In the first of these tasks (Level 1) children were taught to identify emotions (happy, sad, anger, fear) from photographs. The next stage (Level 2)

Figure 6.1.

involved the identification of the same emotions from schematic drawings (see Figure 6.1).

Level 3 requires the child to identify emotions within a given context and Figure 6.2 (i–iv) gives examples of the types of scenario used. For each scene the child is encouraged to point to, colour in, or find a matching sticker for the appropriate emotion.

At Level 4, the task is to identify emotions according to what the characters want, and what they think they are going to get. If the character's wish is fulfilled then he or she will feel happy, if not he or she will feel sad (see Figure 6.3 (i–ii)).

Finally (Level 5), children were shown scenarios in which characters could have true or false beliefs, and in which desires could be fulfilled or unfulfilled. Again the task is to identify the appropriate emotion (see, for example, Figure 6.4 (i–iv)).

Look, the big dog is chasing Dan down the road.

How does Dan feel when the dog chases him?

sad?

happy?

cross?

scared?

Betty's Grandma gives her a teddy for her birthday.

How does Betty feel when her Grandma gives
her a teddy?

sad?

happy?

cross?

scared?

Kim's Daddy has to go away on a trip.

How does Kim feel when her Daddy goes
away?

sad?

happy?

cross?

scared?

*Glenn takes Jacky's pen. Jacky cannot finish her
picture.*

How does Jacky feel when Glenn takes her
pen?

sad?

happy?

cross?

scared?

Figure 6.2.

In the little picture you can see what Tracey wants.

What does Tracey want?

Mummy gives Tracey an apple for lunch.

How does Tracey feel when her Mummy gives her an apple for lunch?

Does she feel

In the little picture you can see what Adrian wants.

What does Adrian want?

Adrian's Mummy has bought him a car book.

How does Adrian feel when his Mummy buys him a car book?

Will he feel

Figure 6.3.

Lucy has bought George a packet of sweets.

This is George.

This little picture shows you what George wants.

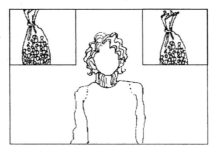

This one shows you what he thinks he will get.

What does George want?

What does George think he will get?

How does George feel?

Does he feel   sad?
                happy?

Look, Lucy gives George the packet of sweets.

How does George feel when Lucy gives him the packet of sweets?

Does he feel   sad?
                happy?

Figure 6.4.

Informational (Belief) Understanding

A similar breakdown of developmental stages was used in teaching children to understand other people's beliefs, knowledge and perception and to help increase the complexity of their developmental play.

In Levels 1 and 2 the tasks involved visual perspective taking. This is the understanding that different people can see different things or that they can see the same thing from different angles. At Level 3 a variety of toys, containers and other objects were used to help children understand that people only know things that they have experienced (directly or indirectly). Children in this group were taught the principle that 'seeing leads to knowing'. Levels 4 and 5 involve the ability to predict actions on the basis of a person's knowledge. Level 4 tests the child's understanding of *True belief*. Here, children are required to predict a person's actions on the basis of where that person believes an object to be. Level 5 requires the child to be able to understand *False belief*. Here children were required to predict a person's actions on the basis of where that person *falsely* believes an object to be. These tasks were taught using both play materials and computerised teaching programmes.

Increasing Pretend Play

Because of the complexity and variety of children's spontaneous play activities, teaching in this group was rather more flexible and varied than in the other two groups, and depended more on the child's current skills and interests. Toys, dressing-up clothes, miniature household equipment and figures, and a variety of different constructional materials, were used to help children progress through the different stages of play.

Level 1 (sensorimotor play) is the stage at which children simply manipulate toys and objects. This stage can include banging, waving or sucking objects. It also includes ritualistic or stereotyped behaviours, such as lining up toys or sorting them by size or colour. Level 2 (functional play) occurs when the child uses toys in a socially conventional way, but with no pretence (e.g. putting a cup on a saucer; pushing a car along). At Level 3 the child was directly encouraged and prompted to engage in pretend-play activities. These included:

(i) *Object substitution*, where one object is made to stand in for another object; for example, a child may pretend that a wooden block is a car.
(ii) *Attribution of pretend properties*, which involves attributing false properties to an object in play; for example, when a child cleans his or her doll's face as if it were dirty.

(iii) *Use of imaginary objects/scenarios,* which involves the use of imaginary objects or actions in play; for example, drinking tea from an empty cup or making a car have an imaginary collision.

At Level 4, the adult performs a pretend action and then asks the child if he or she is *really* doing it or just *pretending.* Level 5 is spontaneous pretend play. This is when children produce one of the forms of pretend play listed in Level 3 but without the need for prompting from the teacher. (For more information on all the training techniques and materials used see Howlin *et al.*, 1998.)

The Results of Teaching Children to 'Understand Minds'

As can be seen from Figure 6.5, significant changes were found in children's ability to understand emotions and informational states after only a relatively brief (two-week) training period, and these improvements were maintained long after intervention ceased (Hadwin *et al.*, 1996).

However, although there was some generalisation to non-taught tasks within the same domain, there was little generalisation to other, non-taught aspects of theory of mind (i.e. children who improved in their

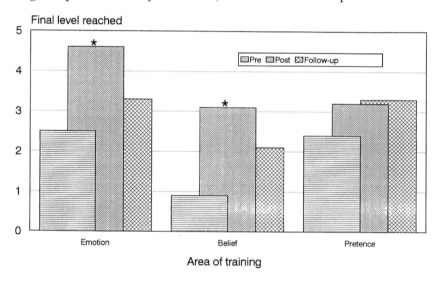

No differences between the groups in initial level. * Change from initial level significant at $p<0.05$

Figure 6.5: Increases in children's level following 'Theory of mind' training.

understanding of emotions after training showed no improvements in their understanding of beliefs, and vice versa). Furthermore, few improvements were found in the development of imaginative play activities and children's spontaneous language usage did not reflect a greater use of mental state terms (Hadwin *et al.*, 1997). Nevertheless, the fact that even brief interventions of this kind can make a significant impact on certain aspects of children's learning is promising. Longer training periods, the involvement of families and schools in therapy, the introduction of the tasks into the children's every day activities, rather than teaching in isolation, and a combined approach to the teaching of emotions, beliefs, play and pretence, could greatly enhance the effectiveness of the methods used and certainly offer the potential for more effective intervention. It is possible, too, that teaching packages specifically designed to increase the ability to 'mindread' could be an important and valuable addition to the educational curricula for many children with autism (Howlin *et al.*, 1998).

THE IMPORTANCE OF PARENTS IN HELPING TO IMPROVE SOCIAL INTERACTIONS

As with studies of language teaching, much systematic work on the development of social skills has taken place in classroom or specialist settings. Although the need to involve parents is widely recognised, this

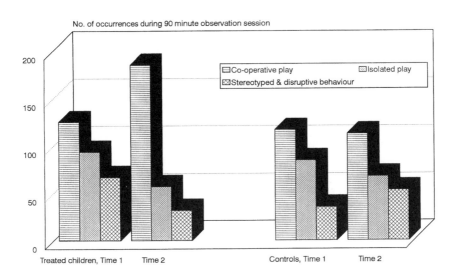

Figure 6.6: Changes in play and social interactions—comparison between treated and control children after 6 months.

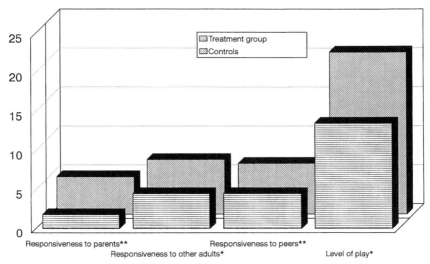

N.B. The higher the rating the greater the level of abnormality. * = group differences significantly at $p<0.05$; **significant at $p<0.01$

Figure 6.7: Parents' ratings of abnormalities in social behaviour and play
after 18 months of treatment.

is less often done in practice. In the home-based study of Howlin and
Rutter (1987a) specific emphasis was placed on teaching parents how to
encourage and elicit joint play activities and social interactions. Observational measures indicated that in the first six months of intervention
mothers in the experimental group became more involved in the child's
activities and they began to direct and praise the child's behaviours more
frequently. There were few changes in the behaviour of mothers in the
control group. Over the same time period children in the experimental
group significantly increased the amount of time in which they spent in
co-operative play activities with their mother, and solitary play, ritualistic
and disruptive behaviours all decreased (see Figure 6.6).

There were no significant improvements in the behaviour of children in
the control group. Over the total 18 months of intervention, parents in the
intervention group reported that they perceived their children as showing fewer abnormalities in their relationships with the family, with other
adults and with their peers. Play behaviour, too, was rated as less deviant.
Control children, in contrast, were generally rated as showing more difficulties in each of these areas (see Figure 6.7).

Problems of Increased Social Awareness

Impaired social awareness is one of the most common problems with
which parents of a child with autism have to cope. However, for some

more able children, especially as they grow older, their greater awareness of socially accepted norms can also give rise to difficulties. Recognition that other children in the family can do things which they are not allowed to do—such as staying out late at night, going on trips with friends, going out with boy/girl friends—can give rise to deep resentment and antagonism. If siblings leave home, or get married, the sense of injustice may be particularly strong. This is even more likely to occur if the other siblings are actually younger than the child with autism, so that excuses such as 'You're not old enough' will simply not work. Alternatively, if the child with autism is younger, then that child may grow up believing that he or she, will also be able to leave home or have a partner as soon as the magic age of 18, or 20, or whatever is attained.

There is no entirely satisfactory solution to problems of this kind, although resentments may be minimised if the child with autism is encouraged to develop his or her independence and to lead as varied a life as possible. Special activity groups, holidays, or even respite care can provide some degree of independence from the family, and although they may not form any strong attachments to the other children whom they meet in these settings, they can at least view themselves as having 'friends'.

Social Demands on Children with Asperger Syndrome

Finally, it is important to consider, separately, the social demands with which more able children, or those with Asperger syndrome, are expected to cope. Although often described as a 'mild' form of autism, the social difficulties experienced by children with Asperger syndrome are, in many cases, just as pervasive and as devastating as those of less able children. Indeed, their particular tragedy lies in the fact that, because of their intellectual ability, they are often painfully aware of their difficulties and differences.

In a number of personal accounts, individuals with Asperger syndrome have described themselves as feeling like aliens from another planet (Jolliffe et al., 1992; Sinclair, 1992) or, in Temple Grandin's words, as being like an 'Anthropologist from Mars' (Sacks, 1993). She is said to have attempted to deal with her difficulties in social understanding by building up

> a vast library of experiences over the years . . . They were like a library of video tapes, which she could play in her mind . . . of how people behaved in different circumstances. She would play these over and over again, and

learn, by degrees, to correlate what she saw, so that she could then predict how people in similar circumstances might act. It is strictly a logical process' she explained. (Sacks, 1993)

However, much social understanding requires us to step beyond the realms of logic. In many cases, the rules governing social interactions are so complex and changeable that for many children with autism life is probably more like the one described in *Through the Looking Glass*. Here, like Alice, they are constantly being given apparently senseless, arbitrary or impossible instructions, which can change from one moment to the next. Whatever they do is likely to lead to problems and, however hard they try, they can never really 'fit in'.

Most children with classic autism are guided through this world by adults who, at least partially, understand the extent of their difficulties. For children with Asperger syndrome, specialist help, or even sympathy, may prove much more difficult to find. Indeed, because of their relatively high cognitive ability, and their *apparently* competent communication skills, this group of children is often least well served or understood. They may well have extensive linguistic difficulties (especially involving abstract or complex concepts); their understanding of the more subtle aspects of social interaction is often profoundly limited, and their stereotyped interests and behaviours also prove a barrier to social integration. Despite this, only a minority receive any specialist provision. Most have to cope in mainstream school with little or no help. Their parents may be dismissed as over-protective, or too lax, and can find it very difficult to get the support or advice they need. Moreover, the children's good vocabulary, and even their well-developed obsessional interests, frequently give the impression that they are capable of far higher levels of achievement than is actually the case. Others' expectations of their social competence tend to be unrealistically high, and when these expectations are not met the children are viewed as negative, unco-operative, rude and manipulative. Seemingly so close to 'normality', there is constant pressure for them to 'fit in', in ways that would never be demanded of a less able autistic child. This can lead to enormous pressure, resulting in extreme levels of anxiety and stress, which in turn can further impede social progress.

Because of their very uneven profile of skills and deficits, such children may require even more highly specialised help than those with global learning difficulties. Unfortunately, such help is rarely available, and although provision for autistic children, generally, has improved markedly over the past few decades, our knowledge of how effectively to help this particular group lags far behind.

7

COPING WITH STEREOTYPED AND RITUALISTIC BEHAVIOURS

STRATEGIES FOR TREATMENT

A Graded Change Approach

Although many different ways of dealing with ritualistic and stereotyped behaviours have been reported in the literature, as far as home-based interventions are concerned, a 'graded change' approach seems generally to be the most effective. Thus, just as stereotypies and routines tend to grow gradually, often almost imperceptibly, over time, programmes to reduce these are best if carried out in gradual and carefully planned stages. Graded change is particularly useful in helping children to cope with environmental changes or alterations in daily routine.

For children with autism, stereotyped and ritualistic activities often play a crucial role in reducing anxiety and providing them with some control over what is otherwise a confusing and unpredictable world (see Jolliffe *et al.*, 1992). If an attempt is made suddenly to restrict or prohibit such behaviours, this can lead to unacceptably high levels of anxiety and distress. Because of the resulting disturbance that ensues, most parents then give in, thereby strengthening rather than weakening the behaviour. Moreover, without careful planning, children may develop replacement routines, which can prove even more disruptive. On the other hand, if no attempt is made to reduce behaviours of this type, then they are very likely to dominate not only the child's activities, but also those of his or her family.

Dominic, for example, was a 4-year-old boy who had been adopted at around 18 months. Although it was not known at that time that he had autism, his adoptive parents had been told to expect difficulties initially because of the disturbance he had experienced in the early months of his life. They had, understandably, given in to his somewhat strange behaviours, attributing these to early deprivation and abuse. However, by the age of 5, his rituals totally dominated the household. The kitchen was 'decorated' with thick, felt tip pen outlines of the wiring system in the local fire station (to which he was always running away). He had developed an obsession with people talking in opposites, so that if his mother wanted him to come in, or take off his shoes she would have to tell him to 'Go outside' or 'Put your shoes on'. He also insisted that stories and fairy tales were told 'in opposites', leading his mother to recount tales of 'Blacklocks and the four mice who ate porridge that was so cold it froze their tongues'. At one stage he insisted that men should live upstairs and women downstairs in the house (as a small boy he could go anywhere). Thus, his father would have to go upstairs immediately he came home from work and was not allowed down until Dominic had gone to bed. In another case, Stevie's resistance to change meant that his parents had never been able to decorate the house or to replace worn-out items of furniture. When he began to attend weekly boarding school, and seemed to become rather more tolerant of change, they decided to refit the kitchen. As expected, on his return home Stevie protested loudly for two days but he eventually calmed down, much to his parents' relief. The next morning, when they entered the kitchen they found that he had drawn all over the newly decorated walls with a large felt tip pen, faithfully reproducing the outlines of the cupboards and fittings that had been replaced.

In the following sections possible approaches to a variety of different stereotyped and ritualistic activities are discussed. As with most interventions for autism, it is important to be aware that much of the work in this area has been based on small group or individual case research; hence, there are no satisfactory guidelines to enable parents to determine which approaches are most likely to work for their particular child, or for specific problems. However, the crucial elements of any programme are early intervention, gradual rather than sudden change, and careful attention to other relevant aspects of the child's environment. Further examples of imaginative ways of dealing with ritualistic and stereotyped behaviours can also be found in Schopler (1995).

STRATEGIES FOR INTERVENTION

Prevention is Better than Later Intervention

Attempts to modify long-standing stereotyped and ritualistic behaviours will almost always result in considerable difficulties and may well require very complex strategies. The more pervasive and entrenched the problems, the more imaginative and resourceful parents will need to be. The earlier intervention begins, therefore, the fewer, and less severe, the subsequent problems are likely to be.

The principal 'rule' is to try to ensure that, from the child's earliest years, stereotyped behaviours are under the control of those caring for the child, rather than parents themselves being dominated by the obsessions. This does not mean that all ritualistic or stereotyped tendencies should be strictly curtailed, but that limits should be set on where, with whom, for how long, or to what extent the behaviour can be tolerated.

The second rule, which admittedly requires some ability to see into the future, is never to allow or encourage behaviours in young children that will be unacceptable in later life. All too often, stereotyped or ritualistic behaviours present difficulties as individuals grow older, not because the intensity or frequency of the behaviours have increased, but because other people's attitudes have changed. Behaviours that are acceptable in a little child (such as a fascination with the feel of women's tights, or continued insistence on removing all clothing) will be viewed very differently when the same individuals reach late adolescence or adulthood.

Joey's fascination with washing machines, for example, had provided his mother with much needed respite when he was a child. However, by the time he was a large, active teenager he was well able to break into other people's houses to indulge his obsession, so that a previously innocuous behaviour became a threat both to himself and others. Adam, whose skill in 'mending' electrical equipment was considered a real party trick at the age of 7 (as when he rewired the video machine and Christmas tree lights together to see if turning on one would trigger the other), by the age of 12 required constant attention and supervision both at and away from home because of his hazardous behaviour.

Without help, parents are unlikely to be able to identify the potential problems related to rituals and routines and in order to avoid distressing a young child, will very naturally tend to tolerate these, perhaps with disastrous results in the future. It is up to professionals who are knowledgeable about autism, and the pattern that behaviours are likely to take in later life, to advise, and, in co-operation with carers, to help develop appropriate strategies for use by families and schools. Coping with an obsession of a few weeks' duration may be difficult, but it is not nearly as difficult as attempting to eliminate a behaviour that has been well entrenched for many years!

The third point is to remain vigilant and sensitive to the emergence of new or potential problems. Most children with autism will develop new interests or rituals over the years. Some of these may be short-lived, others may become very pervasive and disruptive. Knowing when or whether to intervene depends principally on knowledge and understanding of the individual child. In some cases parents know that it is wisest to pay little attention to new behaviours, in that if ignored they will tend to disappear again fairly rapidly. If, on the other hand, parents are aware that *in their child* stereotyped behaviours quickly become entrenched, intervention in the very earliest stages will be crucial if the problems are not to escalate.

RESISTANCE TO CHANGE

Many children with autism, particularly when young, can be very resistant to changes of any kind. When the windows in Giles's house were replaced, for example, he ran after the glaziers, desperately pleading with them to put the old ones back. Other children are unable to tolerate an ornament out of place or a chair in a slightly different position. Often, barely perceptible alterations to the position of a particular object can be the first step in helping the child to accept minor changes. Alternatively, parents might try to extend the limits within which an item can be placed. Suzanne, for example, would become very distressed if items in the house were moved, but often her parents had no clear idea of where exactly they should be positioned. Working together with Suzanne, they used marker pens to delineate the area within which certain items could be placed. To begin with she could tolerate only a few centimetres deviation but gradually the limits were extended, allowing her parents greater and greater leeway in their placement of these particular objects. Additional objects in the house were then treated in the same way. And, although in her own room Suzanne was allowed to restrict the placement of ornaments or other items much more rigidly, she was required to indicate, with a pen or sticker or other marker, where the objects should go, so that at least her mother could clean and tidy the room without provoking a major tantrum.

James would not leave the house unless all the chairs in the kitchen and dining area were placed in a line, a few centimetres away from the wall. If his brothers did not leave for school before him, he would check the kitchen continually in case they had moved something, and on an increasing number of occasions this behaviour had caused him to miss the school bus. In order to try to break this habit his parents began to insist that a *single* chair was left at the kitchen table while he was out; to encourage this they left a small 'prize' on the chair seat (a sweet or biscuit, or a favourite toy) which James could claim when he returned from school. Gradually the number of chairs that had to remain at the table was increased, and James had to guess where the prize would be found each day. Eventually, only one chair, on which he kept his collection of Star Wars figures, was allowed against the wall.

In some cases it needs to be recognised that changes that are enjoyed by normally developing children will be very distressing for the child with autism, and parents and teachers may need to take the decision whether or not to insist on these. Richard was an 8-year-old who became extremely upset by any change, and the beginning of school holidays, or the return to school were always times of considerable trauma for everyone involved. His birthday and Christmas were particularly upsetting days. The situation was helped, to some extent, by minimising the amount of special attention paid to him at such times. Thus, although they would wish him Happy Birthday or Christmas, and leave him with a box of presents, there was no insistence that he should open them. He was also allowed to eat his usual meal (sausages, chips and half a fried tomato) on these days. He would gradually open his presents over the next few days, and as he grew older he became better able to tolerate such occasions. His parents and teachers also agreed on a number of tasks that he could do, whether he was at home or at school, in order to ensure greater consistency between the two settings. So, for example, at school, he always collected the empty milk bottles for the bottle bank, just as he did at home; at home during the holidays he always spent an hour or so each evening doing 'homework' provided by his teachers. Richard was also helped to be better prepared for change by the use of simple calendars. He had always been fascinated by numbers and at the beginning of each term, and immediately at the start of each holiday, he was encouraged to work out how many days were left until the end of term/holiday. The pages in a note pad were carefully numbered, and a 'count down' (peeling off one page per day) began as soon as he returned to his home or his school, so that his interest in this action became a further factor in reducing his anxiety.

Hilda de Clerq (quoted in Peeters, 1997) describes the lengths to which she had to go in order to make Christmas tolerable for her son, Thomas, and the rest of the family:

> The festive season is coming around again . . . I'm really not looking forward to it because Thomas's daily routine is disturbed. But I have found one way of helping him. . . . I show him all the advertising brochures with the toy that Santa can bring, what he can do with the toy, how he can use it. We cut out all the pictures and stick them on pieces of paper. I make him a calendar with white pages so he can tear them off himself, one every day. He can see exactly how long it will be. We stick the picture with the surprise on a sheet of red paper. We then go to the shop to look at the real present because it doesn't look exactly the same as one in the advertisement. And if we can we borrow it from the toy library so I'm sure that it isn't too difficult for him and that he can work it.
>
> The night before Christmas I tell him where he can find the 'surprise' and in what kind of paper it will be wrapped. His brothers and sisters think that

half the fun is lost if they know about things beforehand. But when the big day comes and the red sheet turns up on his calendar, it is a real party for ALL the children. Even for Thomas because now he doesn't fling the paper on the ground, doesn't scream or cry. He has found what he expected. It was predictable. HIS SURPRISE. . . . And then I just melt because I see he is really happy.

Although some children are disturbed by even minor changes to their routine or environment, in other cases it is the unpredictable nature of change, rather than the change itself, that appears to give rise to difficulties. Although a structured and settled daily programme is essential for progress, it is neither possible nor productive to avoid change completely. Thus, as in the case of Thomas described above, the solution is to ensure that the child is made as aware as possible of what is going to happen at any time. Since verbal explanations are rarely adequate, visual representations (in the form of calendars, pictures or written lists) of forthcoming activities, or of planned alterations to the regular routine, are likely to be more effective. Samantha, for example, enjoyed a range of different activities during the week, but any unpredictable alterations could give rise to major disturbance. If a teacher's car were not in the parking area when she arrived at school, or if the person supervising the school crossing had changed, the remainder of the day's activities would be totally disrupted. Increasing her awareness, in advance, of possible changes helped to reduce the problem, at least to some extent. Picture calendars were used to illustrate the next day's activities, and photographs of staff members were used to indicate who would be at school and who would be away. If, as often happened, a teacher was away without prior warning, staff would focus on helping Samantha to find the appropriate photo and place it in the 'Away Today' column.

The danger in using picture calendars or charts with some children is that these, too, may begin to be used in a very rigid fashion. Thus, although each day may include very different activities, if one of these has to be changed or cancelled for some reason, disruption can still occur. Danny's teachers dealt with this by insisting that one or two activities during the course of the week had to be changed around on a weekly basis. While most of the week's timetable would be programmed in advance, pictures of certain activities, such as swimming or horse riding (which were particularly prone to alterations), could not be inserted until the time was confirmed. In turn, this meant that other activities might need to be re-scheduled. Over time Danny became much more able to cope with a flexible timetable, as long as he could always fill in the timetable immediately before the event occurred.

Stuart, had a similar picture timetable, largely filled in by his teachers. However, on each day one slot was left unfilled and Stuart had five cards, illustrating different activities, with which he had to fill in the gaps. Two of these were activities he did not particularly like, but which had to be done (swimming and milk rota); the remainder were things he very much enjoyed (light and sound room, trip to petrol station to fill up the school van, and video session). To begin with he would always put the disliked activities in the final days of the week but later he learned that, to get them over with, it was better to allot them to Monday and Tuesday.

Some children dislike not only general change but change from any one activity to another, and this can happen even if the new activity is one that the child actually enjoys. In such cases, some form of advance warning seems to reduce distress and the behaviours associated with it—such as protests or stereotyped motor mannerisms (Tustin, 1995). Verbal warnings alone are unlikely to be adequate, and are best accompanied by additional visual or auditory cues. For 6-year-old Brian *any* change of activity could cause distress. In the morning he would cry when made to brush his teeth (which he particularly disliked) but he would also cry when told to stop and come and have breakfast. He would cry when beginning any new activity at school, but would protest equally strongly when this came to an end. His teacher decided to use an 'hourglass' filled with coloured oils (these took exactly 5 minutes to move from the top to the bottom of the container) to indicate that the current activity would soon be coming to an end. His fascination with watching the timer reduced his protests about change and his teacher then began to accumulate a collection of different 'timers'. His curiosity to find out which one would be used made him begin to look forward to a change in activities. At home, however, his mother found that allowing him to watch the timer tended to prolong many activities, and this could cause problems for other people—especially in the rush before morning school. She used smaller timers successfully, instead, as a reward for *completed* activities.

DEALING WITH OTHER ROUTINES

The range of stereotyped, ritualistic activities in which children with autism may become involved is probably endless. Fixed rituals around mealtimes are particularly common, with children demanding that food is always prepared at a set time or served in a particular way. Amanda, for example, not only ate a very limited range of foods (mainly fish-fingers, peas and carrots and potato shapes), she also insisted that these were of a particular brand, and would search for the packets before she accepted them. She would only eat at a certain time, only sit in one place at the table and only used specific items of china and cutlery. She insisted on chewing each mouthful of food ten times and each item of food had to be in a particular position on the plate. If any two items touched she would refuse to eat them. Meanwhile she demanded that her father sat with his right foot crossed over his left, and she would be constantly peering under the table to ensure that this demand, too, was complied with. In consequence, mealtimes became ill-tempered, long drawn out affairs that gave little pleasure to anyone.

Her parents began by slightly altering the time of meals. She was told that lunch would be between 11.55 and 12.05, but that it would not be exactly at 12.00, as she had previously insisted. Marks were drawn on the clock face to indicate these limits. After her mother inadvertently broke her favourite plate Amanda was allowed to choose *two* new ones, which were randomly presented at different meals. Next, a half-hour time limit was set on meals. If she had finished within this time she was then allowed to watch a sequence of her current, favourite video. If she did not finish in time she would be left to finish the meal alone. Amanda calculated that this meant she could only chew each mouthful eight times rather than ten and protested that she would suffer from terrible indigestion; nevertheless she usually complied. Finally, the post-meal video was only made accessible if she ate the meal without studying her father's feet. Mealtimes are still somewhat rigid affairs, but at least they are less time consuming and do not involve other members of the family in Amanda's routines.

With older children it is sometimes possible to alter routines by introducing some element of humour or guesswork into the situation. Phillip would become very upset while out on a shopping trip if the shop assistant were not the same as on the previous occasion. One summer holiday had been totally ruined because the deck chair attendant who had been there the previous year had left. His mother attempted to modify this behaviour by suggesting that before they left to go shopping she and Phillip would guess which shops would be the same and which ones would be different. The 'winner' would get to choose a 50p prize before they came home. Phillip soon realised that predicting differences was more likely to win prizes than expectations of stability, and although he continued to protest at change the behaviour did become easier to cope with.

Trouble arose in Gerald's case because of his literal interpretation of his mother's promises when she took him out in the car. If she said 'We're going to the shops' or 'to Auntie Jean's' and they went straight there, all was well. However, if they stopped en route for traffic lights, pedestrians or animals, or any other reason, he would become extremely violent and aggressive. She was on the point of discontinuing outings in the car altogether because of this, but then tried out the strategy described in Table 7.1. Firstly, she predicted a brief stop at a particular point of the journey, but then turned this into a 'guessing' game, whereby Gerald had to guess where they would stop (she would try to comply with these guesses if possible). In this way she gradually reduced his insistence on going *directly* from home to a given destination and helped him to develop a more flexible approach to journeys.

Table 7.1: The use of a graded change strategy to overcome resistance to stopping on journeys

Stages
- Predicted stop of 30 seconds close to home ('next to post office', 'outside ice-cream kiosk', etc.)
- Longer stop (1 minute) at predicted place; journey continues if no resistance
- 1 minute stop, but place not specified in advance
- Several brief stops on journey
- Journey length extended
- Normal shopping trips resumed

Table 7.2: Reduction of stereotyped activities

Problem	Stages of intervention
Collecting coins	1. Reduction in number of rooms where coins allowed. 2. Access to other enjoyed activities (TV, eating, getting into parents' bed) contingent on coins being removed from room. 3. Reduction in numbers of coins allowed in any one place. 4. Coins allowed only in bedroom.
Lining up toy cars	1. Gradual reduction in number of cars from 50 to 20. 2. Further reduction in length of lines to 5 cars only. 3. *Pairs* of cars only allowed in house, though these scattered in various rooms. 4. Cars used in imaginative play.
Motor mannerisms	1. 'Flapping' restricted at certain time of day (e.g. TV or mealtimes). 2. Increase in areas where flapping restricted. 3. Further restrictions to certain times only. 4. Flapping allowed only in own room.
Resistance to environmental change	1. Minor change in angle of single chair. 2. Chair gradually moved away from usual position. 3. Other chairs moved to different angles. 4. Gradual changes in other household items angles of doors, curtains, etc.).
Verbal rituals	1. Routines allowed only after period of non-stereotyped conversation. 2. Number of repetitive sessions per day gradually reduced. 3. Number of repetitive questions per session reduced. 4. Routines allowed briefly at bedtimes only.

In dealing with other routine or stereotyped activities, it is often helpful gradually to introduce rules that make it clear where, with whom, or how long the activity is allowed. This makes it clear to the child that the activity can take place, thereby avoiding an escalation in anxiety and distress, while at the same time placing certain restrictions on the behaviour. Some examples of this approach are outlined in Table 7.2.

Other routines, although not necessarily disruptive when they first appear, may eventually begin to prove more problematical. The previous chapter on social difficulties contains a number of examples of stereotyped behaviours that gave rise to increasing problems as children grew older. Tarquin's nose-squeezing behaviour was another such example. When very young the only physical contact he would accept from his mother was to have her gently squeeze his nose and later he began to reciprocate by squeezing hers. As he grew older the squeezes became increasingly frequent and more forceful. His mother could barely speak when he squeezed her, and as he became a particularly hefty teenager this behaviour in public appeared extremely bizarre. Unfortunately, attempts to persuade his mother that she should perhaps try to discourage the habit were unsuccessful as she did not want to interfere with his only means of expressing 'affection'.

Verbal Routines

The one class of obsessional behaviour that can prove particularly resistant to modification is that of verbal rituals and routines. While it may be relatively easy to restrict the time spent lining up cars or to insist that the collection of coins is kept in a specified place, placing limitations on verbal behaviours is much more difficult. The problems of developing *consistent* management strategies should never be underestimated. It is surprisingly easy to be drawn into stereotyped conversations, before even realising it, and if the subject matter is interesting or novel the individual with autism usually has little problem in finding an audience. Dan, who was fascinated by the subject of albinoism, could readily attract the attention of visitors with his extraordinary knowledge of this subject. Aaron, who spent all his time watching videos or reading about 'Thomas the Tank Engine' showed remarkable skill in turning any conversation around to this topic. Even deliberate attempts to discourage stereotyped conversation can backfire. Adam was a 7-year-old who was obsessed by playing with and talking about electrical equipment. He would become visibly excited whenever anyone tried to talk to him about the dangerousness of this behaviour, and such warnings simply seemed to 'feed' his preoccupation.

If parents are forewarned that such routines may develop, especially in the case of children who are verbally more competent, they may be able to set limits very early in childhood, or when the problem first becomes apparent. Simple but firm 'rules' about (a) *when* a topic can be discussed (e.g. only after answering a few questions about the day at school, or only at bath- or bedtimes); (b) *where* discussions take place (only in the house and never outside); or (c) *with whom* (e.g. with the class teacher, but only at the end of the day's work) can then help to minimise later difficulties. The crucial aspect seems to be to make it clear when the child WILL have the opportunity to indulge in his or her preoccupations as well as when he or she WILL NOT be allowed to do so. It needs to be recognised that attempts to prevent the child from ever talking about his or her special interests, or asking the ritualised questions, are likely to result in over-whelming anxiety and agitation. But, as long as the established rules make it clear that the routine is allowed at specified times, and as long as parents, other carers and teachers keep to their side of the agreement too, then a reasonable degree of control is usually possible. It is also important to try to intervene before the behaviour becomes well entrenched. If complete freedom is allowed in the early years, or if stereotyped discussions or questions reach a level when they totally dominate all other conversations, later intervention becomes far more difficult. Josh had always had a fascination with holes but at the age of 8 he suddenly began asking constant questions about how many holes there were in different things. Answering questions such as 'How many holes are there in snow when it melts?', 'How many holes are there in the ice on the roof?', 'How many holes are there in the hedge?', 'How many holes are in your lace sweater?' proved impossible to answer, although fortunately he did not seem to mind too much how accurate the answer was. Because Josh's parents soon recognised that this behaviour was becoming very fixed and rigid they rapidly intervened, insisting that he could only talk about holes for a maximum of 15 minutes at bedtime. If he thought of 'hole questions' at other times he was to write them down and save them up till later. This strategy soon brought the behaviour under reasonable control.

In contrast, Ricky had been very late to learn to talk, and hence his first phrases—which generally concerned places and distances—were much welcomed by his parents. By the age of 10 his speech was dominated with stereotyped questions, mainly about the distance and direction from his home town to various obscure places on the globe. Few people other than Ricky knew the answers to these queries and incorrect responses would provoke an outburst of rage and often verbal abuse. His parents did their best to impose restrictions on the frequency of questioning but they continued to find this behaviour very difficult, particularly if they were away from home, when his resulting tantrums proved extremely embarrassing.

The position was not helped by his grandparents, who, believing that their daughter's attempts to limit such questions were unfair and unkind, indulged this habit as much as they could whenever they visited.

OBJECT ATTACHMENTS

Many normally developing children form strong attachment to specific objects, such as teddy bears, soft toys, old blankets, pieces of cloth and so forth. For some these can be an important part of the growing-up process, and are especially needed when the child is ill, tired, anxious or unsettled (Boniface & Graham, 1979; Mahalski, 1983). Although the attachment can persist for several years, by the time they reach school age most children are aware that such attachments are not to be exhibited publicly, and they certainly do not interfere with other activities. The attachments of autistic children, while similar in some respects (i.e. they are used for comfort, and tend to be stronger if the child is ill, tired or distressed) are very different in other ways. Firstly, the nature of the object tends to be unusual. These are generally not the soft toys or cloths of the normal child but may be bits of string, certain types of elastic band, left-foot red wellingtons, blue sink plungers, particular makes of baby bottle or a partially dismembered doll's torso. Secondly, the attachment shows little sign of diminishing as the child reaches school age, and may disrupt other activities because of the insistence on carrying it at all times. The object may also become part of other ritualistic or stereotyped routines—for example, the elastic bands might be twisted in a particular way in front of the child's eyes. Loss or removal of the object is likely to cause severe and lasting distress.

One way in which some families deal with this problem is to ensure that the object never disappears, by having vast stocks of replacements continually at hand. In one case the father himself was always sorting through elastic bands in the office to find ones of the 'right' thickness and length for his son. In many others, parents, aunts and uncles, grandparents, nieces and nephews are constantly on the look out for dummies, baby bottles, sink plungers or drinking cups of particular shapes, makes or colours. Unfortunately, keeping cupboards full of the items in question does not tend to be the most effective way of solving the problem. Instead, as with other obsessions, gradual restrictions on where, when and with whom the object is allowed, are generally more successful. Again, too, it is crucial for the success of such programmes that there is consistency and agreement between all the adults involved in the child's care. If an attachment object is restricted at home, then it is not helpful to allow free access in school—or vice versa. If parents allow access to the object only at certain times of day, it is not helpful for other relatives, no matter how well meaning, surreptitiously to offer the object to the child at other times.

In some cases, when the attachment is particularly strong, it may not be possible to remove the object even a tiny distance from the child without causing enormous distress. Five-year-old Patrick, for example, would not relinquish his blanket in any circumstances. As Howlin and Rutter (1987a) describe, his mother could only wash it while he was asleep, and the strength of his attachment (together with the stereotyped hand movements which also accompanied it) effectively prevented him from taking part in most other activities. Because the blanket could not be removed during the day, his mother began to cut small pieces from it at night while he slept. Patrick seemed unaware of the resulting shrinkage, despite the fact that by the end of two months the blanket was reduced to a few threads. Eventually, because he was continually dropping these he began to lose interest in them and the attachment quite suddenly ceased. At the same time, another of his stereotyped behaviours, which involved carrying and twisting picture postcards in his left hand, also vanished, although this problem had never been directly addressed (see Figure 7.1).

In other cases, when carrying a particular object is likely to result in the child being teased, disguise may be a preferable option. Twelve-year-old William had a long-standing fascination with toy and model dinosaurs, and had a vast collection of these at home. When younger, his parents had laid down firm rules about the number of dinosaurs that could be

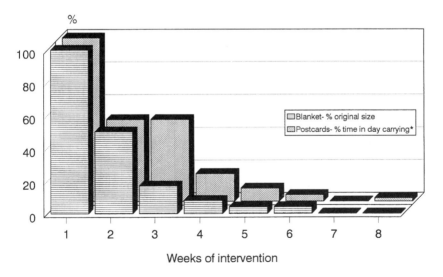

Weeks of intervention

* N.B. Attachment to postcards was never directly addressed

Figure 7.1: Graded change in the reduction of abnormal attachments to objects.

carried around, and by the time he was 10 he was only allowed to take one with him when he was away from home. However, he then selected increasingly larger toys, which instantly attracted other people's attention. His parents supplied him with a duffle bag, decorated with pictures of dinosaurs, in which to keep his 'pet'. This had the advantage of limiting the size of toy that could be carried; it also meant that, in the street at any rate, other children could not see what he was carrying and, therefore, had less opportunity to tease him.

Collecting Objects

Extensive collections of particular objects are another typically autistic characteristic. Tins, bus tickets, leaflets, glass jars, pieces of leaf, string or elastic band, magazines, records and audio or video tapes, spectacles, screws, fuses, stick insects, snails and woodlice are just a few of the items that may be hoarded. As with other obsessions, the collection is usually fairly innocuous to begin with but, if not treated with care, may come to dominate the household. Damion, for example, had accumulated 4,000 computer magazines by the time he was 14, and his room was completely covered by these. He had even put piles together to form make-shift stools and tables. Gerard's interest in stick insects was tolerated while he kept them in the shed, but unknown to his mother he was also bringing jars into his room. Since he was none too careful about replacing the tops, his parents awoke one day to a plague of insects covering the house. Other preoccupations can result in considerable expense for parents. Whereas a single Thomas the Tank Engine book, Star Wars model, or sweater with a Reebok logo on may not cost too much, definitive collections of all the items in a series can prove prohibitively expensive. Life may also be dominated by continual searches for objects of this kind. Other children may 'borrow' items (or money) in order to enhance their collection of, say, computer magazines, coins or model engines.

A total ban on such items is likely to prove counter-productive. Even attempts to remove one or two items surreptitiously from the collection may be instantly spotted and loudly resented. Again, therefore, the most effective way of proceeding is gradually to limit the number of objects in the collection. Janice had an extraordinary collection of glass jars, in which she kept the cut-off tails from toy animals. In addition to the damage this did to her toys, the glass collection was steadily growing, leaving little space in her bedroom for other things. Her father agreed to build a special cupboard in her bedroom for her jars, but once this was full she was not allowed to store any more. Any excess tails had to be kept in a box under the bed. Janice could not bear the thought of her precious tails being 'wasted' in this way, and hence reluctantly agreed not to cut off any more tails, unless these were particularly irresistible.

Byron had collected comics since he was tiny and, according to his mother, had never thrown away a single one, although they were hardly ever read. By the time he was 12 years old his room was full of comics, and he refused to let anyone move them. However, when the family moved house, the comics, too, had to be moved. His parents allowed him to store existing comics in the garage but insisted that no more than two boxes of new comics could be kept in his room from then on. Excess comics could be removed to the garage only if space were made by 'recycling' older ones. Because this plan was agreed *immediately* the family moved house, Byron actually showed remarkably little resistance, and although his collection has not diminished, it has remained static in size now for several years.

Special Interests and Preoccupations

These can also present problems, particularly in the case of more able children in whom the tendency to collect facts can prove just as disruptive

Figure 7.2: Teenage girl's fascination with stools in changing rooms

as collecting objects. Indeed, a child who thinks about, talks about and spends all his time and even money on specific pursuits can be much more difficult to deal with than one who sits quietly lining up bricks or toy cars. Transport, inland waterways, lighting systems, TV test cards, computers, badminton players, greyhounds, stick insects, handwriting, the A3 roadway, arabian stud horses, albinoism, the life cycle of the frog, Moses and the plagues, even the stools in changing rooms (see Figure 7.2) are but some of the interests that may be found.

Families may have to spend much of their free time indulging the child in his or her special interest. Warren's family, for example, had to spend every holiday on canal boats, often in less than picturesque parts of the country. Expense can also be an issue—a regular subscription to several computer magazines can cost many pounds each month. At times, too, the obsession may lead the child into other difficulties. Christopher's preoccupation with the lighting systems on different trains resulted in his attempting to travel on as many routes as possible. As he rarely had the money to pay for his ticket his parents frequently had to travel long distances to bring him home again. He also had a strong interest in handwriting and signatures. As he grew older he developed a remarkable skill in copying people's signatures and by the age of 14 had managed to defraud a number of local banks and building societies out of several thousand pounds—money that was then used to pay for his train tickets.

Once more, it is crucial for parents to be aware that the interest may be reaching a stage when it is becoming out of control. Setting limits early—for example, a strict budget for magazines, or a restriction on the number of outings to visit changing rooms, train stations or canals—can avoid subsequent, major disruptions to family life. In contrast, any attempt to

Table 7.3: Setting limits on a 3-year-old boy's obsession with Thomas the Tank Engine trains

---

1. Picture calendar, indicating when access to 'Thomas' videos and train sets is allowed, produced by parents.
2. Videos 'unavailable', before school; 'Thomas' book read over breakfast instead.
3. Videos restricted to one per evening after school; weekend access unrestricted; unlimited access to train sets.
4. Limits on 'Thomas' clothing imposed; school agree that no 'Thomas' clothes can be worn there. No restrictions at home.
5. Access to 'Thomas' train sets gradually restricted by increasing alternative activities (including 'Thomas' books, board games, etc.).
6. New electric train set provided at home; allowed in conjunction with some 'Thomas' toys; but not train sets
7. 'Thomas' trains moved to grandmother's house; access only available at weekends. Interests in trains, generally, encouraged.

---

reduce behaviour patterns once these are well established is likely to meet with great resentment and resistance.

Table 7.3 presents an example of how one child's overwhelming obsession with Thomas the Tank Engine trains was gradually overcome by his parents, using strategies of this kind. By the time he was 3, they realised that the interest was becoming so pervasive that they had to intervene in some way. At that age their son would wear only Thomas the Tank Engine clothes, spent all his time watching or re-enacting Thomas videos, and talked of almost nothing else.

STEREOTYPED AND REPETITIVE BEHAVIOURS

Touching, spinning, flicking or lining up objects, hand flapping, rocking, licking or smelling things (or people) are all common behaviours in autism. When children are very small such behaviours may not seem unduly bizarre or unacceptable, and they may not be particularly difficult to cope with. However, this can change as they grow older. Chloe had been fascinated with lavatories since infancy and the first thing she would do on visiting anywhere new was to rush to the lavatory and flush it, flapping her arms and hands in glee at the same time. By the time she was in her early teens her insistance on doing this had become much more disruptive and significantly restricted her outside activities. Desmond would approach people and sniff their hands when he met them, a habit which was not particularly disturbing when he was a small boy but which became socially much less acceptable as he grew larger. Behaviours such as rocking and hand flapping, which are relatively common in normally developing infants, may appear innocuous at the age of 3 but can lead to teasing and ostracism by peers at the age of 13.

Unfortunately, there is always a risk that if adults pay too much attention to these behaviours they may be inadvertently reinforced and strengthened. Samantha, for example, used to flap her hands only when she was very excited but as this behaviour made her look increasingly odd as she grew older, her parents and teachers told her to stop each time it occurred. Samantha soon realised that a very effective way of getting attention was to flap ostentatiously any time she was being ignored. In such cases distracting or intrusion techniques may be more effective, especially with younger children. Giving the child something to hold if she is flicking her fingers in front of her eyes, or introducing a novel or interesting toy to a child who is lining up rows of cars or spinning pencils, can help to stop the behaviour temporarily. Restrictions may also be imposed on where the activities are allowed, or how long they can go on for. Howlin and Rutter (1987a) describe how one child's ritual of lining up coins was gradually reduced by limiting the rooms in which this could take place. He loved bathtimes, and was therefore only allowed to have a bath if all coins were removed from the bathroom. Next, because he enjoyed playing in his parents' bed at weekends, coins had to be removed from their room, too. Subsequently the ban was extended to the kitchen, where he liked to eat, and to the sitting room where he watched TV until, eventually, the lines of coins were only allowed in his own bedroom.

Developing new play and constructional skills is particularly important, as stereotyped behaviours of this kind are more likely to occur if children are bored or unoccupied. For older children, alternative and incompatible behaviours can also be encouraged. Simon's parents helped him to bring his hand-mannerisms under control by ensuring that he always wore trousers with large pockets into which he could put his hands. Whenever they saw him flap he would be told 'Hands in pockets' and eventually he began to tell himself what to do if he was aware that he was flapping. When he grew older he also learned to disguise his facial grimacing by always carrying a magazine that could cover his face (see also Chapter 6).

THE USE OF GRADED CHANGE TECHNIQUES IN THE TREATMENT OF OTHER PROBLEM BEHAVIOURS

Ritualistic and stereotyped tendencies may lie at the root of many other behavioural problems, and again it is important to recognise this possibility, and to consider the use of graded change techniques.

Feeding Difficulties

Feeding problems are common in autism and many young children develop extremely rigid eating patterns, existing on a diet of (say) sausages and mashed potatoes; insisting on particular brands of frozen food; or refusing to eat any item that is broken or incomplete (such as a broken biscuit or irregularly shaped piece of bread). Although parents can become very anxious about their children's restricted food intake, studies of the dietary intake of children with autism have indicated that the nutritional and vitamin content is generally no worse than that of their normally developing peers (Renzoni *et al.*, 1995). Close observation often reveals that most children do in fact, eat a considerably wider range of foods than is actually realised. A thorough assessment of the child's eating behaviours *throughout the day* is therefore recommended before any intervention procedures are implemented. This can help to reassure

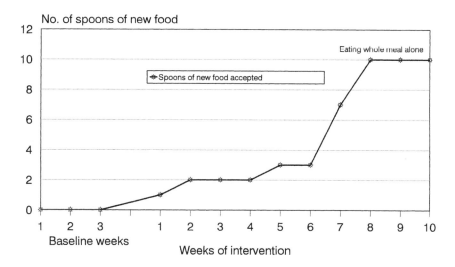

Figure 7.3: Using a graded change approach to overcome resistance to new foods

parents that the child is, in fact, getting enough to eat. It may also help to identify additional foods that the child is willing to accept. For example, if the child is observed to eat certain items (such as crisps or other snacks) outside mealtimes, these items might then be gradually introduced as a part of the regular meal. Although Clive only ate two or three different foods at mealtimes, in the course of the day it was noted that he would eat other items of food including crisps, pieces of bread, and small slices of apple; he would also occasionally take other children's biscuits. Before he received his usual menu, therefore, a small portion of one of these other foods was offered first. Once he began accepting these, small pieces of other food items were also introduced. Howlin and Rutter (1987a) describe the way in which a tiny amount of new food was introduced into 5-year-old Patrick's diet. To begin with only minute quantities were offered, but once these were accepted, Patrick suddenly began to eat more or less the same meals as the rest of the family (see Figure 7.3)

In another case, 4-year-old Adam, who insisted on being spoon fed at home, was observed to feed himself without difficulty at play group. To change this behaviour his mother began by physically prompting him to take one spoonful of food himself first—she then continued to feed him the remainder of the meal as usual. The number of spoonfuls he was required to take himself was steadily increased, and within the course of a week he was completely feeding himself (see Figure 7.4)

Howlin and Rutter (1987a) also describe the procedures used to wean 4-year-old Gary from a baby bottle to a proper drinking mug. Having first

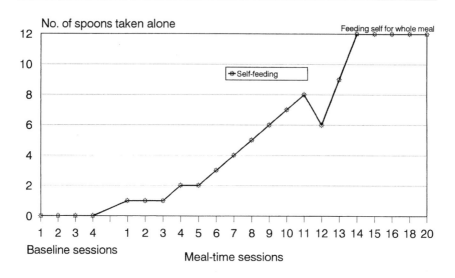

Figure 7.4: Increase in self-feeding using graded change approach

encouraged him to accept a wider range of bottles, a modified baby beaker was introduced, and later he moved on to drinking from ordinary mugs. This technique has subsequently been used successfully with other children, and the process has been made easier by the fact that manufacturers have now produced bottles with interchangeable tops so that the child can progress from a normal bottle to a bottle/cup with a teat, then to one with a hard lid, then to one with no lid at all (see Figure 7.5)

Although many feeding problems can be relatively easily modified by procedures of this kind, parents can understandably become very anxious lest such programmes result in their child refusing to eat at all. If intervention procedures are introduced very gradually and without undue pressure, problems of this kind should not arise. However, children are likely to be very sensitive to their parents' anxiety over such issues and if they realise that non-eating results in increased attention there is a risk that the problem may escalate. Martin, for example, had been hospitalised at the age of 3 for refusing to eat, and had spent some time being drip fed because of this. Thereafter, refusal to eat became his most powerful weapon, and for many years his parents would give in to a wide range of other unacceptable behaviours to avoid further eating problems. It was only when he began attending a special residential school that his eating improved. Staff had been warned in advance that overt attention to his feeding problems would be likely to exacerbate these and hence any mention of food was kept to a minimum. Careful checks were kept on his weight and calorific supplements were added to his drinks; however, at

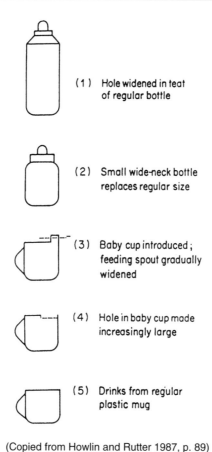

(1) Hole widened in teat of regular bottle

(2) Small wide-neck bottle replaces regular size

(3) Baby cup introduced; feeding spout gradually widened

(4) Hole in baby cup made increasingly large

(5) Drinks from regular plastic mug

(Copied from Howlin and Rutter 1987, p. 89)

Figure 7.5: Stages in reduction of attachment to feeding bottle.

mealtimes the overt attitude to eating was 'Take it or leave it'. If food were not eaten within a set period it would be removed without comment. Martin soon began to eat meals, and although his food intake remains irregular, this is accepted by school staff. Unfortunately at home, because of his parents' understandable anxieties about food, this has continued to be a major problem.

In another case, concerning a five-year-old boy called Robert, the refusal to eat became so severe that surgery was required. A gastrostomy (an operation to create an artificial opening into the stomach) was performed, allowing him to be fed via a tube. Although this was clearly a very unusual and dramatic step to take—and one that parents and doctors had debated over for a long time—the resulting diminution in anxiety over food actually led Robert to try some new foods, whereas previously he would not even tolerate food substances near his mouth. The use of this procedure has also been reported by a family in Australia (Johnson, 1996). Nevertheless, with greater support and more appropriate advice from professionals when problems of this kind *first* arise, such drastic steps should never need to be considered. Severe feeding difficulties, once well established, can be notoriously difficult to treat in any child, not just those who have autism, and hence, with problems of this kind, prompt intervention is particularly crucial.

Rigidity over food can, of course, lead to problems of weight gain as well as weight loss. Bobby developed increasingly complex routines, involving eating snacks and meals at fixed intervals, taking certain numbers of different foods at each meal and having set quantities of sweets and biscuits at other times. He also consumed an apple and a yoghurt following each mealtime or snack on the grounds that these would help him to keep thin. If food were ever denied him he would raid cupboards and even forage in the bin, and by his early teens he weighed well over 14 stones. Attempts by a dietician to change his attitude to eating and to encourage him to take more exercise backfired because, after he had completed a weekly diet sheet which monitored how much he ate and how much exercise he took, he announced that he was clearly doing too many physical activities and needed to do less!

Eventually the problem was tackled by his mother working out a joint contract with him. This specified the number of snacks that could be eaten each day and the amount of food that could be consumed at these times. There was no emphasis on his losing weight, simply on his keeping to the contract. In fact, to prevent him taking foods at other times, the number of snacks per day was increased slightly, although the amount of food consumed on each occasion was reduced. His reward for keeping to the agreed plan was a trip to McDonald's at the end of each week. Other members of the extended family, including several grandchildren, were also limited to eating at set times, and this proved difficult since previously food had always been made readily available to anyone in the house. However, over time, the amount of food consumed at snack times was gradually reduced as was the number of snacks allowed. This regime has not resulted in a significant loss of weight, but neither has his weight increased over recent months and the foraging for food has also stopped.

Sleeping Problems

Other problem behaviours, such as sleeping difficulties, may also be tackled using a graded change approach. Again, Howlin and Rutter (1987a)

Table 7.4: Graded change in the reduction of sleeping problems in 8-year-old boy with epilepsy who refused to sleep alone

---

Stages
- Mother on inflatable mattress next to child's bed
- Mattress moved a few inches from bed
- Distance increased—mother still in reach
- Mattress too far away to touch child
- Mattress at door of child's room
- Mattress in hallway
- Mattress at door of parents' bedroom
- Mother returns to own bed

---

describe how one child's insistence on his mother's remaining with him throughout the night was gradually reduced. The problem had begun when he had a bad attack of influenza, and because he also suffered from epilepsy his mother had decided that she should sleep with him for several nights. However, when he recovered he still insisted that she remain with him each night. The Health Visitor advised his mother that she should just leave him to sleep alone and that as long as she ignored his screams he would eventually accept the situation. In fact, because of his prolonged screaming each night, the neighbours finally called the police because they thought he was being physically abused. It was many months before his mother would even contemplate trying to deal with the problem again, but eventually, with a great deal of support and the help of an inflatable mattress, she was able to return to her own bedroom. The steps involved in this process are described in Table 7.4.

OTHER APPROACHES TO DEALING WITH STEREOTYPED BEHAVIOURS

Often, by the time parents seek professional help, patterns of ritualistic behaviour may have become so intractable that they affect many different aspects of family life. Attempts to solve a wide range of problems at one go usually lead to frustration and failure. The first important step, therefore, is to accept that progress will be slow (although it can also be steady) and this is generally only made possible by working on one aspect of one problem area at a time. Overambitious attempts to eliminate behaviours that have had a strong hold for many years will almost certainly prove unsuccessful. Instead, behaviours need to be carefully broken down into their component parts and these then tackled step by step, with the ultimate goal perhaps taking many months or even longer to achieve.

Rapid Intervention for New Problems

Modifying long-established routines and rituals is neither an easy nor a rapid process, as the examples above illustrate. Moreover, following the successful elimination or reduction of one behaviour there is always a risk that a new behaviour might emerge to take its place. Parents need to be aware of this risk and be prepared to intervene immediately if problems arise. In the case of Patrick, for example, a few weeks after his blanket attachment had faded, he began to carry around toy London buses. From the start his parents ensured that no single bus was allowed to dominate his attention and restrictions were placed on where he could keep the buses and how many he could carry at any one time. They also encouraged the use of the buses in co-operative play activities. This approach ensured that the buses never became as disruptive as his blanket attachment had been, although they could still be used as a source of comfort, and even to encourage reciprocal interactions.

Environmental Modifications

It is clear from personal accounts written by individuals with autism that stereotyped and ritualistic behaviours are extremely important methods of reducing stress and anxiety, and such behaviours are much more likely to occur if children are placed under too much pressure. They are also more frequent in unfamiliar situations, and particularly with unfamiliar people (Runco et al., 1986) and hence stability of environment is a crucial factor. Reducing unnecessary demands on the child, encouraging more flexible attitudes in adults, or making relatively simple modifications to the daily routine or environment can also help significantly to reduce stereotyped behaviours. In mainstream schools, for example, many children with autism become very distressed (and hence more ritualistic) if they are forced to take part in group games or 'join in' at play times, or when they have to scramble to find somewhere to sit at the start of each lesson. If staff can sit back and ask themselves 'Are such activities really necessary?' they may be able to avoid problems that are caused by stress or undue demands. Allowing children to avoid such socially demanding situations, letting them spend play/game times alone in the library or carrying out other tasks and providing them with a set place in which to sit may all have much greater impact than a complex behavioural programme.

It may also be necessary to examine the demands that are made on the child at home. Paul's father insisted that, as soon as they arrived home, each of the children should tell what had happened at school that day.

However, when Paul moved to a new school, where he was under much greater pressure, he became increasingly resistant to talking when he returned home and would repeatedly pace up and down the room in a very agitated and distressed manner. His mother quickly realised that as long as he was allowed to go straight to his room on his return and remain there quietly for half an hour or so, the pacing ceased, and he would then, sometimes, tell them more about his activities during the day.

Ways of Reducing Stress

It is important for parents and others to be aware that intense anxiety can occur if the child is prevented (or has fears of being prevented) from carrying out his or usual routines. Thus, it is essential that it is always made clear to the child when an activity WILL be allowed, as well as when it will not. A graded change approach is usually the most effective way of ensuring that anxiety is kept to a tolerable level, but additional strategies may also be needed. Simple relaxation techniques, which have proved effective in dealing with the fears and anxieties of non-autistic children, can be adapted for use within this group. Basic breathing exercises—such as teaching children to take a few deep breaths in a way that decreases, rather than increases chest tension (many pull in their stomach muscles when they inhale, which simply increases tension) can be a useful way of helping the older child to feel calmer. Distracting techniques, such as looking at a photograph, 'magic eye' post card, or picture of a pleasant or familiar scene, may also be helpful. The picture needs to be small enough to be carried about easily, and may need covering or reinforcing in some way if it is not to fall apart. Alternatively, individually made tapes of music or other relaxing sounds can be used, while massage, aromatherapy, physical exercise, music and dance are among other activities that have been found to be helpful in reducing agitation and distress.

Establishing Self-control

Keeping to rituals and routines may be one of the few ways that a child with autism has of coping with day-to-day stress. As Therese Jolliffe, a woman with autism, now studying for a PhD degree, explains:

> Reality to an autistic person is a confusing, interacting mass of events, people, places, sounds and sights. There seems to be no clear boundaries,

order or meaning to anything. A large part of my life is spent trying to work out the pattern behind everything. Set routines, times, particular routes and rituals all help to get order into an unbearably chaotic life. Trying to keep everything the same reduces some of the terrible fear. (Jolliffe *et al.*, 1992)

Insensitive attempts to remove these support systems may well prove counter-productive and, by increasing anxiety, strengthen the child's need for ritual and routine. With more able children, therefore, it is important to focus on the need to develop more effective self-control strategies as an integral part of any intervention programme. Ben had very rigid eating habits, which his parents knew would cause diffi- culties when he moved to a new school. For many years he had existed almost exclusively on sandwiches but the prospective school insisted on all pupils eating a cooked lunch. After discussion with the Head of Special Needs the following plan was established. Ben would be al- lowed to take sandwiches for the first term but in order to eat them he would have to earn tokens in order to eat these (the necessary tokens were provided as long as he said 'Good Morning' to the teacher and gave his name at registration, so there was no danger of his going without). Alternatively, if he chose *not* to use the tokens for sandwiches, and ate the school lunch instead, he could earn enough tokens to borrow a video from the school library at the weekends. Once he was given real control over what he could eat, Ben became increasingly reluctant to 'waste' his tokens on sandwiches, and by the end of the term was regularly eating the school meals. There is little doubt in his parents' minds that a direct confrontation over school meals would have res- ulted in a very different outcome!

Making Use of Environmental Changes

Alterations to the child's environment or other aspects of daily life also offer scope for change. The move from home to school for example, or from one school to another may provide a valuable opportunity for inter- vention. Even individuals with very fixed routines in one setting may show surprisingly little resistance to modifying these in a totally different environment. However, for such changes to occur it is crucial that every- one works together to ensure that there are no opportunities for the old behaviour patterns to re-establish themselves. If allowed in the new en- vironment the behaviours will be strengthened even further. On the other hand, if different and more appropriate routines are established *from the outset*, major behavioural changes can often be implemented with rela- tively little difficulty. Thus, Jake, who had never slept apart from his parents, settled down without difficulty into a bed of his own when he was transferred to boarding school. Diane, who had always insisted on wearing purple clothes, accepted the green and yellow school uniform without protest. Morgan, who had always been fed by his mother and who had an extremely restricted diet, quickly learned to feed himself with a wide range of different foods when he began attending nursery school. In contrast, William, whose parents were unwilling to inform his new school (the third in two years) that he had Asperger syndrome, in the vain hope that no one would notice, immediately launched into his stereotyped monologues on TV test cards. This quickly resulted in his receiving considerable attention from his teachers. By the time the school realised that this topic had begun to dominate everything, the behaviour was already well established once more.

Ensuring Consistency of Approach

Reducing stereotyped behaviours to an acceptable level can be a very complex process, involving a variety of different strategies. In order to succeed, consistency of approach is essential and help and support are needed from everyone concerned. Adults may need to change their behaviours or expectations as much as the child and, for them, altering the habits of many years may be particularly difficult.

Attention to the General Quality of Life

Stereotyped behaviours are frequently at their worst when children are bored or when their time is unstructured, and there is considerable experimental evidence to indicate that such behaviours increase when individuals are inadequately occupied (Chock & Glahn, 1983). Moreover, attempts to modify rituals or routines without replacing them with alternative behaviours are unlikely to prove successful. Without careful planning there is a real risk of even more disruptive behaviours taking their place. One of the most fundamental elements in any intervention programme for stereotyped or ritualistic behaviours, therefore, is the need to develop and encourage other activities as far as possible. The problem here is that once rituals and routines become established they can prove remarkably resistant to change and any attempts to expand alternative activities may be strongly resisted. Again, a 'graded change' approach may be needed to increase new and alternative behaviours as well as to limit older and maladaptive ones (see Schopler, 1995, for further examples).

Making Use of Special Interests

Although it may sometimes be necessary to eliminate certain ritualistic activities entirely, on the whole, once an acceptable level of control is reached, stereotyped behaviours and interests can have many positive features. They may serve as extremely powerful reinforcers for developing other, more productive activities (Howlin & Rutter, 1987a); they may also be an essential source of comfort or self-occupation for a child with few other interests or abilities. In the hands of imaginative teachers or other adults, obsessions or special skills may be a means of promoting interactions with other children. A child who is particularly good at arithmetic or spelling can be made 'class monitor' to check the accuracy of other children's work. In another case, Robin's remarkable skill in spinning any objects (from tin cans to Mars bars) led to other children in his nursery school queueing up to bring him increasingly bizarre objects each play time and they would fight to be accepted as his 'best friend'. Sean's only topic of interest was the Tin Man (from the Wizard of Oz) but his teacher succeeded in using this as a reward for other pieces of work. She had sets of Tin Man stickers made which he could stick on the end of each piece of work as he finished it. In addition, she made use of his ability to draw and make models of the Tin Man in order to increase his involvement with peers in class projects based around the Wizard of Oz and other fairy stories.

Follow-up studies suggest, too, that if stereotyped skills and interests are appropriately encouraged and developed they can play a crucial role in later social and educational integration (Kanner, 1973). Thus, Temple Grandin (1992a) describes how, as a young child, she would construct 'squeeze machines' to keep her own anxiety and obsessional fears under control. In later years this became the basis for her highly successful cattle-restraining devices, which have won acclaim in the field of animal psychology.

Finally, it is important to remember that stereotyped activities can be an extremely effective means of rewarding alternative behaviours. Premack (1959) was one of the first to demonstrate that the use of ritualistic, stereotyped or other apparently meaningless activities as a reward for more appropriate behaviours may be a very effective strategy in increasing behavioural repertoires. This approach may be particularly valuable for less able children or those with a very restricted range of interests and abilities. Many subsequent studies have shown how stereotypic, obsessional or attachment behaviours can be used to increase more appropriate or constructive activities (Wolery et al., 1985; Sugai & White, 1986). Charlop-Christy and colleagues (Charlop et al., 1990; Charlop-Christy & Haymes, 1996, 1998) found that obsessional interests—including tooth paste caps, coffee swizzle sticks, toy helicopters, photo albums and balloons—all proved more effective reinforcers for decreasing inappropriate and stereotyped behaviours than did traditional differential reinforcement techniques using food rewards.

It is now well established that the use of rituals and obsessions can be highly effective in reinforcing and encouraging more appropriate behaviours. Firstly, there appear to be few if any negative side-effects. Contrary to expectations, stereotyped behaviours DO NOT increase in other settings (Wolery *et al.*, 1985; Charlop *et al.*, 1990). Instead, as alternative skills and interests develop, rituals and preoccupations tend gradually to diminish in frequency or intensity. Secondly, the basic strategy can be adopted for use within many different settings. Thirdly, children do not appear to habituate to reinforcers of this kind in the same way that they satiate to food. Finally, the use of stereotypies or obsessions as reinforcers can avoid the need for more negative strategies, such as 'time out'.

THE SUCCESS OF HOME-BASED PROGRAMMES

It is clear that dealing with stereotyped and ritualistic behaviours is by no means an easy task and successful interventions will require time, patience and often the implementation of several different strategies in tandem. Nevertheless, with appropriate support these techniques can be

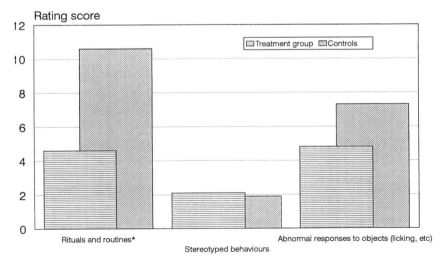

The higher the rating the more abnormal the behaviour. * Difference between groups significant at $p<0.01$

Figure 7.6: Parental ratings of stereotyped and ritualistic behaviours at end of 18-month intervention period.

Table 7.5: Guidelines for dealing with ritualistic or stereotyped behaviours at home

1. *Establish clear and consistent rules* for *where* and *when* the activity is permitted, *who* it can be carried out with or *how long* it can go on for. This ensures that the child knows not only when the behaviour is not permitted but also when it is allowed.

2. *Ensure that change is introduced one small step at a time* so that any distress to the child is kept to a minimum. Do not attempt to deal with too many problems at once. Setting very small goals optimises the chance of long term success.

3. *Explore possible reasons for ritualistic/stereotyped behaviours.* High levels of stereo-typed behaviour are often an indicator of uncertainty, anxiety or distress. Such problems can be significantly reduced by ensuring that the child's daily pro-gramme is predictable, and that the environment is appropriately stimulating and structured.

4. *Intervene without delay.* Establishing parental control over a behaviour that has lasted a few days is a great deal easier than over one that has lasted many months.

5. *As far as possible try to predict problems in advance.* What is acceptable in a 3-year-old may prove a disaster 10 years later.

6. *Help children to predict and hence cope better with change.* Non-verbal means of indicat-ing what will/will not happen are usually more reliable than verbal methods.

7. *Make use of obsessions as far as possible,* either as rewards or as the basis for more sociable activities. Remember that other children are more likely to accept un-usual behaviours if the child also has something at which he or she can excel.

used successfully within the home, resulting in a steady diminution of problems. Howlin and Rutter (1987a) found that parental reports indi-cated a steady decline in many ritualistic behaviours over 18 months of home-based intervention and were significantly lower in cases than con-trols at the end of treatment (see Figure 7.6).

Guidelines for dealing with stereotyped and ritualistic behaviours are summarised in Table 7.5. The principal guidelines for success, however, are early intervention, a graded approach to the introduction of change, the provision of a more appropriate or stimulating environment in order to encourage other activities, and the establishment of basic rules about where, when, who with or for how long ritualistic or stereotyped be-haviours may take place. It is also crucial to try to minimise anxiety and distress (for both parents and child), to aim for gradual but achievable behavioural change rather than dramatic improvements and, finally, to weigh up the potential advantages, as well as obvious disadvantages, of the obsession and, wherever possible, to capitalise on these issues.

The overall aim should generally not be to remove the obsession en-tirely but to ensure that the behaviour no longer intrudes in a distressing or unacceptable way into family life. Once an acceptable level of control is reached, stereotyped behaviours or interests may actually have many beneficial effects.

8

APPROACHES TO DEALING WITH OTHER BEHAVIOURAL PROBLEMS

BEHAVIOURAL STRATEGIES

Parents of children with autism are faced by a range of different behavioural difficulties. These may include disruptive and aggressive behaviours, tantrums, self-injury, over-activity, poorly developed self-help skills, and lack of self-occupation. While none of these is specific to autism—they occur in many other groups of children with disabilities—the rigidity and poor communication skills of the child with autism can make such problems particularly difficult to deal with.

Many books and papers have been written on ways of modifying 'challenging behaviours' in individuals with autism and other developmental disorders (Emerson, 1995; Kiernan, 1993) but until relatively recently such texts have usually focused on specific intervention strategies. These might include time out, extinction, positive or negative reinforcement, differential reinforcement of alternative activities (DRO and DRI), punishment, or a combination of several approaches together. Table 8.1 provides a brief summary of the definitions and use of such techniques.

During the 1980s, however, there was a general change in attitudes towards the use of behavioural methodologies. While recognising the power of these approaches, both for encouraging appropriate behaviours and reducing unwanted ones, an increasing number of professionals expressed concerns about the punitive nature of some of the techniques used. Aversive techniques had been used for many years. Lovaas and his colleagues, for example, used electric shocks, not only to discourage behaviours such as self-injury, but also to increase social interactions (Lovaas *et al.*, 1965a, 1965b). Self-stimulatory and self-injurious behaviours, including pica (eating non-food substances), have also been subject to a variety of aversive treatments, including electric shock, water sprays, squirts of lemon juice, ammonia

Table 8.1: Commonly used behavioural terms

Behavioural terminology	What it means in practice	An example
Time out	Actually means 'Time out from reinforcement'. Ongoing reinforcers cease whenever the unwanted behaviour occurs.	Child (who usually enjoys her meals) fidgeting and throwing food around the table at mealtimes; food is removed for a brief period until child is sitting quietly.
Extinction	The reinforcement (often attention) that usually follows a behaviour no longer does so.	Child begins to sob heart-rendingly each morning when school bus arrives. Observations confirm he is fine when he gets to school. Helping his parents to ignore the sobs, and getting the escort to take him calmly onto the coach results in marked diminution.
Positive reinforcement	Strengthening a behaviour by following it with something desirable.	Child screams for sweets at supermarket check-out queue. Mother gives in out of embarrassment. Screaming behaviour is thereby positively reinforced and is likely to increase in future.
Negative reinforcement	Strengthening a behaviour by taking away something undesirable.	Same scenario as above, except mother is reinforced for giving sweets by cessation of screams and end to her embarrassment.
Differential reinforcement of other/ incompatible behaviours (DRO; DRI)	Reinforcing and hence strengthening an alternative behaviour, preferably one that is incompatible with the undesirable activity.	Child flaps arms whenever excited, especially while watching favourite videos. Is given controller to hold in order to stop/start tapes. This almost automatically cuts down the flapping and child is reinforced by being able to watch videos.
Punishment	Attempts to weaken behaviour by following it with something unpleasant.	Child screams; mum yells or smacks. May have a short-term effect but can actually make the behaviour worse in the long term. If children have no other means of getting attention, any response may be preferable to no response at all. Also, danger of punitive responses escalating.

pellets, noxious tastes, slaps, shouts and hair pulls (Oliver, 1995; Myles *et al.*, 1997).

Not only has a variety of different methods been used to treat behaviours of this kind, but often several different strategies may be employed together, so that it can prove virtually impossible to tease out which one, if any, has a positive effect. In a recent review of treatments for pica, for example, Myles *et al.* (1997) found that the interventions included external devices such as sheet metal helmets, fencing masks and blindfolds; aversive techniques, such as ammonia, water mists and lemon juice; physical restraints and shouting; 'overcorrection' (lengthy cleansing and oral hygiene programmes following the ingestion of non-food substances); as well as various combinations of these approaches.

Although, *perhaps* justifiable in the cases of life-threatening behaviours, the use of such methods with children who are unable to communicate effectively, and whose lives are already stressful, must be considered deeply disturbing. Debate about the ethics of such approaches has become widespread and in 1988 the Autism Society of America called for a total ban on the use of aversive procedures. While some researchers, such as Carr (1991), have argued that such methods are rarely if ever justified, others such as Gerhardt *et al.* (1991) support their use in particular circumstances. Certainly, examples of the abuse of behavioural techniques are not hard to find (Horner *et al.*, 1990; Howlin & Clements, 1995) but, at the same time, cases have also been reported in which students or residents with autism have had to be excluded from existing provision, when mildly aversive techniques, which had previously been effective in controlling their difficult behaviours, were outlawed (see Schopler, 1986, for further discussion).

Although the arguments continue, there is now far more awareness of the dangers to which the unsystematic, uncritical and inadequately supervised use of aversive procedures (including some drug therapies) can lead. There is also wider recognition that, with appropriate and early support for families, speedier access to adequate educational opportunities, the provision of different treatment options, and better legislative protection against abuse and malpractice, the use of such methods, particularly as a form of crisis management, could be greatly curtailed (Schopler, 1995).

The debate has helped to illustrate, too, that specific treatment methods can rarely be judged, in isolation, as being either appropriate or ethically unjustifiable. Instead their value, effectiveness and acceptability will depend on individual circumstances. This, in turn, has shifted the focus of treatment away from *strategies* and onto *functions* (Emerson & Bromley, 1995).

FUNCTIONAL ANALYSIS

As noted in Chapter 4, research has now begun to concentrate more on the need to analyse why challenging behaviours occur, the functions that such behaviours serve for the child, and how he or she might be able to obtain the same ends, but by alternative and more acceptable means. Experimental studies consistently show that many such behaviours serve an important communicative function (Durand, 1990). Indeed, aggression, tantrums, self-injury or destructive behaviours may be the *only* way in which a child with limited linguistic abilities can rapidly, effectively and predictably control his or her environment.

Five main functions of aggressive, self-injurious, stereotyped, or other disruptive behaviours have been identified (Durand & Crimmins, 1988; Durand & Carr, 1991). These are:

- To indicate the need for help or attention
- To escape from stressful situations or activities
- To obtain desired objects
- To protest against unwanted events/activities
- To obtain stimulation

If the primary function of a behaviour can be identified it is then possible to provide the child with alternative means to obtain the same ends. The choice of strategy taught will depend on the child's cognitive and linguistic ability, but might range from teaching him to push a button, lever or switch, or to use signs, symbols, pictures, or words and simple phrases (such as 'Help me'). As long as the newly acquired behaviour has a rapid and predictable impact on the child's environment, this can result in rapid and significant reductions in undesirable behaviours (Durand & Carr, 1991). And, when compared with the use of more traditional behavioural techniques, such as differential reinforcement, or even punishment, the functional analysis approach to problems tends to work far more rapidly and dramatically. There are many other reports of individuals with aggressive or self-injurious behaviours, who, although showing little response to complex behavioural programmes utilising differential reinforcement, reprimands and response interruption, have responded well when functional communication training was introduced.

Nevertheless, despite the huge surge in work on functional analysis in recent years, it is important to be aware that the majority of studies have been conducted in highly intensive experimental settings. Detailed analyses of the possible functions of undesirable behaviours may require considerable time, expertise and technology and are often impracticable within mainstream settings. As Owens and MacKinnon (1993) note,

'Functional analysis isn't as easy as ABC'. Emerson and Bromley (1995) also warn of the problems inherent in this approach. Human behaviour will always be determined by many factors, and by different factors at different times, and they found that often it was not possible to determine the function underlying a particular challenging behaviour. In around 25% of cases, no specific function could be identified, and a third of behaviours appeared to be influenced by multiple factors. Hall (1997), in a highly sophisticated assessment of self-injurious and stereotyped behaviours in 16 children with severe to profound learning disabilities, was able to identify a consistent underlying function for self-injury in only four cases and for stereotyped behaviours in six cases. Moreover, knowledge of the function underlying one class of behaviours is not necessarily of any value in predicting the behavioural function underlying other forms of challenging behaviour shown by the same individual.

A further problem with this type of research is that there has been no evaluation using random control trials. Most studies are based on multiple baseline, single case or small group reports, and although those that have been published are certainly encouraging, there is no way of ascertaining how many unsuccessful studies may also have been conducted. Despite these intrinsic problems, it is apparent that this approach to assessment and treatment can play an important role in reducing challenging behaviours and a number of rating scales or questionnaires have now been produced to assist carers in identifying the possible functions of disruptive behaviours (see Sturmey, 1996). The most widely used of these is the 'Motivation Assessment Scale' (Durand & Crimmins, 1988), which attempts to classify behaviour into four main categories: attention seeking; self stimulatory; escape or avoidance; or as indicating the need for help or assistance. However, there are doubts about the reliability and validity of this scale when used in naturalistic settings and, probably more importantly, the five summary categories cannot encompass all the possible reasons for disruptive behaviours. In particular, they cannot identify idiosyncratic or multi-function causes (Sturmey, 1995).

A somewhat less complex questionnaire, which is described in greater detail in Chapter 5, is the one developed by Schuler et al., (1989). Information from this can be used to help parents or teachers plan ways in which alternative and more acceptable responses might be established.

Approaches involving functional analysis haves now been used successfully in a wide range of studies, in particular to reduce aggressive, self-stimulatory and self-injurious behaviours (see Carr & Durand, 1985; Emerson, 1995; Oliver, 1995) and although most interventions continue to be clinic based there have been increasing attempts to adapt these for use in community settings.

A simplified version of this approach was used with Dominic, an 11-year-old boy with Asperger syndrome and superficially good spoken language skills. For much of the time at his boarding school he was exceptionally well behaved and co-operative, taking an active role in lessons and other school activities. However, from time to time he would 'explode' without warning, and at such times could become extremely aggressive and malicious. As well as apparently random attacks on other children, on one occasion he had deliberately followed another child with a knife and tried to cut off her hair; another time he had systematically destroyed a younger pupil's precious teddy bear, and once he had removed all the belongings from a child's room and thrown them out of the window. Children and staff were becoming increasingly fearful of him and he was eventually threatened with exclusion. All staff were asked to complete the questionnaire, and although their responses were not always consistent, the one reliable finding that emerged was that protests or more disruptive behaviours occurred when attention was given to another child, when another child took something that Dominic considered to be his own property, or when he was stopped from completing a task on which he was working. Identification of these precipitating factors then led the staff to devise strategies that might help to avoid disturbance. Warning him, well in advance, that a task would need to be completed within a set time (but offering him the opportunity to complete it later if possible) reduced his protests about having to leave work unfinished. If he was seen to become agitated when attention was given to another child he was prompted to say 'Can I have a turn now'. If another child took something that he believed belonged to him he was told to report this immediately to a teacher. However, instead of becoming involved in arguments over ownership, the class teacher would simply record his complaint and then provide him with the written account to discuss with his key worker at the end of the day. Attention to his grievances, even if his demands were not actually met, seemed to diffuse his anger, and the frequency of his outbursts significantly decreased.

APPROACHES TO OTHER BEHAVIOURAL PROBLEMS

In a functional analysis approach to treatment, the focus is very much on changing the children's behaviour, so that they can learn to communicate their needs more effectively and by more socially acceptable means. However, in normal daily life, successful intervention will also necessitate changes to other people's behaviours.

In the following sections, examples of the ways in which parents have tackled a range of different problems at home are discussed.

Eating and Sleeping Difficulties

Although difficulties in these areas are often related to stereotyped or ritualistic tendencies (see Chapter 7) problems can also arise for a variety of other reasons. Unnecessary attention to eating difficulties can certainly help to maintain these and parental anxiety about food intake is an understandable problem. However, in many cases, simple record keeping can help to reduce worries of this kind. Carl's mother was concerned that he seemed to eat very little at home, apart from breakfast, although he showed no sign of losing weight. In an attempt to reassure her, staff at school kept a detailed account of what he ate there and it was apparent that on most days he ate not only most of the school lunch but also biscuits and crisps, as well as helping himself occasionally to other children's food. His teachers reported that no encouragement was needed to persuade him to eat at school, although at home his mother would spend up to an hour trying to tempt him with various foods, even allowing him to eat what he wanted directly from the fridge. The school doctor was consulted and she confirmed that Carl was of normal height and weight for a boy of his age. His parents were provided with a calory supplement that could be added to his milk at home, which he readily accepted. Otherwise, he was offered meals at the same time as the rest of the family. The food offered consisted of items he enjoyed at school, and portions were kept small although he could obtain extra if he wished. Once the rest of the family had finished, the meal was removed. Reducing the emphasis on eating (while ensuring that he got enough to eat at school) minimised confrontations, and although Carl did not eat a meal every day at home, the records showed that he generally ate a reasonable amount over any two-day period.

In other cases, introducing much more regular and, possibly, more frequent mealtimes can help. Jane's family never sat down to a meal together and she was provided with food more or less on demand (as indeed were the rest of the family). This could result in her asking for food to be cooked at very inconvenient times of the day or night, with severe tantrums resulting if she did not get her own way. Her mother drew up a chart indicating when she would cook meals (six mealtimes a day were designated initially so that if one meal were missed Jane did not have to wait long until the next) and a timer was used to set the limit for eating meals. No cooking was done at other times, so that the rest of the family also had to comply with the timetable. Once this regime was accepted, the number of mealtimes per day was reduced to three, and eventually the whole family, including Jane, would sit down together at the evening meal.

As with any child, it is important to take account of individual likes and dislikes and there is little point trying to force a child to eat something that he or she really dislikes. Martin's father, for example, had very rigid eating habits and could not tolerate any waste of food. If his son did not finish a meal he would insist on presenting the left-overs at the next mealtime. Naturally, Martin would refuse to eat this, while his father would eventually have to give in when the food began to decay. Battles continued for many months, much to the distress of his mother. Eventually, however, with the help of an intermediary from school, a list was drawn up of the foods he would happily eat and those he would not tolerate. His mother made use of this information in preparing meals for him, and if he did not eat his meal within a set time this was removed without fuss, but no further food or snacks were provided until the next meal. Once the pressure to eat was removed, the problem rapidly diminished.

The texture, or even the colour, of food can be a problem for other children. In these cases it is generally better to try to increase the items eaten within a particular range of foods, rather than battle to persuade the child to eat novel items. Thus, if crisps are a favourite food, the child might be encouraged to eat different types of potato products rather than sticking rigidly to just one type or one brand. Phillip developed an obsession with drinking only clear liquids but, by mixing flavourings with water, his mother managed to get him to accept a variety of different drinks and over time he began to tolerate slightly opaque or coloured liquids too.

For other children, introducing greater routine, structure and predictability into mealtimes can help and this is perhaps one reason why many children eat much better at school than at home. The menu might be discussed beforehand, or chosen from a set of alternatives (perhaps in picture form); mealtimes should be regular, although not absolutely rigid, and made as calm as possible; other children rushing in and out are unlikely to help. A set place to sit, perhaps against the wall so that it is not quite so easy to leave the table, can also be helpful. In other words, in order to improve the *child's* eating behaviour, attention may well need to be given to the general environment, to other people's eating habits and to the food itself.

Sleeping difficulties, which are also common in autism, may respond to a similar approach. Firstly, it can be helpful to keep a record of when, where and how much a child sleeps over the course of the week in order to get a reliable estimate of his or her sleeping habits. When analysed, the sleeping times of children who are said 'never to sleep' are usually found to be within the normal range, although the timing may not be particularly convenient. For children who have developed the habit of always sleeping with their parents, a graded change approach (see Chapter 7) may be helpful. For others, who have difficulties in settling at night, establishing a set bedtime routine is often the most effective form of intervention. The child may need to be warned in advance that 'bedtime' is about to begin (possibly by means of a timer of some sort), so that there is plenty of opportunity to finish ongoing activities. The signal for the bedtime ritual might be a warm drink followed by a story, or a brief video session followed by a bath (or any combination of these in any order). In the majority of cases, the bedroom should be made as pleasant a place as possible, with ready access to favourite toys or objects. Soft lighting or quiet story or music tapes can also prove to be very soothing. However, for children who are very destructive, or who become disturbed by over-stimulation, it may be preferable to keep the room quite bare. Once taken to the room, the child should be settled in bed—again the routine of a song, a story, or even a ritualised 'conversation' can be helpful. Parents should then decide how long they will stay *and keep to this decision.* Falling asleep on the child's bed is not usually helpful, but a clock or timer of some sort to indicate when they are going to depart can sometimes be useful. For some children regular but brief checks to reassure them that all is well can help them to settle and then, over time, the frequency of such visits can be steadily reduced. Any attempts by the child to leave the room should be firmly, but calmly, prevented. For children who tend to fall asleep before getting back into bed, a thin foam mattress, or thick matting on the floor, can avoid the need to disturb them before they are soundly asleep.

In general, the approaches that work well with young, normal children (see Douglas & Richman, 1984) also tend to be effective with children with autism. However, it is crucial that attempts to intervene begin as soon as problems arise. A child who has slept for 13 years in his parents' bedroom will be much more difficult to remove than one who has been there for only three days.

Tantrums and Other Disruptive Behaviours

As indicated earlier, undesirable behaviours of this kind may be the child's most effective means of communicating his or her needs, and very often the goal of intervention is to teach alternative and more acceptable means of communication. However, not all disruptive behaviours can be neatly classified in this way. Moreover, the application of functional analysis approaches does not exclude the need to attend to the child's wider environment, or careful assessment of the behaviour of carers.

Whenever unacceptable behaviours become a source of concern, attention needs to turn first to the general quality of the child's life. If this is impoverished and lacking in appropriate stimulation, or if adults tend to respond *only* to tantrums and rarely to more positive behaviours, a focus on changing the child is unlikely to be effective. It is important, therefore, that parents are provided with help and guidance to ensure that *they* are able to communicate effectively with their child and to provide him or her with the stimulation and encouragement that is required. A child who has access to a range of different and enjoyable activities is far less likely to demand attention by tantrums or disruptive behaviours.

On the other hand, over-stimulation and lack of structure may also increase stress and anxiety, thereby leading to tantrums and aggressive outbursts. It is important, therefore, to try to achieve the correct balance, so that the child is provided with a predictable and stable environment but one that is, at the same time, appropriately varied and stimulating. If stress is a cause of problem behaviours, then, in addition to a careful restructuring of the daily programme and environment, cognitive-behavioural procedures to help develop self-control or promote relaxation may also prove a valuable adjunct to treatment, especially for more able children. (For further details on the use of cognitive behavioural techniques with children or people with learning disabilities, see Ronen, 1997, and Kroese *et al.*, 1997.)

Parents, too, may need help and encouragement to appreciate that, in order to improve their child's behaviour, they should try to attend less to inappropriate behaviours and more to desirable ones. However, although this is easily said, it may prove much more difficult to do. Thus, if a child is sitting quietly and not creating any fuss, the natural reaction of most parents is to breathe a sigh of relief and continue with a task of their own. At such times they are unlikely to want to intervene for fear of disturbing the peace. On the other hand, they may well respond quickly if the child suddenly begins to scream or throw things. It is often difficult to accept that this type of response will only tend to encourage disruption, and few parents of a child with autism will be able to achieve optimal styles of management without at least some professional advice and guidance.

No matter how perfect the family environment, all children, whether they are autistic or not, quickly learn that tantrums or aggressive behaviours are an efficient means of gaining attention. This is particularly true when communication skills are poor and when a well-aimed blow at the TV set, or a sharp pull on mother's hair, are always going to succeed far more quickly than attempts to sign or speak. In such cases it may be necessary to implement additional behavioural strategies.

Extinction procedures
These techniques have been shown to be effective in modifying a great variety of disruptive behaviours. In *principle*, extinction is a very powerful and straightforward technique that simply involves removing any attention or other reinforcement that the child receives for the disruptive behaviour. An example of this is provided in the section on reducing

inappropriate speech in Chapter 5. In *practice*, however, such techniques can be extraordinarily difficult to implement.

Firstly, they cannot be used with dangerous or violent behaviours, when ignoring might endanger the child or someone else. Secondly, when attention or reinforcement is initially withdrawn there may be a tendency for the behaviour to increase, at least in the short term (this is sometimes known as the 'extinction burst'). Thus, if the child finds that a brief screaming attack does not result in a response, he or she may well try to scream louder, or longer, or both. When parents then respond they will have effectively, if unwittingly, succeeded in encouraging the child to react more persistently and more strenuously. Again this may be an unacceptable risk, particularly if the behaviour is dangerous or damaging. Thirdly, if such programmes are to work effectively, consistency is essential. The behaviour must go unrewarded *on each and every occasion* that it occurs, otherwise intermittent attention will be enough to maintain it over a much more prolonged period. Finally, the ability to implement extinction procedures is highly dependent on parents' mood, their general state of mind, and their situation at the time. In the privacy of their own home, after a good night's sleep, and when they are not having to deal with other problems, it may not prove too difficult to ignore the child's behaviour. In the supermarket queue on a Friday evening, after a difficult week at work and/or several sleepless nights, the task is very different. Unfortunately, a single response at such a time is liable to undermine all the earlier efforts.

Time out
This is a term that actually means 'time out from reinforcement', not necessarily, as might be thought, time away from other people or being left in a room alone. Time out is not meant to be a strongly aversive procedure; instead, the aim is to remove ongoing reinforcers whenever the behaviour occurs. Thus, if the child pulls his or her sister's hair while watching the TV, the programme is immediately turned off. If the child gets satisfaction watching his or her mother's agitation during a tantrum, then *her* leaving the room will result in 'time out' from this reinforcement. If the child is always leaving the table at mealtimes, then the food might be removed until he or she is sitting quietly. For more disruptive behaviours the child may need to be removed from the situation, perhaps into the hallway or into a quiet bedroom, so that there is no chance of further reinforcement occurring.

Figure 8.1 illustrates the successful use of time-out procedures with 7-year-old Jamie, a child who would throw a major tantrum or urinate over the carpet whenever he was angry or wanted attention. His mother would *not* accept that her son should get attention when he was quiet but

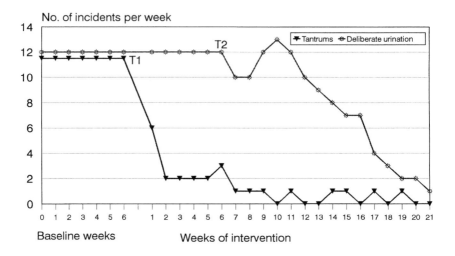

T1 = intervention for tantrums; T2 = intervention for urination

Figure 8.1: The use of 'time out' procedures to reduce frequency of tantrums and deliberate urination in 7-year-old boy.

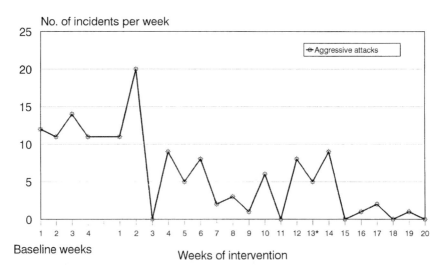

* Time out not used consistently until week 13; before then mother's approach was very variable (ignoring, smacking, shouting etc.)

Figure 8.2: The need for consistency when attempting to use 'time out' procedures.

she did respond with great alacrity to behaviours of this kind. Eventually realising that the problem showed no sign of improving, she agreed to remove him briefly to the bathroom whenever a tantrum occurred. Subsequently she tried the same technique for urination, again with quite rapid success (see Howlin & Rutter, 1987a for further details). However, she was not able to respond with anything like the same degree of consistency when he became aggressive and tried to attack her. At times she would remove him from the situation, at others she would scream or even hit him and in this case it took several months for her to develop a more consistent approach (see Figure 8.2).

A further difficulty with time-out approaches, in addition to the need for consistency, is that they can rarely be used in isolation. Indeed it has been argued that they almost invariably involve a combination of other techniques, including extinction, punishment, and positive and negative reinforcement (Smith, 1987). At times, too, it can be very difficult to establish what reinforcers are in operation, and hence which ones need to be withdrawn or replaced.

When a time-out programme was used to stop Wayne's deliberate smashing of glasses and bottles, it had little effect. Only when it was recognised that his reinforcement seemed to come from watching the fragments of glass and the reflections these made, rather than from

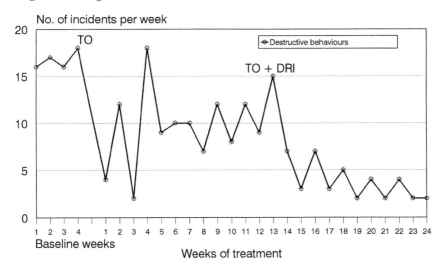

TO = use of time out alone; TO + DRI = use of time out and differential reinforcement of incompatible behaviours

Figure 8.3: The comparative effects of 'time out' and differential reinforcement of incompatible behaviour in reducing destructive behaviours (smashing glass and china).

attention by his mother, was any real progress made. In this case, he was offered an alternative reinforcement, which consisted of the opportunity to wash glass items in large quantities of bubbly washing up liquid, as long as he did not break them (see Figure 8.3).

In some cases, procedures that are assumed to result in *time out* from reinforcement may actually function as positive or negative reinforcers. Durand and Carr (1987) found that the introduction of a 'time out' (i.e. removal of attention) condition, in an experimental setting, resulted in an increase in self-stimulatory behaviours rather than the postulated decrease. This was because the so-called 'time-out' period seemed to signal the removal of task demands, and hence functioned as a negative reinforcer for the child. For many other children with autism, being removed from the room or being left alone can actually be highly motivating. Thus, Stevie's mother began to remove him to his room every time he hit his sister, on the grounds that he would not then get satisfaction from hearing her screams. Unfortunately, he obtained even more satisfaction from being left alone and he rapidly learned to pull his sister's hair whenever he wanted peace and quiet.

There are also other risks. Unless used with caution time-out can sometimes lead to an escalation of punitive procedures, especially in residential or institutional settings (Howlin & Clements, 1995). Once a child begins to be excluded for aggressive attacks, he or she may be removed with increasing frequency, or spend ever longer periods in isolation. There is little good experimental evidence to indicate the optimum time of exclusion periods, but anecdotal reports suggest that without firm controls or written guidelines this time can steadily escalate, leading to a significant diminution in the child's access to other, more appropriate activities.

Differential reinforcement
This technique, which involves the use of rewards to encourage alternative behaviours, is often a more acceptable strategy for both parents and teachers. No aversive element is involved, and the emphasis, as with functional analysis approaches, is on the development of positive behaviours. Differential reinforcement techniques can be used to build up new and desirable behaviours, or to decrease unwanted ones, sometimes simultaneously. For example, Matthew had two main interests in life: one was spinning, one was numbers. Initially his parents had encouraged the spinning 'because it kept him out of mischief'; on the other hand, his interest in numbers proved rather irritating because he was always asking them to solve arithmetic calculations. Realising that this was perhaps not a very constructive approach they decided that they would respond more enthusiastically to his queries about sums; however, they no longer joined in, or encouraged his spinning, except when it was time to go to

bed. Over time, his mathematical skills developed considerably while the spinning virtually disappeared.

If the behaviour that is attended to or otherwise rewarded is incompatible with the unwanted behaviour the results can be particularly effective. For example, Simon's hand flapping and flicking was brought under control when his parents reinforced him for putting his hands in his pockets; Josh, a non-verbal child who made an almost constant moaning sound, was gradually reinforced instead for humming. (For further examples see Schopler, 1995.)

The choice of which behaviours should be replaced or which alternatives should be reinforced are, of course, decisions that can only be made at an individual level. The selection of reinforcers, too, will also be very variable. Rewards that work well with normally developing children may have little effect on a child with autism, and parents and teachers must be willing to contemplate a range of unusual items or activities. Pieces of plumbing or electrical equipment, toothpaste lids, sheets of fractions, or periods of solitude may be far more effective than hugs or sweets, and the child's own ritualistic or stereotyped behaviours are likely to prove particularly powerful.

When searching for effective reinforcement techniques, it is also necessary to bear in mind the power of negative reinforcement. This is not, as is sometimes mistakenly believed, a form of punishment, but is the reinforcement that is obtained when an unwanted or unpleasant behaviour or event ceases. Very often negative and positive reinforcers work in tandem, and it is no use changing one while leaving the other untouched. The child who yells loudly for sweets in the supermarket queue, for example, will be reinforced for his screams if his mother gives in and offers him the sweets. However, she, in turn, will also be reinforced by the termination to her embarrassment. Unless the possible impact of negative reinforcement, particularly for parents, is considered at the same time as deciding on positive reinforcers for the child, behavioural improvements may well prove difficult to achieve.

Self-stimulatory and Self-injurious Behaviours

Autistic children may indulge in a wide range of such behaviours, ranging from hand flapping and flicking, rocking, head banging, eye poking, skin picking, biting, or pica (eating non-food substances). The behaviours may be relatively innocuous or occur only briefly—for example, if the child is very bored or anxious—or they may be serious and persistent, causing physical damage or even danger to life. On the whole, children who are most intellectually handicapped are most likely to indulge in severe self-injurious or stimulatory activities (Hall, 1997).

Behaviours of this kind can have a wide range of different causes and the treatments used in intervention have been equally varied. These have included drugs, aversive techniques and other forms of punishment, differential reinforcement and restraint (see Murphy *et al.*, 1993; Oliver, 1995; Hall, 1997). However, the success or otherwise of these methods is also unpredictable, and what is effective in discouraging self-injury or stimulation in one child may actually serve as a reinforcer for others. Murphy *et al.* (1993), for example, suggest that although restraints such as splints are widely used in attempts to discourage self-injury, they may reinforce and hence increase the rates of these behaviours in some children.

Sometimes, in the case of more able children, extinction procedures can work effectively. Daniel, who was a 7-year-old boy of normal non-verbal intelligence, could be seen to watch his parents carefully for their reaction to his head banging. He never banged unless an adult was present and would also 'test' the floor or furniture first in order to ensure that he did not hurt himself unduly. In his case, simply ignoring the behaviour, while encouraging other attempts to seek attention, worked very rapidly. In other cases, however, especially when the child is profoundly handicapped or the self-injury is more severe, professional help will be required in order to avoid the risks of escalation. Studies of the development of self-injurious behaviours tend to show that these may begin as non-harmful stereotyped responses, often appearing first when the child is ill, or when he or she is left unoccupied. However, what begins as a mild form of self-stimulation can steadily escalate if the child receives greater attention for this than for any other behavioural response. Self-injury is also an extremely effective way of avoiding unwanted demands since few adults will continue to insist that a child completes an activity if this results in head banging or other distressing responses. Moreover, for children who are seriously or profoundly retarded, their repertoire of alternative behaviours may be so limited that the risk of self-injurious or stimulatory behaviours becoming the easiest means of obtaining attention or controlling their environment is particularly high.

Successful programmes have generally involved early intervention, *before* the behaviour becomes a powerful manipulator, together with a detailed functional analysis of the behaviour and careful assessment of the responses of others towards this. However, this can be extremely time consuming and at times, even with highly sophisticated methods of recording and statistical analysis, it can prove very difficult to establish the factors provoking or maintaining self-injury. In some cases (Hall, 1997) parents may fail to realise that a self-stimulatory behaviour has begun to turn into something more serious and harmful. Very often, too, intervention is delayed until the behaviour reaches crisis proportions, and at this stage so many different interventions may be attempted at once that it becomes impossible to determine which, if any, are effective (Davies *et al.*, 1998).

The level of stimulation to which the child is exposed can also be an important factor. Too little stimulation or structure may well exacerbate such behaviours and self-stimulatory behaviours, such as pica, have been found to increase in impoverished environments but decrease if children have greater access to toys and adult attention (Myles *et al.*, 1997). On the other hand, over-demanding or over-stimulating environments may also produce stress, which in turn can result in self-injury or stereotyped behaviours. Duker and Rasing (1989) for example, found that by simplifying the classroom environment and removing extraneous stimulation, rates of stereotypies could be significantly reduced.

Self-injurious or stimulatory behaviours can arise, too, as a result of fears or physical pain. Desensitisation techniques (see below) can be used to help the child deal with particular fears or phobias. Attention also needs to be paid to possible physical factors. Insensitivity to pain, as well as a lack of ability to explain what hurts or where the pain is, can make diagnosis difficult (Biersdorff, 1994), and Gunsett *et al.* (1989) stress the importance of carrying out medical screening *before* any psychological programmes are implemented, especially in individuals who are profoundly handicapped. They found that in a series of 13 cases referred for self-injurious behaviours, 10 had a physical basis for the behaviour. These included limb fractures, hernias, urinary tract infections, ear infections, bowel problems, incorrect medication, toxic levels of anti-convulsants and progressive brain deterioration. Other authors note that stereotyped and self-injurious behaviours may appear following minor illnesses, such as dermatitis and otitis media (Oliver, 1995; Hall, 1997). As children with autism may suffer more frequently from ear infections (Konstantareas & Homatidis, 1987) it is clearly important for the clinician to rule these out as a possible cause of episodic behavioural changes, especially in non-verbal children.

Fears and Phobias

Children with autism may experience extreme fear in many different situations. A particular radiator, a specific corner of the garden, a certain lamp-post in the street, a door or cupboard left open in a particular way, can all cause profound distress, which in turn results in an increase in tantrums and disruptive behaviours or elevated levels of self-injury and stereotypes. In such cases, rather than attempting to addressing the disruptive or injurious behaviours directly, desensitisation procedures may be used to modify the child's fears until they are no longer a source of distress and agitation.

Table 8.2: Reducing a long-standing bath phobia in a 5-year-old boy

---

Stages
- Week 1: New bath left in hallway before being installed. Child allowed to use it as a toy store
- Week 2: Bath placed in bathroom; continues as toy store
- Week 3: Child washed fully clothed standing in bath
- Week 4: Child washed in plastic washing-up basin placed in bath
- Week 5: Child washed while wearing bathing shorts only
- Week 6: Plug placed in bath; child still standing in basin
- Week 7: Water level gradually raised; plastic basin removed
- Weeks 8–10: Child spends increasing time in bath-tub. Also allows hair to be washed without protest for the first time ever

---

Desensitisation involves exposing the child to the feared object or situation, but in such a way as to keep anxiety to a minimum. Again, a graded change approach is most effective. Table 8.2 shows the stages used to overcome 5-year-old Patrick's fear of baths and bathrooms. He had developed this fear during a period in hospital and thereafter refused to be washed except in a baby's plastic bath or the kitchen sink. Hair washing was also described as a 'nightmare'. When his family moved house they immediately took the opportunity to keep his toys in the bathroom in the weeks before the new bath was installed; they then gradually increased his exposure to the bath, and then to water (see Table 8.2).

Graham's fear of balloons had escalated to such an extent that even the expectation of celebrations for Christmas or children's birthdays would provoke extreme anxiety and agitation. Even deflated balloons caused anxiety, so he was encouraged instead to blow bubble gum, or a substitute material that produced non-banging plastic 'balloons'. Subsequently he moved on to thick, inflatable footballs, which were unlikely to burst, and then on to cheaper, thinner ones. Real balloons, which were gradually inflated more and more, were eventually introduced, until he was able to blow up and burst balloons by himself. In order to avoid the fears incubating during the non-party season, his parents always ensured that a few balloons were left hanging in the house at all times.

Daisy had a marked fear of dogs, which was increasingly restricting her parents' ability to take her out. A teacher at school had an old and docile labrador, an ex-guide dog that moved extremely slowly and never barked. Daisy, who was also fascinated with video cameras, was allowed to take a film of the dog, initially being led by his owner and then off the lead. Because she loved to see herself on video Daisy eventually allowed herself to be filmed walking with the teacher and the dog, and finally leading the dog alone. Although she is still obviously agitated if small, yappy dogs come suddenly into view, she no longer refuses to go to parks or other public places, nor will she run out into the road if a dog approaches.

Other fears, which can give rise to considerable practical problems, relate to visiting the doctor or dentist. Some children are so terrified by the latter that they may suffer severe tooth decay, or require a general anaesthetic for even minor procedures. Recognition that this is a common problem for the parents of children with autism is the best solution here. Firstly, families need to elicit the help of a sympathetic dentist or family doctor to whom the child can be taken at regular intervals, preferably long before any treatment is required. Lying on the doctor's couch, being weighed, listening through a stethoscope will all familiarise the child with the sights, sounds and smells of the surgery. At the dentist's, rides up and down on the chair, being allowed to manipulate the lights, spitting into the basin can all be a source of fun. Later, brief oral examinations should cause few problems, so that by the time any treatment is needed the child is well used to the whole procedure. It is, of course, possible to introduce desensitisation procedures at a later stage. Luscre and Center (1996) report on a treatment programme for children who had already had dental phobias. They found that a combination of graded exposure, anxiety-reducing stimuli (such as music or Play Doh), rewards, and modelling (the autistic children watched videos of peers having an examination at the same time) led to rapid improvements. However, with prior planning and gradual and careful exposure from infancy, there should be less need for more elaborate programmes of this kind, at least for the majority of children.

Self-control Techniques

Once carers and teachers have developed successful management strategies to bring problem behaviours under control, the next stage is to try to help the child gain more effective self-control. Frea (1995) gives a number of examples of how self-management strategies can be used to reduce inappropriate social behaviours. Koegel *et al.* (1995) also illustrate how severe stereotypic behaviours could be brought under control by teaching individuals to monitor their own stereotyped movements over increasing periods of time. The children wore wrist watch alarms to signal when they should begin recording and simple counters were used to monitor the frequency of stereotypes. The act of counting, alone, can help to reduce the frequency of unwanted behaviours but children were also prompted to replace the stereotyped behaviour with a more appropriate activity. Even individuals with quite severe learning disabilities have proved able to monitor their behaviours with surprising reliability, and once better awareness of the problem is established it becomes much easier to encourage and reinforce alternative activities. Using techniques of this kind, Koegel and colleagues have reported 'dramatic ' decreases in self-stimulatory behaviour (from 100% to 0% of the time in specific settings).

Self-monitoring devices (counters, pegboards, checklists, etc.) can also be used to record and increase the frequency or duration of on-task behaviours. Sally, for example, needed continual prompting in order to complete even the simplest task, and was constantly bothering teachers and peers for reassurance that she was 'a clever girl'. She was provided with a wrist watch alarm, set for a very brief period of time, and when this sounded she was encouraged to go to the teacher, who would stamp her work with a 'clever girl' marker. Gradually, the timer was set for increasing periods of time, and then Sally was provided with her own stamp so that she could mark each full page of work herself. Eventually direct praise from the teacher was required only at the end of each teaching session.

Daniel was a child who had always had a tendency to strip off all his clothes whenever he could, and as he grew older this became an increasing source of embarrassment for his parents. Eventually they provided him with a wrist watch with an integral thermometer, and when the temperature reached a certain level an alarm would sound. He was allowed to strip down to his undershorts (quite respectable garments in much the same style as other young men's shorts) ONLY when the temperature reached 30 degrees and the alarm sounded. This technique worked remarkably well throughout much of the following year. Unfortunately, in a hot and crowded department store, just before Christmas time the alarm went off unexpectedly, signalling to Daniel that it was time to strip off once more!

However, despite potential difficulties of this kind, self-management strategies can result in much more effective behavioural control. Problems of maintenance and generalisation can be more easily overcome and the active involvement of children in their own intervention programmes helps to foster independence and autonomy, thereby decreasing dependence on adult regulation.

INCREASING OTHER BEHAVIOURS AND SKILLS

Although there are obviously times when intervention has to concentrate on the elimination of unwanted behaviours, on the whole a focus on building up the child's alternative skills results in a more positive and often more effective approach to treatment. There is little point in

Table 8.3: Strategies commonly used to increase behaviours

Behavioural term	What it means in practice	An example
Shaping	Building up a behaviour by progressively rewarding child for closer and closer approximations to that behaviour.	Praising (or otherwise rewarding) the child for putting her toys at the end of the day onto carpeted area of room; then for putting them onto smaller rug; then into large shallow box; finally into toy box.
Prompting	Guiding the child through a required action using physical or verbal guidance. The child is then reinforced for carrying out the action.	Holding child's hand while he is helped to take a spoonful of food. In this case access to the food itself should serve as the reinforcer.
Fading prompts	Gradually reducing the prompts until the child can carry out the action independently.	In the scenario above, the amount of help given to the child would be gradually reduced until he can eat with only minimal help (e.g. hand being placed around spoon in order to 'start him off'; or plate held to stop it moving).
Task analysis	Breaking down the task into its component parts; essential for teaching skills such as washing dressing, etc., which are actually a lot more complex than they might appear.	Child who has difficulty putting on clothes. Adult puts on (say) a jumper and writes down each of the stages involved (lifting it onto head; pushing neck through; holding up arms, etc.), then prompts child through each of these stages in turn.
Backward chaining	Extremely useful technique for teaching new skills; requires careful task analysis. FINAL step in the chain is identified and this taught first, so that child is rapidly rewarded for the completion of task. Then penultimate stage is taught and so on until the task can be completed from the beginning.	Scenario above: child is prompted and rewarded for pulling down the last few centimetres of her jumper (e.g. from waist to above hip level). The next stage is to have her pull jumper from chest; then from under armpits, etc.

Table 8.4: Examples of strategies that can be used to shape and promote more complex skills

Tidying toys	*(Child who refuses to put toys away at end of the day)* 1. Child rewarded for placing toys anywhere on large carpet in play room. 2. Carpet covered by piece of blanket; rewards for placing toys on this. 3. Size of blanket gradually reduced. 4. Blanket replaced by 'garden-tidy'—large plastic sheet with drawstring closure. Toys left on this can be gathered up quickly by pulling the cords.
Visual matching skills	*(Child who consistently posts objects down back of radiator)* 1. Radiator covered by heavy-duty cardboard 'shelf' with slots in through which shapes can be posted (container placed underneath for easy retrieval). 2. Slots made gradually smaller/shallower, thereby restricting object size. 3. Child encouraged to use simple toy 'posting boxes' (i.e. regular shape boxes made easier by covering up more difficult shapes). 4. Complexity of posting toys increased; more complex form boards introduced. 5. Simple jigsaws introduced; complexity gradually increased.
Pre-reading skills	*(Child with well developed visuo-spatial skills)* 1. Child prompted to match photos to a few favourite household items/toys. 2. Simple picture to picture matching tasks introduced. 3. Shape matching follows. Velcro backings help to keep these from sliding around. 4. Complexity of pictures or shapes to be matched increases; size decreases. 5. Names added to bottom of pictures used in matching. 6. Gradually, writing enlarged on one set of pictures (so accompanying picture very small) and picture enlarged on other set (so written label very small). 7. Child able to match cards with written labels only to picture cards. 8. 'Flash cards' used to identify objects around the house.
Tidying clothes	*(Child who drops all his clothes on the floor in the bathroom and refuses to pick these up)* 1. Large shallow toy container placed on bathroom floor. Child allowed special bath-foam if clothes fall in this. 2. Deeper but narrower container provided. 3. Top half of old plastic wash-basket removed so child can easily drop clothes in. 4. This replaced by regular clothes basket (lid removed). 5. Lid re-attached. Child continues to place clothes in each night.

designing complex programmes to minimise self-stimulatory behaviours if the child has no access to other behaviours that can, functionally, take their place.

Zarkowska and Clements (1988) outline a number of very practical
procedures that can be used to teach alternative skills to individuals with
learning disabilities. In her book, *Helping your Handicapped Child*, Janet
Carr (1995) also describes many relatively simple procedures that can be
used to build up the child's behavioural repertoire. Using techniques
such as prompting, shaping, task analysis and chaining (see Table 8.3),
together with reinforcement, she illustrates how parents can help the
child to improve their skills in areas such as dressing, toileting and other
self-help activities. Howlin and Rutter (1987a) also describe how quite
basic behaviours such as shape matching, or even stereotyped activities
such as 'posting' objects down the backs of chairs, could be systematically
shaped into more productive skills. Table 8.4 gives examples of a number
of tasks that have been taught at home by parents utilising methods of
this kind.

Hyperactivity is a problem frequently complained of by the parents of
children with autism, especially when they are younger (in adolescence,
many children tend to become much less active and sometimes even
lethargic). In fact, although some children do show clear symptoms of
hyperactivity, in many other cases it is the lack of ability to engage in any
constructive activities that leads to their tendency to move rapidly from
one task to another, continually to fiddle with or destroy toys or other
objects, or run repetitively back and forth. Jack, for example, spent most
of his day running to and fro across the room, and dents in the wall at
either end bore witness to this. At one stage his parents had resorted to
Ritalin, in the hope that this might improve things, but instead the situation became even worse as Jack then stopped sleeping at night. Once he
started at nursery school, his teachers and parents worked together on a
programme to structure his daytime activities more effectively. Throughout the day, brief periods of time 'on task' were introduced. To begin
with, these were simply sitting long enough to take a few sips of drink
through a straw; standing at a table and blowing a few bubbles with soap
liquid; pressing knobs and levers on a toy that made a variety of different
noises; sitting on a toy train that vibrated; or shaking and blowing various
musical toys. His parents also took turns to organise more out-door activities for him when he was at home. Gradually, the time on-task was
increased (co-operation being rewarded by periods of being allowed to
run up and down the room) and the number of activities was also
enlarged. Although Jack continues to run if not otherwise occupied, he is
now willing to sit for several 10-minute periods during the day, and will
also join his family for meals.

Environmental Modifications

As described in the earlier chapters on communication and rituals, attention to environmental structure can help to reduce or minimise many of the problems associated with autism. Non-verbal forms of communication, such as pictures, photographs, charts or lists, can help the child to make more sense of his or her environment, and can make day-to-day activities more predictable and hence easier to cope with.

Other, very simple, physical aids can also have a considerable impact. For a child who is always attempting to leave the table at mealtimes, a chair placed between the table and the wall may be more difficult to leave than one with no such obstruction; for a little child who is forever getting up at night, side bars on the bed may make the exit just that much more difficult. Appropriately fitted locks on fridges, cupboards and doors can limit access to food or other substances; socket covers on switches may help to reduce the risk for a child who is constantly poking things inside them. A small step-stool for the bath or toilet can make these more accessible and less frightening while potties that play a tune may encourage the child to urinate in the right place. Timers or clocks may be used as signals to indicate that an activity is about to begin, or come to an end, and sticky tape on the inside of basins, baths or smaller containers can help to indicate safe water levels. Electric toothbrushes can help to encourage dental hygiene—these also have wider handles that are often easier to hold. 'Self-tying' shoe laces that automatically curl around each other can reduce the need to tie laces. Other problems with dressing can be minimised by ensuring that skirts or trousers have elasticated waists, avoiding the need to cope with zips or buttons. Velcro fastenings can make life easier for everyone, while T-shirts or jumpers should be kept large and loose—no tight head or arm holes. Dressing can be further helped by sticking or sewing on labels or coloured tags that indicate back and front, left or right.

For children who dislike changes of clothes, a different bag or drawer containing clothes for each day of the week can be useful for establishing the need to change clothing regularly, while simultaneously providing predictability for the child. Rowena always insisted on wearing the same clothes and her mother took great trouble to buy her identical items to wear. However, as she grew older, she also became increasingly resistant to changing her garments and, if possible, would wear the same items day after day. Her mother bought an old set of drawers and painted each one a different colour, so that on Monday she had to take clothes from the red drawer, on Tuesday from the blue one and so on. Because she was intrigued by this, Rowena complied with changing her clothes each night. Gradually her mother began to introduce slight changes into the drawers—a slightly different shade of blue T-shirt, a different label on the jeans, socks with varying tops—and again Rowena eventually began to accept this. Her dress still remains rather limited in range, but as long as she is able to predict, in advance, what she will wear she is much more willing to accept minor changes, and her mother no longer has to buy large sets of identical items each time she goes shopping.

To improve eating behaviours, table mats showing the outline of plates and cutlery can greatly assist in tasks such as setting the table. For children who have problems with fine motor movement, aids designed for people with physical disabilities should also be explored. These include non-slip plates with rubber bases, cups that are easy to hold and will not move around, or knives, forks, spoons and pens with special handles.

If tidiness is a problem, drawers or cupboards might show pictures of the relevant items, or even have a specific item of clothing, such as a T-shirt, attached to the front. Problems of this kind can also be reduced using shaping procedures. Jan would never put toys or clothing away and insisted on dropping everything she used on the floor. In her bedroom, her parents constructed a large, shallow box from cardboard. This covered so much of the floor area that it was almost certain that some items of clothing would find their way in there; a similar box was placed in the living room for toys. Jan had a special reward (songs from her favourite tape in the bedroom, and a particular clip from a Thomas the Tank Engine video in the living room) if any items were in the box when it was time to go to bed. Gradually the size of the containers was reduced until eventually most of her clothes were put in a laundry basket each night, and toys were generally placed in a large toy box.

DRUGS AND DIET

Special Dietary Treatments

From time to time there is widespread publicity in the press about the effectiveness of different dietary treatments for a wide range of childhood problems, including hyperactivity and autism. Donna Williams (1992, 1994), a woman with autism, has also written about the effects that she believes a strict dietary regime has had on her life and on her ability to cope with social interactions. There is little doubt that, for some children, the eradication or reduction of certain additives and colourings does seem to lead to a diminution in overactivity and agitation. Many parents report that 'outlawing' chocolates or artificially coloured drinks has had a major impact on their child's behaviour. Reducing caffeine intake in coffee, tea or Coca-cola may also help. Jo, for example, was delighted when she got to college and found that she could take a cup of coffee whenever she wanted (it had always been restricted at home). Over a period of several months her mood became increasingly agitated and she also developed a mild hand tremor. Initially, her parents thought that the change in mood was due to the stress of attending college. Eventually, they found that she was having a cup of coffee at the end of every lecture (i.e. around seven cups a day); insisting that she took decaffeinated coffee with her to college instead resulted in a rapid improvement.

The possible advantages and disadvantages of more restricted diets, however, need to be very carefully evaluated. Some parents are advised that diets of this kind are necessary on the basis of somewhat spurious analyses of children's hair samples, or poorly controlled tests for allergies, rather than on the basis of detailed behavioural, psychological and physiological assessments. On the assumption that any one of a variety of different foods might be responsible for the child's overactivity or agitation, an exclusion regime then needs to be instituted, which usually involves removing all risk items from the child's diet. This results in the child being restricted to a very limited diet, with risk items being gradually re-introduced in order to assess their impact on the child's behaviour. Although, in some cases, this may help to identify allergic responses, Taylor (1998) suggests that many children are incorrectly identified as being 'allergic'. Moreover, the diet can have unpredicted effects. Giles's parents, for example, had tried out a number of different diets with him when he was younger. They had found that excluding artificial colourings and additives seemed to help; they also restricted his meat intake. He co-operated well with this programme and when he learned to read would check product labels himself. However, at the age of 10 he decided that he should become entirely vegetarian and he began to spend hours scrutinising packets of biscuits, crisps or cakes, or tins and jars of other foods in case they contained any meat derivatives. He would refuse to eat any food unless all the ingredients were listed in detail. He took longer and longer to eat meals because of his insistence on reading all the packaging and his diet became so restricted that his doctor became quite concerned. Eventually his mother had to give up feeding him processed or pre-packaged food entirely and had to cook everything for him herself.

Joshua was a 7-year-old boy with severe learning disabilities whose parents had been told, after a single visit to a private dietician, that he was allergic to all wheat products. His main pleasure in life was food, especially cakes and bread, and he also attended a small school where eating and cooking activities played a central role in the school curriculum. The insistence that he should not eat or even come into contact with wheat products had a major impact on his daily life, resulting in great changes and restrictions to his diet, which had previously been quite varied.

He became disruptive at school because he could not take part in pre-viously enjoyed activities, and at home there were major tantrums every mealtime.

Pharmacological Treatments

When things are particularly bad, or if all other approaches have failed, parents may well turn for help to medication. In a recent review of treat-ments for children with autism Rimland and Baker (1996) note: The vast majority of parents who take their autistic children to medical treatments are offered prescription drugs as the treatment of choice.' While this state-ment may not be true for parents in the UK it is clear that in the USA a wide variety of medication is used to treat or ameliorate many of the problems associated with autism. Surveys of American parents indicate the astonish-ing range of drugs prescribed, and the variation in parental views of their effectiveness. In a study based on data from 6,568 parents, Rimland and Baker (1996) found six particular drugs to be used most frequently, al-though their effectiveness seemed very variable (see Table 8.5).

Another survey, conducted by Aman et al. (1995) and based on replies from 838 carers, found that 33.8% of the sample was taking some form of psychotropic drug or vitamin treatment. When drugs for physical problems were also included, the figure rose to 53%. Ratings of parental satisfaction with the different forms of treatment indicated that anticonvulsants, stim-ulants and antidepressants were most popular—although a number of sud-den deaths have been reported in children given tricyclic antidepressants (Varley & McClellan, 1997). Least favoured by parents were vitamins, mood stabilisers, neuroleptics, antihypertensives and sedatives/hypnotics.

Drugs may be prescribed for many different reasons; the most common tend to be hyperactivity, aggressive and destructive behaviours, self-

Table 8.5: Most often prescribed drugs for children with autism in the USA (from Rimland & Baker, 1996)

Drug	No. prescriptions	% children rated as 'improved'	% rated as 'worse'*
Ritalin	1971	27	47
Mellaril	1668	34	28
Benedryl	1582	26	22
Dilantin	878	24	28
Haloperidol	852	37	39
Tegretol	799	33	24

* Remainder of cases rated as showing no change.

injury, stereotypies and obsessions, anxiety and depression, and sleeping problems. Medication may also be required for associated problems, such as epilepsy. Some drugs, such as fenfluramine and more recently certain selective seretonin uptake inhibitors (fluoxetine and fluvoxamine—Lewis, 1996; McDougle *et al.*, 1996), have been recommended as a means of reducing autistic symptomatology more generally.

Despite the widespread use of so many different drugs, especially in the USA, evaluations are frequently inadequate (Lewis, 1996; McDougle, 1997). Campbell and her colleagues (1996) suggest that only haloperidol, fenfluramine, naltrexone, clomipramine and clonidine have been appropriately investigated.

Haloperidol
The short-term efficacy and safety of haloperidol has been demonstrated in a number of large-scale studies of hospitalised children (Anderson *et al.*, 1989). The drug, which is a neuroleptic, has been found to reduce disruptive, aggressive, non-co-operative and hyperactive behaviours; improvements in language and sociability have also been reported. No deleterious effects on cognitive functioning have been found and in two laboratory-based studies learning is said to have been enhanced (Anderson *et al.*, 1989; Campbell *et al.*, 1978). For children who initially respond well, the long-term effects seem to be good (Perry *et al.*, 1989). However, sedation can occur and the other main side-effect is tardive or withdrawal dyskinesia (Armenteros *et al.*, 1995; Campbell *et al.*, 1997).

Fenfluramine
Fenfluramine hydrochloride is a serotonin-depleting agent and its use in autism was based largely on findings of elevated serotonin levels in some individuals with this condition. Large-scale, multi-centre studies in the USA during the 1980s resulted in reports of significant improvements in activity levels, attention span and motor disturbance (especially stereotyped movements); social, cognitive and sensory skills were also found to improve (Ritvo *et al.*, 1986). Subsequent studies, however, indicated that the response to treatment was very variable, with some children showing few improvements, even though serotonin levels did generally decline (Sherman *et al.*, 1989). The reported improvements in linguistic and cognitive functioning were particularly elusive (Coggins *et al.*, 1988; Ekman *et al.*, 1989) and Beisler and colleagues (1986) found no consistent changes that could be attributed to the drug regime. Later investigations began to indicate a wide range of negative side-effects, including mood disturbances, irritability, agitation, eating and digestive problems, insomnia or lethargy, weight loss, and learning problems (Sherman *et al.*, 1989). By 1996, concerns about side-effects were so widespread that Campbell *et al.* conclude

'fenfluramine is not viewed as a therapeutic agent for autism' although they note that 'it may have beneficial effects in individual patients'.

Naltrexone

This is an opiate antagonist, which has been used in the treatment of autism generally and self-injurious behaviour in particular (see Campbell & Cueva, 1995 and Campbell *et al.*, 1996 for review). The hypothesis underlying the use of this drug was that, in autism, abnormalities of the endogenous opioids could result in cognitive impairments and behavioural difficulties such as social withdrawal, high pain thresholds and lability of mood. Theoretically, the administration of naltrexone should control or reduce behavioural problems, while simultaneously correcting underlying abnormalities in the endogenous opioids (Sahley & Panksepp, 1987). Practically, however, there have been too few double blind/ placebo controlled trials of adequate size to support these views. Campbell *et al.* (1993) report a significant reduction in hyperactivity in 41 hospitalised children, and this has also been found in other studies (Herman *et al.*, 1991; Kolmen *et al.*, 1993). A study by Bouvard *et al.* (1995) also reports improvements in sociability, communication and attention. So far there appear to be few negative side-effects, and no adverse effects on liver function or learning. However, its efficacy in reducing self-injurious behaviour still awaits confirmation (Campbell, 1996; Harris, 1996; Zingarelli *et al.*, 1992; Willemsen-Swinkels *et al.*, 1995).

Clomipramine

This is a serotonin re-uptake inhibitor from the class of tricyclic antidepressants. Its apparent effectiveness in treating obsessive-compulsive disorders and repetitive motor behaviours led to its trials with autistic patients. However, in a recent double blind study of 24 subjects aged between 6 and 18 years, Sanchez *et al.* (1995) found improvements in only a minority of cases. Adverse effects included grand-mal seizures, behavioural toxicity, constipation and severe urinary retention. Not surprisingly, Campbell *et al.* (1996) warn: 'It is recommended that this class of drugs be used judiciously in individuals with autism.'

Clonidine

Used to reduce tics, hyperactivity, impulsivity and inattention in Tourette's syndrome, clonidine has been used more recently with children with autism. However, studies to date have been very small in size, and few conclusions can be drawn about its efficacy or safety. There is some indication that hyperactivity may be reduced, although even here findings are variable (see Campbell *et al.*, 1996) and cardiac problems are also among the possible side-effects.

Stimulants and Selective Serotonin Re-uptake Inhibitors

Methylphenidate (Ritalin)

Stimulant medication has been widely used in the USA to control problems of overactivity and attention. However, there are few, if any, adequately controlled trials of its effectiveness with children with autism. The largest is that of Quintana *et al.* (1995) who used a cross-over, placebo design with 10 children. The trial was conducted over six weeks (two weeks baseline; two weeks placebo or drug; two weeks drug or placebo). A 'modest' improvement in hyperactivity was recorded, and there were no obvious side-effects, although problems such as irritability, tantrums, and stereotyped movements have been noted in other studies (Anderson *et al.*, 1989). Quintana concludes that methylphenidate may have a role in the treatment of children with autism who are hyperactive but that 'further studies with larger samples are warranted'.

Selective serotonin re-uptake inhibitors (SSRIs)

This is a relatively new class of drugs which includes fluoxetine (Prozac) and fluvoxamine. They have gained increased popularity in the treatment of aggression and self-injury in autism; there are also claims that they can reduce repetitive thoughts and behaviours and improve social and communication skills (McDougle *et al.*, 1996). However, recent reviews suggest that SSRIs may also be associated with serious movement disorders (including tardive dyskinesia, dystonia and parkinsonism), seizures, headaches, self-harm, apathy, memory impairment, sleep disturbance and manic disorders (Leonard *et al.*, 1997).

Other medical interventions

Many other pharmacological approaches to the treatment of autism have also been tried over the years—see, for example, updates by Campbell and Cueva (1995) on stimulants and lithium, Connor *et al.* (1997) and Arnold and Aman (1991) on beta blockers, Lewis (1996) on fluoxetine, and McDougle *et al.* (1997) on risperidone. Nevertheless, Campbell *et al.* (1996) warn that 'No conclusions can be made concerning the efficacy and safety of these agents because the findings are based on small sample sizes and open studies without placebo control.'

In conclusion, it seems that although medication may be helpful for some children, much remains to be known about which drugs work best for which problems and for which types of children. Prescribing tends to be very much a 'hit and miss' affair, and negative and unwanted side-effects are a continuing risk. In addition, there are few if any data on the long-term impact of powerful drugs taken from childhood.

Medication will, of course, be required if there are co-existing complications such as epilepsy. However, finding the most appropriate anti-epileptic for an individual child is also often a matter of trial and error, and because of the side-effects many physicians prefer not to prescribe if the child has had only one or two fits. Medication may be necessary, too, for a few very severely disturbed children. For others, medication may be occasionally beneficial for the symptomatic treatment of overactivity, sleeping problems or agitation. Nevertheless, medication alone is unlikely to be effective unless it is combined with other behavioural interventions, as well as close attention to other factors within the child's environment. It is also a mistake to view medical treatments as confined to the use of drugs. Good-quality paediatric care is as important for children with autism as it is for any other young people with disabilities. Visual or hearing impairments, or other physical conditions, may also play a contributory role in the development of behavioural difficulties. Thus, continuing and skilled medical surveillance is yet another crucial element in the package of care required for children with autism and their families.

9

FINDING APPROPRIATE EDUCATION

No matter how much professional help is provided in the early years, and no matter how skilled parents themselves become as therapists, few families with a child with autism will be able to cope adequately without additional help from educational services. Finding the 'right' school, therefore, is of crucial importance.

WHAT IS THE RIGHT SCHOOL AND HOW CAN PARENTS FIND IT?

Unfortunately there is no easy answer to this question, for, as with so many other issues, individual needs and, hence, individual provision can vary widely. Some children can only receive the help they need in highly specialised autistic provision, whereas others require the academic stimulation that only mainstream school can provide. Both mainstream and segregated education have their benefits and drawbacks and these will vary according to the needs of individual children and the severity of their disorder (Howlin, 1994).

Over the last two decades, throughout much of western Europe, Australia and New Zealand, Canada and North America, legislation has swung steadily towards integrated education for all children with disabilities. Although beginning in the USA (see Kellegrew, 1995, and Berkman, 1997, for concise and useful historical accounts) similar movements occurred in many other countries, resulting in the closure or even abolition of specialist schools. However, although clearly desirable on many philosophical and practical grounds, integrated education is far from being a cheap option and may, in fact, make many more demands on resources and teaching expertise than is often acknowledged. Indeed, the failure of integrated services to provide children with autism with appropriately skilled educational help has resulted in many parents using legislation to obtain specialist rather than mainstream provision in order to ensure that their children are placed in 'the least restrictive environment'.

It is also clear that despite greater recognition of the requirements of children with special educational needs, provision still remains very inadequate. A survey of educational authorities in England and Wales (Gilby et al., 1988; Jones & Newson, 1992) found that very few provided any specialist facilities for children with autism. And, although the National Autistic Society now lists over 150 schools, classes, or units for children with autism in the UK these are clearly insufficient to meet the needs of all those who fall within the autistic spectrum.

In the following section, the possible advantages and disadvantages of different forms of provision are briefly discussed. (See Howlin, 1997a, for an expanded version of the following discussion of educational provision and practices.)

Forms of Provision

Specialist schools and units for children with autism

In the UK, the National Autistic Society is directly responsible for five specialist schools for children with autism, and ten others are part of its Accreditation Programme. There are also a number of units or classes run by local education authorities (National Autistic Society, 1995). In other countries where, either for economic or political reasons, there is less state-run segregated provision, small classes or units may be set up by charitable or parental organisations, or as part of a university-based research project. The TEACCH system, which originated in North Carolina (Mesibov, 1992) and which has since spread to many different countries, is an example of the latter.

As in any educational setting, the curriculum and quality of teaching offered within specialist schools or units can be very variable. The physical isolation of some of these schools is, in itself, something of a risk, and without ongoing monitoring or regular inspections, inappropriate and even damaging practices may develop. Howlin and Clements (1995), for example, describe one school for children with autism (which had never been adequately monitored by the local education authority) where behavioural techniques gradually became increasingly punitive over the years, until they reached the stage where children suffered both physical and psychological abuse.

The unique advantage of 'autistic schools', however, lies in the specialist knowledge and expertise of the teachers who work there. They are in a singular position when it comes to developing social and communication skills, minimising ritualistic and stereotyped behaviours, and generally creating the optimal environment for reducing problems and maximising abilities. Recognition of the problems of generalisation faced by many children with autism has also resulted in a particular focus on the link between home and school, which, in turn, promotes greater consistency in treatment and management. Small class sizes and a very high teacher-to-pupil ratio are other advantages. Many such schools also have a strong professional support network, including social workers, family doctors, paediatricians, psychiatrists or psychologists who are able to offer additional help to deal with other aspects of the child's or family's needs.

Many children with autism, even those with severe behavioural disturbances, show rapid improvement when placed in provision of this kind. Nevertheless, there are also drawbacks to segregated units. Firstly, the peer group itself, by its very nature, is unlikely to offer optimal scope for the development of social relationships. Secondly, many parents are concerned about the effects of placing their child with others who are equally or even more severely handicapped, especially as children with autism, like any others, have a propensity for copying undesirable behaviours from their peers.

The third and perhaps most important drawback of specialised autistic units, especially for more intellectually able children, is the limited educational facilities that they are able to offer. Small schools may have a great advantage when it comes to developing a consistent and individualised approach to teaching, but these very factors make it difficult, if not impossible, to offer a wide teaching curriculum. If they have pupils with particular skills in maths, physics, computing or even Greek, few autistic schools will have staff qualified enough in these topics to offer children the opportunity to take external examinations. Since success in later life is highly dependent on the qualifications obtained in school or college, the inability of most autistic schools to provide such opportunities can have serious long-term implications for more intellectually able pupils.

An increasingly popular alternative to separate *schools* is the development of small units, specifically designed to meet the needs of children with autism, but on the same site as a larger school. This may be a mainstream school, or a school for children with other forms of disability, including language disorders, sensory impairments, or learning difficulties. The advantage of such units is that children can benefit from the facilities offered by the parent school while continuing to have access to the individual support and specialist knowledge of the staff in the autistic unit. However, there is no hard evidence for the effectiveness or otherwise of units of this type. Clearly they do work well for some children but integration within the parent school often proves more difficult to achieve in practice than in principle. Thus, pupils and teachers in small units may remain isolated, and indeed sometimes even rejected, from the main body of the school.

Schools for children with severe learning disabilities

Around half of all children with autism have severe to moderate learning problems. Because of this many education authorities argue against placement in highly specialised (and expensive) autistic provision, when places are more readily available in schools for children with more general learning disabilities.

Again, there are several factors in favour of this argument. Firstly, because there are more schools available for children with learning disabilities, the child with autism can be educated relatively close to home, thereby promoting parent–teacher links and avoiding the need for extensive travelling or boarding provision. Secondly, because other pupils also live locally, this should facilitate the development of peer relationships outside school. Finally, because such schools are larger, the physical amenities are often far better.

However, the very unusual profile of relative skills and disabilities found in many children with autism can also lead to problems. Most children with learning disabilities, especially those in the mild to moderately handicapped range, will show a fairly 'flat' profile of abilities. Thus, although delayed in all areas, their social, communication and emotional development will, in general, be on a par with their development in other areas. Teaching can therefore be relatively easily adapted to the child's overall cognitive level. In the case of autistic children, whose developmental profiles are characteristically uneven, this can prove much more difficult. Thus, certain aspects of motor development may be relatively unimpaired; there may be moderate delays in other areas of non-verbal development, while deficits in verbal, social and emotional development may be very profound. If matched with other learning disabled children on the basis of their non-verbal skills, pupils with autism will almost certainly be far more handicapped than their peer group in terms of social and communication development. If matched for social or communication skills then they are likely to be far more capable in terms of their non-verbal abilities. Particularly if placement is in a special needs unit, then much of the staff's time is likely to be taken up with care-taking activities, such as cleaning, feeding or toileting, for the children who are most disabled, and the needs of the physically more able child with autism can easily be neglected.

The dependence of many children with autism on one-to-one teaching, at least for part of the day, together with their inability to work co-operatively with other pupils, also severely limits the opportunities for group teaching. In addition, specific impairments in imagination and imitative skills make play and other joint activities very difficult.

Schools for children with mild learning disabilities or emotional and behavioural difficulties

Although this type of provision should be appropriate for those children with autism whose general intellectual ability falls within the low average to mildly handicapped range, their very uneven developmental profiles can make teaching, and learning, in such settings very difficult. Thus, while the communication and interpersonal skills of children with autism may be much less well developed that those of their peers, their cognitive development, at least in certain areas, may be significantly more advanced, leading to problems for class or group teaching.

Moreover, although many pupils in schools of this kind will have behavioural problems, these are often very different in kind, or have very different causes from the problems shown by autistic children, and hence may require very different approaches to intervention. Similarly, conflicts may arise because of the general ethos of the school. Hence, while an emphasis on the development of independence and self-motivation skills may be important for non-autistic students, those with autism will be unable to make progress without a much more directive input from teachers. The children's limited social understanding also leaves them highly vulnerable to teasing or bullying by more socially competent peers. These are not necessarily insurmountable problems, especially if schools are small and well organised.

With due attention to these risks, accompanied by educational programmes that are specifically adapted to meet the child's cognitive, social and emotional needs, some schools for children with mild learning disabilities, or emotional and behavioural disturbance, can, and do, offer an effective educational environment. Unfortunately, in other cases, such provision may prove, at best, inadequate and, at worst, psychologically or even physically harmful.

Schools and units for children with language disorders

Although placement in a 'Language Unit' might be thought to be very suitable for at least some children with autism, in practice, such provision tends to be very limited. The few schools or units that do exist are often unwilling to accept pupils with a diagnosis of autism, because of the extent of their handicap. The majority of children with developmental language disorders show normal social reciprocity and imaginative play, and impairments in their use of gesture and other non-verbal skills are relatively mild (Bishop, 1994). In contrast, children with autism may have extensive problems in all these areas, even if their expressive language skills appear relatively intact. Thus, again, the skills required for teaching may be very different. In addition, few school-leavers in language units obtain formal qualifications (Haynes & Naidoo, 1991; Mawhood *et al.*, 1998) so that the intellectually able student with autism is unlikely to gain any academic advantages in such provision.

Children with autism in mainstream schools

For the majority of high-functioning children with autism, their chances of living a full and independent life will be dependent on whether they are able to obtain formal academic qualifications at school. Without these they will be unlikely to gain access to further education or subsequently to find suitable employment. With few exceptions, the only way in which this can be achieved will be by attending 'mainstream' school.

The push towards integration, particularly for children with fairly mild problems, has had a significant impact on education at the infant and junior levels and many primary schools have children with a variety of different disabilities on roll. Research evidence suggests that children with less severe or obvious disabilities tend to be more readily accepted by their peers (Howlin, 1994) so that children whose autism is relatively mild are likely to be more easily assimilated. There have also been a number of studies indicating that input from normal peers can have very beneficial impact on the play and social interactions of young children with autism (Lord, 1984; Wolfberg & Schuler, 1993; Quill, 1995). However, such interactions need to be carefully structured and reinforced by teaching staff; the types of play equipment used and the general structure of the classroom are also important, otherwise the enthusiasm of the normal children tends to be short-lived.

Moreover, even when specialist teaching is available, children in integrated classes do not invariably make better progress than those in segregated provision. Harris and her colleagues (1990) compared language development in two groups of children, both enrolled in special pre-school provision. One group attended an integrated class with normal peers; the others were in a small segregated class, exclusively for children with autism. Over the following year all children made better than normative progress in their rate of language development, although the scores of the children with autism remained significantly lower than those of their peers. Contrary to predictions, however, there were no differences in language ability between the autistic children in the integrated and segregated classes.

There are fewer studies of integration involving older, secondary school children but the evidence available suggests that the risk of rejection rises with age. Discrimination by peers and teachers alike tends to increase for a number of reasons. Firstly, because of increasing pressures to perform well in academic 'League Tables' or similar forms of assessment, schools have become more reluctant to accept pupils who are unlikely to do well. If a pupil has disruptive behaviours, these can also have a negative impact on the work of other children. In addition, during adolescence the need to conform to group norms and to be accepted by peers becomes of paramount importance. Those who do not fit in are increasingly likely to be rejected.

Secondly, the structure of secondary school is very different from that of primary school, and poses far more problems for pupils with autism. In primary school, children often remain with the same peer group for six years or more. Almost all lessons are conducted in the same classroom, and many children remain with the same teacher for two years or longer. Schools tend to be relatively small in size, so that teachers become familiar with all the children and their parents; it is possible to keep a careful watch on teasing and bullying, and close liaison between staff members makes it easier to agree on consistent approaches to education and management. Staff are more likely to tolerate 'unusual' behaviours (such as making loud comments in assembly or correcting the teacher in the classroom) and younger pupils accept children who are 'different' more readily than older ones do. In contrast, secondary schools are large, sometimes on split sites, and the majority of other pupils will be unfamiliar to the child. Lessons, classrooms and teachers change at hourly intervals so that most teachers will never get to know the children well, or understand the problems associated with a condition such as autism. Collaboration between teachers, in establishing an appropriate educational programme for a pupil with special needs, can also prove very difficult.

Guy, for example, although academically very gifted, constantly disrupted lessons because he always arrived late, could never find anywhere to sit, and had usually forgotten to bring the necessary books and equipment. After discussions between his mother and the Head of Special Needs it was suggested that he should be allowed to have a fixed desk at which to sit in every lesson—preferably at the back of the class where he would be less of a distraction to other pupils. In each classroom the desk would also contain the minimum equipment necessary for him to cope with the lesson (paper, pens, ruler, etc.). Some teachers were happy to implement these suggestions and in their classes Guy's behaviour improved rapidly. Others refused to change long-established teaching practices and in these classes his behaviour remained highly disruptive and erratic.

Thirdly, the very uneven profile of skills and difficulties shown by the child with autism can prove extremely disconcerting for teachers. Edward was a 14-year-old boy who had developed an interest in classical civilisation in primary school and subsequently became very proficient in ancient Greek. Despite this he was always forgetting to complete homework assignments, invariably came to lessons with the wrong books or equipment, his appearance was always dishevelled and he could not seem to learn even to tie his shoe laces after gym. It proved very difficult for teachers to accept that his apparent lack of compliance was related to his poor organisational abilities or to problems of comprehension, rather than to deliberate laziness or disobedience.

Teachers in secondary school may also be far less willing to make use of unusual teaching strategies than those in primary school. Thomas, for example, had made remarkably good progress in primary school despite a very shaky start, mainly due to his overwhelming obsession with 'Doctor Who', which threatened to disrupt all other activities. His teacher showed remarkable skill in using this obsession to reward an increasing range of alternative activities. Thus, after completing a few arithmetic problems he would be allowed to draw a picture of Doctor Who; later the reward was delayed until he had completed a page or more. Other written work was reinforced in similar ways. She also utilised his interest and knowledge in this topic to encourage group activities with other children and to extend his interest in other areas, from science to geography. At secondary school, however, such flexibility proved much harder to achieve. His teachers had been informed that allowing him to draw a picture of Doctor Who at the end of each piece of work would almost certainly ensure his co-operation, but he was frequently banned from doing this, or even punished. Deprived of his primary motivation, he became increasingly anxious and non-compliant, refusing to complete work assignments and eventually refusing to go to school at all.

Finally, crucial home–school links may also prove much harder to establish. Because Peter had always managed to avoid work of any kind unless firmly pressured into doing it, his junior school teachers and parents had worked hard together to monitor the quantity and quality of his work and to set strict limits on the amount of time he was allowed to complete any project. Each evening his parents received a note from his teacher informing them of the amount of homework to be completed and they filled in a 'time sheet' indicating how long this had taken. When he transferred to secondary school, his Statement of Special Educational Needs stressed his concentration problems and recommended strategies for dealing with these. Unfortunately, few of the teachers at his new school had the time or inclination to monitor his work, or enlist the help of his parents in the same way, with the result that his output declined rapidly and dramatically.

Because of this inability or unwillingness to provide pupils with autism with the very special help that they may need, many children go through multiple changes of school, with little understanding or proper planning. Some have been lucky in finding a sympathetic teacher or school that has been able to offer them the support needed, and this has then enabled them to make the best use of their academic abilities. However, this has more often been due to chance rather than appropriate educational planning. Most others have struggled along miserably throughout the years; unsupported, misunderstood and often mistreated. The following abstracts—one adapted from a letter home, written by a 12-year-old boy attending boarding school, the other taken from a school report on an 11-year-old—indicate all too clearly the types of distress and confusion that can occur (see also Howlin, 1997, for further examples of difficulties).

A letter home

Dear Mummy and Daddy.
Thank you for coming to see me on Saturday . . . I thought what pleasant company you were out with me. But, oh!! How those boys tease!! How they aggravate and Annoy!! My prep books have gone missing again. I told Mrs Jacks but she just said to go and find them. But I don't know where they have hidden them. They say they will put them in the water tank if I tell on them. I will be in real trouble with Mr Roberts if I don't do my prep once again. Last night Howard threw my slippers onto the lawn. I had to go out in my pyjamas to get them . . . I got splinters in my feet again. Will you come and collect me to come home? Please make the decision whether I am to come home . . . It's 10 days to go before the holidays, such a very long time. I don't want to have to come here again ever. I am hoping and hoping you won't say I have to come back.
   With best wishes, your sad son Josh.

A school report

David is a very difficult boy to understand. His written work is very messy and careless but he is making rapid progress in his maths. His reading is good and this term he has shown a lot of interest in books about astronomy. However, he finds it difficult to cope with anything that requires him to use his imagination. He still finds it hard to play with the other children in the playground but at last he is making some effort to join in team games. Unfortunately he never seems able to grasp the right rules. His work would be improved if he just tried to bring the right books and equipment to lessons. And, why is it that a boy of his age and intelligence seems incapable of learning a simple task such as tying his shoe laces?

Therese Jolliffe, now a post-graduate student, writes bitterly of her time in mainstream school and suggests 'Parents of autistic children should never think of sending their children to ordinary schools because the suffering will far outweigh any of the benefits achieved' (Jolliffe *et al.*, 1992). However, even if parents are aware that a school will not be able to cater for their child's social needs, and may even cause him or her considerable emotional stress, they also know that if a child of average or above academic ability is denied access to the normal curriculum, this will severely limit the chances of making good progress in later life.

Clearly much needs to be done to improve existing support systems and the crucial issue is not whether integrated or segregated education is best, but what can be done to ensure that the educational system available to children with autism is able to meet their social, emotional *and educational* needs. Research into effective school environments has consistently indicated that children do best in settings that are well structured, offer appropriately individualised programmes, emphasise 'on-task' activities, have goals that are clear to both teachers and children and that can be modified according to children's needs and abilities (Rutter, 1983). Very similar factors appear to be important in educational programmes for children with autism. Over 20 years ago, Rutter and Bartak (1973) stressed the value of a structured and task-oriented programme that focused directly on educational goals in improving both academic *and* social competence. Directive teacher intervention is usually required (Meyer *et al.*, 1987) as is the use of behavioural strategies to decrease undesirable behaviours and to improve skill levels (Egel *et al.*, 1980). A focus on communication and social skills, and the enhancement of peer relationships, is also important (Brady *et al.*, 1987; Wolfberg & Schuler, 1993; Lord, 1984; Howlin & Rutter, 1987a; Williams, 1989).

SPECIALIST EDUCATIONAL PROGRAMMES FOR CHILDREN WITH AUTISM

There are, of course, many different approaches to teaching children with autism. Some involve integration, some segregation, some a mixture of the two. Many focus specifically on the fundamental impairments associated with autism, especially the cognitive, linguistic, social and motivational deficits, with specific teaching strategies being devised to overcome these problems. Quill (1995), for example, provides much useful information on programmes designed to improve social and communication functioning. Butera and Haywood (1995) describe the 'Bright Start Programme', which concentrates on the development of cognitive and meta-cognitive abilities.

The TEACCH Method

The importance of structured educational programmes for children with autism has been well documented over the last quarter of a century (Fischer & Granville, 1970; Halpern, 1970; Graziano, 1970; Fenichel, 1974). Schopler *et al.* (1971) found that autistic pupils made more progress in structured as compared with unstructured settings, with structure being particularly important in the earlier stages of development. Bartak and Rutter (1973) compared the progress of 50 children with autism in three different educational settings. One was highly structured, with an emphasis on the development of perceptual, motor and cognitive skills; the second focused on psychotherapeutic and regressive therapies; and the third employed a very individualised approach to teaching, in which regimes varied from fairly structured to permissive. They found that children exposed to the structured, task-oriented, more 'academic' programme made better educational progress than children in the other groups; language skills and on-task behaviours were also superior.

The TEACCH programme, developed by Eric Schopler and his colleagues in North Carolina (Schopler, 1997), is now widely used throughout the USA and many parts of Europe (Peeters, 1997). This is an educational approach that is founded on the need for structure. It is not a curriculum as such, more a framework for teaching, that emphasises the need for appropriate environmental organisation and the use of clear visual cues to circumvent communication difficulties. The programme also takes account of developmental levels and the importance of individually based teaching, as well as using other behavioural and cognitive approaches as necessary. The student's daily routine is illustrated by individualised timetables; work and play areas are identified by visual cues (often of different colours) and the tasks to be completed, the amount of work to be achieved and the sequences to be followed are all indicated by visual cues and 'jigs' (or blueprints) (Schopler *et al.*, 1995). There have been many reports of the effectiveness of this approach (Campbell *et al.*, 1996), although there have been no recent comparative evaluations.

In the hands of skilled teachers there is little doubt that such a framework for teaching has many advantages. However, there is a danger that less experienced teachers may apply the approach in a more rigid way than is appropriate, thereby sacrificing individuality and spontaneity. The need to ensure that, over time, students are eventually able to cope within far less structured community settings must also be recognised. Otherwise, the gains achieved using such a highly specialised approach may be lost once the student is exposed to a different environment.

Other Approaches to Teaching

Rita Jordan and Stuart Powell (Powell & Jordan, 1997; Jordan & Powell, 1995) provide many other examples of good teaching practice. The overall aim is to explore how a psychological perspective on the ways in which pupils with autism think and learn may be applied in particular areas of the curriculum. Thus, although there is an emphasis on appropriate structure, there is also a focus on more imaginative and flexible approaches to encourage growth in all areas of the child's development. These include music, dance and drama, computers and outdoor education.

Harris (1995) summarises the changes in teaching practice that have taken place over the last two decades and notes, in particular: the move towards more naturalistic approaches; the use of intrinsic rather than extrinsic reinforcers; the reduction of aversive procedures; the increasing emphasis on social relationships with peers; the development of more effective communication strategies (rather than a focus on speech); and the value of functional assessments in the reduction of behavioural problems.

However, despite the undoubted improvements in education for autistic children in general over this period, much still remains to be done. Many children remain non-verbal, and the advances in technology, which now enable students with severe physical or communication impairments to be integrated within mainstream settings, still need to be further adapted to meet the needs of autistic pupils. Moreover, the benefits and limitations of specific teaching programmes still require much more detailed evaluation if such programmes are to be tailored more specifically to the needs and abilities of different students. In addition, although there can be no doubt that advances in the functional assessments of behaviour and reductions in the use of aversive procedures can only be welcomed, flexibility in both practice and philosophy continues to be required. It has also been suggested that the present non-aversive technology may be insufficient for some students who require more sophisticated, and possibly mildly aversive procedures, in order to gain control over highly dangerous or disruptive behaviours (Harris, 1995).

Parents need to be aware, too, that some claims for the effectiveness of particular educational placements are not necessarily adequately evaluated, nor is any single programme likely to be effective for every child. The Options method, and the teaching approaches advocated by the Higashi School for example, may be very helpful for some children. However, they will not be equally effective for all, and could possibly be damaging for some. Uprooting the whole family, or sending the child away to a foreign country, are not usually the best methods of achieving family cohesion. Claims can be easily made but are much more difficult to justify, and because a particular programme or school does not offer promises of 'miracles' this does not mean that it is ineffective—the teachers may merely be more cautious, or honest, in their judgements. Moreover, no one type of school can be considered to be more or less appropriate, in principle, than another. Success for any child will depend largely on the skills, care and flexibility of the staff involved, rather than the particular type of school.

Although there have been attempts to evaluate the most appropriate types of teaching programme and school environment for children with autism (Newson & Jones, 1994), the small sample size of such studies, together with problems in experimental design, mean that the conclusions are often contradictory or uncertain. There is certainly no firm evidence to support the argument that the majority of children with autism are best educated in special autistic schools—or vice versa. Indeed, because of the heterogeneity of children with autism, it would be surprising if any one approach or system were to be universally effective. As Rutter pointed out many years ago (Rutter & Bartak, 1973), what is needed is task-oriented and highly structured teaching adapted to meet *individual* needs.

It is certain that simply placing a child with autism alongside normal peers will not automatically lead to improvements in either behaviour or cognitive abilities. Furthermore, even special education teachers may require additional in-service training to ensure that they provide an optimum environment for enhancing children's skills. For example, although one of the best indicators of academic gains by children with special needs is the amount of time spent on learning tasks, a number of studies indicate that the frequency of teacher–child interactions, or time on task, can be very low. Thus, Rich and Ross (1989) found that almost half the school day was spent in non-learning activities. Sigafoos *et al.* (1994a, 1994b) note that, even in special educational settings, children were provided with opportunities for interaction and communication in less than 14% of 6,000 observation intervals. The authors also found a strong correlation between the frequency of children's attempts to communicate and teachers' behaviour. When teachers were encouraged to increase opportunities for interaction, particularly for requesting behaviours, these rose significantly; pupil responses also increased.

The impact of teacher skills, the quality of the curriculum, and the extent of children's disabilities are all important variables. Not unexpectedly, integration proves more difficult for pupils with significant disabilities, and while higher functioning children may do well in integrated classrooms, those at a lower level tend to show increased gains in segregated settings (Cole *et al.*, 1991; Semmel & Peck, 1986; Howlin, 1994; Harris *et al.*, 1990).

Teachers working with children with autism in an integrated classroom will need considerable skill if they are to minimise behavioural difficulties and avoid disruption to the rest of the class; they will need patience and understanding in order to cope with the child's inappropriate social responses (such as commenting on their appearance or questioning the accuracy of their statements), and they will need special skills in order to enhance interactions with peers. Thus, not only will teacher intrusion be necessary to increase interactions, but the level of intrusion also needs to be carefully monitored. Meyer *et al.* (1987), for example, found that low level intrusion was more effective in maintaining peer interactions than higher levels of teacher interaction. The essential component is that educational strategies and curricula should be adapted to the specific patterns of skills and disabilities shown by the child with autism. It is also generally more productive (and certainly more rewarding for all concerned) to focus on developing the child's existing skills, rather than attempting to overcome fundamental deficits. Equal emphasis needs to be placed, too, on meeting children's social and emotional needs. For more able children, in particular, this latter goal can prove difficult to achieve. In specialised schooling it is often not possible to provide them with sufficient intellectual stimulation; on the other hand, unless extra support is provided within mainstream school, teasing and bullying by other pupils, and lack of understanding from teachers, may often result in severe emotional stress.

There is good evidence (Rogers, 1996) to show that the most effective educational programmes are those that begin early (between the ages of 2 to 4) and once the right placement is found this can help greatly to reduce the pressure on families. And, if parents, teachers and other professionals work together, this will markedly improve the consistency of management techniques and help to ensure the generalisation and maintenance of newly acquired behaviours.

The appropriateness, or otherwise, of special education facilities will also vary during the course of the child's school life. Thus, while specialist, segregated provision—especially for those with more severe behavioural problems—may be valuable in the early school years, it may be less productive at the secondary school age, where access to the normal school curriculum becomes crucial for entry to further educational and occupational opportunities. Even those in support of integration may find, because of the failure to provide teaching staff with adequate training or support, that it may be preferable for education in the early years to be provided in specialist units. If major difficulties can be brought under control in this way, gradual integration may then be feasible at a later age.

The Range of Educational Provision for Children with Autism

Finally, flexibility of provision is also crucial, and this applies both to the range of provision on offer as well as to the ease with which children are able to move from one type of school to another. As the following examples illustrate, for some children, early education in specialist provision may be required initially, especially if there are marked behavioural or obsessional problems. Once these are under good control, transfer to mainstream school may be possible, thereby offering the child access to a much wider educational curriculum. Other pupils, who are able to cope with mainstream school in the primary years, may then require more segregated provision when they reach secondary school stage. In some cases children may need to be enrolled in two different types of school at the same time.

Kelly, was a 13-year-old girl who had always attended a school for children with autism, but her teachers increasingly felt that they were failing to meet some of her social and academic needs. Because most of the other pupils were boys she had no female peer group with whom to interact, and she was also academically more able than most of the other students. It was arranged for her to spend some sessions in the local girls' school where she began attending music and home economics classes with an aide from her own school. Later she was introduced into gym and arts classes. Although she was not able to cope with more academic subjects, by the end of a year she was able to attend the school unaccompanied and clearly profited socially from her time there.

Dominic had attended mainstream school up to the age of 12 but, because of continuing social and behavioural problems, it was agreed that he would not be able to cope in the local secondary school. Instead he transferred to a unit for children with autism in the grounds of a mainstream school, spending part of his day there and attending some lessons in the main school. As time went on his time in mainstream increased and by the fifth year, with the continuing guidance of staff from the unit, he was able to take several GCSE examinations.

Ben had even more changes of schooling. Initially he went to a normal nursery but then, at the age of 5, he moved to an autistic school where he made good progress for several years. By the time he was 11, however, he became increasingly unhappy and asked to leave. He was transferred to a small private school that had catered for a number of pupils with special needs in the past. Subsequently, he won a place at a well-known boys' public school where small classes, a vigilant attitude to bullying, and a focus on individual skills rather than weaknesses, made it an ideal placement. He excelled at maths and Greek, and because the school did not hesitate to seek professional help if problems arose, he did well in all his exams, eventually gaining a place at university to read biology. His tendency towards outspokenness, and a critical attitude to what he was taught, were accepted by most of his teachers, while his occasionally outrageous remarks in the middle of assembly rather endeared him to other pupils!

Sally, in contrast, attended a specialist autistic school from the age of 4. Her progress was good initially and she learned to speak and to acquire simple academic skills. In adolescence, however, she became increasingly unable to cope with the educational demands of the setting. Although her teachers made every effort to reduce the pressure as far as possible, she remained agitated and distressed. Eventually she was transferred to a school for children with severe learning difficulties where she was considerably more able than most of the other pupils. Her mood rapidly improved and she remained there until she reached school-leaving age. Her parents are confident that in doing this they made the right decision, although academically she failed to make the same amount of progress as she had done in the early years.

Families and children with autism may have to cope with several changes of school—and the trauma these involve—throughout childhood. Unlike normally developing children, the educational needs of a child with autism can fluctuate widely over time. Sometimes, academic progress may be much more rapid than expected; conversely, behavioural, emotional or social difficulties (or changes within the school) may result in disruption to a previously satisfactory placement. Provision may need to be reviewed, and possibly changed, much more often than is the case for other children. A placement that seems appropriate at 5 may be quite wrong by 12, or even by 7. Parents will need to be prepared for the possibility of several changes of school and regular and frequent monitoring of the placement, taking account of the needs of teachers and other pupils, as well as those of the child with autism, will be essential.

Parents require considerable support to guide them through the complex processes whereby their child's educational needs are assessed, and suitable provision recommended. Sometimes for financial reasons, sometimes on other grounds, the judgement of parents with regard to suitable placement may differ significantly from that of professionals. Thus, parents need to be fully aware of their legal rights and the actions they can take if they are dissatisfied. In the UK a comprehensive 'Statement' of the child's Special Educational Needs is a crucial step in ensuring that the appropriate placement is provided. Detailed information on this can be obtained from the Department for Education and Employment. Parents can initiate an assessment of needs themselves before the child reaches school age or at any stage thereafter. If they experience problems, there are a number of special advice and support groups, as well as local or national autistic societies, which can offer them informed and practical advice. They may also be able to advise about legal services if necessary, or to persuade educational authorities to take a more flexible attitude to schooling. For example, the small size and greater structure offered by some independent schools may, in certain cases, make them much more appropriate placements than larger state schools for intellectually able children with autism. Although most parents are not able to afford this option themselves, local authorities can occasionally be persuaded to pay the fees if it can be demonstrated that no suitable alternative exists.

WHAT SCHOOLS NEED TO KNOW

Whatever placement is finally chosen, the crucial factor determining success will be whether the staff have a real understanding of, and sympathy towards, the needs and problems of children with autism.

Increasing Teachers' Knowledge and Understanding of Autism

Apart from among those working in specialist autistic provision, or in schools with a high proportion of children with autistic features, an understanding of autism and the problems associated with it tends to be limited. Few teachers in schools for children with mild to moderate learning disabilities, and even fewer in mainstream schools, will have had any special training in this field. Even educational psychologists, unless they are working primarily with children with special needs, are unlikely to have detailed knowledge about the condition. Since the incidence of autism within the wider spectrum (including children of normal intelligence) is now estimated to be as high as 9 per 1,000 (i.e. almost 1%; National Autistic Society, 1997) it is highly likely that MOST teachers will, in fact, come across several such children in the course of their careers. Although training courses for teachers do now incorporate modules related to children with special needs, the time that can be allotted to any specific condition, such as autism, is very limited. Thus, continuing professional development courses such as those organised by the National Autistic Society or the TEACCH organisation can be crucial in increasing both awareness and professional expertise. In the UK, Birmingham University also offers distance learning programmes specifically in autism.

Recognising children with autism in non-specialist settings

Specialist training can also be vital in helping teachers to identify pupils with autism. This is particularly important for pupils who have managed to cope, often without a formal diagnosis, up to secondary level in mainstream schools. Although such pupils will almost certainly have been singled out, in the past, as having behavioural or emotional difficulties they may well have received little help. Or, if therapy is offered this tends to concentrate on the outward manifestations of problem behaviours or on presumed difficulties within the family. However, real improvements, not only in the child but in teachers' willingness and ability to cope, are only likely to occur if the underlying disorder is recognised, correctly diagnosed and accepted.

The failure to recognise autism can also present problems for staff and pupils in specialist settings. Oliver was an 11-year-old boy with Down's syndrome who had always been extremely difficult to cope with because of his 'stubbornness', his 'lack of co-operation' and his 'failure to join in with other children'. For many years his parents had felt that his progress was very different to that of other children with Down's syndrome and in desperation they finally sought a further diagnostic assessment. This revealed that he was clearly autistic, in addition to having Down's syndrome—a diagnosis that led to a much better understanding of his difficulties both at home and at school (see also Howlin *et al.*, 1995).

Understanding WHY children with autism behave as they do

It is obviously important for teachers to be aware that many difficulties may arise because of children's ritualistic tendencies or their difficulties in communication, particularly abstract understanding. However, a particular problem for staff in mainstream school is the apparent rudeness of a child with autism. Constantly being corrected in class; having one's physical imperfections highlighted; or being faced with direct refusals to co-operate are not easy for any teacher to deal with. However, the knowledge that children may act in this way, not out of deliberate malice but because of an inability to understand the impact of their behaviour on others, can help to make the situation a little more tolerable.

Adopting a Different Approach to Teaching

The mere understanding that a child has autism does not, of course, solve the problem directly, but there are now many books and pamphlets available that may be of help. The series of books edited by Schopler and Mesibov (1983, 1986, 1988, 1992) contain many valuable accounts of teaching techniques. Recently published books by Quill (1995) and Rita Jordan (Jordan & Powell, 1995; Powell & Jordan, 1997) also provide a wealth of information on imaginative and innovative teaching strategies. Together they provide many practical ideas for helping children with autism and their teachers in a variety of educational settings.

The Need for Structure

Since the work of Rutter and Bartak many years ago, numerous studies have stressed the importance of structure in teaching children with autism (Howlin & Rutter, 1987a; Short, 1984; Jordan & Powell, 1995). The TEACCH programme, in particular, illustrates how highly structured teaching programmes can have a very positive impact on both the behaviour and learning abilities of pupils with autism.

The organisation of time

Many studies have shown that ritualistic or other problem behaviours are most likely to occur at times when individuals are not appropriately occupied (Durand & Crimmins, 1991). In the school setting such problems are usually most in evidence if the daily timetable is poorly organised. This means that the programme for the entire school day, including breaks and mealtimes, possibly even trips to the lavatory, should be made absolutely explicit. In addition to the regular school timetable, the student with autism may need to be provided with an extra, personalised time-table indicating the amount of work to be produced by the end of the lesson (or even at particular stages throughout the lesson). Instructions will be easier to follow if pictures or other non-verbal cues are used to indicating the tasks to be completed. It also helps if these require some form of direct interaction from the child. For example, 'tear off' clock faces, indicating the passage of each quarter of an hour, can help students keep a much better track of time than if they are simply asked to watch the clock.

Problems of free time

Although breaks from lessons are designed to provide normal children with the opportunities they need to relax and to interact with their peers, for a child with autism such periods can be extremely stressful. Children who are able to behave quite acceptably when involved in guided and structured activities, frequently appear much more 'odd' or unusual at times of free play. Stereotyped and ritualistic behaviours may become more apparent and exposure to teasing or bullying is a significant risk, especially because staff supervision at such times is greatly reduced.

If, as is often the case, it is simply not possible to offer greater structure or supervision in the playground, avoiding the problem by allowing children *not* to go out to play may be the best solution. Play times, after all, are intended to offer children relief from the pressures of the classroom; they are not designed to increase stress, although this is just what they may do for children with autism. Sports may also be a nightmare for children who lack both the social competence and physical skills to take part in these activities. Caroline, a 13-year-old girl attending a unit for children with mild learning difficulties, became so anxious about having to 'play outside' at break times that she began to complain of sickness and headaches each morning, showing increasing reluctance to leave the house. After discussions between her teachers and parents it was agreed that she would be allowed to remain in the classroom during break, as long as she completed certain chores. Caroline was delighted at the opportunity to be able to do this and she was soon able to remain in the classroom without supervision. In similar cases, the situation has been greatly improved by allowing children to avoid break times or games sessions, by spending the time in the school library or computer room, going home for lunch, or helping in the school 'snack shop'.

The organisation of teaching materials

Many children with autism, even those who are most able, have problems regulating their own progress, or even continuing to work, unless they are continually supervised. Constant attention to the work output of one child is rarely feasible, even in specialist provision where staff ratios are relatively high. Within lesson times, therefore, it may be necessary to attend to the design of work materials in order to ensure that tasks are satisfactorily completed. For constructional tasks, or other relatively simple activities, the student can be presented with trays or boxes containing small quantities of material rather than leaving them to select from a larger display. Once completed, the task can then be placed in another empty container, and returned to a specified 'finished' position. If the amount of material to be worked with is limited, the task requirements clear, and completion marked by the return of equipment to a specific setting, the activity is more likely to be completed without the need for constant prompting. Breaking down a complex task into smaller stages also provides the student with more frequent opportunities for reinforcement. In addition, having a visible 'finishing position' helps the teacher to monitor progress from a distance.

'Post it' stickers, or clocks or timers can also be used to indicate how much work needs to be completed, or when it should be finished. Jennifer had an obsession with plastic timers (the types filled with coloured oils which slowly move from top to bottom) and in order to gain access to these she would have to complete a certain amount of 'work' before the oils reached the bottom. In other cases, a sticker might be placed at the bottom of each page, to be removed by the child when he or she has completed the necessary task.

Thought also needs to be given to the materials used when teaching new tasks or activities. Equipment should be sturdy and durable and, at least initially, should demand minimal effort on the part of the child. If toys needed to be tidied, large containers, adequately labelled (with pictures, or even an actual example of the items to be inserted) can make the task less arduous.

Finally, the setting in which learning is to take place needs to be given due consideration. Most people find concentration difficult if surrounded by crowds or other distractions but autistic children are often expected to learn in noisy, open-plan environments. As indicated earlier, Guy's difficulties in settling in the classroom were greatly helped if he were allowed to have his own table at the back of the room. Other, more active pupils may find it easier to remain still if they are seated in the corner of a room, with their back to the wall and a table in front of them, so that it is less easy for them simply to get up and walk away. Movable screens can help to provide some degree of privacy, or freedom from distraction, when children are engaged in specific teaching tasks. These can also serve as a visual cue for 'on task' activities; while being easily removable at other times.

Homework

This can be another major problem in mainstream settings, and generally requires close liaison between home and school. In Roger's case, for example, homework instructions were written in his 'Home–School book' each night, as were details of the books to be taken home. Before leaving school each evening his form tutor checked that he had the necessary books and his parents ensured that homework was adequately completed. Once this arrangement was working satisfactorily, Roger was encouraged to write down homework instructions for himself and every night, before leaving school, he ticked off the books that he needed as he packed them. By the beginning of the second term, Roger needed little additional help to monitor homework assignments.

Learning the Rules

Most children at school develop some sort of sixth sense for understanding what is appropriate and what is not, or which games/clothes/popstars are 'in' and which are 'out' at any time. How they do so is poorly understood; the important thing is they do it so easily and so well. For autistic children, who have difficulty understanding or following even explicit social rules, making any sense of these unwritten and often apparently inexplicable rules is virtually impossible. Even if they do eventually realise that a particular 'craze' or sport or type of clothing is in vogue, by the time they have obtained all the necessary equipment it will almost certainly have long gone out of fashion.

Other children get themselves into trouble because, in their desperation to make friends, they will do whatever anyone asks of them—and are unable to recognise the difference between children laughing at or with them. Tales abound of children, especially in mainstream school, getting into serious trouble for following the instructions of their peers: to call their teacher by an insulting nickname; to remove their clothes in the middle of assembly; or even, in one case, to defecate in the school piano (immediately admitting to this when confronted).

Because of the complexity of even apparently simple social interactions it is impossible to provide any child with a full understanding of why and how he or she should behave. Nevertheless, there are some fundamental rules that can help to enhance acceptability in school. Dressing appropriately (which may mean parents keeping a careful look out for the latest fashions); never removing clothes in public; urinating only in private; never doing things that are known to be 'naughty' or 'silly' however many children ask you to; not correcting teachers however wrong they may be; not informing teachers about the activities of other children without discussing this first with parents; and not commenting on people's physical characteristics, are all simple guidelines that can make the difference between tolerance and rejection. Learning to wait and watch what other children do before taking action, can also help. Temple Grandin (1995) notes that although she always had problems understanding social interactions, she would store up memories of how other people had acted, and then, when similar situations arose, would replay the scenes in her imagination like 'tapes in a video cassette' in order to guide her what to do.

As noted in the chapter on social behaviour, there is often little to be gained by offering detailed explanations of *why* it is best to keep quiet about particular things, or *why* certain behaviours are unacceptable. This may have no impact on the child's behaviour and may well lead to prolonged and futile arguments. At least in the initial stages of dealing with a problem it is often preferable to lay down a simple rule and insist that this is kept. Explanations can be given later, when the behaviour is under better control.

Overcoming Problems of Understanding

As noted many times throughout this book, verbal instructions are rarely an adequate means of communication for the child with autism. Even

very able pupils may continue to have problems with abstract or hypo-
thetical concepts, and dealing with change can be a particular problem—
usually because the child is not adequately prepared for this. At secondary school, for example, frequent and daily changes in the timetable can
be a nightmare. Having a personal timetable (in a folder or diary) that
they can carry around with them, with instructions about where lessons
will be held and what books or equipment will be needed, can be of
considerable help. A simple chart displayed at home can also be a useful
reminder of what equipment they need to take to school on a particular
day. Checklists, which children have to complete or tick off themselves,
can also be valuable. If these have a tendency to get lost, then laminated
pieces of strong card, indicating the lessons and books needed for each
day, might be firmly attached to the child's rucksack or tied to the locker
door.

Visual materials, such as photographs, can also help children to cope
with alterations in routine. Fran, a 14-year-old in an autistic unit, was
always extremely upset by changes in staffing. Her class teacher collected
photographs of all the staff in the school and each day she was encouraged to stick up on a board the pictures of those who were 'in' and,
below, the pictures of those who were 'off'. This significantly reduced her
agitation, especially if it were known in advance that someone would be
away so that their pictures could be placed in the appropriate section
before she left for home.

As noted in the chapter on communication skills, stick on/peel off
pictures can also be used to indicate changes to the regular timetable.
'Picture calendars', or ordinary calendars for the more able pupils, are
invaluable for preparing for major disruptions to the school routine, such
as holidays or trips away, and the complexity of these materials can easily
be modified to suit the ability of the children involved.

Visual cues can help children to dress appropriately or to keep better
track of their belongings. A coloured label discretely sewn at the front of
T-shirts or jumpers can help to indicate which way round clothes should
go, while a bright identifying mark on bags, clothing or other belongings
can also help to reduce losses. Sally's mother, for example, used to stick or
sew 'Happy Eater Faces' on all her clothes, as she was continually losing
things. These helped to motivate Sally to collect her things before leaving
school, and also ensured that her belongings were readily identifiable by
all the staff.

Visual 'jigs' of the sort used in industrial settings to indicate the correct
placements of objects can also be helpful in increasing tidiness or for
acquiring new skills. Placing a knife, fork and plate on a plastic mat that
has the items already drawn on it makes setting a place at table much
easier; if mats are laid out for everyone, a whole table can be set with only

minimal prompting. Such cues can also be helpful in ensuring that equipment is put away properly, or even helping with activities such as dressing. Richard, an adolescent with many physical problems in addition to his autism, was supplied with special orthopaedic shoes to wear at school. Because he had great difficulty putting these on the correct feet, even with colour cues, his teacher drew the outline of each shoe, correctly positioned, on a mat by her desk. Each morning Richard matched his shoes to the outline and then simply stepped into them.

Making Use of Additional Resources

For teachers who are already under great pressure, designing or implementing even very simple strategies can seem difficult if not impossible. However, help might be forthcoming from a number of additional sources (see Howlin, 1997a). These can include other professionals such as psychologists, psychiatrists, social workers or other professionals who may already know a lot about the individual child, or about autism more generally. Enlisting the advice and help of teachers who are actually working in specialist autistic provision can also prove very helpful, as can a visit to an autistic unit. Even other pupils may be used as extra sources of support, while any advice or information that parents can offer should also be seized on. They will have far greater insight into their child's difficulties than anyone else and are also likely to have evolved effective strategies for dealing with or avoiding many problems. Finally, if problems are to be minimised it is important that staff agree on the ways to approach problems and that they attempt to work together to deal with these. Consistency in management is of crucial importance and disagreements between staff will jeopardise even the best constructed intervention programmes.

ADOPTING A FLEXIBLE APPROACH TO TEACHING

Although the inflexibility of children with autism is a characteristic feature, educational systems can, at times, prove equally resistant to change. As noted above, allowing pupils to avoid activities that are beyond their levels of competence can significantly reduce unnecessary confrontation. After all, few schools would insist on a child in a wheelchair joining in sports activities unless he or she wanted to, yet group games may be just as impossible for a child with autism. Having classmates fighting each other because no one wants the child with autism to be in their team does little to enhance self-esteem or peer interactions.

Avoiding core curriculum subjects may be more of a problem, but if a child has a particular difficulty in certain topics then the relevant teachers should be made aware of this, and helped to modify their teaching and expectations accordingly.

Flexibility is also important when it comes to developing existing abilities to the highest possible level. If these are in maths or Greek, then there should be few problems. However, other special abilities may be more difficult to exploit: for example, a child who does nothing but spin objects, or who only draws high-rise buildings, or who can read at an adult level of accuracy but without comprehension. Teachers may argue, with some justification, that such skills are of little value in themselves, and may even try to discourage them. Nevertheless, because they are of such inherent interest they can be very potent in motivating the child with autism to complete a range of other activities (see Chapter 8).

Avoiding Undue Pressure

The need for structure and stimulation is paramount in almost every teaching situation and because most children with autism are lacking in self-motivation (at least when it comes to work) a certain degree of pressure will be needed throughout the school day. If the pressure becomes excessive most children will communicate this through their behaviour, and a sudden or unexplained upsurge in temper tantrums, aggression, agitation or self-injury should always be considered as a possible indicator of stress. If this proves to be the case, the curriculum will need to be carefully examined and, if necessary, modified until a more appropriate level is reached. Once an equilibrium is established, then the pressure may be gently increased once more. At times, however, particularly in the case of more able children attending mainstream schools, the strain of having to co-operate, to conform and to compromise may not be so readily apparent. The child may continue to work and behave well at school, showing his or her disturbance only at home. Michael's teachers, for example, could not believe his mother's tales of life at home. At school he never said or did anything out of place; at home he was a complete tyrant, dictating to his family what they should eat, where they should sit, what music they should listen to or what they should watch on TV. If his wishes were not complied with he would instantly become verbally and physically abusive. Examination of the pattern of these behaviours indicated that they were much worse during term time, especially towards the end of term when the children had exams. The situation was not improved by the family's rather chaotic lifestyle, which did not really matter so much during holidays but did adversely affect his ability to do homework during term time. His school attempted to reduce the pressure on him to some degree, but this proved difficult as he was about to take public examinations. His parents also tried, though with little success, to introduce a certain degree of structure into their lives at home. Eventually, however, it became clear that the levels of disturbance could not be effectively reduced by these means and for the final three years of schooling he moved to a boarding school which offered him the calmness and consistency, but gentle pressure, that he so badly needed.

In cases where the academic pressures are not so great, or when the home situation proves more amenable to change, it can be much easier to reduce unnecessary demands. Again, if teachers take care to listen and act upon parents' views (rather than dismiss them as exaggerated, or as evidence of parental incompetence) a great deal can often be achieved.

The Need for Parent–Teacher Co-operation

Finally, no matter how good or effective a school placement, the child's progress is likely to be compromised unless teachers and parents can work together and respect each others' views and practices. The need for consistency of approach, whatever the skills or problems being worked on, has been stressed repeatedly in previous chapters. If parents feel that decisions about school placement have been forced upon them without due consultation, it will take them a very long time to be able to work comfortably with teachers or to try to continue school-based interventions in the home. Unresolved conflicts about the suitability of the placement will result in continuing arguments and disagreements, with parents remaining highly critical of what the teachers are doing, and vice versa. Thus, decisions about educational placements should be made in full consultation with parents. They, in turn, need to take part in decisions about needs, goals, educational options and the various advantages and disadvantages these offer. By focusing on family priorities, actively listening to each other, and engaging in continuing negotiations about goals and strategies, parents and educationalists can create home–school environments in which both sides feel valued, understood and respected (Bailey, 1987; Wood, 1995).

10

FAMILY ISSUES

WORKING WITH PARENTS AS THERAPISTS

Recognition of the importance of parents working in co-operation with professional therapists is not new. Over 20 years ago, studies by Lovaas and his colleagues (Lovaas, 1977) demonstrated clearly that no matter how effective clinic-based interventions might be, the results were often short-lived unless parents themselves were actively involved in treatment at home. The value of parents as co-therapists for their children has now been demonstrated in very many studies (see Howlin & Rutter, 1987a; Mullen & Frea, 1995, for reviews). Recent work suggests, too, that parental motivation and participation can be further increased if families and professionals work together, not only in carrying out treatment procedures, but also in analysing the possible functions of problem behaviours and testing hypotheses about causation and intervention. To this end, Frea *et al.* (1993) have produced a simple functional assessment form designed specifically to assist parents in understanding why problem behaviours may occur (see Table 10.1). This focuses on what was happening immediately before the problems occurred (e.g. the child being told to do something or having an ongoing activity interrupted), what happens subsequently (child receives attention, or is ignored or removed, etc.), and why the parent thinks the child acted as he or she did (to get out of something, to obtain attention, avoid having to do something, etc.). Understanding the possible reasons why a behaviour occurs can help families to participate more effectively in decision making, as well as encouraging greater consistency in the implementation of treatment plans.

Not only does active participation in problem solving improve co-operation between families and professionals, but this type of analysis can also help to increase parents' understanding of their children's problems. Perceptions of problem behaviours as provocative, aggressive or deliberately disruptive may be radically revised once it is realised that they may be the child's only effective form of communication. This can often help parents to see the world more from the child's point of view,

Table 10.1: A 'Before', 'After' and 'Why' chart for understanding behaviour (adapted from Frea *et al.*, 1993)

Date:	BEHAVIOUR X						
TIME							
PLACE (K = kitchen, G = garden etc.)							
WHAT HAPPENED IMMEDIATELY BEFORE THE BEHAVIOUR?							
X was told to do something							
Activity was changed/interrupted							
X was moved							
X was left alone							
Other							
WHAT HAPPENED AFTERWARDS?							
X given attention							
X given something he wanted							
X had something taken away							
X was removed from room/area							
X was ignored							
Other							
WHY DO YOU THINK IT HAPPENED?							
To get out of doing something							
Because activity changed							
To get something							
To get attention							
To avoid a particular person, place or thing							
Other							

and to examine how they might act or feel if they, too, were unable to express their needs, could not understand what was happening around or to them, or had no means of letting other people know that they were afraid, anxious, confused or distressed. From such a perspective, the behaviours of children with autism may appear far less challenging and easier to understand.

Despite the importance of parent–professional collaborations, it is also important to be aware that inappropriate attempts to engage families in therapy can prove counter-productive. Parents may not necessarily agree with professional goals; they may come from very different cultural backgrounds, or they may have little motivation to employ treatment strategies which they view as irrelevant, unnecessary or impractical. Professionals, in turn, may have limited insight into family needs and values, and can easily fail to appreciate the resources, time, skill or energy that is required to implement programmes in a consistent and effective way.

There is now a large body of research showing that professionals should not attempt to force their own values on families; instead they need to try to approach the family from a systems perspective in order to engage in *collaborative* goal setting. This may require a degree of compromise and flexibility which some professionals can find difficult to accept (even though they may well expect this of parents). Davies *et al.* (1998), for example, discuss the difficulties of working within a behavioural framework when parents insist the problems (in that case, severe self-injury) are due to the child's being influenced by a malignant force. Clinicians may also need to change their own role expectations or to modify strong beliefs about intervention processes. Unless this is done, failure is almost inevitable (Wood, 1995; Bailey, 1987).

The Need for Early Diagnosis, Information and Advice

The importance of early diagnosis has already been discussed in some detail in Chapter 3. However, it is clear from recent research surveys that parents continue to face delays and difficulties in their attempts to obtain a diagnosis . Not only do such difficulties have a deleterious effect on parent–professional relationships, but delays in diagnosis can mean that parents are denied the help and support they need to deal with practical problems at home. Lack of information about likely problems, and what the first indicators of these might be, can also result in the emergence of difficulties that might otherwise have been avoided.

In their study of almost 1,300 families, Howlin and Moore (1997) found that, as well as problems in obtaining a diagnosis, the majority of parents felt that they had subsequently received little specialist help or support. For most families, making contact with appropriate educational services was considered to be the greatest benefit; links with parent groups were also helpful. For a few, simply being given a diagnosis was felt to be the most important form of help. Practical, home-based help of any kind was almost non-existent, despite good evidence that early help with management can help to reduce, or even avoid, the development of subsequent problems (Howlin & Rutter, 1987a). In many cases access even to basic information was lacking. Not only did parents experience difficulties in obtaining advice on managing day-to-day difficulties, they also expressed the need for information on many other practical issues. These included explanations about the processes involved in assessing the child's special educational needs; information on respite care, local facilities and support groups, or on the financial benefits and allowances for which they might be eligible. Many families remained unclear about the roles and responsibilities of the numerous professionals involved; they also requested *comprehensible and straightforward* definitions of the terminology used in describing the child's abilities or needs, or in explaining the possible causes of problems. The vagueness of terms such as 'autistic tendencies' or 'traits' was considered to be particularly irritating. Others said they would have appreciated advice on relevant reading materials that would help them, as parents, to understand more about their child's difficulties and ways in which they might deal with these. As one parent remarked: 'It took us a long time to find out this sort of information, much of which was gleaned from other parents who had also found things out the hard way.'

Genetic Implications

Delays in diagnosis may also have more extensive implications. As discussed in Chapter 2, if one child in the family has autism, other siblings may also be affected to some degree. If the diagnosis of the child with autism is late, recognition of, and hence intervention for other children's difficulties may be delayed as well.

Professionals also need to recognise that, within the wider family, there may be other members with autistic tendencies, which can affect their flexibility, understanding, social relationships, or the ability to compromise and collaborate. Parents who have difficulty accepting professionals' views concerning therapy, management or eduction are all too often dismissed as 'unco-operative' or even inadequate. However, it may well be that fault lies within the clinicians, who are not conveying information in an appropriate way or are failing to take account of innate difficulties that may well be associated with an autistic-spectrum disorder.

If advice is disregarded, if confrontation over school or other management issues occurs, or if parents seem unable to work together, the professional involved needs to explore why he or she is failing to engage families or to provide them with the support they need. Godfrey's father had many stereotyped and ritualistic behaviours and found change of any kind difficult to tolerate. He could not bear it if any of the children did not finish their meal and insisted that food was replaced, meal after meal, until it was finally eaten. The other children developed various strategies to deal with this (including carrying plastic bags into which they could push their food), but Godfrey, who was autistic, had no such wiles. The resulting battles greatly distressed his wife, but she was unable to change his attitude. On the other hand, she had far more difficulties in controlling Godfrey's tantrums because her husband had no problem in totally ignoring these, and so they very rarely occurred in his presence. The therapist, although entirely disagreeing with the father's attitude to food, did not say so. Instead she pointed out that since his strategy of ignoring the tantrums worked so effectively, he might also try this with the food—that is, simply taking no notice of the leftover food and letting his wife remove it without comment. This advice (and the fact that his wife began to give Godfrey much smaller meals and avoided any of the foods he disliked) was so effective that his father eventually agreed to keep to this strategy even though he continued to insist that the old one 'had worked perfectly well'.

In another case, a father with very rigid and obsessional tendencies decided that his son must go to a particular school. When the educational psychologist did not agree to this he embarked on a series of highly vituperative letters about her and the education authority, which were widely distributed to local services and the press. The initial reaction of her employers was to place a legal injunction on him but the psychologist recognised that this would have little, if any effect. Instead, she arranged for the man to visit a number of different schools, taking his son with him, so that the father could see what was going on. The child himself seemed particularly happy in one school, and accepting this his father agreed to 'give it a try'. Meanwhile the psychologist promised not to exclude entirely the possibility of the child's attending the other school at some time in the future. Eventually his father became so used to the staff and routines of the new school that no further mention was ever made of his original plans.

Sometimes, of course, a more direct approach may be needed. Joe's father had many social difficulties and obsessional characteristics, and a very rigid way of organising his life. Joe, who had Asperger syndrome, was badly teased and bullied at school and his father was constantly telling him to 'stand up for himself' and to hit any boy who teased him. Joe had none of the social, physical or cognitive skills necessary to look after himself in this way and there was a real fear that if he did hit out he would get himself into even deeper trouble. Despite many sessions together, the father could simply not understand why the psychologist involved considered this advice inappropriate. In the end, she decided to dispense with explanations and simply insisted that he must *not* give instructions of this kind because his son could get badly hurt. At the same time she promised to make sure that the school took a much more active role in preventing bullying. While expressing total disagreement with her principles, the father did, in fact, agree to do what she said as long as she intervened in the school.

Studies of the genetic background in autism also reveal another risk to families, that of depression. As discussed in Chapter 2, rates of depressive-type illnesses are somewhat higher in this group, and not just because parents have to cope with the stress of raising a child with a developmental disorder. In working with families, therefore, it is particularly important that professionals avoid imposing too many additional stresses on their lives, and that they are alert to indications of depression. If sensitive to issues of this kind, professional therapists will avoid imposing unnecessary burdens, and will be able to adjust therapeutic interventions as necessary; they should also be in a better position to advise parents or other family members if they feel the need to seek further help on their own behalf.

Outcome and Planning for the Future

Among the questions that almost every parent asks or will want to ask when first told that their child has autism, are: 'What will happen as he or she grows older?'; 'Will she always need special care?'; 'Will he find work, make friends or get married?'; 'Will he "end up" in some sort of institution; become violent and aggressive, or develop a psychiatric illness such as schizophrenia?' Although it is never possible to predict, with any accuracy, what will happen to a 2-, 3- or 4-year-old child in 10 or 20 years' time, thorough assessments, even in early childhood, can give some indications as to future outcome and how much parents can realistically expect. Long-term outcome studies have shown that children who are profoundly handicapped in their communication, social and motor development are unlikely ever to achieve independent living, and their families will need help to come to terms with this from the time the child is very young. However, this does not mean that he or she cannot be helped to make considerable progress, and with support and appropriate education a great deal can be done gradually to increase skills, and minimise the development of unwanted behaviours.

For those who have moderate cognitive impairments, the combination of developmental delays and their autism is always likely to impose restrictions on what they are able to achieve. It is an unfortunate fact of life that any one with a disability, whether this is physical or intellectual, will be relatively disadvantaged when it comes to obtaining adequate education, finding work or gaining access to appropriate accommodation. If the picture is complicated by autism, the difficulties will be compounded even further. Thus, although some autistic people with

moderate learning disabilities should be able to live reasonably independent lives, their ability to do so will depend heavily on the support
that they receive from external agencies. For parents, the development
of close links with social and educational services from an early age can
be crucial in ensuring that their children are provided with the optimum
chances of success in later life.

Somewhat paradoxically, outcome is often most difficult to predict in
children whose cognitive and linguistic impairments are within the normal range. Follow-up studies show clearly that it is *only* children within
this group who tend to do well as they grow older; on the other hand, the
level of independence achieved by many still remains very low. Finding
appropriate education can be particularly difficult, and families may have
to endure many changes of school throughout childhood. Support in
college and work may be particularly hard to find. As adults, only a
minority manage to find suitable work, develop a range of social contacts,
or obtain satisfactory accommodation and support, although there is
some evidence that the numbers who manage to do so are gradually
increasing (see Howlin, 1997, for a more detailed discussion of outcome
in adult life).

Unfortunately, families of these children can suffer even greater disadvantages than those whose children are much more clearly disabled. It
may be harder to obtain a formal diagnosis, and the age of diagnosis in
this group tends to be much later than for children with more obvious
disabilities (Howlin & Moore, 1997). It can prove very difficult to enlist
the support systems that are available for children with severe learning
disabilities, and appropriate education, in particular, can be extremely
difficult to achieve. Families of more able children are often left to cope
with little or no support from educational or social services, despite the
fact that, within this group, the provision of early help and adequate
education can have a significant impact on later outcome. The aim of
professionals should be (a) to ensure that everything necessary is done to
obtain appropriate educational provision, (b) to help families cope with
the variety of different problems that are likely to arise throughout childhood, and (c) to encourage their hopes and aspirations in a realistic way.
Few families will easily forgive a clinician who has promised much more
for their child than can ever be achieved; at the same time, unduly
pessimistic estimates of the child's potential abilities can also be damaging. Keeping an open mind (within reasonable limits), making the best of
the opportunities that are offered, and never undermining parents' confidence in themselves or their child, are crucial elements for any
therapeutic practice.

The following is an example of the problems that professionals might
face in getting the right balance between undue gloom and excessive

optimism. One of the first questions asked by 4-year-old Adrien's father, following diagnosis, was whether he should keep his son's name down for his old (and extremely prestigious) public school. The clinician involved suggested that it was probably unlikely that Adrien would gain entrance there as the competition was so intense; however, he advised the father to wait, rather than take any irretrievable steps at this stage. Adrien later went to a specialist school for children with autism and his father withdrew the application. At the age of 11, however, having made good progress, Adrien then transferred to a small private school. At 13 he succeeded in passing the entrance examination for another school, which although not quite so famous as his father's was in fact the same school that his consultant had attended.

Increasing Independence

Whatever children's level of ability, help should also be provided to encourage independence, not only for their sakes, but also for parents and siblings. Assistance in finding suitable baby sitters, or other forms of respite help, can help parents maintain their own relationship, as well as offering a brief break from other family ties. Later, special holiday schemes that can accommodate children with learning or other disabilities may be explored.[1] More regular breaks can be achieved via some form of 'share a family' scheme. These are schemes whereby another family (sometimes one that also has a handicapped child, sometimes not) takes over the child's care for occasional nights or weekends. Respite care may also be available through other Social Services provision, such as small group homes. Opportunities of this kind can enable parents to spend more time together as a couple, or with their other children; they also help the child with autism to experience brief separations on a planned and predictable basis. If, as children grow older, lengthier or more permanent separations are needed (as for boarding school or residential care) they are then more likely to be able to cope with these without undue stress or anxiety.

The National Autistic Society in the UK organises a number of other schemes which may enable children and parents to spend brief periods of time apart. These include a befriending scheme, which helps to provide companions for outings or visits outside the home. There is also a 'Parent

---

[1] The National Autistic Society in the UK publishes a Holiday Resource List, providing information on organisations and centres that offer holidays appropriate for people with autism and Asperger syndrome. This can be obtained from the National Autistic Society Information Centre, 393 City Road, London EC1V 1NE, UK.

to Parent Link' service, which allows families to make contact with others in similar circumstances. If families wish to make use of this scheme they can be put in touch with parents who have undergone special training, and who continue to receive support from the NAS.

Finally, although financial problems may be relatively low on many families' lists of priorities, worries about money do not help to improve family functioning. It is important, therefore, that if benefits are available, families are provided with *full* details about these and with advice about how to obtain them. It can be difficult, especially when applying for discretionary benefits, to persuade officials who may have little under-standing of autism that the family of a child with this condition (especially if he or she has no obvious physical or cognitive difficulties) may be just as much in need of help with transport, or additional allowances, as the family of a child who is deaf or blind or unable to walk. Again, because they have developed an expertise in making successful claims of this kind, the National (or local) Autistic Society should be approached for advice about the best way to fill in application forms, or to deal with staff involved in the dispensation of benefits.

Even relatively minor benefits, such as a 'Disabled Parking Permit' can make the difference between parents being able to go shopping with their child, or take him or her on family outings. Brian and Godfrey were brothers with autism, whose single mother had been unable to take them out on her own. Their lives were transformed when she received financial help to buy a car and was granted a permit that allowed her to park close to local shops. In another case, however, where the mother was also struggling by herself to cope with two children with autism (one with severe learning difficulties and the other with additional visual impair-ments) the request for a parking permit was turned down on the grounds that both children were able to walk independently. A request for special-ist educational provision had also been rejected some weeks earlier. For the mother this proved the final straw, and some days later she failed to pick up the children from school. She became too depressed to care for them and both are now in the care of the local authority.

Eliciting Help from Other Services

Although most children with autism have few additional medical prob-lems, help from family doctors or dentists is almost certain to be required from time to time. Practitioners working in these areas are unlikely to have much, if any, knowledge about autism and may in fact be quite anxious if they have to deal with a child with this condition. The doctor and dentist may thus have to be desensitised to their patient, in much the same way as the child needs to become accustomed to them. Regular, brief visits, long before any form of treatment is required, are the best way of dealing with the problem on both sides. Children can get used to the smells and sounds of the surgery, familiarise themselves with the equipment, and perhaps undergo brief 'examinations', with the doctor using a stethoscope, or the dentist peering at their teeth. Then, by the time any treatments or investigations are needed, anxiety should be reduced to a minimum.

As well as getting to know individual patients better, clinicians can be helped to learn more about the needs of children with autism or Asperger syndrome if they have access to relevant written information. Pamphlets published by the National Autistic Society on these conditions give brief but concise guidelines on the nature of the disorder, explaining in particular the children's social and communication problems, and their difficulties in coping with change. Some parents always carry a few of these leaflets around with them so that they can offer them to other people when, or preferably before, problems arise.

It is also helpful if family doctors are aware of the possible genetic risks to other children in the family. Thus, if a sibling is slow to talk, is developmentally delayed or is experiencing problems at school, these problems should be taken seriously and action taken as soon as possible. Reassurance that 'He/she will grow out of it' or 'It's just a stage' will be of little help, and is very likely to delay the provision of appropriate interventions which might otherwise significantly reduce the long-term impact of these problems. The risks of depressive type illness should also be born in mind so that, again, treatment can be offered as soon as needed. Finally, sometimes doctors may find it very difficult to communicate with a parent, or they may encounter 'stubbornness' or lack of co-operation. Instead of striking the family from the surgery's list (as has happened in a number of cases) the possibility that the mother or father may be affected by an autistic-spectrum disorder should also be considered. Being more concrete and explicit, offering better explanations, taking the parent systematically through the processes to be followed, can all result in improved relationships all round.

'Familiarisation' strategies will, of course, be more difficult to implement if the child needs help from specialist services. Nurses and consultants in large hospitals may be unable to spend much time with any of their patients, and the extra patience needed for a child with autism can prove very difficult. Jonah was a large 7-year-old, with minimal language, who had broken his leg and required in-patient treatment. He was very distressed and disturbed by this dramatic change to his daily routine, and his screams and cries were equally distressing for nurses and other patients. He was constantly trying to get out of bed and on several occasions managed to disentangle himself from the traction apparatus used to immobilise the limb. He was rapidly discharged from hospital to his home—a fourth-floor flat where the lift was usually out of order. His mother was unable to take him out or to leave the flat herself and because of this missed several follow-up appointments. When the fracture had finally healed it was found that the leg was badly distorted and required resetting. In view of the earlier trauma, his mother refused another operation and he is now left with considerable difficulties in walking. In contrast is the case of John, a child with severe asthma, for whom hospital admissions were equally traumatic. He caused great consternation by biting through his drip equipment, or struggling against injections, even when he was severely ill. Nurses at the hospital carefully taught his parents how to recognise the first signs of an attack and provided them with all the equipment they might need at home if problems arose. If his parents felt they could not cope, a nurse or doctor would attend without delay, and in this way the need for hospital visits significantly diminished.

As well as helping families to cope with some emergencies themselves, consultants need to listen to the advice families give about their own child. If a mother says 'He hates white coats', much unnecessary disruption may be avoided if the clinician agrees to wear normal clothing. When Kevin's mother told the dental hospital 'He doesn't like waiting', warning them what the consequences might be if the appointment was not on time, no one really believed her. After a 15-minute wait Kevin began to protest in his usual way, by head banging. He aimed straight for the large fish tank in the waiting room, with fatal accuracy—as far as the fish were concerned.

THE EFFECTS ON FAMILIES OF HAVING A CHILD WITH AUTISM

There can be little doubt that raising a child with autism leads to many increased pressures on families. They tend to be under greater strain than parents of children with Down's syndrome or other forms of mental handicap, and may experience even higher levels of stress than those caring for a child with a terminal illness, such as cystic fibrosis (Siegel, 1997; Koegel *et al.*, 1992c; Moes, 1995). Social isolation and stigma are often cited as being particular problems, and Bristol (1984, 1987) outlines a number of other factors that make caring for a child with autism uniquely stressful. Among these are the *ambiguity* of the disorder—the contrast between a normal physical appearance and severe disability in other areas; its *severity and duration*—autism is a life long disorder which affects every aspect of a child's functioning; and *societal reactions*—parents of an autistic child do not receive the same sympathy or understanding as those with a child with an obvious physical disability, or an easily recognisable condition such as Down's syndrome. Negative reactions become even more pronounced as the child gets bigger and older and parents may well be held directly responsible for their child's inappropriate or unacceptable behaviour in public.

Parents, particularly mothers, tend to have strong feelings of guilt and inadequacy and may often blame themselves for the child's difficulties. Guilt can focus on what they did before the birth (having an occasional drink or cigarette), at birth (accepting medication or other interventions) or afterwards (not stimulating children adequately and leaving them alone because they seemed so contented). Or, with increasing knowledge about the genetics of the disorder, they may feel responsible if any one else in their family has similar characteristics.

Even parent training programmes, although designed to alleviate the burden on families, may, if not sensitively conducted, serve to increase rather than diminish feelings of incompetence. Rodrigue *et al.* (1993) note that any such programmes need to stress that although changes in parent strategies may be necessary in order to bring about improvements, this is due to the child's condition and not because of the parents' deficiencies. Parent-training programmes can be particularly stressful if professionals have unrealistic expectations of what can be achieved. Hourly behavioural recordings may be relatively easy to complete in a clinic setting; they may be quite impossible at home given all the other demands of family life. Bristol (1984) recommends that professionals should encourage a 'family-oriented rather than an autistic centred home', meaning that therapy should take account of the needs of the wider family, rather than concentrating specifically on the child.

Although some studies have reported higher rates of depression and marital breakdown in the families of children with autism, these findings are not consistent. In a review of studies in this area, Koegel and colleagues (1992c) report few differences in the psychological health of mothers of children with autism and mothers of normally developing children. Nor is there any clear evidence that divorce rates are higher than the national average. Bristol found that the responses of the parents whom she studied were very similar to those of 'well-adjusted' families. The principal differences were in their greater emphasis on 'moral-religious' issues, and a lower participation in social and recreational activities.

Nevertheless, although, *on average,* parents of children with autism may not show significant levels of disturbance, some families certainly find the strain much more difficult to cope with than others. High stress levels are associated with a number of different factors, such as a lack of help and support, as well as variables within the child. These include poor social responsiveness, temperamental difficulties and behavioural disturbance. In turn, parents who have high stress levels are likely to interpret their child's behaviour more negatively and to expect more problems (Kasari & Sigman, 1997).

Bristol suggests that the keys to coping include a close knit, supportive home environment, being able to express feelings openly, and active participation in activities outside the home. Support from family, friends, other parents of children with handicaps and, above all, a sympathetic spouse were crucial in minimising stress. Parents involved in family support schemes, such as the programmes offered by TEACCH, had significantly lower stress levels than other parents.

Practical help in order to develop effective intervention strategies at home is also important for increasing parents' feelings of competence, as well as improving their children's behaviour. In our own behaviourally based work with families (Howlin & Rutter, 1987a) we found, like Bristol, that attention also needs to be paid to other aspects of family life. Difficulties with marital relationships or with other children often require attention, and parents may need the opportunity to talk about their own feelings of grief or guilt or confusion. Sometimes, too, more expert help may be required (for example, if a parent becomes very depressed), and it is important for therapists working within a family to recognise when additional, specialist counselling or medication may need to be provided.

Effects on Siblings

Many parents suffer great anxiety about the effects that having an autistic sibling may have on their other children. Most feel that the non-autistic child has a 'raw deal' when it comes to having a fair share of their time and attention. Many are concerned, too, about the interference of the child with autism in siblings' other activities, particularly in their interactions with friends. However, just as a number of studies have found surprisingly low rates of severe disruption to family life, research into the impact on siblings also suggests that levels of disturbance are generally low. DeMyer (1979) found few differences between siblings of autistic children and normal controls, with similar numbers in each group showing some signs of emotional disturbance, or reporting problems of teasing or bullying. However, more children in the autistic group reported feelings of being neglected (30%) or of having worries and anxieties about their sibling (18%); 15% of parents also reported difficulties in eating and toileting which they believed were attributable to the effects of having a sibling with autism. McHale and her colleagues (1984) studied 30 children with an autistic sibling, 30 with a learning disabled sibling and 30 with a normal sibling. The children were aged between 6 and 15 years at the time of the study. The relationship between siblings and the children with autism or other handicaps was actually rated as more positive by parents than the relationship between normal siblings, with the 'autistic' siblings being rated as more supportive and accepting and as less hostile. Rodrigue (1993) found no differences in academic competence between siblings of children with Down's syndrome or autism and other studies have described siblings as showing greater tolerance, better awareness of prejudice and as being more certain about their own future and goals; they may also demonstrate higher levels of dedication and self-sacrifice. Mates (1990) reported that these children scored more highly on measures of self-concept, and there were no apparent effects on friendships or the quality of their lives more generally; self-concept measures were higher than average, interpersonal and caretaking skills were good, and academic attainments were not affected. Other studies have also found that the social adjustment scores of children with autistic siblings tend to be similar to those of other children.

However, many of these studies have also reported some negative findings. Mates found that general family activities were restricted; others have described feelings of guilt, isolation and anxiety about the condition generally; some children were concerned about the possible risks to their own offspring; others worried that they might 'catch' autism themselves. Rodrigue found somewhat higher rates of behavioural and emotional problems, although these were still within the normal range. Closer analysis of the findings in the McHale study also revealed large individual differences between children; thus, although average rates of disturbance were low, the range was very wide, with some children having quite serious problems. On the whole, disturbance in siblings tended to be related to poorer relationships between parents, with older siblings showing greater disturbance than younger ones. Worries about the handicapped child's future, perceptions of parental favouritism and feelings of rejection were all associated with negative sibling responses. Positive reactions were correlated with better understanding of the nature of the handicap and positive reactions by parents and other peers.

In a small group for siblings run at the National Autistic Society in London (Howlin 1997a) a similar picture emerged. Although all had some complaints (mainly related to the child with autism having temper tantrums, being noisy, interfering with their belongings or being ritualistic), 9 out of the 10 children involved were able to identify some positive characteristics. In six cases the sibling was described as making them laugh, even as being cuddly and friendly. Others considered the fact that the child spent a lot of time alone to be a positive asset! In some cases the

autistic child's obsessional interests were considered 'a good thing' because they meant that the family always had to 'go to interesting places,
like going rock climbing, going on trains and to the fair'. However, three
members of the group had serious anxiety for the future, mainly concerning the need for a suitable residential placement in adulthood. Most children had experienced some problems with their peers. In some this was
due to teasing; for example, if they ever made a mistake at school other
children would respond with jeers such as 'You're going the same way as
your brother' or 'You're just as stupid as he is'. Others complained that
peers were 'too sympathetic . . . sort of pitying', which they found very
irritating. Nevertheless, only one child out of the group, an 11-year-old
girl with a younger brother, expressed real anger or bitterness. For her,
life at home was described as 'total chaos . . . everything's a problem',
and she could find nothing positive whatsoever to say about her brother.

Overall these studies are encouraging in indicating that siblings do not
necessarily experience a disturbed and miserable childhood because of
the presence of a child with autism. However, the picture is a complex
one that is not always easy to disentangle. Fisman *et al.* (1996) have
conducted a longitudinal, comparative study of the siblings of children
with pervasive developmental disorders, such as autism, children with
Down's syndrome, and normally developing children. They found significantly more sibling problems in the developmentally disordered
group; parents, too, showed higher levels of distress and depression.
Moreover, while marital satisfaction, lack of parental depression, a cohe-
sive family and a warm, non-conflictual sibling relationship were protective factors for the Down's and normal control siblings, this was not
necessarily the case in the PDD group. The authors suggest that these
findings suggest the importance of a transactional mechanism, rather
than the identification of single risk or protective factors in predicting
sibling adjustment.

Reducing the impact on siblings

While individual personality and family factors are clearly important,
there are a number of practical steps that can be taken to minimise the
negative impact on siblings. Opportunities for open and honest discussions within the family, about feelings towards the child with autism,
seem to be particularly crucial. Most normally developing children have
no qualms about declaring that they hate their brothers or sisters from
time to time—even that they wish they were dead or had never been
born. However, a child with a disabled sibling may feel very guilty about
even thinking such thoughts, never mind expressing them openly. Children may also harbour feelings of guilt that they themselves may have

caused the autism. Howlin (1988) cites the case of a twin, who for years had believed that she had caused her sister's autism because she had hit her on the head with a book when she was little, but she had always been too frightened to tell anyone.

Another decisive factor is the attitude of parents. If they are positive towards and accepting of the child with autism and able to value his or her positive asserts, as well as being open about the difficulties, other children are likely to adopt a similar attitude. However, acceptance of the child with autism also needs to be tempered by fairness. If the affected child is seen as 'getting away with everything'; if he or she destroys their belongings or interferes in their other activities; if the parents are left with no time at all to give to their other children, then resentments are almost certain to develop. Most siblings, even if they are much younger than the child with autism, soon realise that the rules governing their behaviour are different to the rules that are applied to them, and with adequate explanation seem able to accept this without too much difficulty. However, it is when there are *no* rules that problems occur. Thus, parents should be clear that certain behaviours will not be tolerated and they need to ensure that there are boundaries for the autistic child in the same way as there are for his siblings (although, of course, the basic ground rules may be very different). As long as the child is not too severely handicapped, the allocation of specific 'chores' can help reduce feelings of unfairness. These may be very simple demands—one child simply had to straighten the mats on the dining table (which he tended to do anyway because he disliked anything being crooked); another had to collect the milk from the door; another was responsible for feeding the dog (which he did at exactly the same time and with the same amount of food each day). If established when the child is young, such routines soon tend to become part of the daily pattern of activities and may be gradually extended over time.

Privacy is another important factor. Having somewhere safe to keep toys or other possessions, being able to read, watch television or do homework in peace, or have friends to visit are basic needs for most children and may be even more necessary for siblings of a child with a disability. If at all possible, a separate bedroom, which can be locked if necessary, and to which the autistic child is not allowed access except with permission, should be provided. If not, individual space and possessions should be clearly demarcated from the time the child is very young. One mother placed a line of bricks down the middle of the room to indicate which bit of the bedroom belonged to each child; later this was reduced to a line drawn on the carpet. If a room is shared, locks on certain cupboards or drawers may be required in order to keep belongings safe. If other children need to do homework, they should be able to do so without noise and interruption. If it is feasible, the autistic child might be provided with some alternative activity at such times (such as watching a video in another room or 'helping' in the kitchen). Again, if 'quiet times' become part of the children's routines from the time they are very young, these should be accepted without too much difficulty.

For many children with autism, opportunities to mix with their peers out of school are very limited. Thus, their siblings' friends may be the only other children with whom they come into contact. Such interactions can be very important, especially for young children, who can be drawn into social games or make-believe play in this way. However, firmer boundaries may have to be drawn as they grow older. Dawn, for example, had always played in the neighbourhood with her older sister and friends, but when the sister's interest switched from bicycles to boys, Dawn's presence was no longer appreciated. Because she had never done anything independently of her sister in the past, this rejection was extremely distressing. In principle, therefore, encouraging some independent activities, again from an early age, or ensuring that the other sibling spends some time alone with his or her own friends, can help to minimise problems of this kind.

As children grow older, teasing or even rejection by peers because they have a brother or sister who is 'weird', 'mad' or 'mental' becomes an increasing risk. This seems to be somewhat reduced if friends have been used to the autistic child from a young age and are accustomed to his or her unusual ways. For older children, being able to explain coherently to their peers what autism is, and how it affects their sibling, can be enormously helpful. Hence, they will need clear explanations and advice about the condition if they are to pass this information onto others. Fromberg (1984) gives a moving account of the years spent with his autistic brother and notes how much basic information about autism, and about ways of dealing with difficult behaviours, would have helped in reducing his own feelings of upset and anger, as well as increasing his sense of competence and understanding. Again leaflets published by the National Autistic Society can be useful. Books for or about siblings, such as those by Davies (1993, 1994a, 1994b) or Harris (1994), may also provide valuable help.

Access to a reasonable amount of parents' time is another important factor in minimising resentment and jealously. This can be very difficult to manage, especially if the child with autism is very disturbed and demanding. However, if parents work together on this it may be possible for them to share out their time more effectively, perhaps by taking turns to look after the autistic child while the other parent spends time with the rest of the family. The use of other family members, other parents of children with a disability, baby sitters, family support workers, 'befrienders', respite care facilities, or special after school or holiday provision can also help to free up more time. Even having just one day, or half day a month to look forward to, when they can have their parents' undivided attention or do things they want to do together, can significantly increase children's tolerance.

It is also important that the autistic child's rituals and routines are not allowed to dominate or interfere with the rest of family life. A child who refuses to let anyone else have the television on, watches the same video hour after hour, insists that everyone else eats or sits, or even talks in a particular way, or has the whole family visiting the local train station every weekend will not be greatly loved by his brothers or sisters. While the child with autism should be able to watch things he or she likes, or visit places of special interest, there should be a fixed time, place and frequency for these activities, with other children also getting their turn. Jeremy's parents, for example, allowed their four children to choose an activity in turn for one weekend each a month. Although Jeremy's choice was always to go looking for King George V post boxes, the others tolerated this because they had their own activities for the other three weekends. Simon's parents were aware of his obsessionality, especially over TV programmes, from an early age. On alternate nights after school, therefore, he and his sister had the choice of what they would watch. If it was the other's turn and they thus had to miss a favourite programme, this would be videoed, and could be watched at the weekend. Although routines of this kind can be very difficult to introduce if the child with autism has already acquired total domination over the family's viewing habits, if established early enough they can prove relatively easy to maintain and adapt.

Almost all studies of families with a disabled child conclude that it is crucial to avoid placing too great a burden of care, either practically or psychologically, on siblings. There can be a tendency for some parents to rely over much on their other children either for practical help within the home, or for emotional support. There may also be a desire for their other children to succeed, in order to compensate in some way for the sense of 'loss' that having a child with a disability can entail. Equitable sharing of household activities, between *both* parents and *all* children can help to reduce strain all round. Financial and residential plans for the future of the child with autism should also be made on the assumption that this will eventually be the responsibility of social or other statutory services. A 10-year-old girl may be happy to agree to her parents' request for her autistic brother to live with her when they die; she may feel very differently 20 years later. And, if such a promise is ever extracted, the guilt at not being able to keep it can be life-long.

Care also needs to be taken if siblings attend the same school. It can be all too easy for teachers to complain about the child with autism to, or in front of, their brothers or sisters, or to make unfavourable comparisons.

One boy used to have to take home a note each day, documenting his brother's many misdemeanours; another was actually made to take his autistic brother home if his behaviours became too disruptive. Such insensitivity will do little to improve sibling's tolerance, and singling them out in front of other pupils in this way further increases the chances of rejection and teasing. Although not inevitable, the risk of problems of this kind leads many families to seek separate schools for their child with autism and his or her siblings.

Therapy for siblings, and siblings as therapists

Moreover steps are taken to minimise the impact on siblings some children will need individual counselling and help on their own behalf. As long as intervention is offered early enough, rather than waiting until resentment and jealousies have gone too deep, such intervention can have significant effects (McHale *et al.*, 1984).

However, if good relationships can be maintained siblings may prove very effective therapists for their brother or sister. Many families report that as a younger sibling begins to talk and play and becomes more demanding, the child with autism is often 'forced' into becoming more sociable and communicative. Siblings may also be able to make use of the autistic child's special skills. Dominic, for example, always took his autistic brother to school chess matches with him because of his skill in the game. For some reason, no one seemed to mind that many of the moves were suggested by the brother, although they would certainly have objected to anyone else doing the same. Gerry's brother always scored extremely highly on fruit machines, and hence was a useful source of money when they visited arcades. Anthony, a 16-year-old with autism offered his sister help with her maths homework in return for her help with his dog phobia. Howlin and Rutter (1987a) also found that if siblings were involved in home-based treatment, they could prove very competent and consistent partners in intervention programmes.

In a number of other studies siblings have been systematically trained to use behaviourally based strategies with the autistic child. The tasks taught have included basic self-care and domestic skills (Lobato & Tlaker, 1985; Swenson-Pierce *et al.*, 1987), academic skills (Schreibman *et al.*, 1983) as well as a variety of other behaviours (Colletti & Harris, 1977). More recently emphasis has shifted to the teaching of play and social skills (Coe *et al.*, 1991; Celiberti & Harris, 1993) and it is clear that even in these more complex areas, siblings can prove very effective therapists. However, as with any home-based programme, sensitivity and careful judgement must be used if siblings are employed in this way. Although self-esteem and feelings of competence may be enhanced, it is also possible inadvertently to increase feelings of pressure and responsibility. Rather than focusing specifically on siblings as therapists, therefore, it may be better to encourage parents and siblings to decide together which behaviours need to be changed, and what techniques they should try to use, consistently and co-operatively, to deal with these.

Parents' Views of Intervention

As already noted, one of the greatest changes in approaches to the treatment of autism over recent years has been the move away from clinic-based, professionally directed programmes to therapeutic strategies, carried out within naturalistic, home-based settings. Such programmes are clearly more effective than other interventions in establishing long-term gains, and can be used to increase a wide range of abilities, including social and communication skills, as well as to reduce unwanted behaviours such as rituals and obsessions, tantrums, aggression and self-injury (see Lovaas, 1977, Koegel & Koegel, 1995, Howlin & Rutter, 1987a, for reviews). Nevertheless, there is a risk that interventions of this kind, if not sensitively conducted, might impose unnecessary stress on families. The impact on families involved in highly intensive, child-oriented therapy of the type used in the intervention programmes of Lovaas and

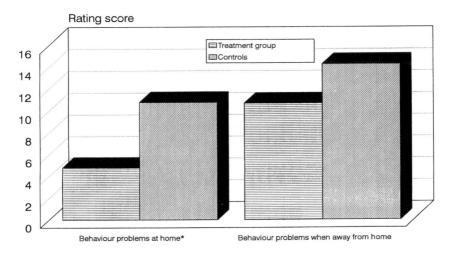

N.B. The higher the rating the more severe the behaviour. * Difference between groups significant at $p < 0.01$

Figure 10.1: Parental ratings of disruptive behaviours at home and when out— comparison between cases and controls at end of 18 months.

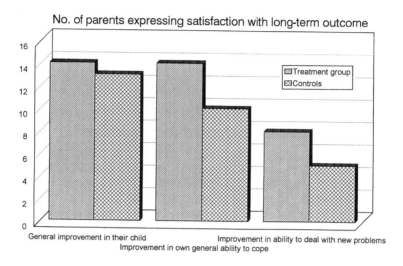

No. of parents expressing satisfaction with long-term outcome

Figure 10.2: Parents' longer-term views of treatment effectiveness

his colleagues has not, so far, been investigated. However, less intensive programmes, with a greater emphasis on *family* functioning, suggest that in the majority of cases the general effects are very positive. Koegel and his colleagues (1996) studied two groups of parents involved in home-based interventions. In one group the emphasis was on the training of specific skills, using traditional reinforcement procedures; in the other the focus was on the development of greater motivation and responsivity to multiple cues, using naturally occurring reinforcers. Parents in the latter group rated themselves as being happier, experiencing less stress and as having more positive interactions with their child following treatment. There was also greater generalisation to other aspects of family life. In the home-based study of Howlin and Rutter (1987a) the focus was also on a wide range of skills and behaviours; naturalistic reinforcers were used as far as possible, and the aim was to improve the consistency of parental approaches to their child, rather than imposing more stringent be-havioural programmes. Again, as compared with control families, these parents rated themselves as being significantly more favourable towards therapy. Parents in the treatment group recorded fewer behaviour prob-lems both in and outside the home, following the 18 months of interven-tion (Figure 10.1). Few felt that the demands on their time, or on family life generally, had been excessive and they did not perceive intervention as unduly intrusive (Figure 10.2). They also reported more positive changes in their children's behaviour (Figure 10.3).

An independent assessment of parents' coping techniques showed, too, that parents in the treatment group were using more efficient strategies

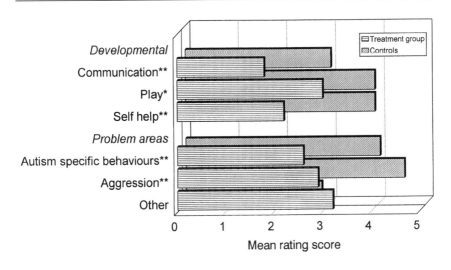

Ratings are based on a 7-point scale. 1/2 = strategies sensible and efficient; 3/4 = inefficient or no strategies used; 5+ = inappropriate and inefficient or likely to exacerbate the behaviour. * Group difference significant at $_p$<0.05; ** p,0.01

Figure 10.3: Effectiveness of coping strategies used by parents.

(Figure 10.4). However, although a longer term follow up, after 18 months, indicated that parents in the treatment group felt more competent in coping with their child's problems, the differences were no longer significant. Parents also tended to perceive their child as making less progress, and as showing fewer significant improvements than independent, observational data actually indicated. There were difficulties, too, in generalising treatment approaches to newly developed behavioural problems. It may be, that in order to maintain parents' views of their own competence at a high level, contact with therapists needs to be maintained, in some form or other, over a much longer period. Even when effective ways of coping have been established, parents' ability, or perhaps motivation, to use these skills in the absence of external support can present difficulties.

Both this and the Koegel study demonstrate that, for maximum effectiveness, the focus of therapy needs to be on the amelioration of family problems more generally. The overall goal should not be simply to increase specific skills in the child, or to reduce problem behaviours to a specified level (although these are clearly important aims) but to produce widespread positive gains throughout the family's lives (Koegel *et al.*, 1996). This requires much more flexibility on the part of therapists, with programmes being led more by family needs than by prescribed procedures. Although long-term goals will need to be set in advance, careful

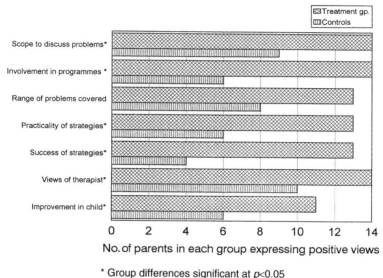

Figure 10.4: Parents' satisfaction with different aspects of therapy.

monitoring of progress and of parents' abilities to meet these goals can mean that planned programmes may need to be significantly modified if therapy is to produce real advantages. In many cases it may prove more effective to encourage parents to use strategies and techniques they have already developed, and to help them do so more efficiently, rather than introduce novel techniques. Most parents, after all, do the 'right' thing at least some of the time—the problem is to help them use appropriate strategies with greater consistency. Thus, rather than expect parents to use novel or more complex behavioural techniques, it may be much more effective (and less stressful for them) if they are encouraged to use existing methods in a more systematic and planned way. In the programme described by Howlin and Rutter (1987a) the only methods that were actively discouraged were punitive techniques such as shouting or smacking, and even here it was often found better to demonstrate the effectiveness of other strategies before appearing to criticise or undermine existing approaches.

Throughout that study, it was also apparent that more stringent behavioural programmes might well have had a more rapid or extensive impact, *had they been rigorously carried out.* However, it was also evident that, in most instances, the required degree of rigour or consistency would never be achieved. Even if this were possible in the short term, it became evident that any additional stressors or problems could easily result in rapid disruption and the potential loss of any previous gains.

Instead, the aim was for steady and achievable, albeit sometimes slow, progress. As demonstrated both in this book and in the more detailed description of the programme provided by Howlin and Rutter (1987a), this 'compromise' approach can in fact lead to many and long-lasting gains. It even made it possible to persuade partners with severe marital difficulties (who disagreed on virtually everything else) to work together in devising a consistent approach to the treatment of their child.

Transitions

Many different types of intervention programme have been reported as being successful for families with an autistic child, although it is still not possible to determine the variables that may be most effective for particular children, families or problems. The majority of families, however, as the survey by Howlin and Moore indicated, have to get by with little or no specialist help. Appropriate educational provision is often the most that families can hope for. Although certainly a crucial component of care, even the best of schools is unlikely to be able to meet all the family's needs. Additional support and guidance is particularly likely to be needed in the months following diagnosis; in the early years when behavioural problems may be at their most severe; when children first go to school, but not with their normal peers; when they move into adolescence and are unable to take any part in normal teenage activities; when they take their first holiday or period of respite care away from the family; when they go to college; or when they eventually leave home.

The concept of 'chronic sorrow' was first introduced by Olshanski in 1962, who suggested that parents can never fully resolve the grief that the birth of a disabled child brings. This grief waxes and wanes over time in response to changes in their child, other family stresses and life events. Research by Wikler et al. (1981) also supported the view that events such as those listed above can rekindle feelings of grief and bereavement in parents, for at each stage they are reminded once again of the 'normal' child they have lost. Siegel (1997) offers a helpful and sensitive review of work in this area, but it is important to be aware that some parents remain deeply sceptical of such theories. The fact is that at these times families are often in urgent need of *practical help and support*, which is frequently unobtainable. Hypotheses about parental grief reactions (even if true) should not be used as an excuse for inaction, and they may understandably be regarded by parents who cannot obtain the help they need as a rather pathetic defence. Unfortunately, because over the years the child's needs may have to be met by various different agencies—health, education or social services—consistency of support is often lacking. Even within any one service, frequent changes of staff can mean that parents have to recount the same, often lengthy history, many times over in order to explain their problems or to elicit the required help. There can be particular problems in the transition to adult-based services, as knowledge about developmental disorders such as autism is often sparse, and the child-based help that was almost automatically available through educational services suddenly disappears.

In many cases, the lack of appropriate provision or help for older children—especially those who are more able—can lead to parents becoming very over-protective. Many believe, quite correctly, that if they do not provide the necessary protection no one else will, and that without such support their child is likely to get into serious difficulties. After numerous episodes of bullying by local youths (including one occasion when they had forced him to consume a large quantity of marihuana-cake) the mother of one 17-year-old boy simply refused to let him out unaccompanied. Her request for additional support for him at college was turned down on the grounds that he was 'quite capable of standing up for himself'. As she said: 'I know that they (the professionals) think that I'm just a neurotic mum who is unable to let go. . . . They're probably right, but whenever I've tried to let him fend for himself some disaster has occurred. They won't accept that he still needs support and until they do I'm not prepared to take any more risks.'

All too often, usually because of financial restraints, practical help for families is provided only on a crisis basis—when things have finally broken down or are in imminent danger of doing so. However, there can be little doubt that the early provision of clear and practical advice on how to avoid or deal with potential problems *before these actually emerge* could do much to improve the quality of life for children with autism and their families. Thereafter, support or intervention at those stages of development that are known to be associated with stress and upheaval could well reduce the impact on families. Knowing that they can quickly and reliably contact a professional who is familiar with their background, and who will help to co-ordinate health, social or educational services if necessary, can significantly improve families' sense of adequacy and control. It may also encourage them to allow more able children with autism or Asperger syndrome to develop greater independence as they grow older.

CONCLUSIONS

It is now well over 50 years since Kanner and Asperger first described the conditions that were subsequently named after them. In that time much has been learned about the nature of autism and its possible causes. The progress in genetic research and in complex brain imaging technology, for example, is particularly encouraging, although it is likely to be some time before such findings will benefit individual families. In the last half century, too, clinical and research experience has taught us much about strategies that can be used to improve educational and intervention programmes and to enhance children's inherent skills and abilities. Recognition that social and communication deficits, and the need for ritual and routine, underlie much behavioural disturbance has had a considerable impact. This has led to a greater appreciation of the difficulties experienced by children with autism, and better understanding of, and sympathy for their problems. In turn this has resulted in a much more positive approach to treatment, and a marked decline in the use of aversive techniques. Awareness that effective and early intervention can help greatly to minimise, or even avoid secondary problems has also been crucial. Much, however, remains to be achieved. In many cases, practical help for families is still extremely limited, and is often only available on a crisis basis, when problems have become too difficult for them to cope with. A far greater emphasis on *preventative* interventions is needed in order to ensure that:

 (i) families have access to early and specialist diagnostic facilities, as soon as they are aware that all is not well
 (ii) early diagnosis is backed up by clear information for parents on the nature and course of the condition generally, and, more specifically, on what the outcome is likely to be for their own child
(iii) parents are alerted to the sorts of problems that may emerge with time and are provided with practical advice on how to deal with these in order to prevent their escalation
(iv) guidance is provided on how to obtain appropriate and effective educational support, thereby ensuring that families have access to skilled and continuing professional help

Unfortunately, financial support for preventative work, not only in the field of autism, but for many other childhood disorders, remains very limited. All too often provision depends on *where* families live, or on what services and schools are available in their particular locality rather than on research-based evidence. Access to help may also depend on the persistence and determination of individual parents. We have learned much about what to do and how to help families—the crucial need now is to ensure that such help is made more readily available to all.

Appendix 1

COGNITIVE AND LANGUAGE TESTS THAT CAN BE USED FOR CHILDREN WITH AUTISM

This is not meant as a comprehensive list, but includes tests that have been found useful in follow-up and research studies.

TESTS OF GENERAL ABILITY

Bayley Scales of Infant Development (Bayley, 1993; The Psychological Corporation: London)
Age range: 1–42 months
Normative sample: American
Type: Mainly non-verbal tests; useful for very young or very delayed children. Provides IQ and mental age scores.

Merrill-Palmer Pre-School Performance Scale (Stutsman, 1931; NFER-Nelson: Windsor)
Age range: 18 months to 6 years
Normative sample: American
Type: Verbal and non-verbal tests but verbal items can be omitted. Despite having very old norms has been shown to have good predictive validity in this group (as long as child is able to complete several different tasks). Requires little or no verbal understanding; materials tend to maintain children's interest and hence useful for non-verbal children. Provides IQ, mental age and percentile scores.

Wechsler Pre-school and Primary Scale of Intelligence: Revised UK Edition (WPPSI-R UK). (Wechsler, 1990; The Psychological Corporation: London)
Age range: 3–7 years

Normative samples: UK (but many other editions available)
Type: Verbal and non-verbal tests mostly requiring some verbal comprehension. Assesses Performance, Verbal and Full Scale IQ. Experience suggests that only the most able autistic children in this age group can cope with the materials. (Merrill-Palmer is often more viable option.) Provides IQ, age equivalent and standard scores.

Wechsler Intelligence Scale for Children: Third UK Edition (WISC-III UK). (Wechsler, 1992; The Psychological Corporation: London)
Age range: 6–16 years
Normative samples: UK (but many other editions available)
Type: Verbal and non-verbal tests, almost all requiring some verbal comprehension. Supplies helpful profile of skills and difficulties. Assesses Performance, Verbal and Full Scale IQ. Younger children tend to cope better with the Performance Scale, but older, more able subjects may do better on the Verbal Scale. Provides IQ, age equivalent and standard scores.

Raven's Progressive Matrices (Raven; NFER-Nelson: Windsor)
Age range: Child to older adults
Normative samples: American; British and many others
Type: Test of perceptual ability. Requires little or no verbal ability/explanation, but tasks themselves difficult for most very young and/or delayed children. Colour form usually best for young children and Board form (in which pieces attached with velcro) can be particularly useful in this group. Provides age equivalent scores.

Kaufman Assessment Battery for Children (Kaufman, 1983; NFER-Nelson: Windsor)
Age range: 30 months to 12.5 years
Normative samples: American.
Type: Mixture of verbal and non-verbal tests. Assesses sequential processing, simultaneous processing and achievement. Supplies helpful profile of skills and difficulties which can then be used for designing educational programmes. Provides percentile ranks, age equivalent and standard scores.

Leiter International Performance Scale Battery (Leiter, 1948, 1979; NFER-Nelson: Windsor)
Age range: 2–18 years
Normative samples: European and USA
Type: Non-verbal tests; largely involving matching and sequencing. Developed specifically for use with children with hearing/linguistic problems; however level of conceptual understanding required can present

difficulties for young autistic children. Works best with older/more able group. Provides IQ and Mental Age scores.

TESTS OF LANGUAGE AND PLAY

Reynell Language Scales: Third Revision (Edwards *et al.*, 1997) NFER-Nelson: Windsor)
Age range: 1–7 years
Normative samples: British
Type: Scored from observations of child and structured tasks with toys and pictures. Provides age equivalent and standard scores for Comprehension and Expression. Even quite young children seem to enjoy the materials. Low age ceiling the main drawback.

British Picture Vocabulary Scale (Dunn, Dunn, Whetton Pintilie, 1982; 1997; NFER-Nelson: Windsor)
Age range: 2.5–18 years
Normative samples: British (based on American PPVT)
Type: Assesses verbal comprehension. Provides age equivalent and standard scores + percentiles, etc. Child is required to identify one picture from a set of four. Not very useful/interesting for very young or very linguistically delayed children. In older, more verbal group, the wide age range is valuable; and a short version is also very quick and easy to administer. However, because of very circumscribed nature of task, may not provide very accurate assessment of linguistic functioning within the wider social context.

Expressive One Word Vocabulary Test (Gardner, 1982, 1990; Western Psychological Services: Los Angeles)
Age range 2–15 years *Upper extension:* to 18 years
Normative samples: American
Type: Assesses expressive vocabulary. Provides age equivalent and standard scores + percentiles, etc. Child is required to name individual pictures. Again, not very useful/interesting for very young or very delayed children. Wide age range is useful, although some items very 'American'. Like BPVS, nature of task very circumscribed.

Test of Reception of Grammar (TROG)
Age range: 4.0–12.11 years
Normative samples: British
Type: Assesses grammatical understanding. Provides age equivalent, standard scores and percentiles. Child selects one picture from set of

three. Useful for more verbal children; one of few well-standardised tests of grammatical ability, although again skills tested rather circumscribed. Provides age equivalent, standard scores and percentiles.

Symbolic Play Test: Second Edition (Lowe & Costello, 1988; NFER-Nelson: Windsor)
Age range: 1–3 years
Normative samples: British
Type: Scored from observations of child and structured tasks with toys. Provides age equivalent scores for symbolic play. Enjoyed by quite young children but low age ceiling the main drawback.

REFERENCES

Agrotou A. (1988). A case study: Lara. *Journal of British Music Therapy*, **2**, 17–33.

Alvin J. (1968). *Music Therapy for the Autistic Child*. Oxford: Oxford University Press.

Aman M.G., van Bourgondien M.E., Wolford P.L. & Sarphare G. (1995). Psychotropic and anticonvulsant drugs in subjects with autism: prevalence and patterns of use. *Journal of the American Academy of Child and Adolescent Psychiatry*, **34**, 1672–1681.

American Psychological Association (1994). *Resolution on Facilitated Communication*. August 1994.

Anderson L.T., Campbell M., Adams P., Small A.M., Perry R. & Shell J. (1989). The effects of Haloperidol on discrimination learning and behavioral symptoms in autistic children. *Journal of Autism and Developmental Disorders*, **19**, 227–239.

Anderson S.R., Avery D.L., DiPietro E.K., Edwards G.L. & Christian W.P. (1987). Intensive home-based early intervention with autistic children. *Education and Treatment of Children*, **10**, 352–366.

APA (1980). *Diagnostic and Statistical Manual of Mental Disorders (DSM-III)*, 3rd Edition. Washington, DC: American Psychiatric Association.

APA (1994). *Diagnostic and Statistical Manual of Mental Disorders (DSM-IV)*, 4th Edition. Washington DC: American Psychiatric Association.

Arnold L.E. & Aman M.G. (1991). Beta blockers in mental retardation and developmental disorders. *Journal of Child and Adolescent Psychopharmacology*, **1**, 361–373.

Arendt R.E., MacLean W.E., Halpern L.F. & Youngquist G.A. (1991). The influence of rotary/vestibular stimulation upon motor development of non-handicapped and Down Syndrome Infants. *Research in Developmental Disabilities*, **12**, 333–348.

Armenteros J.L., Adams P.B., Campbell M. & Eisenberg Z. (1995). Haloperidol related dyskinesis and pre- and peri-natal complications in autistic children. *Psychopharmacological Bulletin*, **31**, 363–369.

Arrow P. (1993). My experience with auditory Integration Training at the Light and Sound Centre, London. *Communication*, **27**, (No. 3), 8–10.

Arvidsson T., Danielsson B., Forsberg P., Gillberg C., Johanssen M. & Kjellgren G. (1997) Autism in 3–6 year old children in a suburb of Goteborg, Sweden. *Autism: The International Journal of Research and Practice*, **1**, 163–174.

Asperger H. (1944). Autistic psychopathy in childhood. Translated and annotated by U. Frith (Ed.). In: *Autism and Asperger Syndrome* (1991). Cambridge: Cambridge University Press.

Attwood T., Frith U. & Hermelin B. (1988). The understanding and use of interpersonal gestures by autistic and Down's syndrome children. *Journal of Autism and Developmental Disorders*, **18**, 241–257.

Ayres J.A. (1979). *Sensory Integration and the Child*. Western Psychology Services. Los Angeles, California.

Bailey A.J., Bolton P., Butler L., Le Couteur A., Murphy M., Scott S., Webb T. & Rutter M. (1993). Prevalence of fragile X anomaly amongst autistic twins and singletons. *Journal of Child Psychology and Psychiatry*, **34**, 673–688.

Bailey A., Phillips W. & Rutter M. (1996). Autism: towards an integration of clinical, genetic and neurobiological perspectives. *Journal of Child Psychology and Psychiatry*, **37**, 89–126.

Bailey A., Le Couteur A., Gottesman I., Bolton P., Simenoff E., Yuzda E. & Rutter M. (1995). Autism as a strongly genetic disorder: evidence from a British twin study. *Psychological Medicine*, **25**, 63–77.

Bailey D.B. (1987). Collaborative goal-setting with families: Resolving differences in values and priorities for services. *Topics in Early Childhood Special Education*, **7**, 59–71.

Bailey T. and the International Molecular Genetic Study of Autism Consortium (1998). A full genome screen for autism with evidence for linkage to a region on chromosome 7q. *Human Molecular Genetics*, **7**, 571–578.

Baron-Cohen S. (1995). *Mindblindness: An Essay on Autism and Theory of Mind.* Cambridge, Massachusetts. The MIT Press.

Baron-Cohen S., Cox A., Baird G., Swettenham J., Nightingale N., Morgan K., Drew A. & Charman T. (1996). Psychological markers in the detection of autism in infancy in a large population. *British Journal of Psychiatry*, **168**, 158–163.

Baron-Cohen S. & Howlin P. (1993). The theory of mind deficit in autism: Some questions for teaching and diagnosis. In: S. Baron-Cohen, H. Tager-Flusberg, & D.J. Cohen (Eds), *Understanding Other Minds.* Oxford: Oxford University Press.

Barrera F.J. & Teodoro G.M. (1990). Flash bonding or cold fusion? A case analysis of gentle teaching. In A.C. Repp & N.N. Singh (Eds). *Current Perspectives on the Use of Aversive and Non-Aversive Interventions with Developmentally Disabled Persons*, (pp. 199–214). Sycamore, IL: Sycamore.

Bartak L. & Rutter M. (1973). Special educational treatment of autistic children: A comparative study. I: Design of study and characteristics of units. *Journal of Child Psychology and Psychiatry*, **14**, 161–179.

Bauman M. (1991). Microscopic neuroanatomic abnormalities in autism. *Pediatrics*, **31**, 791–796.

Bauman M. & Kemper T. (Eds) (1994). *The Neurobiology of Autism.* Baltimore: Johns Hopkins.

Bebko J.M., Perry A. & Bryson S. (1996). Multiple method validation study of facilitated communication: II Individual differences and subgroup results. *Journal of Autism and Developmental Disorders*, **26**, 19–42.

Beisler J.M., Tsai L.Y. & Stiefel B. (1986). Brief report: The effects of Fenfluramine on communication skills in autistic children. *Journal of Autism and Developmental Disorders*, **16**, 227–234.

Benjamin S., Seek A., Tresise L., Price E. & Gagnon M. (1995). Case study: Paradoxical response to naltrexone treatment of self-injurious behavior. *Journal of the American Academy of Child and Adolescent Psychiatry*, **34**.

Berkman M. (1977). The legal rights of children with disabilities to education and developmental services. In: Cohen D.J & Volkmar F.R. (Eds), *Handbook of Autism and Pervasive Developmental Disorders* (2nd Edition). New York: Wiley, pp 808–821.

Bernard-Opitz V. (1989). Computer assisted instruction for autistic children. *Journal of Child and Adolescent Psychiatry*, **17**, 125–130.

Bernard-Opitz V., Ross K. & Tuttas M.L. (1990). Computer assisted instruction for autistic children. *Annals of Academy of Medicine*, **19**, 611–616.

Bettison S. (1996). The long-term effects of auditory training in children with autism. *Journal of Autism and Developmental Disorders*, **26**, 361–374.

Bettelheim B. (1967). *The Empty Fortress: Infantile Autism, and the Birth of the Self.* New York: Free Press.

Bidet B., Leboyer M., Descours B., Bouvard M.P. & Benveniste J. (1993). Allergic sensitization in infantile autism. *Journal of Autism and Developmental Disorders*, **23**, 419–420.

Biersdorff K.K. (1994) Incidence of significantly altered pain experience among individuals with developmental disabilities. *American Journal on Mental Retardation*, **98**, 619–631.

Bignell L. (1991). Higashi Update. *Communication*, **26**(2), 9.

Biklen D. (1990). Communication unbound: Autism and praxis. *Harvard Educational Review*, **60**, 291–315.

Birnbrauer J.S. & Leach D.J. (1993). The Murdoch early intervention program after 2 years. *Behavior Change*, **10**, 63–74.

Bishop D.V.M. (1994) Developmental disorders of speech and language. In: M. Rutter, E. Taylor & L. Hersov (Eds), *Child and Adolescent Psychiatry: Modern Approaches*, 3rd Edition (pp. 546–568). Oxford: Blackwell.

Bligh S. & Kupperman P. (1993). Brief Report: Facilitated communication evaluation procedure accepted in a court case. *Journal of Autism and Developmental Disorders*, **23**, 553–557.

Boatman M. & Szurek S. (1960). A clinical study of childhood schizophrenia. In: D. Jackson (Ed.), *The Etiology of Schizophrenia*. New York: Basic Books.

Bolton P., Macdonald H., Pickles A., Rios P., Goode S., Crowson M., Bailey A. & Rutter, M. (1994). A case-controlled family history study of autism. *Journal of Child Psychology and Psychiatry*, **35**, 877–900.

Bolton P.F., Murphy M., MacDonald H., Whitlock B., Pickles A. & Rutter M. (1997). Obstetric complications in autism: Consequences or causes of the condition? *Journal of the American Academy of Child and Adolescent Psychiatry*, **36**, 272–281.

Bondy A. & Frost L. (1996). Educational approaches in pre-school: Behavior techniques in a public school setting. In: E. Schopler and G.B. Mesibov (Eds), *Learning and Cognition in Autism* (pp. 311–334). New York: Plenum Press.

Boniface D. & Graham P. (1979). The 3-year old and his attachment to a special soft object. *Journal of Child Psychology and Psychiatry*, **20**, 217–224.

Bouvard M.P., Leboyer M., Launay J-M., Recasens C., Plumet M-H., Waller-Perotte D. *et al.* (1995). Low-dose naltrexone effects on plasma chemistries and clinical symptoms in autism: a double-blind, placebo-controlled study. *Psychiatry Research*, **58**, 191–201.

Brady M.P., Shores R.E., McEvoy M.A., Ellis D. & Fox J.J. (1987). Increasing social interactions of severely handicapped autistic children. *Journal of Autism and Developmental Disorders*, **17**, 375–390.

Bristol M. (1984). Family resources and successful adaptation to autistic children. In: Schopler E. & Mesibov G (Eds), *The Effects of Autism on the Family*. New York: Plenum Press (pp. 289–310).

Bristol M. (1987). Mothers of children with autism or communication disorders: successful adaptation and the ABCX model. *Journal of Autism and Developmental Disorders*, **17**, 469–486.

Brocklehurst-Woods J. (1990). The use of tactile and vestibular stimulation to reduce stereotypic behaviors in two adults with mental retardation. *American Journal of Occupational Psychology*, **44**, 536–541.

Brown J. & Prelock P.A. (1995) The impact of regression on language development in autism. *Journal of Autism and Developmental Disorders*, **25**, 305–310.

Brua B. & Link H. (1997). A checklist for alternative therapies. *Communication*, **31**(1), 14.

Butera G. & Haywood H.C. (1995). Cognitive education of young children with autism: an application of Bright Start. In: E. Schopler & G. Mesibov (Eds), *Learning and Cognition in Autism*. New York: Plenum Press.

Campbell M. (1996) Resolved: autistic children should have a trial of naltrexone. *Journal of the American Academy of Child and Adolescent Psychiatry*, **35**, 246–247.

Campbell M., Anderson L.T., Mier M. *et al.* (1978) A comparison of haloperidol and behavior therapy and their interaction in autistic children. *Journal of the American Academy of Child and Adolescent Psychiatry*, **17**, 640–655.

Campbell M., Anderson L.T., Small A.M., Adams P., Gonzalez N.M. & Ernst M. (1993). Naltrexone in autistic children: behavioral symptoms and attentional learning. *Journal of the American Academy of Child and Adolescent Psychiatry*, **32**, 1283–1291.

Campbell M., Armenteros J.L., Malone R.P., Adams P.B., Eisdenberg Z.W. & Overall J.E. (1997). Neuroleptic-related dyskinesis in autistic children: a prospective, longitudinal study. *Journal of the American Academy of Child and Adolescent Psychiatry*, **6**, 835–844.

Campbell M. & Cueva J.E. (1995). Psychopharmacology in child and adolescent psychiatry: a review of the past seven years. Part II. *Journal of the American Academy of Child and Adolescent Psychiatry*, **34**, 1262–1272.

Campbell M., Schopler E., Cueva J.E. & Hallin A. (1996). Treatment of autistic disorder. *Journal of the American Academy of Child and Adolescent Psychiatry*, **35**, 134–143.

Cantwell D.P., Baker L. & Rutter M. (1979). Families of autistic and dysphasic children. I: Family life and interaction patterns. *Archives of General Psychiatry*, **36**, 682–688.

Carr E.G. (1991). Replacing factionalism with functionalism. *Journal of Autism and Developmental Disorders*, **21**, 277–279.

Carr E. & Durand V. (1985). The social communicative basis of severe behavior problems in children. In: Reiss, S. & Bootzin, R. (Eds), *Theoretical Issues in Behavior Therapy*. New York: Academic Press.

Carr E.G. & Kemp D.C. (1989). Functional equivalence of autistic leading and communicative pointing: analysis and treatment. *Journal of Autism and Developmental Disorders*, **19**, 561–578.

Carr J. (1995) *Helping your Handicapped Child*, 2nd Edition. London, Penguin.

Carrier J. (1976). Application of a non-speech language system with the severely language handicapped. In: Lloyd L.L. (Ed.), *Communication Assessment and Intervention Strategies*. Baltimore: University Park Press.

Celiberti D.A. & Harris S.L. (1993). Behavioral intervention for siblings of children with autism. *Behavior Therapy*, **24**, 573–599.

Charlop M.H. (1986). Setting effects on the occurrence of autistic children's immediate echolalia. *Journal of Autism and Development Disorders*, **16**, 473–483.

Charlop M.H, Kurtz P.F. & Casey F. (1990). Using aberrant behaviors as reinforcers for autistic children. *Journal of Applied Behavior Analysis*, **23**, 161–181.

Charlop M.H. & Milstein J.P. (1989). Teaching autistic children conversational speech using video modeling. *Journal of Applied Behavior Analysis*, **22**, 275–285.

Charlop M.H., Schreibman L. & Thibodeau M.G. (1985). Increasing spontaneous verbal responding in autistic children using a time delay procedure. *Journal of Applied Behavior Analysis*, **18**, 155–156.

Charlop M.H. & Trasowech J.E. (1991). Increasing autistic children's daily spontaneous speech. *Journal of Applied Behavior Analysis*, **24**, 747–761.

Charlop M.H. & Walsh M.E. (1986). Increasing autistic children's spontaneous verbalizations of affection: an assessment of time delay and peer modeling procedures. *Journal of Applied Behavior Analysis*, **19**, 307–314.

Charlop-Christy M.H. & Haymes L.K. (1996). Using obsessions as reinforcers with and without mild reductive procedures to decrease inappropriate behaviours of children with autism. *Journal of Autism and Developmental Disorders*, **26**, 527–543.

Charlop-Christy M.H. & Haymes L.K. (1998). Using objects of obsession as token reinforcers for children with autism. *Journal of Autism and Developmental Disorders*, **28** 189–198.

Chen S. & Bernard-Opitz V. (1993). Comparison of personal and computer assisted instruction for children with autism. *Mental Retardation*, **31**, 368–376.

Chock P.N. & Glahn T.J. (1983). Learning and self-stimulation in mute and echolalic children. *Journal of Autism and Developmental Disorders*, **14**, 365–381.

Chung S.Y., Luk F.L. & Lee E.W.H. (1990). A follow-up study of infantile autism in Hong Kong. *Journal of Autism and Developmental Disorders*, **20**, 221–232.

Coe D.A., Matson J.L., Craigie C.J. & Gosssen M.A. (1991). Play skills of autistic children: assessment and instruction. *Child and Family Behavior Therapy*, **13**, 13–40.

Coe D., Matson J., Fee V., Manikam R. & Linarello C. (1990). Training nonverbal and verbal play skills to mentally retarded and autistic children. *Journal of Autism and Developmental Disorders*, **20**, 177–187.

Coggins T.E., Morisset C., Krasney L., Frederickson R., Holm V.A. & Raisys V.A. (1988). Brief report: Does fenfluramine treatment enchance the cognitive and communicative functioning of autistic children? *Journal of Autism and Developmental Disorders*, **18**, 425–434.

Colby K.M. (1973). The rationale for computer-based treatment of language difficulties in non-speaking autistic children. *Journal of Autism and Childhood Schizophrenia*, **3**, 254–260.

Coldwell R.A. (1991). Intellectually handicapped children: development of hieroglyphic symbols. *Australian Educational Computing*, Sept. 10–12.

Cole K.N., Mills P.E., Dale P.S. & Jenkins J.R. (1991). Effects of pre-school integration for children with disabilities. *Exceptional Children*, **58**, 201–215.

Colletti G. & Harris S.L. (1977). Behavior modification in the home: siblings as behavior modifiers, parents as observers. *Journal of Abnormal Child Psychiatry*, **5**, 21–30.

Connor D.F., Ozbayrak K.R., Ma Y. & Fletcher K.E. (1997). A pilot study of nadolol for overt aggression in developmentally delayed individuals. *Journal of the American Academy of Child and Adolescent Psychiatry*, **36**, 826–834.

Cook E.H., Kieffer J.E., Charak D.A. & Leventhal B.L. (1993). Autistic disorder and post-traumatic stress disorder. *Journal of the American Academy of Child and Adolescent Psychiatry*, **32**, 1292–1294.

Cottrell D.J. & Summers K. (1990). Communicating an evolutionary diagnosis of disability to parents. *Child Care, Health and Development*, **16**, 211–218.

Creak M. (1963). Childhood psychosis: a review of 100 cases. *British Journal of Psychiatry*, **109**, 84–89.

Crossley R. & Remington-Gurley J. (1992). Getting the words out: Facilitated Communication training. *Topics in Language Disorders*, **12**, 29–45.

Cummins R.A. (1988). *The Neurologically Impaired Child: Doman-Delacato Techniques Reappraisal*. London: Croom Helm.

Daley D., Cantrell R., Cantrell M. & Aman L. (1972). Structuring speech therapy contingencies with an oral apraxic child. *Journal of Speech and Hearing Disorders*, **37**, 22–32.

Dalrymple N.J. (1995). Environmental support to develop flexibility and independence. In: A. Quill (Ed.), *Teaching Children with Autism: Strategies to Enhance Communication and Socialization* (pp. 219–242). New York: Delmar.

Davies J. (1993). *Children with Autism: A Booklet for Brothers and Sisters*. Child Development Research Unit, University of Nottingham.

Davies J. (1994a) *Able Autistic Children—Children with Asperger's Syndrome: A Booklet for Brothers and Sisters*. Child Development Research Unit, University of Nottingham.

Davies J. (1994b). *Siblings of Children with Autism: A Guide for Families*. Child Development Research Unit, University of Nottingham.

Davies M., Howlin P., Bernal J. & Warren S. (1998). A multi-disciplinary approach to the treatment of severe self-injury. *Child Psychology and Psychiatry Review*, **3**, 26–32.

Delacato C.H. (1974). *The Ultimate Stranger: The Autistic Child*. New York: Doubleday.

DeLong G.R. & Dwyer J.T. (1988). Correlation of family history with specific autistic subgroups: Asperger's syndrome and bipolar affective disease. *Journal of Autism and Developmental Disorders*, **18**, 3–30.

DeMyer M.K. (1979). *Parents and Children in Autism*. New York: John Wiley.

DeMyer M.K., Barton S., DeMyer W.E., Norton J.A., Allan J. & Steele R. (1973). Prognosis in autism: a follow-up study. *Journal of Autism and Childhood Schizophrenia*, **3**, 199–246.

Devilliers J. & Naughton J. (1974). Teaching a symbol language to autistic children. *Journal of Consulting and Clinical Psychology*, **42**, 111–117.

Dewart H. & Summers S. (1988). *Pragmatics Profile of Early Communication Skills*. Windsor: NFER.

DiLavore P., Lord C. & Rutter M. (1995) Pre-linguistic Autism Diagnostic Observation Schedule (PL/ADOS). *Journal of Autism and Developmental Disorders*, **25**, 355–379.

Dodge K., Schlundt D., Schocken I. & Delugach J. (1983). Competence and children's sociometric status: the role of peer group entries. *Merrill-Palmer Quarterly*, **29**, 309–306.

Douglas J. & Richman N. (1984). *My Child Won't Sleep*. Harmondsworth, Middlesex: Penguin.

Dura J.R., Mulick J.A. & Hammer D. (1988). Rapid clinical evaluation of sensory integrative therapy for self injurious behaviour. *Mental Retardation*, **26**, 83–87.

Durand B.M. (1990). *Severe Behavior Problems: A Functional Communication Approach*. New York: Guilford Press.

Durand B.M. & Carr E.G. (1987). Social influences on 'self stimulatory' behavior: analysis and treatment application. *Journal of Applied Behavior Analysis*, **20**, 119–132.

Durand B.M. & Carr E.G. (1991). Functional communication training to reduce challenging behavior: maintenance and application in new settings. *Journal of Applied Behavior Analysis*, **24**, 251–254.

Durand B.M. & Crimmins D.B. (1988). Identifying the variables maintaining self-injurious behavior. *Journal of Autism and Developmental Disorders*, **18**, 99–117.

Durand B.M. & Crimmins D.B. (1991). Teaching functionally equivalent responses as an intervention for challenging behaviour. In B. Remington (Ed.), *The Challenge of Severe Mental Handicap: A Behaviour Analytic Approach* (pp. 71–96). Chichester: Wiley.

Egel A.L., Koegel R.L. & Schreibman L. (1980). Review of educational treatment procedures for autistic children. In L. Mann and D. Sabatino (Eds), *Fourth Review of Special Education* (pp. 109–149). New York: Grune & Stratton.

Ehlers S. & Gillberg C. (1993). The epidemiology of Asperger Syndrome: a total population study. *Journal of Child Psychology and Psychiatry*, **34**, 1327–1350.

Eisenberg L. (1956). The autistic child in adolescence. *American Journal of Psychiatry*, **1112**, 607–612.

Eisenberg L. (1972). The classification of childhood psychosis reconsidered. *Journal of Autism and Childhood Schizophrenia*, **2**, 338–342.

Eisenmajer R., Prior M., Leekham S., Wing L., Gould J., Welham M. & Ong B. (1996). Comparison of clinical symptoms in autism and Asperger's disorder. *Journal of the American Academy of Child and Adolescent Psychiatry*, **35**, 1523–1531.

Ekman G., Miranda-Linne F., Gillberg C., Garle M. & Wetterberg L. (1989). Fenfluramine treatment of twenty children with autism. *Journal of Autism and Developmental Disorders*, **19**, 511–532.

Elliott R.O., Dobbin A.R., Rose G.D. & Soper H.V. (1994). Vigorous aerobic exercise versus general motor training: effects on maladative and stereotypic behavior of adults with autism and mental retardation. *Journal of Autism and Developmental Disorders*, **25**, 565–576.

Emerson E. (1990). Some challenges presented by severe self-injurious behaviour. *Mental Handicap*, **18**, 92–98.

Emerson E. (1995). *Challenging Behaviour: Analysis and Intervention*. Cambridge: Cambridge University Press.

Emerson E. & Bromley J. (1995). The form and function of challenging behaviours. *Journal of Intellectual Disability Research*, **39**, 388–398.

Fenichel C. (1974). Special education as the basic therapeutic tool in treatment of severely disabled disturbed children. *Journal of Autism and Childhood Schizophrenia*, **4**, 177–186.

Fenske E.C., Zalemski S., Krantz P.J. & McClannahan L.E. (1985). Age at intervention and treatment outcome for autistic children in a comprehensive intervention program. *Analysis and Intervention in Developmental Disabilities*, **5**, 5–31.

Finnerty J & Quill K. (1991). *The Communication Analyzer*. Lexington, MA: Educational Software Research.

Fischer I. & Granville, B. (1970). Programmed teaching of autistic children. *Archives of General Psychiatry*, **23**, 90–94.

Fisman S., Wolf L., Ellison D., Gillis B., Freeman T. & Szatmari P (1996). Risk and protective factors affecting the adjustment of children with chronic disabilities. *Journal of the American Academy of Child and Adolescent Psychiatry*, **35**, 1532–1541.

Folstein S. & Rutter M. (1977a). Infantile autism: a genetic study of 21 twin pairs, *Journal of Child Psychology and Psychiatry*, **18**, 297–321.

Folstein S. & Rutter M. (1977b). Genetic influences and infantile autism. *Nature*, **265**, 726–728.

Fombonne E. (1998). Epidemiological studies of autism. In: F. Volkmar (Ed.), *Autism and Developmental Disorders*. New York: Cambridge University Press.

Fombonne E., Talan I., Bouchard F. & Lucas G. (1989). A follow-up study of childhood psychosis. *Acta Paedopsychiatrica*, **52**, 12–25.

Fombonne E., Bolton P., Prior J., Jordan H. & Rutter M. (1997). A family study of autism: cognitive patterns and levels in parents and siblings. *Journal of Child Psychology and Psychiatry*, **38**, 667–683.

Frea W.D. (1995) Social-communicative skills in higher-functioning children with autism. In: Koegel R.L. & Koegel L.K. (Eds), *Teaching Children with Autism*. Baltimore: Paul H. Brookes.

Frea W.D., Koegel R.L. & Koegel L.K. (1993). *Understanding Why Problem Behaviors Occur: A Guide for Assessing Parents in Assessing Causes of Behavior and Designing Treatment Plans*. Santa Barbara: University of California Press.

Frith U. (1991). *Autism and Asperger Syndrome*. Cambridge: Cambridge University Press.

Frith U., Soares I. & Wing L. (1993). Research into the earliest detectable signs of autism: what parents say. *Communication*, **27**(3), 17–18.

Fromberg R. (1984). The sibling's changing roles. In: E. Schopler and G. Mesibov (Eds), *The Effects of Autism on the Family*. New York: Plenum Press.

Gagnon L., Mottron L. & Joanette Y. (1997) Questioning the validity of the semantic–pragmatic syndrome diagnosis. *Autism*, **1**, 37–57.

Gardner J. (1976). *Three Aspects of Childhood Autism*. Unpublished PhD thesis, University of Leicester.

Garreau B., Barthelemey C., Sauvage D., Leddet I. & LeLord G. (1984). A comparison of autistic syndromes with and without associated neurological problems. *Journal of Autism and Developmental Disorders*, **14**, 105–111.

Gath A. (1985) Parental reactions to loss and disappointment: the diagnosis of Down's syndrome. *Developmental Medicine and Child Neurology*, **27**, 392–400.

Gerhardt P.F., Holmes D.L., Alessandri M. & Goodman M. (1991). Social policy on the use of aversive interventions: empirical, ethical and legal considerations. *Journal of Autism and Developmental Disorders*, **21**, 265–276.

Ghaziuddin M., Tsai L.Y. & Ghaziuddin N. (1992). Brief report: A comparison of the diagnostic criteria for Asperger's Syndrome. *Journal of Autism and Developmental Disorders*, **22**, 643–651.

Gilby K., Jones G.E. & Newson E. (1988). Autistic children in ordinary mainstream schools. Report to the Departments of Health and DES. (Available from Child Development Research Unit, Nottingham University.)

Gillberg C. (1984). Infantile autism and other childhood psychoses in a Swedish urban region: epidemiological aspects. *Journal of Child Psychology and Psychiatry*, **25**, 35–43.

Gillberg C. (1991). Clinical and neurobiological aspects of Asperger syndrome. In: U. Frith (Ed.), *Autism and Asperger Syndrome* (pp. 122–146). Cambridge: Cambridge University Press.

Gillberg C.L. (1992a). The Emanuel Miller Memorial Lecture 1991. Autism and autistic-like conditions: subclasses among disorders of empathy. *Journal of Child Psychology and Psychiatry*, **33**, 813–842.

Gillberg C. (1992b). Epilepsy. In: C. Gillberg & M. Coleman (Eds), *The Biology of the Autistic Syndromes*, 2nd Edition (pp. 60–73). Oxford: MacKeith Press.

Gillberg C. & Coleman M. (1992) *The Biology of the Autistic Syndromes*, 2nd Edition. Oxford: MacKeith Press.

Gillberg C. & Gillberg C. (1989). Asperger's syndrome: some epidemiological considerations: A research note. *Journal of Child Psychology and Psychiatry*, **30**, 631–638.

Gillberg C., Ehlers S., Schaumann H., Jakobsson G., Dahlgren S.O., Lindblom R., Bagenholm A., Tjuus T. & Blidner E. (1990) Autism under age 3 years: a clinical study of 28 cases referred for autistic symptoms in infancy. *Journal of Child Psychology and Psychiatry*, **31**, 921–934.

Gillberg C., Johansson M., Steffenburg S. & Berlin O. (1997). Auditory integration training in children with autism. Brief report of an open pilot study. *Autism*, **1**, 97–100.

Gillberg C. & Steffenburg S. (1987). Outcome and prognostic factors in infantile autism and similar conditions: a population-based study of 46 cases followed through puberty. *Journal of Autism and Developmental Disorders*, **17**, 272–288.

Gillberg C., Steffenburg S., Wahlstrom J., Sjostedt A., Gillberg I.C., Martinsson T., Liedgren S. & Eeg-Olofsson O. (1991). Autism associated with a marker chromosome. *Journal of the American Academy of Child and Adolescent Psychiatry*, **30**, 489–494.

Goldfarb W. (1961). *Growth and Change of Schizophrenic Children*. New York: Wiley.

Goode S., Howlin P. & Rutter M. (1998). A cognitive and behavioural study of outcome in young adults with autism (in preparation).

Goode S., Rutter M. & Howlin P. (1994). A twenty-year follow-up of children with autism. Paper presented at the 13th Biennial Meeting of the International Society for the Study of Behavioural Development, Amsterdam, The Netherlands.

Gordon C.T., State R.C., Nelson J.E., Hamburger S.D. & Rapoport J.L. (1993). A double-blind comparison of clomipramine, desipramine and placebo in the treatment of autistic disorder. *Archives of General Psychiatry*, **50**, 441–447.

Gould G.A., Rigg M. & Bignell L. (1991). *The Higashi Experience: The Report of a Visit to the Boston Higashi School*. London: National Autistic Society Publications.

Grandin T. (1992a). An inside view of autism. In: E. Schopler and G. B. Mesibov (Eds), *High Functioning Individuals with Autism* (pp. 105–125). New York: Plenum Press.

Grandin T. (1992b). Calming effects of deep pressure in patients with autistic disorder, college students and animals. *Journal of Child and Adolescent Psychopharmacology*, **2**, 63–72.

Grandin T. (1995). How people with autism think. In: E. Schopler and G.B. Mesibov (Eds), *Learning & Cognition in Autism* (pp. 137–158). New York: Plenum Press.

Gray C.A. (1995). Teaching children with autism to 'read' social situations. In A. Quill (Ed.), *Teaching Children with Autism: Strategies to Enhance Communication and Socialization* (pp. 219–242). New York: Delmar.

Graziano A.M. (1970). A group-treatment approach to multiple problem behaviors of autistic children. *Exceptional Children*, **36**, 765–770.

Green G. (1994). The quality of the evidence. In: H.C. Shane (Ed.), *Facilitated Communication: The Clinical and Social Phenomenon* (pp. 157–226). San Diego, EA: Singular Press.

Green G. (1996) Evaluating claims about treatments for autism. In: C. Maurice, G. Green & S.C. Luce (Eds), *Behavioral Intervention for Young Children with Autism*. Austin, Texas: Pro-Ed.

Groden J. & LeVasseur P. (1995). Cognitive picture rehearsal: a system to teach self control. In K. Quill, *Teaching Children with Autism: Strategies to Enhance Communication and Socialization* (pp. 287–306). New York: Delmar.

Gunsett R.P., Mulick J.A., Fernald W.B. & Martin J.L. (1989). Brief report: Indications for medical screening prior to behavioral programming for severely and profoundly retarded clients. *Journal of Autism and Developmental Disorders*, **19**, 167–172.

Hadwin J., Baron-Cohen S., Howlin P. & Hill K. (1996). Can we teach children with autism to understand emotions, belief, or pretence? *Development and Psychopharmacology*, **8**, 345–365.

Hadwin J., Baron-Cohen S., Howlin P. & Hill K. (1997). Does teaching theory of mind have an effect on social communication in children with autism? *Journal of Autism and Developmental Disorders*, **27**, 519–539.

Hagerman R.J. (1990). The association between autism and Fragile X syndrome. *Brain Dysfunction*, **3**, 219–227.

Hall S. (1997). *The Early Development of Self-Injurious Behaviour in Children with Developmental Disabilities*. Unpublished PhD thesis; University of London.

Halle J.W., Baer D.M. & Spradlin J.E. (1981). An analysis of teachers' generalized use of delay in helping children: a stimulus control procedure to increase language use in handicapped children. *Journal of Applied Behavior Analysis*, **14**, 389–409.

Halpern W.I. (1970). The schooling of autistic children: preliminary findings. *American Journal of Orthopsychiatry*, **40**, 665–671.

Hamilton-Ely S.P. (1990). The Option method. *Communication*, **24**, 6–7.

Harris J.C. (1996). Autistic children should have a trial of naltrexone: negative. *Journal of the American Academy of Child and Adolescent Psychiatry*, **35**, 248–249.

Harris S.L. (1994). *Siblings of Children with Autism: A Guide for Families*. USA: Woodbine House.

Harris S.L. (1995). Educational strategies in autism. In: E. Schopler and G. Mesibov (Eds), *Learning and Cognition in Autism* (pp. 293–309). New York: Plenum Press.

Harris S.L., Handleman J.S. & Alessandri M. (1990). *Journal of Applied Behavior Analysis*, **23**, 297–305

Harris S., Handleman J.S., Kristoff B. Bass L. & Gordon R. (1990). Changes in language development among autistic and peer children in segregated and integrated preschool settings. *Journal of Autism and Developmental Disorders*, **20**, 23–32.

Harrison J.E. & Bolton P.F. (1997). Annotation: Tuberous sclerosis. *Journal of Child Psychology and Psychiatry*, **38**, 603–614.

Hauck M., Fein D., Waterhouse L. & Feinstein C. (1995). Social initiations by autistic children to adults and other children. *Journal of Autism and Developmental Disorders*, **25**, 579–596.

Hawkins D. (1995) Spontaneous language use. In: R.L. Koegel & L.K. Koegel (eds) *Teaching Children with Autism*. Baltimore: Paul H. Brookes.

Haynes C. & Naidoo S. (1991). *Children with Specific Speech and Language Impairment. Clinics in Developmental Medicine*. Oxford: Blackwell.

Heimann M., Nelson K., Tjus T. & Gillberg C. (1995). Increasing reading and communication skills in children with autism through an interactive multimedia computer programme. *Journal of Autism and Developmental Disorders*, **25**, 459–480.

Hemsley R., Howlin P., Berger M., Hersov L., Holbrook D., Rutter M. & Yule W. (1978). Treating autistic children in a family context. In: M. Rutter & E. Schopler (Eds), *Autism: A Reappraisal of Concepts and Treatment*. New York: Plenum.

Hemsley R. & Carr J. (1980). Methods of increasing behaviour with the severely retarded. In: W. Yule and J. Carr (Eds), *Behaviour Modification for the Severely Retarded*. London: Croom Helm.

Herman B.H., Asleson G.S., Borghese I.F. *et al.* (1991). Acute naltrexone in autism: Selective decreases in hyperactivity. In: *Scientific Proceedings, 38th Annual Meeting of the American Academy of Child and Adolescent Psychiatry*. San Francisco, October 15–20.

Hewett F. (1965). Teaching speech to an autistic child through operant conditioning. *Journal of Orthopsychiatry*, **35**, 927–936.

Hingtgen J. & Churchill D. (1968). Differential effects of behavior modification in four mute autistic boys. In: *Proceedings of Indiana University Colloquium on Infantile Autism*.

Hobson R.P. (1990). On psychoanalytic approaches to autism. *American Journal of Orthopsychiatry*, **60**, 324–336.

Hooker D. & Hare C.C. (Eds) (1973). Constitutional inadequacies. In: *Childhood Psychosis: Initial Studies and New Insights*. [Revised from the original published in: *Genetics and the Inheritance of Integrated Neurological and Psychiatric Patterns* (1954)].

Horner R.H., Dunlap G., Koegel R.L., Carr E.G., Sailor W., Anderson J., Albin T.W. & O'Neill R.E. (1990). Toward a Technology of 'Nonaversive' Behavioural Support. Reprint: Association for Persons with Severe Handicaps from *JASH*, **15**(3), 1990, pp. 125–132. Bild Publications.

Hoshino Y., Kaneko M., Yashmina Y., Kuashiro H., Volkmar F. & Cohen D. (1987), Clinical features of autistic children with setback course in their infancy. *Japanese Journal of Child and Adolescent Psychiatry*, **24**, 191–196.

Holopf M. & Bolton P. (1995). A case of autism associated with partial tetrasomy 15. *Journal of Autism and Developmental Disorders*, **25**, 749–755.

Howlin P. (1987). Behavioural approaches to language. In: W. Yule & M. Rutter (Eds), *Language Development and Disorders*. Oxford: MacKeith Press.

Howlin P. (1988). Living with impairment: the effects on children of having an autistic sibling. *Child Care, Health and Development*, **14**, 395–408.

Howlin P. (1989). Changing approaches to communication training with autistic children. *British Journal of Disorders of Communication*, **24**, 151–168.

Howlin P. (1994). Special educational treatment. In: M. Rutter, E. Taylor & B. Hersov (Eds), *Child and Adolescent Psychiatry: Modern Approaches*, 3rd Edition. Oxford: Blackwell.

Howlin P. (1997a). *Autism: Preparing for Adulthood*. London: Routledge.

Howlin P. (1997b). Prognosis in autism: Do specialist treatments affect outcome? *European Child and Adolescent Psychiatry*, **6**, 55–72.

Howlin P. (1998). A survey of specialist autism diagnostic services in the UK. *Autism, International Journal of Research and Practice*, **2**, 205–211.

Howlin P., Baron-Cohen S., Hadwin J. & Swettenham J. (1998). *Teaching Children with Autism to Mindread. A Practical Manual for Parents and Teachers*. Chichester: Wiley.

Howlin P. & Clements J. (1995). Is it possible to assess the impact of abuse on children with pervasive developmental disorders? *Journal of Autism and Developmental Disorders*, **25**, 1–17.

Howlin P. & Cross P. (1994). A comparison of language tests in young normal children. *European Journal of Communication Disorders*, **29**, 279–288.

Howlin P. & Goode S. (1998). Outcome in adult life for people with autism and Asperger syndrome. In: F. Volkmar (Ed.), *Autism and Pervasive Developmental Disorders*. New York: Cambridge University Press.

Howlin P. & Jones D.P.H. (1996). An assessment approach to abuse allegations made through facilitated communication. *Child Abuse and Neglect*, **20**, 103–110.

Howlin P. & Moore A. (1997). Diagnosis in autism: a survey of over 1200 patients. *Autism: The International Journal of Research and Practice*, **1**, 135–162.

Howlin P. & Rutter M. (1987a). *Treatment of Autistic Children*. Chichester: Wiley.

Howlin P. & Rutter M. (1987b). The consequences of language delay for other aspects of development. In: W. Yule & M. Rutter (Eds), *Language Development and Disorders*. Oxford: MacKeith Press.

Howlin P., Wing L. & Gould J. (1995). The recognition of autism in children with Down's Syndrome: Implications for intervention and speculations about pathology. *Developmental Medicine and Child Neurology*, **37**, 398–414.

Hoyson M., Jamieson B. & Strain P.S. (1984). Individualised group instruction of normally developing and autistic-like children: a description and evaluation of the LEAP curriculum model. *Journal of the Division of Early Childhood*, **8**, 157–171.

Ingenmey R. & van Houten R. (1991). Using time delay to promote spontaneous speech in an autistic child. *Journal of Applied Behavior Analysis*, **24**, 591–596.

Irlen H. (1995). Viewing the world through rose tinted glasses. *Communication*, **29**(1), 8–9.

Jenkins J.R., Speltz M.L. & Odom S.L. (1985). Integrating normal and handicapped pre-schoolers: effects on child development and social interaction. *Exceptional Children*, **52**, 7–17.

Johnson D. (1996). Letter to Editor. *Autism Research Review*, **10** (1), 7.

Johnson M.H., Siddons F., Frith U. & Morton J. (1992). Can autism be predicted on the basis of infant screening tests? *Developmental Medicine and Child Neurology*, **34**, 316–320.

Jolliffe T., Landsdown R. & Robinson T. (1992). *Autism: A Personal Account*. London: The National Autistic Society.

Jones G. & Newson E. (1992). *Summary Report on the Provision for Children and Adults with Autism in England and Wales*. Unpublished report: Child Development Research Unit, Nottingham University.

Jones J.L., Singh N.N. & Kendall K.A. (1990). Effects of gentle teaching and alternative treatments on self-injury. In: A.C. Repp & N.N. Singh (Eds), *Current Perspectives on the Use of Aversive and Non-aversive Interventions with Developmentally Disabled Persons* (pp. 215–230). Sycamore, IL: Sycamore.

Jones J.L., Singh N.N. & Kendall K.A. (1991). Comparative effects of gentle teaching and visual screening on self-injurious behaviour. *Journal of Mental Deficiency Research*, **35**, 37–47.

Jones R.S.P. & McCaughey R.E. (1992). Gentle Teaching and applied behavior analysis. A critical review. *Journal of Applied Behavior Analysis*, **25**, 853–867.

Jordan R.R. (1990). *The Option Approach to Autism: Observer Project Report*. London: National Autistic Society.

Jordan R. & Libby S. (1997). Developing and using play in the curriculum. In Powell, S. & Jordan R. (Eds), *Autism and Learning: A Guide to Good Practice*. London: David Fulton.

Jordan R. & Powell S. (1995). *Understanding and Teaching Children with Autism*. Chichester: Wiley.

Jordan R. & Powell S. (1990a). Teaching autistic children to think more effectively. *Communication*, **24**(1), 20–22.

Jordan R. & Powell S. (1990b). Improving thinking in autistic children using computer presented activities. *Communication*, **24**(1), 23–25.

Jordan J., Singh N.N. & Repp A.C. (1989). An evaluation of gentle teaching and visual screening in the reduction of stereotypy. *Journal of Applied Behavior Analysis*, **22**, 9–22.

Jorde L.B., Hassdtedt S.J., Ritvo E.R., Mason-Brothers A., Freeman B.J., Pingree C., McMahon W.M., Peterson B., Jenson W.R. & Moll A. (1991). Complex segregation analysis of autism. *American Journal of Human Genetics*, **49**, 932–938.

Kanner L. (1943). Autistic disturbances of affective contact. *Nervous Child*, **2**, 217–250.

Kanner J. (1951). The conception of wholes and parts in early infantile autism, *American Journal of Psychiatry*, **108**, 23–26.

Kanner L. (1973). *Childhood Psychosis: Initial Studies and New Insights*. New York: Winston/Wiley.

Kasari M. & Sigman M. (1997). Linking parental perceptions to interactions in young children with autism. *Journal of Autism and Developmental Disorders*, **27**, 39–59.

Kaufman B.N. (1977). *To Love is to be Happy With*. New York: Fawcett Crest.

Kaufman B.N. (1981). *A Miracle to Believe in*. New York: Doubleday.

Kaufman B.N. (1976). *Son-rise*. New York: Warner.

Kellegrew D.H. (1995). Integrated school placements for children with disabilities. In: R.L. Koegel & L.K. Koegel (Eds), *Teaching Children with Autism*. Baltimore: Paul H. Brookes.

Kern L., Wacker, D.P., Mace, F.C., Falk, G.D., Dunlap, G. & Kromrey, J.D. (1995). Improving the peer interactions of students with emotional and behavioral disorders through self-evaluation procedures: a component analysis and group application. *Journal of Applied Behavior Analysis*, **28**, 47–59.

Kiernan C. (1983). The use of non-vocal communication systems with autistic individuals. *Journal of Child Psychology and Psychiatry*, **24**, 339–376.

Kiernan C. (Ed.) (1993). *Research to Practice? Implications of Research on the Challenging Behaviour of People with Learning Disability.* Clevedon: BILD.

Kirchner D.M. (1991). Reciprocal book-reading: a discourse-based intervention strategy for the child with atypical language development. In: T.M. Gallagher (Ed.), *Pragmatics of Language: Clinical Practical Issues.* San Diego: Singular Press.

Kitahara K. (1983). *Daily Life Therapy* (Vol. 1), Tokyo: Musashino Higashi Gakuen.

Kitahara K. (1984a). *Daily Life Therapy* (Vol. 2), Tokyo: Musashino Higashi Gakuen.

Kitahara K. (1984b). *Daily Life Therapy* (Vol. 3), Tokyo: Musashino Higashi Gakuen.

Klin A. (1994). Asperger syndrome. *Child and Adolescent Psychiatric Clinics of North America,* **3**, 131–148.

Klin A. (1991) Young children's listening preferences in regard to speech: a possible characterisation of the symptom of social withdrawal. *Journal of Autism and Developmental Disorders,* **12**, 29–42.

Klin A. & Volkmar F.R. (1997). Asperger's syndrome. In: D. Cohen & F. Volkmar (Eds), *Handbook of Autism and Pervasive Developmental Disorders* (2nd Edition). New York: Wiley (pp. 94–122).

Klin A., Volkmar, F.R., Sparrow, S.S., Cicchetti, D.V. & Rourke, B.P. (1995). Validity and neuropsychological characterization of Asperger Syndrome. *Journal of Child Psychology and Psychiatry,* **36**, 1127–1140.

Kobayashi R., Murata, T. & Yashinaga, K. (1992). A follow-up study of 201 children with autism in Kyushu and Yamguchia, Japan. *Journal of Autism and Developmental Disorders,* **22**, 395–411.

Koegel R.L. & Koegel L.K. (1995) *Teaching Children with Autism.* Baltimore: Paul H. Brookes.

Koegel R.L., Koegel L.K. & Parks D.R. (1995) 'Teach the individual' model of generalization: autonomy through self-management. In: R.L Koegel & L.K. Koegel (Eds), *Teaching Children with Autism.* Baltimore: Paul H. Brookes.

Koegel R.L. Bimbela, A. Schreibman, L. (1996) Collateral effects of family training on family interactions. *Journal of Autism and Developmental Disorders,* **26**, 347–360.

Koegel L.K., Koegel R.L., Hurley C. & Frea W.D. (1992a). Improving social skills and disruptive behavior in children with autism through self-management. *Journal of Applied Behavior Analysis,* **25**, 341–353.

Koegel R.L., Koegel L.K. & Schreibman L. (1991). Assessing and training parents in teaching pivotal behaviors. In: R. Prinz (Ed.), *Advances in Behavioral Assessment of Children and Families.* London: Jessica Kingsley.

Koegel R.L., Koegel L.K. & Surratt A.V. (1992b). Language intervention and disruptive behavior in pre-school children with autism. *Journal of Autism and Developmental Disorders,* **22**, 141–153.

Koegel R.L., O'Dell M.C. & Dunlap G. (1988). Producing speech use in non-verbal autistic children by reinforcing attempts. *Journal of Autism and Developmental Disorders,* **18**, 525–538.

Koegel R.L., Schreibman L., Johnson J., O'Neill R.E. & Dunlap G. (1984). Collateral effects of parent training on families with autistic children. In: R.F. Dangel & R.A. Polster (Eds), *Parent Training: Foundations of Research and Practice* (pp. 358–378). New York: Guilford Press.

Koegel R.L., Schreibman L., Loos L.M., Dirlich-Wilhelm H., Dunlap G., Robbins F.R. & Plienis A.J. (1992c). Consistent stress profiles in mothers of children with autism. *Journal of Autism and Developmental Disorders,* **22**, 205–216.

Kolmen B.K., Feldman H.M., Handman B.L. & Janosky, J.E. (1993). Naltrexone in young autistic children: a double-blind, placebo-controlled crossover study.

Journal of American Academy of Child and Adolescent Psychiatry, **34**, 223–231.

Konstantareas M. (1987). Autistic children exposed to simultaneous communication training: a follow-up. *Journal of Autism and Developmental Disorders*, **17**, 115–131.

Konstantareas M.M. & Homatidis S. (1987). Ear infections in autistic and normal children. *Journal of Autism and Developmental Disorders*, **20**, 591–593.

Konstantareas M., Oxman J. & Webster C. (1978). Iconicity: effects on the acquisition of sign language by autistic and other severely dysfunctional children. In: P. Siple (Ed.), *Understanding Language Through Sign Language Research*. New York: Academic Press.

Kozloff M.A. (1984). A training program for families of children with autism: responding to family needs. In: E Schopler & G Mesibov (Eds), *The Effects of Autism on the Family* (pp. 163–186). New York: Plenum Press.

Krantz P.J., MacDuff M.T. & McClannahan L.E. (1993). Programming participation in family activities for children with autism: parents' use of photographic activity schedules. *Journal of Applied Behavior Analysis*, **26**, 137–138.

Krantz P.J. & McClannahan L.E. (1993). Teaching children with autism to initiate to peers: effects of a script-fading procedure. *Journal of Applied Behavior Analysis*, **26**, 121–132.

Kroese B.S., Dagnan D. & Loumidis, K. (1997). *Cognitive Behaviour Therapy for People with Learning Disabilities*. London: Routledge.

Krug D.A., Arick J. & Almond P. (1980). Behavior checklist for identifying severely handicapped individuals with high levels of autistic behavior. *Journal of Child Psychiatry and Psychology*, **21**, 221–229.

Kuntz J., Carrier J. & Hollis J. (1978). A non-vocal system for teaching retarded children to read and write. In: C. Meyers (Ed.), *Quality of Life of Severely and Profoundly Retarded People: Research Foundations for Improvements*. Washington: American Association on Mental Deficiency.

Kurita H. (1985). Infantile autism with speech loss before the age of 30 months. *Journal of the American Academy of Child and Adolescent Psychiatry*, **24**, 191–196.

Lainhart J.E., Piven J., Wzorek M., Landa L., Santangelo S.L., Coon H. & Folstein S.E. (1997). Macrocephaly in children and adults with autism. *Journal of the American Academy of Child and Adolescent Psychiatry*, **36**, 282–290.

Layton T.L. (1988). Language training with autistic children using four different models of presentation. *Journal of Communication Disorders*, **21**, 333–350.

Layton T.L. & Watson L.R. (1995). Enhancing communication in non-verbal children with autism. In: K. Quill (Ed.), *Teaching Children with Autism: Strategies to Enhance Communication and Socialization*, (pp. 73–104). New York: Delmar.

Le Couteur A., Bailey A., Goode S., Pickles A., Robertson S., Gottesman I. & Rutter M. (1996). A broader phenotype of autism: the clinical picture in twins. *Journal of Child Psychology and Psychiatry*, **37**, 785–802.

Leff P. T. & Walizer E.H. (1992). The uncommon wisdom of parents at the moment of diagnosis. *Family Systems Medicine*, **21**, 147–167.

LeLord G., Muh J.P., Barthelemey C., Martineau J. & Garreau B. (1981). Effects of pyridoxine and magnesium on autistic symptoms: initial observations. *Journal of Autism and Developmental Disorder*, **11**, 219–230.

Leonard H.L., March J., Rickler K.C. & Allen A.J. (1997). Pharmacology of the selective serotonin reuptake inhibitors in children and adolescents. *Journal of the American Academy of Child and Adolescent Psychiatry*, **36**, 725–736.

Lepper M. (1981). Intrinsic and extrinsic motivation in children with autism. In: W. Collins, (Ed.), *Aspects of the Development of Competence* (pp. 155–214). Hillsdale, NJ: Erlbaum.

Lewis M.H. (1996). Brief report: Psychopharmacology of autism spectrum disorders. *Journal of Autism and Developmental Disorders*, **26**, 231–235.

Libby S., Messer D., Jordan R. & Powell S. (1996). Using photographs to encourage spontaneous pretend play in children with autism. Paper presented at 5th International Congress Autism—Europe. Barcelona, 3–5 May.

Lister-Brook S. (1992) *The Early Detection of Autism*. Unpublished PhD thesis, London University.

Lobato D. & Taker A. (1985). Sibling intervention with a retarded child. *Education and Treatment of Children*, **8**, 221–228.

Lockyer L. & Rutter M. (1969). A five to fifteen year follow-up study of infantile psychosis: III. Psychological Aspects. *British Journal of Psychiatry*, **115**, 865–882.

Lockyer L. & Rutter M. (1970). A five to fifteen year follow-up study of infantile psychosis: IV. Patterns of Cognitive Abilities. *British Journal of Social and Clinical Psychology*, **9**, 152–163.

Lord C. (1984) The development of peer relations in children with autism. *Applied Developmental Psychology*, **1**, 165–230.

Lord C. (1996). Facilitating social inclusion: examples from peer intervention programs. In: E. Schopler & G. Mesibov (Eds), *Learning and Cognition in Autism*. New York. Plenum Press.

Lord C. (1997). Diagnostic instruments in autism spectrum disorders. In: D. Cohen & F. Volkmar (Eds), *Handbook of Autism and Pervasive Developmental Disorders*, 2nd Edition. (pp. 461–483). New York: Wiley.

Lord C. & Pickles A. (1996). Language level and nonverbal social-communicative behaviors in autistic and language delayed children. *Journal of the American Academy of Child and Adolescent Psychiatry*, **35**, 1542–1550.

Lord C. & Rutter M. (1994) Autism and pervasive developmental disorders. In: M. Rutter, E. Taylor & B. Hersov (Eds), *Child and Adolescent Psychiatry: Modern Approaches*, 3rd Edition (pp. 569–591). Oxford: Blackwell.

Lord C., Rutter M. & DiLavore P. (1996) *Autism Diagnostic Observation Schedule— Generic (ADOS-G)*. Unpublished MS, University of Chicago.

Lord C., Rutter M., Goode S., Heemsbergen J., Jordan H. & Mawhood L. (1989). Autism Diagnostic Observation Schedule: a standardized observation of communicative and social behavior. *Journal of Autism and Developmental Disorders*, **19**, 185–212.

Lord C., Rutter M. & Le Couteur A. (1994). Autism Diagnostic Interview— Revised: a revised version of a diagnostic interview for care-givers of individuals with possible pervasive developmental disorders. *Journal of Autism and Developmental Disorders*, **24**, 659–686.

Lord C. & Schopler E. (1985). Differences in sex ratios in autism as a function of measured intelligence. *Journal of Autism and Developmental Disorders*, **15**, 185–193.

Lord C., Storuschuk S., Rutter M. & Pickles A. (1993). Using the ADI-R to diagnose autism in preschool children. *Infant Mental Health Journal*, **14**, 234–252.

Lotter B. (1974a). Factors related to outcome in autistic children. *Journal of Autism and Childhood Schizophrenia*, **4**, 263–277.

Lotter B. (1974b). Social adjustment and placement of autistic children in Middlesex: a follow-up study. *Journal of Autism and Childhood Schizophrenia*, **4**, 11–32.

Lotter V. (1966). Epidemiology of autistic conditions in young children. I: Prevalence. *Social Psychiatry*, **1**, 163–173.

Lovaas O., Schaeffer B. & Simmons J.Q. (1965a). Experimental studies in childhood schizophrenia: building social behavior in autistic children by use of electric shock. *Journal of Experimental Research in Personality*, **1**, 99–109.

Lovaas O. (1977). *The Autistic Child: Language Development through Behavior Modification*. New York: Wiley.

Lovaas O.I. (1978). Parents as therapists for autistic children. In: M. Rutter & E. Schopler (Eds), *Autism: A Reappraisal of Concepts and Treatment*. New York: Plenum Press.

Lovaas O.I. (1987). Behavioral treatment and normal educational and intellectual functioning in young autistic children. *Journal of Consulting and Clinical Psychology*, **55**, 3–9.

Lovaas O.I. (1993). The development of a treatment—research project for developmentally disabled and autistic children. *Journal of Applied Behavior Analysis*, **26**, 617–630.

Lovaas O.I. (1996). The UCLA young autism model of service delivery. In: C. Maurice (Ed.), *Behavioral Intervention for Young Children with Autism* (pp. 241–250). Austin, Texas: Pro-Ed.

Lovaas O.I., Freitag G., Gold., V.J. & Kassorla I.C. (1965b). Experimental studies in childhood schizophrenia: analysis of self-destructive behavior. *Journal of Experimental Child Psychology*, **2**, 67–84.

Lovaas O.I. Koegel R., Simmons J. & Stevens J. (1973). Some generalization and follow-up measures on autistic children in behavior therapy, *Journal of Applied Behavior Analysis*, **6**, 131–166.

Luscre D.M. & Center D.B. (1996) Procedures for reducing dental fear in children with autism. *Journal of Autism and Developmental Disorders*, **26**, 547–556.

McClenny C., Roberts J. & Layton T. (1992). Unexpected events and their effect on children's language. *Child Language Teaching and Therapy*, **8**, 229–264.

McCracken R.A. & McCracken M.J. (1986). *Stories, Songs, and Poetry to Teach Reading and Writing: Literacy Through Language*. Winnipeg, Canada: Peguis.

McLean L. & McLean J. (1974). A language training program for non-verbal autistic children. *Journal of Speech and Hearing Disorders*, **39**, 186–193.

Macdonald H. & Macdonald A. (1991). Option Method. *Communication*, **25**, 5–6.

McDougle C.J., Naylor S.T., Cohen D.J., Volkmar F.R., Heninger G.R. & Price L.H. (1996). A double blind, placebo-controlled study of fluvoxamine in adults with autistic disorder. *Archives of General Psychiatry*, **53**, 1001–1008.

McDougle C.J. (1997). Psychopharmacology. In: D.J. Cohen & F.R. Volkmar (Eds), *Handbook of Autism and Pervasive Developmental Disorders*, 2nd Edition (pp. 707–729). New York: Wiley.

MacDuff G.S., Krantz P.J. & McClannahan L.E. (1993). Teaching children with autism to use photographic activity schedules: maintenance and generalisation—a complex response chain. *Journal of Applied Behavior Analysis*, **26**, 89–97.

McEachin J.J., Smith T. & Lovaas O.I. (1993). Long-term outcome for children with autism who received early intensive behavioral treatment. *American Journal of Mental Retardation*, **97**, 359–372.

McGee J.J. (1985). Gentle teaching. *Mental Handicap in New Zealand*, **9**, 13–24.

McGee J.J. (1990). Gentle teaching: The basic tenet. *Mental Handicap Nursing*, **86**, 68–72.

McGee J.J. & Gonzalez L. (1990). Gentle Teaching and the practice of human interdependence: a preliminary group study of 15 persons with severe behavioral disorders and their caregivers. In: A.C. Repp & N.N. Singh (Eds), *Current Perspectives on the Use of Aversive and Non-Aversive Interventions with Developmentally Disabled Persons* (pp. 237–254). Sycamore, IL: Sycamore.

McGee J.J. Menolascino P.E., Hobbs D.C. & Menousek P.E. (1987). *Gentle Teaching: A Non-Aversive Approach to Helping Persons with Mental Retardation*. New York: Human Science Press.

McGhee P. (1983). Humor development: towards a life span approach. In: P. McGhee & J. Goldstein (Eds), *Handbook of Humor Research*. New York: Springer Verlag.

McHale S., Simeonsson R. & Sloan J. (1984). Children with handicapped brothers and sisters. In: E. Schopler & G. Mesibov (Eds), The Effects of Autism on the Family (pp. 251–276). New York: Plenum Press.

Mahalski P. (1983). The incidence of attachment objects and oral habits at bedtime in two longitudinal samples of children age 1.5 to 7 years. *Journal of Child Psychology and Psychiatry*, **24**, 283–296.

Manjiviona J. & Prior M. (1995). Comparison of Asperger Syndrome and high functioning autistic children on a test of motor impairment. *Journal of Autism and Developmental Disorders*, **25**, 23–40.

Marans W.D. (1997). Developmentally based assessments: communication assessment. In: D. Cohen & F. Volkmar (Eds), *Handbook of Autism and Pervasive Developmental Disorders*, 2nd Edition (pp. 427–447). New York: Wiley.

Maratos O. (1996). Psychoanalysis and the management of pervasive developmental disorders, including autism. In: C. Trevarthen, K. Aitken, D. Papoudi & J. Robarts (Eds), *Children with Autism: Diagnosis and Interventions to Meet Their Needs*. London: Jessica Kingsley.

Marshall N.R. & Hegrenes J.R. (1970). Programmed communication therapy for autistic, mentally retarded children. *Journal of Speech and Hearing Disorders*, **35**, 70–83.

Marshall N. & Hegrenes H. (1972). The use of the written word as a communication system for non-verbal autistic children. *Journal of Speech and Hearing Disorders*, **39**, 186–194.

Martineau J., Barthelemy C., Garreau B. & Lelord G. (1985). Vitamin B6, Magnesium and combined B6Mg: therapeutic effects in childhood autism. *Biological Psychiatry*, **20**, 467–477.

Martineau J., Barthelemy C., Cheliakine C. & Lelord G. (1988). Brief report: An open middle-term study of combined vitamin B6-Magnesium in a subgroup of autistic children selected on their sensitivity to this treatment. *Journal of Autism and Developmental Disorders*, **18**, 435–447.

Mason S.M. & Iwata B.A. (1990). Artifactual effects of sensory integrative therapy on self injurious behaviour. *Journal of Applied Behavior Analysis*, **26**, 361–370.

Mates T.E. (1990) Siblings of autistic children: their adjustment and performance at home and in school. *Journal of Autism and Developmental Disorders*, **20**, 545–553.

Matson J.L., Sevin J.A., Fridley D. & Love S.R. (1990). Increasing spontaneous language in three autistic children. *Journal of Applied Behavior Analysis*, **23**, 227–233.

Maurice C., Green G. & Luce S.C. (Eds) (1996). *Behavioral Intervention for Young Children with Autism*. Austin, Texas: Pro-Ed.

Mawhood L. (1995). *Autism and Developmental Language Disorder: Implications from a Follow-up in Early Adult Life*. Unpublished PhD thesis, University of London.

Mawhood L., Rutter M. & Howlin P. (in preparation). A comparative follow-up study of young adults with autism and severe developmental language disorders.

Mayer-Johnson Co. (1997). *Augmentative Communication Products*. Solana Beach, Ca: USA.

Mesibov G.B. (1992). Treatment issues with high-functioning adolescents and adults with autism. In: E. Schopler & G.B. Mesibov (Eds), *High Functioning Individuals with Autism*. New York: Plenum Press.

Mesibov G.B. (1993). Treatment outcome is encouraging: comments on McEachin et al. *American Journal of Mental Retardation*, **97**, 379–380.

Mesibov G.B. & Schopler E. (Eds) (1992). *High Functioning Individuals with Autism* (pp. 143–156). New York: Plenum Press.

Meyer L.M., Fox A., Schermer A., Ketelsen D., Montan N., Mayer K. & Cole D. (1987). The effects of teaching intrusion on social play interactions between children with autism and their non-handicapped peers. *Journal of Autism and Developmental Disorders*, **17**, 315–322.

Miller J.N. & Ozonoff S. (1997). Did Asperger's cases have Asperger Disorder? A research note. *Journal of Child Psychology and Psychiatry*, **38**, 247–251.

Minshew N.J., Sweeney J.A. & Bauman M.L. (1997). Neurological aspects of autism. In: D.J. Cohen & F.R. Volkmar (Eds), *Handbook of Autism and Pervasive Developmental Disorders*, 2nd Edition (pp. 344–369). New York: Wiley.

Mittler P., Gillies S. & Jukes E. (1966). Prognosis in psychotic children: report of a follow-up study. *Journal of Mental Deficiency Research*, **10**, 73–83.

Moes D. (1995). Parent education and parenting stress. In: R.L. Koegel & L.K. Koegel (Eds), *Teaching Children with Autism*. Baltimore: Paul H. Brookes.

Muller J. (1993). Swimming against the tide. *Communication*, **27**, 6.

Muller P.A. (1993). *Autistic Children and Music Therapy: The Influence of Maternal Involvement in Therapy*. Unpublished PhD thesis, University of Reading.

Mullen K.B. & Frea W.D. (1995). A parent-professional consultation model for functional analysis. In: R.L. Koegel & L.K. Koegel (Eds), *Teaching Children with Autism*. Baltimore: Paul H. Brookes.

Murphy G.H., Oliver C., Corbett J.A., Hales J., Head D. & Hall S. (1993). Epidemiology of self injury: characteristics of people with severe self injury and initial treatment outcome. In: C. Kiernan (Ed.), *Research to Practice Implications of Research on the Challenging Behaviour of People with Learning Disability*. Clevedon: BILD.

Mundy P. (1993). Normal vs high functioning status in children with autism: commentaries on McEachin, Smith and Lovaas. *American Journal of Mental Retardation*, **97**, 381–384.

Myles B.S, Simpson R.L. & Hirsch N.C. (1997). A review of the literature on interventions to reduce pica in individuals with developmental disabilities. *Autism*, **1**, 77–96.

National Autistic Society (1995). *Schools, Units and Classes for Children with Autism*. London: National Autistic Society.

National Autistic Society (1997) *Approaches to Autism*. London: National Autistic Society.

Nelson K. (1973). Structure and strategy in learning to talk. *Monographs of the Society for Research in Child Development*, **38**, 1–2, serial no. 149.

Newson E. & Jones G.E. (1994). *An Evaluative and Comparative Study of Current Interventions for Children with Autism*. Unpublished report. Child Development Research Unit, Nottingham University.

Newton C., Taylor G. & Wilson D. (1996) Circles of friends: an inclusive approach to meeting emotional and behavioural needs. *Educational Psychology in Practice*, **11**, 4.

O'Brien G. & Yule W. (1995) *Behavioural Phenotypes*. Cambridge: MacKeith Press.

O'Gorman G. (1970). *The Nature of Childhood Autism*, 2nd Edition. London: Butterworth.

Oke N.J. & Schreibman L. (1990). Training social initiations to a high-functioning autistic child: assessment of collateral behavior change and generalization in a case study. *Journal of Autism and Developmental Disorders*, **20**, 479–497.

Oliver C. (1995). Self-injurious behaviour in children with learning disabilities: recent advances in assessment intervention. *Annotation: Journal of Child Psychology and Psychiatry*.

Olsson B. & Rett A. (1985). Behavioral observations concerning differential diagnosis between the Rett Syndrome and autism. *Brain and Development*, **7**(3), 281–289.

Olsson B. & Rett A. (1990). A review of the Rett Syndrome with a theory of autism. *Brain and Development*, **12**, 11–15.

Osterling J. & Dawson G. (1994) Early recognition of children with autism: a study of first birthday home video tapes. *Journal of Autism and Developmental Disorders*, **24**, 247–259.

Owens R.G. & MacKinnon S. (1993). The functional analysis of challenging behaviours: some conceptual and theoretical problems. In: R.S.P. Jones and C.B. Eayrs (Eds), *Challenging Behaviour and Intellectual Disability: A Psychological Perspective*. Avon: BILD Publications.

Ozonoff S. & Miller J.N. (1995). Teaching theory of mind: a new approach to social skills training for individuals with autism. *Journal of Autism and Developmental Disorders*, **25**, 415–433.

Ozonoff S., Rogers S.J. & Pennington B.F. (1991b). Asperger's syndrome: evidence of an empirical distinction from high-functioning autism. *Journal of Child Psychology and Psychiatry*, **32**, 1107–1122.

Paisey T.J., Whitney R.B. & Moore J. (1989). Person-treatment interactions across nonaversive response-deceleration procedures for self-injury: a case study of effects and side effects. *Behavioral Residential Treatment*, **4**, 69–88.

Peeters T. (1997). *Autism: From Theoretical Understanding to Educational Intervention*. London: Whurr.

Perner J. (1991). *Understanding the Representational Mind*. London: MIT Press.

Perry M. (1991). Learning and transfer: instructional conditions and conceptual change. *Cognitive Development*, **6**, 449–468.

Perry R., Campbell M., Adams P. *et al.* (1989). Long-term efficacy of haloperidol in autistic children: continuous vs discontinuous drug administration. *Journal of the American Academy of Child and Adolescent Psychiatry*, **28**, 87–92.

Perry R., Cohen I. & DeCarlo R. (1995). Case study: deterioration, autism and recovery in two siblings. *Journal of the American Academy of Child and Adolescent Psychiatry*, **34**, 232–237.

Pfeiffer S. & Nelson D. (1992) The cutting edge in services for people with autism. *Journal of Autism and Developmental Disorders*, **22**, 95–105.

Pfeiffer S.I., Norton J., Nelson L. & Shott S. (1995). Efficacy of vitamin B6 and magnesium in the treatment of autism: a methodology review and summary of outcomes. *Journal of Autism and Developmental Disorders*, **25**, 481–494.

Pickles A., Bolton P., Macdonald H., Bailey A., LeCouteur A., Sim C.-H. & Rutter M. (1995). Latent class analysis of recurrence risks for complex phenotypes with selection and measurement error. A twin and family history study of autism. *Journal of Human Genetics*, **57**, 717–726.

Pierce K. & Schreibman L. (1995). Increasing complex social behaviors in children with autism: effects of Peer-Implemented Pivotal Response Training. *Journal of Applied Behavior Analysis*, **28**, 285–295.

Piper E. & Howlin P. (1992). Assessing and diagnosing developmental disorders that are not evident at birth: parental evaluations of intake procedures. *Child Care, Health and Development*, **18**, 35–55.

Piven J., Arndt S., Bailey J. & Andreasen N. (1996). Regional brain enlargement in autism: a magnetic resonance imaging study. *Journal of the American Academy of Child and Adolescent Psychiatry*, **35**, 530–536.

Piven J., Gayle J., Chase J., Fink B., Landa R., Wzorek M. & Folstein S.E. (1990). A family history study of neuropsychiatric disorders in the adult siblings of autistic individuals. *Journal of the American Academy of Child and Adolescent Psychiatry*, **29**, 177–183.

Porter R. & Schroeder S. (1980). Generalisation and maintenance of skills acquired in non-speech language imitation program training. *Applied Research in Mental Retardation*, **1**, 71–84.

Powell S. & Jordan R. (Eds) (1997). *Autism and Learning: A Guide to Good Practice*. London: David Fulton.

Prekop J.L. (1984). Zur Festhalte Therapie bei Autistischen Kindern. *Der Kinderarzt*, **15**(6), 798–802.

Premack V. (1959). Towards empirical behavior laws: 1: Positive reinforcement. *Psychological Review*, **66**, 11–17.

Premack D. & Premack A. (1974). Teaching visual language to apes and language deficient persons. In: R. Schiefelbusch & L. Lloyd (Eds), *Language Perspectives—Acquisition, Retardation and Intervention*. London: Macmillan.

Prizant B.M. (1995). Foreword. In: K.A. Quill (Ed.), *Teaching Children with Autism. Strategies to Enhance Communication and Socialization*. New York: Delmar.

Prizant B.M. (1996). Brief Report: communication, language, social and emotional development. *Journal of Autism and Developmental Disorders*, **26**, 173–178.

Prizant B., Schuler A., Wetherby A. & Rydell P. (1997). Enhancing language and communication development: language approaches. In: D. Cohen & F. Volkmar (Eds), *Handbook of Autism and Pervasive Developmental Disorders*, 2nd Edition (pp. 572–605). New York: Wiley.

Quill K. (1995). Enhancing children's social-communicative interactions. In: *Teaching Children with Autism: Strategies to Enhance Communication and Socialization* (pp. 163–192). New York: Delmar.

Quill K.A., Gurry S. & Larkin A. (1989). Daily Life Therapy: a Japanese model for educating children with autism. *Journal of Autism and Developmental Disorders*, **19**, 637–640.

Quine L. & Pahl J. (1987). First diagnosis of severe handicap: a study of parents' reactions. *Developmental Medicine and Child Neurology*, **29**, 232–242.

Quintana J., Birnbrauer B., Stedge D., Lennon S., Freed J. Bridge J. & Greenhill L. (1995). Use of Methylphenidate in treatment of children with autistic disorder. *Journal of Autism and Developmental Disorders*, **25**, 283–294.

Quirk-Hodgson L. (1995). Solving social-behavioral problems through the use of visually supported communication. In K.A. Quill (Ed.), *Teaching Children with Autism: Strategies to Enhance Communication and Socialization* (pp. 265–286). New York: Delmar.

Raiten D.J. & Massaro T. (1986). Perspectives on the nutritional ecology of autistic children. *Journal of Autism and Developmental Disorders*, **16**, 133–144.

Rapin I. & Allen A. (1983). Developmental language disorders: nosological considerations. In: U. Kirk (Ed.), *Neuropsychology of Language Reading and Spelling* (pp. 155–184). London: Academic Press.

Raven J.C. (1992). *Standard Progressive Matrices* (1992 edition). Oxford: Oxford Psychology Press.

Redefer L.A. & Goodman J.F. (1989). Brief Report: pet facilitated therapy with autistic children. *Journal of Autism and Developmental Disorders*, **19**, 461–468.

Renzoni E., Beltrami V., Sestini P., Pompella A., Menchetti G. & Zappella M. (1995). Brief Report: Allergological evaluation of children with autism. *Journal of Autism and Developmental Disorders*, **25**(3), 327–334.

Rich H.L. & Ross S.M. (1989). Students' time on learning tasks in special education. *Exceptional Children*, **55**, 508–515.

Richer J. & Zappella M. (1989). Changing social behaviour: the place of Holding. *Communication*, **23**(2), 35–39.

Rimland B. (1988a). Comparative effects of treatment on children's behavior: drugs, therapies, schooling and several non-treatment events. *Autism Research Review International*, Publication 34b (revised).

Rimland B. (1988b). Physical exercise and autism. *Autism Research Review International*, **2**, 3.

Rimland B. (1992). A facilitated communication horror story. *Autism Research Review International*, **6**(1), 1–7.

Rimland B. (1994a). Comparative effects of treatment on children's behavior (drugs, therapies, schooling, and several non-treatment events). *Autism Research Review International*, Publication 34b.

Rimland B. (1994b). Information pack on vitamins/allergies and nutritional treatments for autism. *Autism Research Review International*, Information Pack P24.

Rimland B. (1995). *Studies of High Dose Vitamin B6 in Autistic Children and Adults—1965–1994*. San Diego, CA: Autism Research Institute.

Rimland B. (1995b). Sensory Integration therapy: does it work? *Autism Research Review*, **9** (2), 5.

Rimland B. & Baker S.M. (1996). Brief report: Alternative approaches to the development of effective treatments for autism. *Journal of Autism and Developmental Disorders*, **26**, 237–241.

Rimland B. & Edelson S.M. (1994). The effects of Auditory Integration Training on autism. *American Journal of Speech-Language Pathology*, **5**, 16–24.

Rimland B. & Edelson S.M. (1995). Brief report: A pilot study of auditory integration training in autism. *Journal of Autism and Developmental Disorders*, **25**, 61–70.

Rinaldi W. (1992). *Social Use of Language Programme*. Windsor: NFER.

Risley T & Wolf M. (1967). Establishing functional speech in echolalic children. *Behaviour Research and Therapy*, **5**, 73–88.

Ritvo E.R, Freeman B.J., Yuwiler A. *et al.* (1986). Fenfluramine treatment of autism: UCLA collaborative study of 81 patients at nine medical centers. *Psychological Bulletin*, **22**, 133–140.

Rodrigue J.R., Geffken G.R. & Morgan S.B. (1993). Perceived competence and behavioral adjustment of siblings of children with autism. *Journal of Autism and Developmental Disorders*, **23**, 665–674.

Rodrigue J.R., Morgan S.B. & Geffken G. (1990). Families of autistic children: psycho-social functioning of mothers. *Journal of Clinical Child Psychology*, **19**, 371–379.

Roeyers H. (1996). The influence of nonhandicapped peers on the social interaction of children with a pervasive developmental disorder. *Journal of Autism and Developmental Disorders*, **26**, 303–320.

Rogers S.J. (1996). Brief report: Early intervention in autism. *Journal of Autism and Developmental Disorders*, **26**, 243–246.

Rogers S.J. & DiLalla D.L. (1990). Age of symptom onset in young childen with pervasive developmental disorders. *Journal of the American Academy of Child and Adolescent Psychiatry*, **29**, 863–872.

Rogers S.J. & DiLalla D.L. (1991). A comparative study of the effects of a developmentally based preschool curriculum on young children with autism and young children with other disorders of behavior and development. *Topics in Early Childhood Special Education*, **11**, 29–47.

Ronen T. (1997). *Cognitive Developmental Therapy with Children*. Chichester: Wiley.

Rosenthal-Malek A. & Mitchell S. (1997) The effects of exercise on the self-stimulatory behaviors and positive responding of adolescents with autism. *Journal of Autism and Developmental Disorders*, **27**, 203–212.

Rourke B. (1989). *Nonverbal Learning Disabilities: The Syndrome and the Model*. New York: Guilford Press.

Rumsey J.M., Rapoport J.L. & Sceery W.R. (1985). Autistic children as adults: psychiatric, social and behavioral outcomes. *Journal of the American Academy of Child and Adolescent Psychiatry*, **24**, 465–473.

Runco M.A., Charlop M.H. & Schreibman L. (1986). The occurrence of autistic children's self-stimulation as a function of familiar versus unfamiliar stimulus conditions. *Journal of Autism and Developmental Disorders*, **16**, 31–44.

Ruttenberg B.A., Kalish B.I, Wenar C. & Wolf E.G. (1977). *Behavior Rating Instrument for Autistic and Other Atypical Children* (rev. edition). Philadelphia: Developmental Center for Autistic Children.

Rutter M. (1983). School effects on pupil progress, research findings and implications. *Child Development*, **54**, 1–29.

Rutter M. (1985). Infantile autism and other pervasive developmental disorders. In: M. Rutter & L. Hersov (Eds), *Child and Adolescent Psychiatry: Modern Approaches*, 2nd Edition (pp. 545–566). Oxford: Blackwell.

Rutter M. (1996). Autism research: prospects and priorities. *Journal of Autism and Developmental Disorders*, **26**, 257–275.

Rutter M., Bailey A., Bolton P. & Le Couteur A. (1993). Autism: syndrome definition and possible genetic mechanisms. In: R. Plomin & G.E. MacClearn (Eds), *Nurture and Psychology* (pp. 269–284). Washington, DC: APA Books.

Rutter M., Bailey A., Bolton P. & Le Couteur A. (1994). Autism and known medical conditions: myths and substance. *Journal of Child Psychology and Psychiatry*, **35**, 311–322.

Rutter M. & Bartak L. (1973). Special educational treatment of autistic children: a comparative study. II, Follow-up findings and implications for services. *Journal of Child Psychology and Psychiatry*, **14**, 241–270.

Rutter M., Greenfield D. & Lockyer L. (1967). A five to fifteen year follow-up study of infantile psychosis: II, Social and behavioural outcome. *British Journal of Psychiatry*, **113**, 1183–1199.

Rutter M. & Lockyer L. (1967). A five to fifteen year follow-up study of infantile psychosis: I, Description of sample. *British Journal of Psychiatry*, **113**, 1169–1182.

Rutter M. & Lord C. (1987). Language disorders associated with psychiatric disturbance. In: W. Yule & M. Rutter (Eds), *Language Development and Disorders*. Oxford: MacKeith Press.

Rutter M., Mawhood L. & Howlin P. (1992). Language delay and social development. In: P. Fletcher & D. Hall (Eds), *Specific Speech and Language Disorders in Children* (pp. 63–78). Cambridge: Cambridge University Press.

Rutter M. & Schopler E. (1992). Classification of pervasive developmental disorders: some concepts and practical considerations. *Journal of Autism and Developmental Disorders*, **22**, 459–482.

Rutter M. & Sussenwein F. (1971). A developmental and behavioral approach to the treatment of preschool autistic children, *Journal of Autism and Childhood Schizophrenia*, **1**, 376–397.

Rydell P.J. & Mirenda P. (1994). The effects of high and low constraint utterances on the production of immediate and delayed echolalia in young children with autism. *Journal of Autism and Developmental Disorders*, **24**, 719–730.

Rydell P.J. & Prizant B. (1995). Assessment and intervention strategies for children who use echolalia. In: K.A. Quill (Ed.), *Teaching Children with Autism: Strategies to Enhance Communication and Socialization* (pp. 105–132). New York: Delmar.

Sacks O. (1993). A neurologist's notebook: an anthropologist on Mars. *New Yorker*, 27th December, pp. 106–125.

Sahley T.L. & Panksepp J. (1987). Brain opioids and autism: an updated analysis of possible linkages. *Journal of Autism and Developmental Disorders*, **17**, 201–216.

Sanchez L.E., Adams P.B., Uysal S, Hallin A., Campbell M. & Small A.M. (1995). A comparison of live and videotape ratings: clomipramine and haloperidol in autism. *Psychopharmacological Bulletin*, **31**, 371–378.

Schleien S.J., Mustonen T. & Rynders J.E. (1995). Participation of children with autism and non-disabled peers in a cooperatively structured community art programme. *Journal of Autism and Development Disorders*, **25**, 397–415.

Schoen S.F. & Sivil E.O. (1989). A comparison of procedures in teaching self-help skills: increasing assistance, time delay, and observational learning. *Journal of Autism and Developmental Disorders*, **19**, 57–72.

Schopler E. (1985). Convergence of learning disability, higher level autism, and Asperger's syndrome. *Journal of Autism and Development Disorders*, **15**, 359.

Schopler E. (1986). Editorial: Treatment abuse and its reduction. *Journal of Autism and Development Disorders*, **16**, 99–104.

Schopler E. (Ed) (1995). *Parent Survival Manual: A Guide to Crisis Resolution in Autism and Related Developmental Disorders*. New York: Plenum Press.

Schopler E. (1997). Implementation of TEACCH Philosophy. In: D.J. Cohen & F.R. Volkmar (Eds), *Handbook of Autism and Pervasive Developmental Disorders*, 2nd Edition (pp. 767–798). New York: Wiley.

Schopler E., Brehm S.S., Kinsbourne M. & Reichler R.J. (1971). Effects of treatment structure on development in autistic children. *Archives of General Psychiatry*, **20**, 174–181.

Schopler E. & Mesibov G.B. (Eds) (1983). *Autism in Adolescents and Adults*. New York: Plenum Press.

Schopler E. & Mesibov G.B. (Eds) (1984). *The Effects of Autism on the Family*. New York: Plenum Press.

Schopler E. & Mesibov G.B. (1986). Introduction to social behavior in autism. In: E. Schopler & G.B. Mesibov (Eds), *Social Behavior in Autism* (pp. 1–11). New York: Plenum Press.

Schopler E. & Mesibov G.B. (Eds) (1988). *Learning and Cognition in Autism*. New York: Plenum Press.

Schopler E. & Mesibov G.B. (Eds) (1992). *High Functioning Individuals with Autism*. New York: Plenum Press.

Schopler E., Mesibov G. & Kunce L.J. (1997). *Asperger Syndrome or High Functioning Autism?* New York: Plenum Press.

Schopler E., Mesibov G.B. & Hearsey K. (1995). Structured teaching in the TEACCH system. In E. Schopler & G. Mesibov (Eds), *Learning and Cognition in Autism* (pp. 243–267). New York: Plenum Press.

Schopler E. & Reichler R.J. (1971). Parents as co-therapists in the treatment of psychotic children. *Journal of Autism and Childhood Schizophrenia*, **1**, 87–102.

Schopler E., Reichler R.J. & Renner B.R. (1986). *The Childhood Autism Rating Scale (CARS) for Diagnostic Screening and Classification of Autism*. New York: Irvington.

Schopler E., Reichler R.J. & Renner B.R. (1988). *The Childhood Autism Rating Scale (CARS)*. Los Angeles: Western Psychological Services.

Schreibman L. (1996). Brief report: The case for social and behavioral intervention research. *Journal of Autism and Developmental Disorders*, **26**, 247–250.

Schriebman L., O'Neill R.E. & Koegel R.L. (1983). Behavioral training for siblings of autistic children. *Journal of Applied Behavior Analysis*, **16**, 129–138.

Schuler A.L., Peck C.A., Willard C. & Theimer K. (1989). Assessment of communicative means and functions through interview: Assessing the communicative capabilities of individuals with limited language. *Seminars in Speech and Language*, **10**, 51–61.

Schuler A., Prizant B. & Wetherby A. (1997) Enhancing language and communication development: prelinguistic approaches. In: D. Cohen & F. Volkmar (Eds),

Handbook of Autism and Pervasive Developmental Disorders, 2nd Edition (pp. 539–571). New York: Wiley.

Secan K.E., Egel A.L. & Tilley C.S. (1989). Acquisition, generalization, and maintenance of question-answering skills in autistic children. *Journal of Applied Behavior Analysis*, **22**, 181–196.

Semmel M.I. & Peck C.A. (1986). Effects of special education environments: beyond mainstreaming. In: C.J. Meisel (Ed.), *Mainstreaming Handicapped Children: Outcomes, Controversies, and New Directions* (pp. 165–192). Hillsdale, NJ: Erlbaum.

Shane H. (1994). *Facilitated Communication: The Clinical and Social Phenomenon*. San Diego: Singular Press.

Sheinkopf S.J. and Siegel B. (1998). Home-based behavioral treatment of young children with autism. *Journal of Autism and Developmental Disorders*, **28**, 15–23.

Sherman J., Factor D.C., Swinson R. & Darjes R.W. (1989). The effects of fenfluramine (hydrochloride) on the behaviors of fifteen autistic children. *Journal of Autism and Developmental Disorders*, **19**, 533–544.

Short A. (1984). Short-term treatment outcome using parents as therapists for their own autistic children. *Journal of Child Psychology and Psychiatry*, **25**, 443–485.

Short A & Schopler E. (1988). Factors relating to age of consent in autism. *Journal of Autism and Developmental Disorders*, **18**, 207–216.

Siegel B. (1997). Coping with the diagnosis of autism. In: D.J. Cohen & F.R. Volkmar (Eds), *Handbook of Autism and Pervasive Developmental Disorders*, 2nd Edition (pp. 745–763). New York: Wiley.

Sigafoos J., Kerr M. & Roberts, D. (1994a). Inter-rater reliability of the Motivation Assessment Scale: failure to replicate with aggressive behaviour. *Research in Developmental Disabilities*, **15**, 333–342.

Sigafoos J., Roberts D., Kerr M., Couzens D. & Baglioni A.J. (1994b). Opportunities for communication in classrooms serving children with developmental disabilities. *Journal of Autism and Developmental Disorders*, **24**, 259–280.

Sigafoos J., Kerr M., Roberts D. & Couzens D. (1994c). Increasing opportunities for requesting in classrooms serving children with developmental disabilities. *Journal of Autism and Developmental Disorders*, **24**, 631–646.

Sinclair J. (1992). Bridging the gap: an inside out view of autism (Or, do you know what I don't know?). In: E. Schopler & G.B. Mesibov (Eds), *High Functioning Individuals with Autism* (pp. 294–302). New York: Plenum Press.

Smalley S., Burger F. & Smith M. (1994). Phenotypic variation of tuberous sclerosis in a single extended kindred. *Journal of Medical Genetics*, **31**, 761–765.

Smalley S., Smith M. & Tanguay P. (1991). Autism and psychiatric disorders in tuberous sclerosis. *Annals of New York Academy of Science*, **615**, 382–383.

Smalley S.L., Tanguay P.E., Smith M. & Gutierrez G. (1992). Autism and tuberous sclerosis. *Journal of Autism and Developmental Disorders*, **22**, 339–355.

Smith B., Chung M.C. & Vostanis P. (1994). The path to care in autism: is it better now? *Journal of Autism and Developmental Disorders*, **24**, 551–564.

Smith M. (1987) Treatment of pica in an adult disabled by autism by differential reinforcement of incompatible behaviour. *Journal of Behaviour Therapy and Experimental Psychiatry*, **18**, 285–288.

Smith T. (1996). Are other treatments effective? In: C. Maurice, G. Green & S.C. Luce (Eds), *Behavioral Intervention for Young Children with Autism*. Austin, Texas: Pro-Ed.

Sparrow S.S., Balla D. & Cicchetti D.V. (1984). *Vineland Adaptive Behavior Scales*. Circle Pines, Minnesota: American Guidance Service.

Spence J. (1980). *Social Skills Training with Children and Adolescents: A Counsellor's Manual*. Windsor: NFER.

Spence S.H. (1991). Developments in the assessments of social skills and social competence in children. *Behaviour Change*, **8**, 148–166.

Stahmer A.C. (1995) Teaching symbolic play skills to children with autism using pivotal response training. *Journal of Autism and Developmental Disorders*, **25**, 123–142.

Stallard P., Lenton S. (1992) How satisfied are parents of pre-school children who have special needs with the services they have received? A consumer survey. *Child: Care, Health and Development*, **18**, 197–205.

Steffenburg S. (1990). *Neurobiological Correlates of Autism*. M.D. thesis, University of Goteburg.

Steffenburg S. (1991) Neuropsychiatric assessment of children with autism. *Developmental Medicine and Child Neurology*, **33**, 495–511.

Steffenburg S., Gillberg C., Helgren L., Anderson L., Gillberg I., Jakobsson G. & Bohman M. (1989). A twin study of autism in Denmark, Finland, Iceland, Norway, and Sweden. *Journal of Child Psychology and Psychiatry*, **30**, 405–416.

Stehli A. (1992). *The Sound of a Miracle: A Child's Triumph over Autism*. London: Fourth Estate Publications.

Stone W.L. & Caro-Martinez L.M. (1990). Naturalistic observations of spontaneous communication in autistic children. *Journal of Autism and Developmental Disorders*, **20**, 437–453.

Stott D.H., Moyes F.A. & Henderson S.E. (1984). *Test of Motor Impairment*. Guelph: Brook International.

Sturmey P. (1995). Analog baselines: a critical review of the methodology. *Research in Developmental Disabilities*, **16**, 269–284.

Sturmey P. (1996). *Functional Analysis in Clinical Psychology*. Chichester: Wiley.

Sugai G. & White W.J. (1986). Effects of using object self-stimulation as a reinforcer on the pre-vocational work rates of an autistic child. *Journal of Autism and Developmental Disorders*, **16**, 459–474.

Swenson-Pierce A., Kohl F.L. & Egel A.L. (1987). Siblings as home trainers: a strategy for teaching domestic skills to children. *Journal for the Association for Persons with Severe Handicaps*, **12**, 53–60.

Swettenham J. (1995). Can children with autism be taught to understand false beliefs using computers? *Journal of Child Psychology and Psychiatry*, **37**, 157–166.

Szatmari P., Archer L., Fisman S., Streiner, D.L. & Wilson F. (1995). Asperger's syndrome and autism: differences in behavior, cognition, and adaptive functioning. *Journal of the American Academy of Child and Adolescent Psychiatry*, **34**, 1662–1671.

Szatmari P., Bartolucci G., Bremner R.S., Bond S. & Rich S. (1989). A follow-up study of high functioning autistic children. *Journal of Autism and Developmental Disorders*, **19**, 213–226.

Szatmari P., Jones M.B., Tuff L., Bartolucci C.G., Fisman S. & Mahoney W. (1993). Lack of cognitive impairment in first-degree relatives of children with pervasive developmental disorders. *Journal of the American Academy of Child and Adolescent Psychiatry*, **32**, 1264–1273.

Szatmari P., Tuff L. & Finlayson J.A.J. (1990). Asperger's syndrome and autism: neurocognitive aspects. *Journal of the American Academy of Child Psychiatry*, **29**, 130–136.

Szurek S. & Berlin I. (1956). Elements of psychotherapeutics with the schizophrenic child and his parents. *Psychiatry*, **19**, 1–19.

Tantam D. (1991). Asperger's syndrome in adulthood. In: U. Frith (Ed.), *Autism and Asperger Syndrome* (pp. 147–183). Cambridge: Cambridge University Press.

Taylor E. (1998) Annotation: Treatment of hyperkinetic disorder. *Journal of Child Psychology and Psychiatry* (in preparation).

Taylor B.A. & Harris S.L. (1995). Teaching children with autism to seek information: acquisition of novel information and generalization of responding. *Journal of Applied Behavior Analysis*, **28**, 3–14.

Thorp D.M., Stahmer A.C. & Schreibman L. (1995). Effects of sociodramatic play training on children with autism. *Journal of Autism and Developmental Disorders*, **25**, 265–283.

Tinbergen N. & Tinbergen E.A. (1983). *Autistic Children: New Hope for a Cure*. London: Allen & Unwin.

Tjus T., Heimann M, & Nelson K.E. (1998). Gains in literacy through the use of a specially designed multimedia computer strategy: positive findings from 13 children with autism. *Autism: The International Journal of Research and Practice*, **2**, 139–154.

Tompkins, G.E. & Webeler M. (1983). What will happen next? using predictable books with young children. *The Reading Teacher*, (February), pp. 489–502.

Trevarthen C., Aitken K., Papoudi D. & Roberts J.M. (1996). *Children with Autism. Diagnosis and Interventions to Meet Their Needs*. London: Jessica Kingsley.

Tsai L.Y., Tsai M.C. & August G.J. (1985). Brief report: Implications of EEG diagnoses in the subclassifcation of infantile autism. *Journal of Autism and Developmental Disorders*, **15**, 339–344.

Tsaltas M.O. & Jefferson T. (1986). A pilot study on allergic responses. *Journal of Autism and Developmental Disorders*, **16**, 91–92.

Turk J. & Graham P. (1997) Fragile X syndrome, autism and autistic features. *Autism: The International Journal of Research and Practice*, **1**, 175–198.

Tustin R.D. (1995). The effects of advance notice of activity transitions on stereotypic behavior. *Journal of Applied Behavior Analysis*, **28**, 91–92.

Twachtman D.D. (1995) Methods to enhance communication in verbal children. In: K.A. Quill (Ed.), *Teaching Children with Autism: Strategies to Enhance Communication and Socialization* (pp. 133–162). New York: Delmar.

Udwin O. (1986). *An Evaluation of Alternative and Augmentative Systems of Communication Taught to Non-verbal Cerebral Palsied Children*. Unpublished PhD thesis, University of London.

US Bureau of Justice Statistics (1987). In: *Adolescents* (Fall 1989). Princeton. New Jersey: The Robert Wood Johnson Foundation.

Van Berkelaer-Onnes I. (1994). Play training for autistic children. In: J. Hellendorn, R. van der Kooij & B. Sutton-Smith (Eds), *Play and Intervention*. New York: State University of New York Press.

Varley C.K. & McClellan J. (1997). Two additional sudden deaths with tricyclic antidepressants. *Journal of the American Academy of Child and Adolescent Psychiatry*, **36**, 390–394.

Venter A., Lord C. & Schopler E. (1992). A follow-up study of high functioning autistic children. *Journal of Child Psychology and Psychiatry*, **33**, 489–507.

Volkmar F.R. & Cohen D.J. (1989). Disintegrative disorder of 'late onset' autism. *Journal of Child Psychology and Psychiatry*, **30**, 717–724.

Volkmar F.R. & Cohen D.J. (1991). Comorbid association of autism and schizophrenia. *American Journal of Psychiatry*, **148**, 1705–1707.

Volkmar F., Stier D. & Cohen D. (1985). Age of recognition of pervasive developmental disorders. *American Journal of Psychiatry*, **142**, 1450–1452.

Walker M. (1980). *Makaton Vocabulary* (revised edition). Surrey: The Makaton Vocabulary Development Project.

Warren P.R., Margaretten M.C., Pace N.C. & Foster A. (1986). Immune abnormalities in patients with autism. *Journal of Autism and Developmental Disorders*, **16**, 186–197.

Watson L.R. (1987). Pragmatic abilities and disabilities of autistic children. In: T.L. Layton (Ed.), *Language and Treatment of Autistic and Developmentally Disordered Children.* Springfield, IL: Charles C. Thomas.

Wechsler D. (1990a). *Wechsler Intelligence Scale for Children—Third UK Edition (WISC-III UK).* Sidcup, Kent: The Psychological Corporation.

Wechsler D. (1990b). *Wechsler Pre-school and Primary Scale of Intelligence: Revised UK Edition (WPPSI-R UK).* Sidcup, Kent: The Psychological Corporation.

Welch M. (1988). *Holding Time.* London: Century Hutchinson.

Wellman H.M. (1990). *The Child's Theory of Mind.* Cambridge: MIT Press.

Wetherby A., Schuler A. & Prizant B. (1997) Enhancing language and communication development: theoretical foundations. In: D. Cohen & F. Volkmar (Eds), *Handbook of Autism and Pervasive Developmental Disorders,* 2nd Edition (pp. 513–538). New York: Wiley.

WHO (1978). *International Classification of Diseases. ICD-9* (9th edition). Geneva: World Health Organisation.

WHO (1992). *International Classification of Diseases. ICD-10* (10th edition). *Diagnostic Criteria for Research.* Geneva: World Health Organisation.

Wikler L (1981). Chronic stresses of families of mentally retarded children. *Family Relations,* **30**, 281–288.

Willemsen-Swinkels S.H., Buitelaar J.K. Nijhof G.J. & van Engeland H. (1995). Failure of Naltrexone Hydrochloride to reduce self-injurious and autistic behavior in mentally retarded adults: double blind placebo controlled studies. *Archives of General Psychiatry,* **52**, 766–773.

Willemsen-Swinkels S.H., Buitelaar J.K. & van Engeland, H. (1997). Children with a pervasive developmental disorder, children with a language disorder and normally developing children in situations with high- and low-level involvement of the caregiver. *Journal of Child Psychology and Psychiatry,* **38**, 327–336.

Williams D. (1992). *Nobody Nowhere.* London: Corgi Books.

Williams D. (1994). *Somebody Somewhere.* London: Corgi Books.

Williams T.I. (1989). A social skills group for autistic children. *Journal of Autism and Developmental Disorders,* **19**, 143–156.

Wimpory D. & Cochrane V. (1991). Criteria for evaluative research with special reference to Holding Therapy. *Communication,* **25**(2), 15–7.

Wing L. (1981). Asperger's syndrome: a clinical account. *Psychological Medicine,* **11**, 115–129.

Wing L. (1993). The definition and prevalence of autism: a review. *European Child and Adolescent Psychiatry,* **2**, 61–74.

Wing L. (1996). Autistic spectrum disorders *British Medical Journal,* **312**, 327–328.

Wing L. & Gould J. (1978). Systematic recording of behaviors and skills of retarded and psychotic children. *Journal of Autism and Childhood Schizophrenia,* **8**, 79–97.

Wing L. & Gould J. (1979). Severe impairments of social interaction and associated abnormalities in children: Epidemiology and classification. *Journal of Autism and Developmental Disorders,* **9**, 11–29.

Wolery M., Kirk K. & Gast D.L. (1985). Stereotypic behavior as a reinforcer: Effects and side-effects. *Journal of Autism and Developmental Disorders,* **15**, 149–162.

Wolf L.C., Noh S., Fisman S.N. & Speechley M. (1989). Brief report: Psychological effects of parenting stress on parents of autistic children. *Journal of Autism and Developmental Disorders,* **19**, 157–166.

Wolfberg P. (1995). Enhancing children's play. In: K.A. Quill (Ed.), *Teaching Children with Autism: Strategies to Enhance Communication and Socialization* (pp. 193–218). New York: Delmar.

Wolfberg P.J. & Schuler A.L. (1993). Integrated play groups: a model for promoting the social and cognitive dimensions of play. *Journal of Autism and Developmental Disorders*, **23**, 1–23.

Wolff S. (1991). Schizoid personality in childhood and adult life. 1: The vagaries of diagnostic labelling. *British Journal of Psychiatry*, **159**, 615–620.

Wolff S. & McGuire R.J. (1995). Schizoid personality in girls: a follow-up study. What are the links with Asperger's syndrome? *Journal of Child Psychology and Psychiatry*, **36**, 793–818.

Wood M. (1995). Parent–professional collaboration and the efficacy of the IEP process. In: R.L. Koegel & L.K. Koegel (Eds), *Teaching Children with Autism*. Baltimore: Paul H. Brookes.

Woolley H., Stein A., Forrest G.C. & Baum J.D. (1989). Imparting the diagnosis of life threatening illness in children. *British Medical Journal*, **298**, 1623–1626.

Yoder P. & Layton T. (1989). Speech following sign language training in autistic children with minimal verbal language. *Journal of Autism and Developmental Disorders*, **18**, 217–230.

Yule W. (1993). The methodology of the study. In: R. Cochrane (Ed.), *Proceedings of a Conference on the Evaluation of Conductive Education*. Birmingham University, June 1993.

Zanolli K., Daggett J. & Adams T. (1996) Teaching preschool age autistic children to make spontaneous initiations to peers. *Journal of Autism and Developmental Disorders*, **26**, 407–422.

Zappella M. (1988). Il legame genitore-bambino come base della terapia dei bambini autistici. In: P. De Giacomo & M. Scacella (Eds), *Terapie dell'Autismo*. Bari: Ed. Scient.

Zarkowska E. & Clements J. (1988). *Problem Behaviour in People with Severe Learning Disabilities: A Practical Guide to a Constructional Approach*. London: Croom Helm.

Zingarelli G. *et al.* (1992). Clinical effects of naltrexone on autistic behavior. *American Journal on Mental Retardation*, **97**, 57–63.

INDEX

Index compiled by Sylvia Potter